The Esperanto Movement

Contributions to the Sociology of Language

32

Joshua A. Fishman
Editor

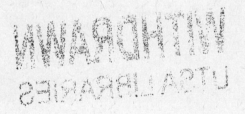

MOUTON PUBLISHERS · THE HAGUE · PARIS · NEW YORK

The Esperanto Movement

Peter G. Forster

MOUTON PUBLISHERS · THE HAGUE · PARIS · NEW YORK

Library of Congress Cataloging in Publication Data

Forster, Peter G. (Peter Glover), 1944-
   The Esperanto movement.
   (Contributions to the sociology of language; 32)
   Bibliography:·p.
   Includes index.
   1. Esperanto. I. Title. II. Series.
PM8205.F6   499´.992   81-22427
ISBN 90-279-3399-5   AACR2

ISBN 90 279 3399 5
© Copyright 1982 by Mouton Publishers. The Hague. All rights reserved, including those of translation into foreign languages. No part of this book may be reproduced in any form – by photoprint, microfilm, or any other means – nor transmitted nor translated into a machine language without written permission from the publisher. Typesetting: Grestun Graphics, Abingdon. – Printing: Krips Repro, Meppel. – Binding: Lüderitz & Bauer Buchgewerbe GmbH, Berlin.
Printed in The Netherlands

Jacket design by Jurriaan Schrofer

For
Suzie, Faiwell, and Yasuza

The Esperanto Anthem

La Espero	Hope
En la mondon venis nova sento,	A new feeling has come into the world,
Tra la mondo iras forta voko;	A mighty call sounds through the world;
Per flugiloj de facila vento	On the wings of a light wind
Nun de loko flugu ĝi al loko.	Let it now fly from place to place.
Ne al glavo sangon soifanta	Not to a sword, thirsting for blood
Ĝi la homan tiras familion:	Does it draw the human family:
Al la mond' eterne militanta	To the world, eternally at war
Ĝi promesas sanktan harmonion.	It promises sacred harmony.
Sub la sankta signo de l'espero	Beneath the sacred symbol of hope
Kolektiĝas pacaj batalantoj,	Gather warriors for peace,
Kaj rapide kreskos la afero	And the cause grows rapidly
Per laboro de la esperantoj.	Through the efforts of the hopeful.
Forte staras muroj de miljaroj	The walls of ages stand fast
Inter la popoloj dividitaj;	Between the divided peoples;
Sed dissaltos la obstinaj baroj,	But the unyielding barriers will leap apart
Per la sankta amo disbatitaj.	Breached by the sacred love.
Sur neŭtrala lingva fundamento,	On the basis of a neutral language,
Komprenante unu la alian,	Understanding one another,
La popoloj faros en konsento	The peoples will form in agreement
Unu grandan rondon familian.	One great family circle.
Nia diligenta kolegaro	Our diligent colleagues
En laboro paca ne laciĝos,	Will not tire in their work for peace,
Ĝis la bela sonĝo de l'homaro	Until the beautiful vision of humanity
Por eterna ben' efektiviĝos.	Is realised, for eternal blessing.

Preface

The present work is a revised version of my thesis, 'A Sociological Study of the Esperanto Movement', which was accepted by Hull University for the degree of Doctor of Philosophy in 1977. For publication in its present form the text has been revised, reworded, and updated in a number of places. The history of Esperanto is naturally an ongoing process, and new events will have occurred by the time of publication; but an attempt has been made to make the chronicle as up-to-date as possible. It is hoped that the analysis presented here will prove useful to Esperantist and non-Esperantist alike.

It is pleasing to be able to record that, while this is an academic account, it has been carried on with the full cooperation of the people studied. First and foremost I have to acknowledge the assistance of those who gave of their time to fill in my questionnaires. Moreover, at the highest organisational level, whether nationally or internationally, full cooperation was secured. I should like to thank particularly Professor Ivo Lapenna, sometime President of the Universal Esperanto Association; Dr. Bernard Cavanagh, sometime President of the British Esperanto Association; and Mr. John Leslie and his successor Mr. Herbert Platt, secretaries of the British Esperanto Association, for their interest and assistance. In particular Mr. Platt has patiently answered all my inquiries on my numerous visits to the London office. During my stay at the Central Office of the Universal Esperanto Association in Rotterdam I was assisted by Dr. Victor Sadler, Mr. Simo Milojević, and Mr. Robert Moerbeek. I am also indebted to numerous Bulgarian Esperantists, particularly Mr. Kuncho Valev and Mr. Nikola Aleksiev, who provided assistance on a short study-visit to Bulgaria.

In the academic world, I would like to acknowledge the help of

Professor Ian Cunnison, Dr. Colin Campbell, Mr. Bernard Golden, Professor Richard Osborne, Professor Valdo Pons, Dr. Richard Wood, Dr. Ulrich Lins, Mr. Ed Strauss, Mr. Farnham Rehfisch, Dr. John Peel, Dr. Edward Evans, and Professor Joshua Fishman.

Ms. Ethel Prent provided information about the Workers' Esperanto Movement, and Mr. Henry Meulen about the Ido movement. Ms. Eileen Lee typed a previous version, and Mr. Coverson F. Malemia the present manuscript.

The British Council provided a grant under the Younger Research Workers' Interchange Scheme to enable me to visit the Esperanto library in Rotterdam. The University of Hull provided financial assistance for a visit to the World Esperanto Congress in Helsinki in 1969. The University of Malawi provided a grant for the final typing of the text.

I am grateful to all who have helped in the realisation of this book. Mention here does not necessarily imply agreement with or approval of its contents. Any faults are my own. I hope that this publication will stimulate further serious research into this unique speech community.

Zomba, Malawi
17 September 1980

Note on Quotations

Where sources written in Esperanto are quoted in the text, these have been translated into English. This has also been done in the case of parallel texts in French and Esperanto, though sources written in French only have been quoted in the original. In all quotations, any emphasis is in the original unless otherwise stated.

In all cases the translation is my own. Where songs and poems have been translated, a more or less literal rendering has been given, and no attempt has been made to create any poetic effect.

Contents

List of Tables

Abbreviations

The following abbreviations used in the text are also widely used in Esperantist publications. They are therefore mostly abbreviations of the Esperanto titles of the institutions concerned. Both English and Esperanto titles are given here, and further information can be obtained by looking up the English titles in the Glossary (p.395).

BEA   *Brita Esperantista Asocio*
      British Esperanto Association
CED   *Centro de Esplorado kaj Dokumentado*
      Research and Documentation Centre
CO   *Centra Oficejo*
      Central Office
D   *Delegito*
      Delegate
EANA *Esperanto-Asocio de Norda Ameriko*
      Esperanto Association of North America
ELNA *Esperanto-Ligo por Norda Ameriko*
      Esperanto League for North America
ICK   *Internacia Centra Komitato*
      International Central Committee
IEL   *Internacia Esperanto-Ligo*
      International Esperanto League
IPE   *Internacio de Proletaj Esperantistoj*
      International of Proletarian Esperantists
KKK   *Konstanta Kongresa Komitato*
      Permanent Congress Committee
KR   *Konstanta Reprezentantaro*
      Permanent Representatives

LK   *Lingva Komitato*
       Language Committee
MEM *Mondpaca Esperantista Movado*
       World Peace Esperanto Movement
SAT *Sennacieca Asocio Tutmonda*
       World Association of Non-Nationalists
SEU *Sovetlanda Esperantista Unuiĝo*
       Soviet Esperanto Union
TEJO *Tutmonda Esperantista Junulara Organizo*
       World Esperantist Youth Organisation
UEA *Universala Esperanto-Asocio*
       Universal Esperanto Association

Introduction

Esperanto is often thought of as a marginal phenomenon in relation to society as a whole, yet it is a more interesting subject of study than might appear at first sight. In particular, it is generally seen by its supporters as 'more than a language'. The definition given in the *Shorter Oxford English Dictionary*, i.e. 'name of an artificial language invented for universal use' will probably represent the limits of most people's knowledge of the subject. In Britain, at any rate, the reaction to hearing the name 'Esperanto' is often that it represents a lost cause, a dead or dying movement. Yet, such comments apart, Esperanto is of interest because of the widespread organisational implications postulated for the language; likewise the millenarian ideals which some of its supporters think can be realised through Esperanto. The 'Hymn' quoted on page vii is a good example of the latter.[1]

It is hardly surprising that the Esperanto movement is little known to the outside world. In the first place, although there is extensive documentation on the subject, the bulk of such printed material is written in Esperanto. As Esperanto is widely thought to be marginal, if its continued existence is even admitted, few outsiders have troubled to learn enough Esperanto to penetrate such literature. But in any case, as will be shown, Esperanto organisations represent a unique phenomenon and are difficult to categorise sociologically. It is hoped in the present work to indicate the features of the Esperanto movement which make it worthy of serious scholarly attention. The perspective adopted is sociological, but it is hoped that those of a wider range of interests will profit from consideration of the subject. It will be apparent that Esperanto provides interesting material for students of comparative linguistics, international politics, peace and conflict research, and contemporary European history. In the same way, material in this study has been drawn from other disciplines. However, no claim is here made to specialist knowledge of any field but the sociological.[2] But my principal aim has been to *translate*, in an anthropological as well as a linguistic sense,[3] so as to present the history of Esperanto (interpreted sociologically) to a wider public than is presently aware of it. This study is based on a close investigation of the Esperanto movement from its inception in 1887 to the present day. The principal source material has been printed documents, which are abundant whether in the form of pamphlets, periodicals, booklets, or full-length volumes. But these have not been used in isolation, since contrary to many people's belief the Esperanto movement continues to exist. Advantage of this fact has been taken, and participant observation and questionnaires have been used to supplement documentary sources. For the purpose of collecting material I have attended a number of Esperanto meetings in Yorkshire and Humberside, plus two national and two international Esperanto congresses. I have also made a comprehensive survey by questionnaire of the membership of the British Esperanto Association.[4] It is worth putting on record that, with very few exceptions, Esperantists have shown themselves to be highly cooperative in a venture of this kind.

Within this framework, the more specific problem to be investigated will be the way in which Esperanto is linked to certain value orientations. The question of the wider claims made for Esperanto will be central throughout this study. This will lead to consideration of issues such as the Esperantists' self-conception as an 'Esperantist people' in its own right as well as the problem of the definition of 'neutrality'.

A study of a social movement cannot be undertaken satisfactorily without a declaration of the author's own involvement in it. I must declare that I am in basic sympathy with (though not uncritical of) the aims of the Esperanto movement. I have myself been a member of the British and the Universal Esperanto Association since 1959 (approximately), but I was not particularly active in the movement before commencing this research in 1968. I did attend meetings of the Manchester Esperanto Society in a purely personal capacity between 1962 and 1966, but was not otherwise very active. Yet this admission inevitably gives rise to questions about the degree of objectivity possible. The question can be debated as to whether the believer or the disbeliever is in the best position to study religion,[5] or whether an anthropologist who is a total outsider is at an advantage or disadvantage compared with someone who has been brought up in the society concerned. It is, however, my belief that such debates have little fruitful outcome. Those who wish to investigate a given problem will do so anyway. The *difference* between an insider's and an outsider's report must be acknowledged, but it is impossible to say that overall the one is superior to the other. It has, too, been recently suggested in certain quarters that orthodox academic sociology has displayed a conservative bias and must be replaced by a critical/radical/insurgent/partisan approach to the study of society.[6] I should like to stress that, although my sympathies undoubtedly lie with the people about whom I am writing, and though my value judgements will have inevitably intervened in the present investigation, I do not see this work as part of such a tradition. It is true that in recent years there has been much debate about the question of 'value-free' sociology. Yet however interesting the questions might have been for clarification of the philosophy of sociology, the sociology of knowledge, and the status of 'theory', remarkably few guidelines have been given for an alternative tradition of empirical investigation: indeed, the possibility of such investigation has at times been denied. This work should therefore be judged as an exercise in academic sociology. It is, however, hoped that it can help to inform value judgements about Esperanto.

Esperanto can be summarised grammatically in its 'sixteen rules' (see Appendix I). As such it might appear to resemble a technical aid, analogous to devices such as shorthand and the Morse Code. Yet many of its supporters make much wider claims for Esperanto. A quasi-religious fervour is often associated with the language, and Esperanto is frequently linked by its speakers with the cause of world peace. Particular significance has been attached to the annual World Esperanto Congresses as a means of contributing to solidarity across national frontiers. There is also noticeable a remarkable veneration for Dr. Zamenhof, the inventor of Esperanto and initiator of organised support for it.

The perspective here employed is sociological, yet it is at once apparent that Esperanto fits uneasily into established sociological categories. Various possibilities suggest themselves, especially 'voluntary association', 'sect', 'cult', and 'social movement'. Organised support for Esperanto contains features of all such types, though none of them fits the bill exactly. Organised support for Esperanto indeed contains many features of the voluntary association. Esperanto associations might simply be conceived of as clubs, with expressive functions predominating. Many local Esperanto associations describe themselves as clubs. Yet Esperanto is appealed to in wider terms, and its supporters mostly wish it to have a considerable influence upon the course of history. The evangelical, conversionist fervour of many members suggests something more than a mere club. Esperanto might alternatively be seen as having some sectarian characteristics. A sect is defined by Wilson as 'the small religious group in which membership is voluntary and conditional upon some mark of merit.'[7] Yet membership in an Esperanto organisation is not conditional upon some mark of merit: it is not even a requirement to be able to speak Esperanto, though it is an advantage for effective participation in the movement to be able to do so. And although the founder of Esperanto wished to associate it with his own religious ideals, this interpretation has not proved popular and Esperanto organisations have emphasised their religious neutrality. On the other hand, organised support for Esperanto resembles the broader conception of sectarianism adopted by Wallis. Wallis suggests that the concept of sect 'has to do with groups, organised around a common ideology, which in a variety of ways cut themselves off from, or erect barriers between themselves and the rest of society.'[8] Broadly speaking this definition would fit the Esperanto movement as interpreted by certain of its members, though others would reject it. Indeed, since 1957 it has been a deliberate policy of leaders of the Esperanto movement to avoid any suggestion of sectarianism.

In some respects, the sociological category of 'cult' is applicable. Yinger[9] suggests that the chief characteristics of such bodies are small size, search for a mystical experience, lack of organisational structure, and presence of a charismatic leader. As such, he points out, the cult represents a sharper break than does the sect from the dominant religious tradition of a society, and it also tends to be unstable. This type bears a resemblance to the early stages of organised international support for Esperanto, while still under

Zamenhof's leadership. At the beginning of the twentieth century the founder of Esperanto wished to associate it with a universal religion. This was derived from certain intellectual currents in Judaism, but was transposed into the much broader cultural context of international relations in Europe. In the event, however, Zamenhof's attempts to obtain substantial support for his religious ideals were completely unsuccessful, and the mainstream Esperanto movement quickly became secularised.

The Esperantists themselves refer to their organisations collectively as the Esperanto 'movement' (*movado* in Esperanto). This term will be employed here, while recognising that some sociologists have adopted a narrower definition. Smelser,[10] for instance, regards social movements as worthy of detailed consideration only when they become part of the conventional social order: when they are successful. This is a view followed by Banks, who refers to social movements as 'self-conscious and successful attempts to introduce innovations into a social system'.[11] Others, such as Heberle,[12] treat social movements strictly within the framework of political sociology; yet others, such as Kornhauser,[13] refer to 'mass' social movements. The Esperanto movement is in no sense a mass movement, it has a highly ambiguous attitude towards politics, and its aims have not been achieved in an instrumental sense. Many who emphasise the expressive component of the movement – the intrinsic value of its social relationships – would claim it to be successful, but this is a different matter from saying that its aims have been achieved. In one respect, however, sociological categories derived from the study of social movements are very clearly applicable. The perspectives of the Esperanto movement can be clearly articulated in accordance with Smelser's distinction between norm- and value-oriented movements.[14] While some Esperantists emphasise its advantages for trade, conferences, travel, and the like (norm-oriented), others emphasise an idealistic attitude, seeing Esperanto as contributing to world peace, justice, and brotherhood of mankind (value-oriented). This distinction is suggested here as an analytical one, and some Esperantists refuse to draw the distinction. It does, however, have an important basis in the history of Esperanto. The diffuseness of the aims of the Esperanto movement constitutes an important source of difficulty in assigning it to a sociological type. In particular there is the problem of identifying the distinctive variant of innovation that Esperanto represents. An answer is therefore needed to the question, 'What is wrong with the world for which Esperanto is put forward as a solution?'.

A movement to support any given cause derives from a situation of strain. This notion implies that there are certain social situations which predispose a group of individuals to come together to propose some resolution or at least mitigation of a problem that has been identified. The question arises as to who suggests that there is such a strain, and how such an innovator succeeds in recruiting a following.

There are differing views on the subject of the nature of strain in a society. One dogmatic Marxist view is committed to the standpoint that it has been scientifically established that the only significant source of strain can be related to the class struggle. From such a point of view, any other position can be relegated to the category of 'petty bourgeois',[15] at best a distraction from the revolutionary cause. An alternative viewpoint might argue that it is highly debatable whether the course of history would develop in such an obvious way with such certainty. Various areas of strain might be perceived in a social system, but it cannot be said automatically that one is objectively valid and others not. As Aron points out:

In the first place, it must be recognised that the idea of an immediate apprehension of objects, of an authentic reality, is itself an illusion which could only apply to a type of life mechanically adapted to its environment, either by instinct or by omniscience. Man, who is neither animal nor god, and who conceives real objects and values, can only interpret the world in terms of the meaning he attributes to his own existence. The notion of "fleeing from existence" has only a psychological, not a logical sense. The *petit bourgeois* who refuses to be a proletarian, because he regards culture and sentiments as more important than the amount of his wages, may be cowardly or blind in the view of Marxists, but from the standpoint of logic he merely has a different scale of values. The proletarian who transforms his situation by religious faith, and looks forward to a future life, may be resigned and stupid in the eyes of the unbeliever, but the criticism is just as metaphysical as the belief. Logically, it is a matter of different conceptions of the world. All self-awareness, and consciousness of one's own situation, implies a metaphysic and a moral theory, and what Marx regarded as authentic reality is only the expression of a particular philosophy.[16]

Esperanto is in any case not incompatible with some versions of Marxist philosophy, as seen by its vitality in many Communist countries. But even a different kind of radical view can reveal the complexities of social reality. In his useful discussion of power, Lukes draws attention to the problem of the dimensions involved:

The one-dimensional view of power offers a clear-cut paradigm for the be-havioural study of decision-making power by political actors, but it inevitably takes over the bias of the political system under observation and is blind to the ways in which its political agenda is controlled. The two-dimensional view points the way to examining that bias and control, but conceives of them too narrowly; in a word, it lacks a sociological perspective within which to examine, not only decision-making and non-decision-making power, but also the various ways of suppressing latent conflicts within society.[17]

Lukes aims to provide a solution to the problem which he out-lines. His three-dimensional view

...allows for consideration of the many ways in which *potential issues* are kept out of politics, whether through the operation of social forces and insti-tutional practices or through individuals' decisions.[18]

Yet despite social controls, it is possible for strain to be pointed out. Becker suggests that this is the province of the 'moral entre-preneur'. The latter's function is to create rules in a given social situation (or to enforce existing ones); he can articulate grievances and propose solutions. As Becker puts it,

Even though a practice may be harmful in an objective sense to the group in which it occurs, the harm needs to be discovered and pointed out. People must be made to feel that something ought to be done about it. Someone must call the public's attention to these matters, supply the push necessary to get things done, and direct such energies as are aroused in the proper direction to get the rules created.[19]

As well as leaders, a movement also requires followers. In his discussion of charismatic leadership, Worsley points out the need for a leader to have a relevant message. He cites the example of speakers in Hyde Park:

What these people lack, however, is a *relevant* message. It is not that they
lack any message at all, for they often have quite definite messages, including
some very radical ones. But they are in fact figures of entertainment, even fun,
rather than serious potential leaders of movements and organizations, precisely
because they possess only the technical trappings of personal leadership rather
than the content. . . . Without the message, there can be no serious content to
the communication. And it cannot be *any* message; it must, firstly, speak to
unsatisfied wants in the hearers, and, secondly, offer them some promise of
eventual fufilment.[20]

Likewise, Friedland points out: 'it is only when the message
conveyed by charismatics to social groups is relevant and meaningful within the social context that authority emerges'.[21]

The question remains as to what constitutes the definition of
social relevance. This admittedly is problematic when theoretical
frameworks originally devised for the study of political social movements are employed, since the term 'social movement' is frequently
reserved for those which are successful, i.e. have become part of
the conventional social order. As already noted, this is the view
taken by Banks, based on similar strictures by Smelser. Discussion
might, however, centre on a movement which may not have become
part of the established social order, such as the Esperanto movement here considered. The term 'social movement' is sometimes
considered inadequate for treatment of such phenomena, but it
has been retained here for convenience. As already noted, strain of
any kind needs to be articulated by someone; the Marxian notion
of 'class consciousness' recognises this. But rather than implying
that there are 'objective' conditions of strain, it might be more
accurate to consider the extent to which any given situation is
perceived of as problematic. It is necessary to ask, 'by whom is
this situation regarded as problematic?'. If the matter of 'relevance'
is to have a part to play in the discussion, it is useful to consider the
extent to which a given situation is thought of as one of strain, and
how far a given solution to the problem is forthcoming. Billington
proposes the useful notion of 'perceived strain'.[22] This incorporates
a subjective element, the actors' definition of the situation, and
avoids any overtones of 'objective' or 'true' solutions.

This perspective will be adopted here so as to enable consideration of a movement which has succeeded in perpetuating its

existence but has not, apart from spasmodic successes, become part of the established social order. A movement of this kind can often be regarded by outsiders with contempt or at least amusement, and supporters of it are frequently labelled as 'cranks'. The concept of a crank will be taken up in the conclusion, but at this stage it can be noted that even Lukes's three-dimensional view of power might be extended further. If the three-dimensional view points to the ways in which potential issues are kept out of politics, the analysis of power might be extended further to consider the ways in which the *radical agenda for change* is drawn up. Thus if Lukes's three-dimensional analysis is a radical view, it is even possible to conceive of a four-dimensional analysis which would be a 'cranky' view. In the latter view could be included anarchists and pacifists, for instance, and it will be seen that if interpreted in a value-oriented manner Esperanto would qualify for inclusion here.

Esperantists have tended traditionally to have a lukewarm, even hostile, attitude to governments as sources of support (though this has not invariably been the case). The emphasis has been on recruiting individuals, so that the movement would eventually become an effective force in the world. The practice of converting individuals to the cause is typical of religious organisations, which see every individual soul as worthy of salvation. Yet there also exist a number of nonreligious movements: vegetarianism, pacifism, and more recent currents of opinion which have striven to create 'alternative' societies.[23] These represent a distinctive form of subversive activity which stands apart from the more obvious kind of political action. Its adherents may not totally reject politics, but will have greater faith in other means of changing the world. It might be suggested that, by the side of the dominant value system, there exist established forms of deviance. By the side of capitalism there are established ways to oppose capitalism through socialist organisations. While one set of dominant values exists, there frequently exists a tradition of radical thought which indicates what it is important to oppose and how to set about it. Yet by the side of political radicalism, there remain the 'cranky' organisations. Such organisations have, not surprisingly, proved elusive for the sociologist. Killian[24] has already pointed out that little emphasis has been placed in modern sociology upon social movements of any kind, and Banks[25] further suggests an explanation of such neglect in terms of the functionalist domination of twentieth-century sociological thought. This has made for a concentration on static phenomena, to the neglect of problems arising from the study of social movements, involving a dynamic perspective. If this is true for politically radical movements, which are relatively easy to identify, then it must be even more true of the study of the alternative subversive tradition here outlined.

Esperanto can be seen to be easily associated with this tradition. Vegetarianism, cooperative communities, nudism, pacifism, and similar causes have been linked by various individuals and groups to Esperanto. Yet at the same time there is nothing intrinsically subversive about Esperanto, and by no means all of its supporters would consider it in any way radical in implication. Yet the more subversive interpretation of Esperanto remains a significant feature among some of its supporters. In the succeeding chapters an examination will be made of the variations in orientation of Esperantists during the history of the organised movement, and a general assessment of the tradition of thought to which Esperanto belongs will be made in the conclusion.

NOTES

1.   The 'Hymn' is reproduced in numerous places. See, for instance, L.L. Zamenhof, *Originala verkaro*, 1929, p.586. *Originala verkaro* will be referred to hereinafter as OV.
2.   On the desirability of a certain amount of naivety about other disciplines, the approach adopted here follows that of M. Gluckman (ed.) *Closed Systems and Open Minds; The Limits of Naivety in Social Anthropology*, 1964.
3.   For the notion of 'translation' in anthropology see J. Beattie, *Other Cultures*, p.31.
4.   See Chapters 11–12.
5.   See, for instance, R. Horton, 'Ritual man in Africa', *Africa*, 1964, pp.85–104.
6.   I have stated my own position on such questions in a different context. See P. Forster, 'Empiricism and imperialism: a review of the New Left critique of social anthropology', in *Anthropology and the Colonial Encounter*, ed. by T. Asad, 1973.
7.   B.R. Wilson, *Sects and Society*, 1961, p.3.
8.   R. Wallis, *Sectarianism*, 1975, p.5.
9.   J.M. Yinger, *Religion, Society and the Individual*, 1957, pp.154–155.
10.   N.J. Smelser, *Social Change in the Industrial Revolution*, 1959.
11.   J.A. Banks, *The Sociology of Social Movements*, 1972, p.17.
12.   R. Heberle, *Social Movements: An Introduction to Political Sociology*, 1951.
13.   W. Kornhauser, *The Politics of Mass Society*, 1959.

14.   N.J. Smelser, *Theory of Collective Behavior*, 1962, Ch. IX, X, and *passim*.

15.   The term is used rather loosely; strictly speaking, 'bourgeois socialism' is the term actually applied by Marx to the kind of movement here considered:

'A part of the bourgeoisie is desirous of redressing social grievances, in order to secure the continued existence of bourgeois society.

'To this section belong economists, philanthropists, humanitarians, improvers of the condition of the working class, organisers of charity, members of societies for the prevention of cruelty to animals, temperance fanatics, hole-and-corner reformers of every imaginable kind. This form of socialism has, moreover, been worked out into complete systems'. K. Marx and F. Engels, *Manifesto of the Communist Party*, 1848, reprinted in *Marx and Engels: Basic Writings on Politics and Philosophy*, ed. by L.S. Feuer, 1959.

16.   R. Aron, *German Sociology*, 1964, pp.63–64.

17.   S. Lukes, *Power: A Radical View*, 1974, p.57.

18.   *Ibid.*, p.24.

19.   H.S. Becker, *Outsiders*, 1963, p.162.

20.   P. Worsley, *The Trumpet Shall Sound* (second edition) 1968, pp.xii–xiv.

21.   W.H. Friedland, 'For a sociological concept of charisma', *Social Forces* 43, October 1964, pp.18–26.

22.   R.H.C. Billington, 'The women's education and suffrage movements, 1850–1914: innovation and institutionalisation', unpublished Ph.D. thesis, Hull, 1976, pp.19–21.

23.   On this subject see particularly A. Rigby, *Alternative Realities*, 1974.

24.   L.M. Killian, 'Social movements', in *Handbook of Modern Sociology*, ed. by R.E.L. Faris, 1964, pp.426–455.

25.   Banks, *op. cit.*, p.43.

PART I

The World Esperanto Movement

1

Size and Spread of the Esperanto Speech Community

In order to introduce the subsequent discussion of the developments in the history of Esperanto, an attempt will be made in this chapter to assess the scale and geographical distribution of support for the language. This task is beset with difficulties. In the first place, sociological studies tend to concentrate in practice upon a social movement as it exists within the confines of a single society, or at most a small number of societies. Although many social movements are international in scope, it still makes perfect sense in most cases to examine them within the confines of a given society. Yet in the case of Esperanto, the whole *raison d'être* of the movement is international contact of some kind. The organised movement to promote Esperanto is itself international, and it conducts its business in Esperanto. This does not preclude the formation of national organisations to promote the language; yet the focus of attention for Esperanto tends to be the annual World Esperanto Congress,[1] and particular stress is placed upon the social relations which the movement facilitates within an international context.

The Esperanto movement, therefore, has to be considered within the general framework of international relations. This is a difficult exercise, since a wide range of detailed historical and sociological knowledge of many societies would be required in order to look at Esperanto in every country into which it has penetrated. This task has been lightened by various procedures.

In the first place, as will soon become apparent, although Esperanto is intended as a world language, for a long period of its history its base has tended to be European. Nearly all world Esperanto congresses have been held in Europe, and the headquarters of international organisations to promote Esperanto have always been in that continent. Thus particular attention will be focused upon the context of international relations within Europe, and the consequences of European relations for the Esperanto movement. It will be apparent that, since Esperanto is expected to help to promote peaceful international relations, the two world wars will be of particular significance for the development of Esperanto.

In the second place, attention will be focused, for the international movement, not so much upon the relationship between Esperanto and the wider society in each country in the world, as upon the internal dynamics of the international movement. The way in which the organised Esperanto movement developed, from one World Congress to the next, will be a particular area of concern. It will however be recognised that such development has taken place within the broader context of European relations, and this will be noted where relevant. Thus the significance of the two world wars, the League of Nations, the Third International, the United Nations, and the 'Cold War' will be considered in their relation to the organised world Esperanto movement.

Third, the case of the Esperanto movement in relation to one particular society will also be investigated in relation to the dominant values and general recent history of that society. For convenience, Great Britain will be the society in which such questions are examined in particular detail.

Part I will therefore deal with the dynamics of the international Esperanto movement, and Part II with Esperanto in Britain. The British movement has, of course, played its part in the international movement, and this will be noted where relevant.

As an appropriate background for the examination of such questions, certain statistical information will be presented in this chapter about the scale and spread of adherents of Esperanto. Many observers have already noted the difficulty of such an exercise. Durrant remarks that

Figures cannot be given with the same degree of definiteness as, say, for the number of motor-cars licensed for the road, where the existence of a motor-car, and payment for the right of use, are complete and finite facts. In dealing with an acquired language there is no such simple standard. This will be obvious if, instead of taking Esperanto, we consider some other language, such as French, and try to assess how many people speak it. Are we to take for our conclusions the number of people living in France and her colonies? If so, this would not be realistic, as the majority of the inhabitants of the overseas territories speak only their own native tongues. Or should we also take into account everyone in other countries who has had French lessons in school? This would be equally misleading. In any event the number would be difficult to establish; further, the majority would have forgotten their lessons in which their degree of proficiency was often too dubious. It is similarly impossible to arrive at any authoritative figures for people knowing any system of shorthand, or, as another example, the Morse Code.

These difficulties beset anyone attempting to gather statistics of the number of Esperantists, where an overwhelming proportion of instruction and use has been the outcome of private initiative, of which no national society could be expected to secure and maintain up-to-date details. Of those who have participated in courses, some have emerged proficient and joined their national or sectional societies, some have remained unaffiliated — and these constitute the greatest number — while others have been less bright or diligent and have consequently not advanced far in their study.[2]

It is also important to exercise caution in relation to claims made by the Esperantists themselves. As Bodmer remarks:

We should accept figures about its [Esperanto's] spread and popularity, when given by Esperantists themselves, with the caution we should adopt towards data about the vitality of Erse or Gaelic when those who supply them are Celtic enthusiasts.[3]

This stricture is particularly important in relation to the number of 'unorganised' Esperantists. Esperanto supporters are always at pains to point out that the number of Esperanto organisations is only the 'tip of the iceberg': that there are many more speakers of Esperanto who are outside the movement. That some such speakers will exist cannot be denied. Not all or even most of those who take Esperanto courses or teach themselves Esperanto through generally available textbooks end up joining the movement. There are also many competent speakers who lapse in their membership. However, the degree to which it is possible to use Esperanto without being a member of the organised movement is severely limited. It is possible to buy and borrow Esperanto books, or to maintain personal contacts already established through Esperanto; but it is not possible to form new contacts effectively without being a member of some kind of association. There is hardly anywhere where it is possible simply to use Esperanto in the course of everyday activities. This assertion needs to be modified for one or two countries, especially in Eastern Europe, where command of the language is comparatively widespread, but on the whole the *effective* number of Esperantists is that of organised supporters. There are various kinds of organisation to promote and/or use Esperanto; some of these are small and loosely structured, while others are firmly established with a degree of bureaucratisation. In most countries there are local Esperanto groups in many centres of population. Most countries have national associations to promote Esperanto. There is also a world Esperanto association. There are in addition various specialist associations, for groups such as Catholics, railwaymen, scientists, chess-players, and several others. It is possible to be a member of any such group without belonging to any other Esperanto association.

It is true that since the Second World War attempts to consolidate a unified world Esperanto association have on the whole been successful; but at other times this has not always been the case. There have been disagreements on matters such as whether a world Esperanto movement should be based on national representation or not; and problems have arisen in relation to political neutrality. There are also formidable difficulties about the reliability of published statistics. Even in recent times, many figures seem to be rounded, suggesting that they are estimates rather than accurate counts. Other factors making for unreliability of statistics include internal disputes, bringing into existence rival national associations; exchange control problems; disputes between national and world organisations; political disapproval of Esperanto in certain countries; and the practice of certain national associations of returning separate figures for their youth movement. There are also problems relating to divided countries such as Ireland, Germany, and Korea. It has not always been clear, for instance, whether recent figures for 'Germany' include both East and West. Membership of the international movement can suddenly increase dramatically from one year to the next simply because a pre-existing national body in the country concerned has become affiliated to the world movement. Similarly, it can suddenly decline if an affiliated national association fails to submit full statistics.

Despite these reservations, some assessment of the state of Esperanto in various countries will be made for various periods in history. Nothing more than a general overview is here attempted. An exhaustive sociography of Esperanto would go further, would examine each national collectivity of Esperantists and assess the available statistics. This would be the subject of a book in itself, so here an attempt is made only to examine the scale on which the activities analysed in subsequent chapters are operating.

The founder, Zamenhof, originally issued a list of addresses (*Adresaro*) of those who had successfully passed a simple test of Esperanto in the first available textbooks. This was issued continually until the beginning of the twentieth century. The list was not cumulative, so the figures presented in Table 1 refer only to *new* Esperantists. Four different series are taken:[4]

1. Nos. 1–1,000, issued 1889.
2. Nos. 3,001–3,602, issued 1896 (covering 1/1/93–1/10/95).
3. Nos. 4,661–5,025, issued 1900 (covering January 1899–January 1900).
4. Nos. 9,261–11,199, issued 1905 (covering 1/1/04–1/1/05).

Table 1. *Statistics derived from Zamenhof's* Adresaro

(a) The first thousand recorded Esperantists. These were distributed nationally as follows; percentage in parentheses, as a proportion of total number of names recorded in the list.

Russia	925	(93%)	Britain	9	(1%)
Germany	26	(3%)	France	5	(1%)
Austria-Hungary	19	(2%)	Sweden	5	(1%)

Less than 1% (actual number in brackets): United States (4), Turkey (2), Spain (2), China (1), Rumania (1), Italy (1).

(b) 1 January 1893–1 October 1895

Russia	486	(81%)	Germany	13	(2%)
France	60	(10%)	Austria-Hungary	4	(1%)
Sweden	18	(3%)	Portugal	4	(1%)

Less than 1%: Argentina (3), Bulgaria (2), United States (2), Belgium (2), Britain, Turkey, Algeria, Egypt, South Africa, Australia, Denmark, Netherlands (1 each).

Table 1 (continued).
(c) January 1899–January 1900

Russia	209	(57%)	Austria–Hungary	8	(2%)
France	72	(20%)	Brazil	4	(1%)
Bulgaria	36	(10%)	Switzerland	3	(1%)
Belgium	12	(3%)	Spain	2	(1%)
Rumania	10	(3%)	United States	2	(1%)

Less than 1%: Britain, Sweden, Netherlands, Chile, Tunisia (1 each).

(d) 1 January 1904–1 January 1905

Russia	520	(27%)	Germany	31	(2%)
France	491	(25%)	Sweden	24	(1%)
Britain	308	(16%)	Mexico	24	(1%)
Austria–Hungary	211	(11%)	Belgium	21	(1%)
Bulgaria	81	(4%)	Switzerland	19	(1%)
Algeria	65	(3%)	United States	11	(1%)
Spain	44	(2%)	Netherlands	10	(1%)

Less than 1%: Tunisia (8), Malta (7), Brazil (7), Turkey (6), Canada (5), Denmark (5), Australia, India, New Zealand (3 each), Rumania, South Africa, Indochina, Dominica (2 each), China, Argentina, Portugal, Chile, Tahiti, Syria, Tonkin, Philippines, Ceylon, Guadeloupe, Cape Verde, Dominican Republic, Norway (1 each).

There was, in the late nineteenth century, no organised association of Esperantists on an international scale, though from the start the movement began to recruit internationally. Apart from figures derived from the list of addresses already mentioned, another source of statistical information is found in subscriptions to the official organ of Esperanto, called *La Esperantisto*. Table 2 gives an indication of the national distribution of such subscriptions; percentages (to the nearest whole number of percentage points) are out of the total number of subscribers.[5]

Even though some subscriptions were collective rather than individual, the total number reached by *La Esperantisto* can be seen to be small. The figures of 335 and 373 are scarcely large in relation to the vast population of the Russian empire. Taking these

Table 2. *Subscriptions to* La Esperantisto

| | December 1892 | | December 1894 | |
	N	%	N	%
Australia	–	–	1	0
Austria	–	–	4	1
Belgium	1	0	–	–
Brazil	1	0	–	–
Bulgaria	3	1	7	1
Finland	–	–	8	1
France	10	2	27	5
Germany	124	23	92	15
Great Britain	1	0	1	0
Italy	4	1	5	1
North America	6	1	4	1
Norway	–	–	1	0
Portugal	1	0	13	2
Russia	335	62	373	63
Spain	2	0	4	1
Sweden	56	10	55	9
Switzerland	–	–	1	0
Total	544		596	

figures together with those derived from the list of addresses, it can be seen that the overwhelming majority of supporters, from the beginning, resided in Russia. This proportion diminished as Esperanto gradually spread to other countries, but the Russian contingent still remained substantial. Up to the mid-1890s Germany also seems to have been an important source of recruits, though by the turn of the century German recruitment was much reduced. The strength of support for Esperanto in Sweden until the mid-1890s is also significant: as a proportion of the population of the country concerned, it would rate higher than Russia.

From the early 1890s onwards, particularly significant was the growth of support for Esperanto in France. French recruitment steadily increased in the late nineteenth and early twentieth centuries. As French recruitment increased, so too did the strength of Esperanto in Bulgaria initially, and later in Britain and Austria-

Hungary. By 1904 Esperanto was steadily spreading to ever more countries.

The number of Esperanto clubs and groups in various countries can give some indication of the strength of Esperanto in various parts of the world. Stojan presents the information shown in Table 3 for 1912 and 1926.[6]

Table 3. *Figures for Esperanto groups*

	Number of Esperanto groups	
	1912	1926
Country		
France	226	101
Germany	273	441
Slavic countries	165	475
Britain	152	144
Spain	76	47
Hungary	42	47
Netherlands	31	51
Japan	26	181
United States	150	47
Continent		
Europe	1,245	1,492
Asia	39	191
The Americas	247	76
Africa	16	6
Oceania	28	11
Total	1,575	1,776

Stojan's figures for 1926 are derived from a survey by Dietterle,[7] in what appears to be the only systematic attempt to present a general statistical overview of the Esperanto organisations. This survey was conducted from Germany and almost certainly reflects better access to German information. Dietterle attempted to avoid exaggeration, but his procedures did not necessarily eliminate double-counting. Tables 4 and 5 are based on Dietterle's research. Table 4 indicates the number of Esperantists and Esperanto groups

Table 4. *Esperanto in European countries, 1928 (Dietterle's statistics)*

Country	Groups	Individuals	Density (individuals)	Base population (millions)
Albania	0	6	7.2	0.837
Austria	96	7,696	1,184.0	6.5
Belgium	26	3,359	447.9	7.5
Bulgaria	35	1,744	317.1	5.5
Czechoslovakia	116	8,967	622.7	14.4
Denmark	17	990	291.1	3.4
Estonia	16	784	712.7	1.1
Finland	15	825	229.2	3.6
France	101	5,237	128.6	40.7
Germany	441	30,868	488.4	63.2
Gibraltar	0	4	193.8	0.020638
Great Britain	144	7,855	173.8	45.2
Greece	3	1,968	298.1	6.6
Hungary	47	3,052	359.1	8.5
Iceland	0	24	235.2	0.102
Ireland	1	343	114.3	3.0
Italy	43	5,341	131.9	40.5
Latvia	10	1,498	832.2	1.8
Liechtenstein	0	1	93.3	0.010716
Lithuania	18	780	339.1	2.3
Luxemburg	0	2	7.7	0.261
Malta	0	7	30.8	0.227
Monaco	0	1	45.1	0.022153
Netherlands	51	6,649	886.5	7.5
Norway	5	380	135.7	2.8
Poland	51	4,690	158.4	29.6
Portugal	2	79	13.2	6.0
Rumania	15	1,912	109.9	17.4
San Marino	0	1	77.2	0.012952
Spain	47	3,591	168.6	21.3
Sweden	28	1,436	235.4	6.1
Switzerland	39	1,821	455.3	4.0
Turkey	0	49	3.6	13.6
USSR*	95	5,726	40.0	147.0
Yugoslavia	30	1,994	166.2	12.0
Total Europe	1,492	109,680		

* Dietterle's figure for the Soviet Union is an underestimate, according to Drezen.[8] In 1926 the Soviet Esperanto Union claimed 527 groups and a total of 16,066 organised Esperantists. This would produce a density of 109.3.

Table 5. *Non-European countries with at least 100 Esperantists,*
1928 (Dietterle)

Country	No. of individual Esperantists	Density	Base population (millions)
Japan	6,903	109.6	63.0
United States	4,845	41.4	117.1
Brazil	1,182	29.6	39.9
Australia	1,087	175.3	6.2
Argentina	445	43.2	10.3
Uruguay	416	244.7	1.7
China	393	1.2	318.7
New Zealand	324	249.2	1.3
Palestine	252	284.1	0.887
Cuba	207	57.5	3.6

World total: 126,575
European total: 109,680
Percentage of Europeans: 87%

for each European country, while Table 5 indicates the principal
sources of strength outside Europe. The figures for 'density' are
arrived at by dividing the number of Esperantists reported for the
country concerned by its population in millions (*pro rata* for
countries of less than a million population). The population figures
are based on the nearest available census to 1926, and are drawn
from the *Statesman's Yearbook*.

Taken in absolute terms, these figures suggest consolidation,
and in most cases expansion, of Esperanto in the larger European
countries – and in some smaller ones too, such as The Netherlands.
The French contribution appears to be slightly weaker than at the
turn of the century. German and Russian support for Esperanto
has increased considerably. Esperanto remains an overwhelmingly
European movement, the only strong non-European contingent (in
terms of total numbers) being Japan.

In the interwar years, problems arose in the organisation of the
world Esperanto movement, on the kind of structure to be adopted.
The dispute was as to whether this should be a federation of
national associations, or whether it should recruit members inde-

pendently of nationality. By 1922 a unified, 'umbrella' committee had been set up, though it operated in addition to, rather than instead of, the existing organisations. In Table 6[9] figures for various national societies are presented together with the total number of

Table 6. *Membership of national societies, 1923–1931*

National society	Number of members			Density		
	1923	1927	1931	1923	1927	1931
Argentina	357	338	300	34.7	32.8	26.3
Belgium	700	570	900	93.3	76.0	111.1
Brazil	210	290	250	6.8	7.3	6.2
Bulgaria	600	2,000	500	109.1	363.6	90.9
Catalan	450	600	300	(included with Spain)		
Czechoslovakia	1,100	500	300	154.7	90.3	68.0
Czechoslovakia (Sudetenland)	1,127	800	700			
Denmark	200	240	250	58.8	70.6	69.4
Estonia	378	382	350	343.6	347.3	318.2
Finland	620	220	70	172.2	61.1	18.9
France	800	1,292	1,587	19.7	31.7	38.8
Germany	3,531	2,230	2,114	55.9	35.3	33.4
Great Britain	1,500	1,200	1,957	33.2	26.5	42.4
Hungary	200	450	650	23.5	52.9	74.7
Italy	1,825	1,825	950	45.1	45.1	23.1
Japan	2,100	2,100	2,100	33.3	33.3	32.1
Latvia	–	110	150	–	61.1	78.9
Lithuania	500	1,115	1,195	217.4	484.8	497.9
Netherlands	295	325	1,300	39.3	43.3	164.6
Norway	200	100	100	71.4	35.7	35.7
Poland	700	689	–	23.6	23.3	–
Spain	425	300	400	41.1	42.3	30.6
Sweden	439	281	800	72.0	46.1	131.1
Switzerland	270	459	650	67.5	114.8	158.5
Yugoslavia	–	860	1,118	–	71.7	80.4
Total	18,527	19,276	18,982			
Universal Esperanto Association	6,352	9,100	8,835			

members of the Universal Esperanto Association (UEA), which recruited on a supernational basis.

The list is not complete, since not all national associations made their membership figures available. For 1923 and 1927 figures for density have been based on the same figures for base population as were used in Tables 4 and 5. 1931 figures for density have used as their base the population figures shown in the 1932 *Statesman's Yearbook*.[10]

The figures for total number of members represent a fairly steady support for Esperanto internationally during the period considered in Table 6. There is overall neither a dramatic increase nor a dramatic decline; there are, however, numerous local fluctuations, which are often quite substantial. For all the years under consideration, Germany represents the strongest support for Esperanto in numerical terms. A non-European country, Japan, comes in second place.

Figures for total number of members are of considerable significance to the extent that they determine which nations contribute most members to the international movement. Yet it can be seen that certain other nations have a particularly strong movement *as a proportion of their total population*. In order to elucidate this matter, figures for density will be examined. Tables 7 and 8 indicate the ten nations where density of penetration of Esperanto has been strongest, using figures already presented in Tables 4 and 6.

Table 7.   *Density of penetration of Esperanto, 1926 (Dietterle's statistics)*

1. Austria	(1,184.0)	6. Germany	(488.4)
2. Netherlands	(886.5)	7. Switzerland	(455.3)
3. Latvia	(832.2)	8. Belgium	(447.9)
4. Estonia	(712.7)	9. Hungary	(359.1)
5. Czechoslovakia	(622.7)	10. Lithuania	(339.1)

A number of interesting features are revealed by these tables. It appears that, despite the relatively better information available for Dietterle for the German figure, this was not sufficient to put Germany in first place for density of penetration. It seems, too, that had figures for Austria been available for Table 6, this country would also have been in a fairly high position in Table 8. From a general overview of these figures it is evident that the density of penetration of Esperanto was particularly high during the period

Table 8. *Density of penetration by membership of national societies, 1923–1931*

1923
1. Estonia (343.6)
2. Lithuania (217.4)
3. Finland (172.2)
4. Czechoslovakia (157.4)
5. Bulgaria (109.1)
6. Belgium (93.3)
7. Sweden (72.0)
8. Norway (71.4)
9. Switzerland (67.5)
10. Germany (55.9)

1927
1. Lithuania (484.5)
2. Bulgaria (363.6)
3. Estonia (347.3)
4. Switzerland (114.8)
5. Czechoslovakia (90.3)
6. Belgium (76.0)
7. Yugoslavia (71.7)
8. Denmark (70.6)
9. Finland (61.1)
10. Latvia (61.1)

1931
1. Lithuania (497.9)
2. Estonia (318.2)
3. Netherlands (164.6)
4. Switzerland (158.8)
5. Sweden (131.1)
6. Belgium (111.1)
7. Bulgaria (90.9)
8. Yugoslavia (80.4)
9. Latvia (78.9)
10. Hungary (74.5)

1923–1931 in those countries which established or re-established their independent existence immediately or shortly after the First World War. One consequence of this had been the officialisation of a number of what were previously minority languages, some of which (Finnish, Estonian, and Hungarian) were also not Indo-European. Such minority language communities have provided a fruitful field for the development of Esperanto. A further factor is noteworthy. Apart from Germany and Austria, all nations represented in Tables 7 and 8 are either (a) other countries speaking minority languages (Netherlands, Sweden, Norway, Denmark, and Bulgaria) or (b) countries divided internally by language (Belgium and Switzerland). Recruitment to the movement has continued to be stronger than average from those countries which speak minority languages.

Towards the end of the 1930s the number of Esperantists in the world was much diminished by Nazi and Stalinist pressures. The world movement recovered slowly after the Second World War, though a unified international movement was consolidated for the first time. This simplifies presentation of statistics, since the Universal Esperanto Association now constitutes an amalgam of representation through national associations and direct membership. Members of affiliated national associations become 'associate members' of the Universal Esperanto Association. On the whole, membership continues to be predominantly European, and until very recently European preponderance tended to increase. This change appears to stem partly from a conscious campaign by UEA to widen the basis of recruitment outside Europe, and partly from a decline in European membership. Table 9 shows some recent figures for European predominance.

In Table 10, each European country is considered separately. Those with no Esperantists recorded for any of the years under consideration are omitted. Figures for number of members refer to UEA membership, counting full and associate members together.[11] In the case of figures for density, however, if membership of a national Esperanto association as recorded in the UEA yearbook for the year concerned (whether or not affiliated to UEA) is higher than the recorded total UEA membership figure for that country, this figure is the one used to calculate density. To save space the base population is given only for 1964.

Table 9.   *Membership of UEA, in Europe and rest of world*

	1954		1964		1974		1979	
	N	%	N	%	N	%	N	%
Europe*	12,738	75	27,336	85	28,631	88	25,402	82
Rest of world	4,263	25	4,851	15	3,802	12	5,408	18
Total	17,001		32,187		32,433		30,810	

* 'Europe' in the sense here considered excludes the Soviet Union and Turkey; as membership in both of these countries is very small, this should not make for difficulties in comparing with data which include them.

Table 11 shows the ten countries with the highest density of penetration, in the manner employed in Table 8. Figures are presented for each of the four years under consideration.

The trend shown seems fairly clear. Luxemburg, Monaco, Vatican City, and possibly Iceland may perhaps be seen as freak results, since their small size has the effect that the national association rather than the local group is the unit of allegiance, with the effect of swelling the figures for national membership. In other respects it can be seen that penetration of Esperanto is highest in those European countries which speak minority languages: Scandinavian countries, The Netherlands, and, increasingly, the smaller East European countries. Lifting of Stalinist pressures has helped the latter considerably in re-establishing their movements. A great increase in membership can be seen for Bulgaria, Hungary, Czechoslovakia, and Poland in this connection. Yet this trend is not universal, and it is useful to examine some European countries with a noticeably *low* penetration of Esperanto. Table 10 shows no members at all for isolationist Albania, except in 1979. Also in Rumania, where Esperanto continued to meet with official disapproval (on linguistic, not political grounds) membership of UEA is negligible.

Weakness is evident also in a number of capitalist countries. In Portugal, where Esperanto organisations were virtually illegal until Spínola's *coup d'état*, membership has been very low. Ireland, Spain, and Greece also show low membership. In the larger European countries (Britain, Italy, West Germany, and France) the

Table 10a.   *Membership of UEA in European countries,*
1954-1979

	1954	1964	1974	1979
Albania	0	0	0	1
Austria	580	306	380	384
Belgium	433	618	664	679
Bulgaria	4	4,719	5,184	4,208
Cyprus	2	1	1	0
Czechoslovakia	31	103	1,231	1,257
Denmark	1,200	1,021	546	470
Finland	317	270	498	637
France	1,064	2,040	1,435	1,263
Germany (D.R.)	0	2,413[b]	15	530
Germany (F.R.)	446[a]		1,565	1,444
Gibraltar	1	0	0	0
Gt. Britain and N.I.	1,585	1,367	1,379	1,124
Greece	9	13	431	14
Hungary	5	3,382	3,239	3,237
Iceland	38	24	22	40
Ireland (Republic)	23	7	34	7
Italy	1,321	1,310	1,575	1,438
Luxemburg	1	1	3	102
Malta	0	2	0	46
Monaco	0	26	35	2
Netherlands	1,174	1,299	1,152	842
Norway	864	613	507	469
Poland	5	3,392	4,361	4,266
Portugal	56	43	31	175
Rumania	1	6	13	36
Spain	523	721	742	485
Sweden	1,847	1,573	1,497	1,682
Switzerland	344	363	393	394
Vatican	0	0	0	1
Yugoslavia	864	1,703	1,698	169
Total	12,738	27,336	28,631	25,402

[a] For 1954, figures for Saarland were enumerated separately. These have been added to the West German figure.
[b] West and East German figures were not indicated separately, but most of this figure relates to West Germany.

Table 10b.   *Base figures for density where different from those in*
Table 10a

	1954	1964	1974	1979
Austria	–	–	–	1,863
Belgium	–	–	–	1,400
Czechoslovakia	–	3,270	–	3,600
Denmark	–	–	–	600
France	–	–	–	1,287
Germany (D.R.)	–	–	1,600	1,100
Germany (F.R.)	3,098*	–	–	1,500
Great Britain	–	–	–	1,256
Greece	–	–	–	400
Iceland	204	204	204	50
Ireland (Republic)	–			25
Italy	–	–	–	1,600
Luxemburg	–	–	120	–
Malta	–	–	15	–
Norway	–	–	–	500
Poland	1,100	–	–	4,621
Spain	–	–	–	550
Sweden	–	–	–	1,700
Yugoslavia	3,300	3,500	–	1,500

* Includes figures separately returned for Saarland.

tendency has been one of decline. UEA appears to be increasingly
relying on smaller European countries for recruits; even here, some
traditional areas of strength (Denmark, Norway and The Netherlands) have declined, and only the large influx from Eastern Europe
seems to have saved UEA from a decline in membership. As will be
seen, this has created certain tensions relating to the definition of
'political neutrality'.

In order to illustrate the European predominance in UEA, Table
12 shows the number and density of UEA members in those non-
European countries with at least 100 members of UEA.

New Zealand forms an interesting exception to the trend for
Esperanto to be more popular in countries speaking a minority
language.

Table 10c.   *Density of Penetration in Europe, 1954–1979*

		Density			Population
	1954	1964	1974	1979	1964 (millions)
Albania	0	0	0	0.4	1.6
Austria	84.1	43.1	50.7	248.4	7.1
Belgium	49.2	66.5	67.8	142.9	9.3
Bulgaria	0.5	575.5	595.8	483.7	8.2
Cyprus	3.9	1.7	1.6	0	0.574
Czechoslovakia	2.3	224.6	86.1	241.6	14.1
Denmark	279.1	212.7	107.1	117.6	4.7
Finland	75.5	58.7	106.0	135.5	4.6
France	24.9	41.9	27.6	24.2	48.7
Germany (D.R.)	0	(?)	94.1	65.5	17.0
Germany (F.R.)	58.2	41.7	25.2	24.4	62.0
Gibraltar	41.7	0	0	0	0.024
Gt. Britain and N.I.	31.2	25.3	24.6	22.5	54.1
Greece	1.2	1.5	49.0	43.5	8.5
Hungary	0.5	334.9	308.5	302.5	10.1
Iceland	1,307.6	1,090.9	940.1	227.3	0.187
Ireland (Republic)	7.7	2.5	11.3	7.8	2.8
Italy	27.8	25.9	29.1	28.4	50.5
Luxemburg	3.3	3.1	340.0	286.5	0.323
Malta	0	6.2	47.2	150.8	0.321
Monaco	0	1,300.0	1,521.7	87.0	0.020
Netherlands	109.7	108.3	84.7	61.0	12.0
Norway	254.1	165.7	126.8	125.0	3.7
Poland	40.0	108.0	129.4	133.5	31.4
Portugal	7.1	5.2	3.8	19.9	8.3
Rumania	0.1	0.3	0.6	1.7	18.8
Spain	17.9	24.0	21.9	15.4	30.1
Sweden	256.5	207.0	182.6	207.3	7.6
Switzerland	73.2	67.2	62.4	61.6	5.4
Vatican	0	0	0	1,000.0	0.001
Yugoslavia	195.3	189.2	82.8	69.1	18.5

In 1964 a survey of local groups was carried out by UEA.[12] This
provides a useful complement to figures for UEA membership since
many local group members are not members of their national
association and thus do not appear in UEA membership figures.

Table 11. *Density of penetration of UEA membership by nation, 1954–1979*

1954		1964		1974		1979	
1. Iceland	(1,307.6)	1. Monaco	(1,300.0)	1. Monaco	(1,521.7)	1. Vatican City	(1,000.0)
2. Denmark	(279.1)	2. Iceland	(1,090.1)	2. Iceland	(940.1)	2. Bulgaria	(483.7)
3. Sweden	(256.5)	3. Bulgaria	(575.5)	3. Bulgaria	(598.5)	3. Hungary	(302.5)
4. Norway	(254.1)	4. Hungary	(334.9)	4. Luxemburg	(340.0)	4. Luxemburg	(286.5)
5. Yugoslavia	(195.3)	5. Czechoslovakia	(224.6)	5. Hungary	(308.5)	5. Austria	(248.4)
6. Netherlands	(109.7)	6. Denmark	(217.2)	6. Sweden	(182.6)	6. Czechoslovakia	(241.6)
7. Austria	(84.1)	7. Sweden	(207.0)	7. Poland	(126.8)	7. Iceland	(227.3)
8. Finland	(75.5)	8. Yugoslavia	(189.2)	8. Norway	(126.8)	8. Sweden	(207.3)
9. Switzerland	(73.2)	9. Norway	(165.7)	9. Denmark	(107.1)	9. Malta	(150.8)
10. Germany (F.R.)	(58.2)	10. Netherlands	(108.3)	10. Finland	(106.0)	10. Belgium	(142.9)

Table 12a.   *UEA membership in non-European countries*
(with at least 100 members), 1964

Country	Members N	Density	Base population (millions)
Argentina	357	17.0	21.0
Australia	272	24.5	11.1
Brazil	1,094	15.4	71.0
Canada	178	9.3	19.2
Israel	190	79.2	2.4
Japan	1,454	95.1	15.3
New Zealand	319	118.1	2.7
United States	407	3.4	192.0

Table 12b.   *Non-European membership (as above), 1979*

Country	Members N	Density	Base population (millions)
Argentina	378	16.2	23.4
Australia	251	18.6	13.5
Brazil	1,094	9.9	110.1
Canada	261	11.3	23.0
Israel	253	81.6	3.1
Japan	1,475	13.0	113.1
Korea (South)	277	8.0	34.7
Mexico	127	2.0	62.3
New Zealand	206	66.5	3.1
United States	711	3.5	203.2

Table 13 presents the number and membership of local groups, together with a figure for density based on group membership. Most figures for base population are not presented, as they already appear in Tables 10 and 12. Where the base population has not already been given, this is indicated in parentheses after the figure for density. The survey was not as complete as could be wished, as many did not reply in certain countries, especially the Soviet Union.

Table 14 is based on the same figures, but presents a rank ordering of the ten countries with the highest density of penetration by local group membership.

There are a few differences in detail, but generally the figures for group membership substantially confirm the picture that is presented by UEA figures. The European predominance is still noticeable; 86% of local group members reside in Europe.

Table 13. *Local group membership, 1964*

(a) Europe

Country	No. of groups	No. of group members	Density
Austria	38	573	80.7
Belgium	13	550	59.1
Bulgaria	139	6,025	734.8
Czechoslovakia	101	3,280	232.6
Denmark	40	923	196.3
Finland	9	191	41.5
France	52	1,693	34.8
Germany (F.R.)	122	2,034	32.8
Great Britain	59	1,443	26.7
Hungary	101	2,418	230.2
Italy	44	1,237	24.5
Malta	1	5	13.6
Monaco	1	40	2,000.0
Netherlands	68	1,593	132.8
Norway	25	504	136.2
Poland	69	3,493	111.2
Spain	30	1,710	56.8
Sweden	59	1,553	204.3
Switzerland	14	258	47.8
USSR	1	?	—
Yugoslavia	84	1,614	87.2

Table 13 (continued).
(b) Outside Europe

Country	No. of groups	No. of group members	Density
Argentina	11	730	42.9
Australia	3	270	11.0
Brazil	41	510	33.1
Canada	7	185	9.6
Congo (Leopoldville)	1	15	1.1 (13.6 m.)
Ethiopia	1	20	0.9 (21.5 m.)
Indonesia	12	?	—
Iran	1	8	0.4 (22.5 m.)
Japan	75	2,148	22.6
Korea (South)	5	243	22.1 (11.0 m.)
Mexico	2	50	1.3 (38.4 m.)
Morocco	1	22	1.9 (11.6 m.)
Mozambique	1	25	3.8 (6.6 m.)
New Zealand	24	424	157.0
South Africa	1	24	1.4 (17.5 m.)
United States	41	435	2.3
Uruguay	1	70	26.9 (2.6 m.)
Venezuela	1	30	3.7 (8.1 m.)
European total	1,070	31,137	
World total	1,299	36,346	

Table 14. *Rank ordering of density of penetration of Esperanto,
by local group membership*

Country	Density	Country	Density
1. Monaco	2,000.0	6. Denmark	196.3
2. Bulgaria	734.8	7. New Zealand	157.0
3. Czechoslovakia	232.6	8. Norway	136.2
4. Hungary	230.2	9. Netherlands	132.8
5. Sweden	204.3	10. Poland	111.2

SPECIALIST ASSOCIATIONS

It is worth noting that, in addition, a number of associations exist for the purpose of linking Esperanto to special interests, whether ideological, recreational, occupational, or otherwise. These hold conferences of their own, often within the framework of the world congresses of the general movement. The following lists have been taken from the UEA handbook for 1954, 1964, 1975, and 1979. In the case of the latter three years the number of members was usually also recorded and this information has been reproduced here. The omission of an association does not necessarily mean that it has ceased to exist, merely that it has ceased for one reason or another to be listed in UEA returns.

1954

Catholics, Christians (Protestant), doctors, Quakers, railwaymen, science, Scouts, stamp-collectors, teachers, Universal League (an association linking Esperanto with world federalism).

1964

Architects and builders (137), authors, blind (591), Buddhists, Catholics (1,320), chess players (700), Christians (Protestant) (1,300), geography (340), journalists (316), lawyers (112), medical (250), nudists (250), photo, cinema, and tape amateurs, Quakers (160), railwaymen (2,500), science (680), Scouts, students (300), teachers, Universal League (13,634), veterans (671).

1974

Biblical and Oriental scholars, blind (550), car drivers (850), Catholics (1,100), chess players, Christians (Protestant) (1,250), journalists (350), medical (350), musical (80), ornithologists (220), philatelists (80), post and telecommunications (600), Quakers

(180), railwaymen (2,852), science (604), Scouts, tourism (356), veterans (763).

1979

Baha'i (175), Biblical and Oriental Scholars, blind (572), Buddhists, car drivers (1,150), Catholics (1,200), chess players, Christians (Protestant) (1,250), journalists (350), mathematicians (90), medical (350), musical (90), nudists (94), ornithologists (300), philatelists (60), philologists (151), post and telecommunications (700), Quakers (300), radio amateurs, railwaymen (2,816), Rotary, science (604), Scouts, teachers, tourism (302), veterans (910).

The number of members of the Universal League in 1964 was large because membership could be obtained by paying a single subscription. The veterans comprise an association of long-standing members, who learnt Esperanto at least 40 years ago.

THE WORLD ASSOCIATION OF NON-NATIONALISTS

The above figures do not include the non-nationalists (*Sennacieca Asocio Tutmonda*, SAT), a broad socialist Esperantist body which has at times discouraged its members from cooperating with the neutral movement. Table 15 indicates its strength for various years.[13]

It is intended that statistics presented in this chapter should serve as an introduction to the extent and distribution of support for the organised Esperanto movement. In the succeeding chapters the movement will be related to its social context in the principal countries where events took place that had repercussions for the international movement.

Table 15.   *The World Association of Non-Nationalists*

Country	1923	1927	1931	1948	1954	1964
Austria	304	244	182	140	77	61
Belgium	43	88	89	63	55	99
Bulgaria	40	0	9	74	4	4
Czechoslovakia	83	148	126	194	0	0
Danzig	3	1	11	—	—	—
Denmark	0	0	7	159	103	72
Estonia	15	15	18	—	—	—
Finland	24	38	27	54	59	16
France	253	271	310	779	587	534
Germany	1,063	1,450	1,081	1,890	559*	409*
Great Britain	24	164	245	148	122	101
Greece	0	0	0	0	1	0
Hungary	49	0	18	90	6	10
Iceland	0	1	4	2	4	1
Italy	31	0	2	19	30	27
Latvia	0	26	15	—	—	—
Lithuania	6	29	10	—	—	—
Luxemburg	0	0	0	0	0	1
Netherlands	10	67	322	1,588	801	498
Norway	23	25	32	50	40	21
Poland	65	39	47	61	2	15
Portugal	24	13	26	122	17	30
Rumania	26	0	2	0	0	0
Saarland	1	1	6	22	12	—
Spain	36	90	135	4	23	21
Sweden	15	43	262	223	243	173
Switzerland	11	23	37	16	13	26
Turkey	0	3	2	1	0	0
USSR	70	1,609	40	0	0	12
Yugoslavia	24	32	11	7	214	182
Europe total	2,243	4,420	3,076	5,706	2,972	2,313
Outside Europe	85	110	162	257	234	170
World total	2,328	4,530	3,238	5,963	3,206	2,483

* Includes a few members in the German Democratic Republic.

NOTES

1. For a list of World Esperanto Congresses see Appendix IV.
2. E.D. Durrant, *The Language Problem: Its History and Solution*, 1943, pp.117–118.
3. E. Bodmer, *The Loom of Language*, 1944, p.461.
4. L.L. Zamenhof, *Adresaro de la personoj kiuj ellernis la lingvon Esperanto*, Series I, 1889; *Adresaro de la Esperantistoj*, Series XVI, 1896; Series XX, 1900; Series XXV, 1905.
5. Taken from A. Holzhaus, *Doktoro kaj lingvo Esperanto*, 1969, p.285.
6. P.H. Stojan, *Bibliografio de internacia lingvo*, 1929, p.438.
7. J. Dietterle, 'Tutmonda statistiko esperantista', *Esperanto*, July–August 1928, pp.134–156.
8. E. Drezen, *Historio de la mondolingvo* (third edition), 1967, p.201.
9. A modified version of a table appearing in *Esperanto*, October 1932, p.146.
10. To save space these are not presented here; they can be arrived at by dividing the number of members for the relevant society by the appropriate figure for density, for each country concerned.
11. All figures are taken from UEA official returns, as published in UEA Yearbook (*Jarlibro*) and the periodical *Esperanto* for the year following.
12. Centro de Esplorado kaj Dokumentado, *Listo de lokaj Esperanto-societoj*, 1964.
13. Figures are taken from the Yearbook (*Jarlibro*) of SAT.

2

The Background of the Esperanto Language

The publication of Esperanto and the gathering of its earliest followers will be examined in both its intellectual and its political context. The intellectual context is that of a tradition of advocacy of constructed languages for both philosophical and more practical purposes. Although in popular usage 'Esperanto' and 'international language' are treated as practically synonymous, Esperanto is in fact only one of a large number of such proposals. Guérard[1] lists 97, and his list is complete only up to 1921. There is, however, a wide variation of extent of development of such languages. Whereas some authors have merely presented certain guidelines about how such a language is to be constructed, others have prepared detailed grammars and vocabularies. Yet Esperanto has undoubtedly acquired both the largest following and the most extensive development as a language. This has included the development of a wide range of literary work, both original and translated.[2]

Thus attention will be concentrated on Esperanto (and off-shoots from it). In view of this it will also be necessary to examine the political context in which Esperanto was developed. Esperanto was published in Poland in 1887, in the part which formed a section of the repressive Tsarist Russian empire. Thus supporters of Esperanto were liable to receive unfavourable attention from the Censorship, and eventually formally organised bodies to promote Esperanto were suppressed in Russia entirely. This situation of conflict with dominant powers has had important consequences for the ethos of Esperanto organisations.

The earliest known philosophical statement on the subject of universal language appears to be that of René Descartes. This appears in a letter dated 20 November 1629,[3] written to Father Mersenne. Descartes referred here to a proposal for a constructed language which Mersenne had sent him, but did not say who the author was. Descartes made favourable remarks on the proposal, and outlined certain desirable principles on which a constructed language would be based. The new language would be devoid of grammatical irregularities, but would be designed for philosophical rather that everyday purposes. It would provide a system of universal symbols for things and notions, in a manner analogous to numbers. These would be easy to learn, write, and pronounce. Although designed as a philosopher's language initially, it would have a democratising effect on philosophical knowledge: '*les paysans pourroient mieux iuger de la vérité des choses que ne font maintenant les philosophes*'. Descartes did not sketch how this scheme would work in practice. The earliest writers to do this were two British scholars, Dalgarno and Wilkins.

George Dalgarno (1626?–1687), an Aberdeen schoolteacher, was interested in various linguistic innovations such as deaf and dumb language and shorthand. His proposal for a philosophical language was published as the *Ars Signorum*,[4] in 1661. It consisted of a logical classification of 'notions'. All knowledge was placed within 17 divisions, and to each of these was assigned a capital letter, thus A (beings and things); H (substances); E (events); K (political matters). Subdivisions were indicated by a small letter, from either the Roman or the Greek alphabet (Ke = judicial matters; Ku = war). Two further divisions could be made, thus words were formed with a total of four letters.

Dalgarno's proposals never had a wide circulation, but they influenced John Wilkins, Bishop of Chester (and brother-in-law of Oliver Cromwell) to produce his own scheme.[5] Wilkins (1614–1672), like Descartes, drew the analogy with numbers and also with mathematical and astronomical symbols. His scheme, published in 1668, was also based on classification of human thought, with 40 different basic classes, which in turn had their subdivisions. These could be expressed either as a pasigraphy – a system of ideographs analogous to Chinese characters – or by Roman and Greek letters in a manner similar to Dalgarno's system. Unlike Dalgarno, Wilkins also devised means of indicating parts of speech, such as distinction of object and adverb, and an ending was provided for the plural.

Dalgarno and Wilkins did not appear to obtain any disciples for their own schemes. These depended for their validity upon the philosophical systems of the authors concerned, neither of which gained popularity in its own right. Quite different was the idea of Gottfried Wilhelm Leibniz (1646–1716). Leibniz's proposals for a universal language have remained influential, though much of his work on this subject was not published until after his death. Leibniz early developed an interest in the subject of philosophical language and published some of his first thoughts on the matter at the age of 20.[6] He later became acquainted with the work of Dalgarno and Wilkins, and with Descartes's letter already referred to. He found that the proposals by Dalgarno and Wilkins were insufficiently philosophical. At various times he became interested in the idea of a language which, rather than being read as words, would consist of signs which would remind users of the thing or the idea signified. In accordance with this proposal, he developed an interest in ideographic languages such as Chinese and ancient Egyptian. He presented a 'logical calculus' based on the notion that all concepts were combinations of simple ideas. In this scheme, prime numbers are taken as symbols of simple ideas, and multiples of these as symbols of combinations of concepts.

Leibniz discovered that the problem of working out a scheme of this kind was more complicated and difficult than he had originally thought. Accordingly he developed a significant shift of interest away from a language constructed totally from elements represented by arbitrary symbols (an *a priori* language). He did not reject such a scheme as an ultimate aim, but until this was realised he saw that a provisional auxiliary universal language would still be useful. This was to be based upon the existing living languages, or rather Latin, the language of scholarship. Leibniz proposed to analyse grammatical and lexical complications into their simplest elements. There would be only one declension and conjugation, and these in turn would be made as simple as possible. Inflections would be reduced to the minimum, as in most cases they merely repeat information already supplied by prepositions or pronouns. Leibniz also reduced the number of parts of speech. Every noun is equivalent to an adjective accompanied by the word *ens* [being] or *res* [thing]. Thus *idem est homo quod ens humanum* [man is the same thing as human being]. Likewise every verb can be reduced to the single verb *to be* and an adjective, thus *scribit* [writes] becomes *est scribens* [is writing].

Leibniz merely made suggestions for a language of this kind, rather than compiling a detailed grammar and vocabulary. Yet his shift of interest from an *a priori* philosophical language to an *a posteriori* simplification of Latin (albeit reshaped for philosophical use) was a development of considerable importance. Proposals based on *a priori* principles depended for their validity on the author's philosophical system, and thus were unlikely to develop a following beyond that of their author. They were in addition very difficult to memorise. But *a posteriori* languages would be based on languages already in existence. They could claim to be simpler and more philosophically sound than natural languages, but need never make the claim of absolute perfection. Thus proposals of this kind were able to obtain wider support. In addition, the use of Latin as the sole medium of scholarly discourse was beginning to wane in the seventeenth century, leaving a gap to be filled. The role of a universal auxiliary could be particularly easily filled by a simplified version of Latin, with which scholars were still familiar. As will be seen, various proposals for reformed Latin continued to have their followers.

Yet proposals for a neo-Latin language for philosophers have not gained widespread support. The group for whom they have been intended is small and has consisted of people who would be unlikely to agree with any one scheme in all its details. Thus support was larger for proposals for which the inventor was prepared to organise a more broadly based following, consisting of those who would be more likely to accept the proposed scheme uncritically.

Thus a remarkable amount of support was obtained for a completely arbitrary scheme by Jean Sudre (1817–1866). Sudre, who was also a pioneer of telephony, proposed an artificial language derived from the seven basic notes of the sol-fa musical scale.[7] This scheme was known as Solresol. As well as being spoken in the ordinary way, this language could also be played on a musical instrument. If the seven notes were replaced by the seven basic colours of the spectrum, the language could be made specially suitable for signalling messages. A method was also devised by which the seven notes could be transformed into seven movements of the hand, in order to make the language suitable for the deaf and dumb. Sudre originally publicised the scheme at the age of 20, though he continued to perfect it until his death, after which his widow continued to promote it. Sudre was active in promoting his system and had some measure of success in England and especially France. Victor Hugo expressed his approval of Solresol, and Sudre was presented to the court of Napoleon III. Sudre's widow formed a society for promoting Solresol in Paris, which still existed at the beginning of the twentieth century. The language was totally arbitrary, depending neither on *a priori* philosophical systems nor on *a posteriori* simpification of Latin or modern languages. It serves as an interesting example of how even a bizarre scheme can gain *some* supporters, provided that it is treated not only as a book to be published but also as a cause to be promoted.

A much larger following was obtained for a proposal by Johann Schleyer (1832–1912) of Konstanz, Germany, published in 1878.[8] This was the first scheme to be used as a spoken language and to develop a formal organisation of any size. Schleyer was a Catholic priest who, especially in later life, saw his work as divinely ordained. He was also inspired by philanthropic motives for the brotherhood of mankind. The scheme was known as Volapük [world speech]. Schleyer claimed that the idea of Volapük came to him as a revelation during a sleepless night. Schleyer also edited the journal *Sionsharfe*, concerned with Catholic poetry, and began to use this as a forum for popularisation of his idea. He published the scheme as a book in 1880,[9] which he destined to 'all educated people the world over' (*aller Gebildeten der ganzen Erde*). In 1881 Schleyer began to issue the newssheet *Volapükabled*. The number of supporters grew steadily, mostly in German-speaking countries. The first Volapük society was founded in Alberweiler, Württemberg, in 1882. By 1889 there were 283 Volapük clubs or societies throughout the world, and 25 Volapük journals (seven of which appeared entirely in Volapük). The number of Volapükists was estimated in that year to be one million, though this is almost certainly a wild exaggeration. It is also not clear whether a Volapükist was someone who was proficient in the language or merely a supporter of the idea. Yet Volapük developed the paraphernalia of an international language movement (such as identification badges), which Esperanto was later to acquire.[10]

Schleyer wished to develop Volapük so that it could translate the most subtle and complex meanings, and emphasised the richness of its vocabulary. His followers were proud of his talents as a poet and musician, and also maintained that he was an accomplished polyglot. It was claimed that he could speak 50 languages, though this was later increased to 83. Volapük contained many arbitrary elements and depended for its viability upon the maintenance of Schleyer's authority. There were intricate schemes of declension and conjugation: but, in contrast to those of highly inflected natural languages, these were completely regular and free of exceptions. Particularly arbitrary was the vocabulary. This was derived from European languages, mostly from English, but words were usually shortened because of Schleyer's preference for monosyllables. Thus English 'knowledge' became *nol*, and 'compliment' became *plim*. The vocabulary did not conform to an *a priori* philosophical system, though certain classes of words were indicated by special prefixes and suffixes. Thus the suffix *-af* denoted some animals, while birds had the suffix *-it*. The prefix *lu-* had a vaguely pejorative connotation (*bien* 'bee' but *lubien* 'wasp'; *vat* 'water' but *luvat* 'urine'). *The suffixes -al* and *-el* both indicated a 'a person concerned with'; but whereas *-el* was the normal form, *-al* indicated a sense of superiority. Thus *sanel* 'doctor' but *Sanal* 'The Saviour'. The normal word for 'inventor' was *datuvel*, but Schleyer had the title of *Datuval*.

As already noted, Volapük received support mainly from German-speaking countries, in the first instance. In 1885 interest spread to France, where Volapük attracted the attention of Dr. Auguste Kerchkoffs, teacher of modern languages at the Paris Commercial High School. Kerchkoffs published manuals of Volapük in French, and founded the *Association française pour la propagation du Volapük*. Unlike Schleyer, Kerchkoffs was interested in Volapük as a simple and practical language, suitable for use in commerce, rather than developing the language as a subtle means of expression.

Initially the Volapükists did not have much opportunity to make use of the language. Schleyer called a Volapük congress at Friedrichshafen (on Lake Constance) in August, 1884. Nearly everyone there was a German-speaker and the proceedings were conducted in German. This congress elected a committee to prepare a second, more international congress, which was organised for August, 1887, in Munich. Two hundred Volapükists were present. This Congress founded a formal organisation concerned with Volapük – the *Volapükaklub Valemik* [Universal Association of Volapükists]. The latter instituted the International Volapük Academy (*Kadem*

Bevünetik Volapüka). Schleyer became Grandmaster of the Academy for life, and Kerchkoffs was elected as Director. The Academy was intended to discuss reform proposals, and conflict soon arose on this issue. Schleyer was ready in principle to recognise the authority of the Academy, as he himself referred to it certain questions. Kerchkoffs also initiated certain discussions of reforms, but Schleyer objected to the fact that the Academy refused to give him the power of veto. Nonetheless, the Academy continued to vote on reforms and decided to call a third Volapük congress in Paris in 1889, where the proposed changes would be ratified. It was decided that the entire proceedings of this Congress would take place in Volapük. Schleyer objected to the proposal to let the Congress ratify the changes, and refused to recognise it. Yet the Congress went ahead, again with about 200 participants. A set of Statutes of the Academy was drawn up during the Congress, which included a proposal that Schleyer should have delaying powers, but not veto. Schleyer again objected, claiming that Volapük was his private property and that nobody could amend it without his consent.

The practical use of Volapük during the Paris congress revealed certain weaknesses, and reformist pressures were thereby strengthened. Schleyer continued to refuse to accept the new Statutes of the Academy and eventually refused to recognise the Academy altogether. He formed a new Academy consisting only of those prepared to accept his authority. As a result of the secession, support for Volapük diminished rapidly; by 1900 the names of only 159 orthodox Volapükists appeared in an address list of supporters. The number of journals and societies also rapidly diminished, though one journal survived till 1960.

There were many disagreements among those who wished for reforms in Volapük. Without the authority of Schleyer, there was little other justification for many of the elements in Volapük. As Director of the (reformist) Academy, Kerchkoffs attempted to obtain agreement on a reformed grammar: but many other Academicians proposed other projects, and it was impossible to reach agreement. Eventually Kerchkoffs resigned the directorship in 1891. His place was taken in 1893 by V.K. Rosenberger, a railway engineer from St. Petersburg and pioneer of Volapük in Russia. Reforms continued to be discussed, and there were three principal schools of thought among reform Volapükists. Some proposed their own modifications of Volapük, whilst retaining the basic feature of mixed *a priori* and *a posteriori* elements.[11] These schemes differed considerably not only from orthodox Volapük but also from one another, and their sole supporter tended to be their author. A second possibility was to support Esperanto instead, and many did this, notably Leopold Einstein and, under his influence, other supporters of Volapük in Nuremberg.[12] *La Esperantisto*, the first Esperanto periodical, contained a series of articles criticising Volapük, during the period 1889–1890.[13] These were printed as a parallel text in German and Esperanto, so they could be understood by non-Esperantists.[14]

There remained a third option. Some ex-Volapükists continued to support the idea of an international language but for various reasons were unwilling to support Esperanto (one reason possibly being the Esperantists' reluctance to consider reforms). Rosenberger did try to recruit Zamenhof to the remains of the Volapük Academy shortly after the break with Schleyer, and again in 1894 (when Zamenhof proposed some reforms in Esperanto). Zamenhof refused to join, though he was originally prepared to consider doing so if the name was changed to 'Volapük–Esperanto Academy'. Rosenberger refused to do this and there was no cooperation with Esperantists.[15] The Volapük Academy now turned its attention to the principal viable alternative to Esperanto, a reformed version of Latin. Rosenberger initiated discussion on this question, and on the election of a new Director (the Rev. A.F. Holmes, an American) in 1898, this commitment was strengthened by a change of name to *Akademi internasional de lingu universal*.[16] The new project was known as Idiom Neutral. A vocabulary of this project appeared in 1902, in German,[17] but attracted little support since by this time Esperanto had become firmly established. Also there was disagreement among supporters of Idiom Neutral. After the schism in the Esperanto movement in 1908, some transferred their allegiance to the new project, Ido. In 1908, too, Holmes was succeeded in the directorship by the Italian logician, Giuseppe Peano. Peano had since 1903 been working on the idea of simplified Latin, *Latino sine Flexione*. After his attention was drawn to Leibniz's discussion of the subject he developed this interest further and in 1908 read a paper on reformed Latin to the Turin Academy of Sciences. This began in standard Latin, but suggestions for simplifications were proposed, and immediately incorporated as Peano continued. The speech ended in *Latino sine Flexione*, or Interlingua. After Peano was elected to the ex-Volapük Academy, it became the *Academia pro Interlingua*. The new Academy did not confine itself to Peano's project, being concerned with a wide range of neo-Latin proposals in the hope of producing an eventual synthesis.

Thus when Zamenhof was confronted with the problem of strife between ethnic groups distinguished by language, there already existed a recognisable tradition of thought on the subject of inter-national language; indeed, Volapük had received widespread sup-port in German-speaking countries. Yet it presented a number of difficulties, especially to the non-German-speaker. The dissent that followed the 1889 Volapük congress made for irretrievable loss of authority for Schleyer's scheme, and no unified opposition to Esperanto was possible: indeed, there is evidence of some support for Esperanto from disillusioned Volapükists.

Zamenhof had been aware of some earlier attempts at construc-tion of world auxiliary languages: but it appears that he found all previous projects that he was aware of unsatisfactory. Zamenhof investigated Volapük while a student; although Volapük had the advantage of being designed as a fully constructed language for all the needs of everyday life, not merely those of philosophical dis-quisitions, Zamenhof found it unsuitable. He objected to its many arbitrary features, to its pronunciation, and to its general difficul-ties for the beginner.

If there were general factors in nineteenth-century Europe favourable to the development of world language projects, there were also some factors quite specific to the development of Esper-anto by Zamenhof in nineteenth-century Poland. Such conditions will also be seen as relevant to the religious and quasi-religious value orientations associated with Esperanto. Zamenhof's family background is also relevant to such questions.[18] Ludwig Lazar[19] Zamenhof was born in 1859, the eldest son of a Jewish family; he eventually had four brothers and three sisters. Zamenhof was born and brought up in Bialystok (Byelostok in the Russian form), where the family resided until 1873, moving to Warsaw in that year. A characteristic feature of Bialystok[20] was considerable strife between ethnic groups. A number of factors contributed to this. Poland was partitioned between 1795 and 1914, and originally

Bialystok had been assigned to the Prussian section. In 1807 the town was transferred to Russian control. Bialystok had also been a centre for Jewish settlement since the eighteenth century, settlement having originally been encouraged by manorial overlords. Although the status of Jews declined after Bialystok passed to Prussia, and then to Russia, it was still possible to engage in trade. Throughout the nineteenth century Jewish settlement continued; in 1856, out of a total population of 13,787, there were 9,547 Jews (69%). The four main ethnic groups — Jews, Russians, Poles and Germans — displayed considerable hostility towards one another. Language was the most obvious point of difference between them. Religion was also a factor: the Jews were religiously distinct; while the Russians were Orthodox, the Poles were Catholic, and the Germans Protestant. This situation evidently made a strong impression on the young Zamenhof, who early looked for a solution to the problem. He was impressed by the Bible story of the Tower of Babel, and at the age of ten wrote a five-act tragedy on this theme, with the scene set in Bialystok. In this manner Zamenhof conceived of the idea of a need for 'mutual understanding'; if the ethnic groups could understand one another, he hoped that tension would be reduced.

Zamenhof was also able to find intellectual justification for his ideas. This came from various sources. Firstly, the Bialystok Jews were a group among whom *Haskalah*[21] had become influential, by virtue of German connections. *Haskalah* was the particularly Jewish version of the Enlightenment. It derived from the general Enlightenment in eighteenth-century Europe but also had its own specific objectives relating to Jewish problems. It was assimilationist and stressed the value of secular education, especially languages. It was rationalistic in outlook, stressing Reason as the measure of all things. In common with other Enlightenment ideas, it was deistic, and rejected the claims of any religion to absolute truth. The Russian government could be seen as a supporting force in the realisation of these ideals. A further influence was undoubtedly Positivism.[22] After the quelling of the 1863 rising against foreign rule, attention in Polish intellectual circles was diverted away from romantic nationalism to the problem of the development of a modern industrial society. Comte's system had profound impact on the intellectual and literary life of Poland in the 1860s, especially among younger writers. Thus the phenomenon of 'Warsaw Positivism' developed. The new Realism found expression particularly in fiction literature, and it is significant that some of the earliest translations of novels into Esperanto were from the works of members of this school (Swietochowski, Prus, Orzeszko, Sienkiewicz, and Reymont, among others).[23] There are also passages in Comte's *Système de politique positive* which stress the importance of language and religion as integrative factors in the social group.[24] Thus both *Haskalah* and Positivism were supportive of the application of a rationalistic, scientific outlook to contemporary problems; yet at the same time neither was totally hostile to religion, opposing only traditional religious dogmas.

Zamenhof grew up in this environment, though he did not accept all these currents of opinion uncritically. His family relationships were significant in this respect. Zamenhof's father was a gifted intellectual and follower of *Haskalah*, but somewhat authoritarian in disposition. He was a linguist, and had found remarkable favour on the part of the Russian authorities, despite being a Jew. In 1857, at the age of 20, he had founded his own school in Bialystok. This had failed to prosper, but he had succeeded in obtaining a teaching post at state schools, in geography and modern languages. He continued this work after the family had moved to Warsaw, but took on the additional work of censorship for the Tsarist authorities — for which his command of languages was a qualification.

Although Zamenhof shared a number of his father's interests, notably in languages, there was also evidence of disagreement on some philosophical issues, and, on the matter of Esperanto, the relationship for a time showed considerable strain. On religion and ethnic identity Zamenhof and his father differed. While his father was secularistic in outlook, though still observing Jewish customs, Zamenhof found a need for belief in God, and received support in this from his mother. Zamenhof was more concerned than his father with social problems experienced by the Jews and was against the idea of assimilation. He began to attach importance to the idea of a 'Jewish people' and took the view that peoples do not normally give up their identity. Later in life (in 1909), despite his heavy involvement in the business of the Esperanto movement and language, Zamenhof found time to work on proposals to reform the grammar and orthography of Yiddish.[25] It is not surprising that Zionist ideals attracted the interest of Zamenhof. This interest developed after 1879, when Zamenhof left school and began training for the medical profession, one of the few professions open to Jews. Until 1881 Zamenhof studied in Moscow; he then returned to study in Warsaw, for financial reasons. It was particularly during the Moscow period that Zamenhof took an interest in Jewish affairs. He collaborated with the journal *Russkiy Yevrey* [The Russian Jew] and became active in the Zionist movement, founding some of the first Zionist groups. Also during 1881–1882 he contributed a series of articles to the periodical *Razsvet* [Dawn] on pogroms in Warsaw and how the Jews should react to them. He advocated the idea of a homeland for the Jews but initially did not insist that this should be in Palestine; he eventually accepted the goal of a homeland in Palestine for the sake of unity. These articles were written under the anagram 'Gamfezon'.[26] Zamenhof gradually became disillusioned with Zionism, finding it unrealisable, and saw the role of Jewish people increasingly as one of uniting humanity. He eventually rejected the idea of Jewish nationalism, writing in 1914 that, although nationalism on the part of the oppressed was more pardonable than nationalism on the part of the oppressor, he was in principle opposed to all nationalism.[27] His ideas developed towards the proposal for a world religion which is examined in Chapter 3.

On the more specific issue of the development of an international language, Zamenhof also came into conflict with his father. His father was not immediately hostile: Zamenhof performed well in school and was particularly good at languages, an interest which his father shared. Zamenhof drew on his linguistic ability to develop the first draft of his project for a universal language, and recruited a number of his classmates to the cause. In 1878 they held a banquet to initiate the new language. The boys made short speeches in the new language and sang a hymn of human brotherhood:

Malamikete de las nacjes,	Enmity of the nations
Kadó, kadó, jam temp' está!	Fall, fall, it is already time!
Lat tot' homoze en familje	The whole of humanity in a family
Konunigare so debá.	Must unite themselves.[28]

Zamenhof's native language was Russian, but he learnt to speak

Polish and German fluently. He also became quite proficient in French, and studied a number of other languages with varying degrees of success (these included Latin, Greek, Hebrew, Yiddish, and English). However, his father felt that a concern with international language would brand Zamenhof as a crank, and that he ought to devote his attention to the serious business of the medical profession. Zamenhof was able to support his ideas from a respectable intellectual tradition: Descartes, Leibniz, and others had advocated the idea of an artificial language. But an important basis of political domination in Tsarist Russia was the principle of 'divide and rule', and this provided an inexpedient background in which to indulge ideas of uniting humanity. Zamenhof's father made him promise to leave the matter of international language while he was a student; he handed over the notes that he had made, which his father impounded in a cupboard. On his return home from Moscow he discovered that his father had burnt the manuscripts. The relationship suffered severe strain, but Zamenhof remembered most of the contents and was allowed to work on Esperanto again. He obtained his medical degree in 1885 and began to practise in Veisiejai. Of his experience in general practice Zamenhof remarks,

Having practised there [Veisiejai] for the duration of four months, I became convinced that I was totally unsuitable for general medical practice, because I was too impressionable and the sufferings of the patients (particularly the dying) tormented me too much.[29]

Zamenhof therefore decided to return to his studies and train as an oculist; he studied in Warsaw and Vienna and opened an oculist's practice in Warsaw in 1886. He had received little financial reward for his work as yet and did not have the means to publish his project. However, in 1886 he met Klara Zilbernik, daughter of a businessman in Kovno; she expressed sympathy for Zamenhof and his ideals. Her father had initial reservations but eventually agreed to their marriage.[30] They married in 1887, and the first textbook of Esperanto was published in that year. The publication received considerable financial support from Zamenhof's father-in-law. Zamenhof's father also gave support to the extent of getting the publication through the Censorship as a harmless eccentricity. The publication, known nowadays as the *Unua Libro* [First Book] appeared in Russian,[31] Polish, German, and French. Significantly, Zamenhof's name did not appear on it. The text was entitled 'Dr. Esperanto: International Language – Introduction and Complete Handbook' in the language in which it appeared. The pseudonym 'Esperanto' (present participle in noun form of the verb *esperi* 'to hope') means simply 'a hopeful person', and it was only through usage that this became the name of the language.

Zamenhof never prospered as an oculist and for a long time claimed to be virtually destitute. The main cause of this seems to have been his need in 1887 to part with 5,000 roubles as a bribe to a high official, in order to prevent the dismissal of his father for leaving uncensored an article offensive to the Tsar. In 1889 the family was 'without a copeck';[32] Zamenhof's wife and child then accepted help from Zilbernik, and even for his own needs Zamenhof claimed that 'I simply and literally did not even have anything to eat; very often I did not have a main meal'.

Eventually Zilbernik again came to the rescue, and it was only in 1901 that Zamenhof finally succeeded in supporting himself entirely from his practice. There were a number of possible reasons for this. Zamenhof had difficulties as a Jew; he was suspected by richer people of having 'cranky' ideas and succeeded in attracting only poor patients, who paid low fees or no fees; clearly, too, Zamenhof's heart was in Esperanto rather than medical practice, and he cut down his medical commitments to the minimum in favour of Esperanto.

Zamenhof became very active in promoting his invention and in collecting a band of followers. He regarded Esperanto not merely as a language but as a cause to be promoted. The *Unua Libro* was thus at one and the same time a textbook of the language and a manifesto for a social movement. It carried on its title page the slogan 'for a language to be universal, it is not sufficient to call it such'. Zamenhof had not only to organise his followers, but also to discipline them. Lacking the authority of an already existing speech community, Esperanto could be subject to criticism and suggestion for improvements. Like the author of any world language project, Zamenhof had to deal with such issues as whether Esperanto in its original form was sufficiently 'easy', 'logical', or 'beautiful'. As already noted, Volapük rapidly lost support after reformist pressures. The existing structure of Esperanto can in a sense be seen as part of the ideology of the movement; changes in the structure of the scheme proposed would be ideological changes. Thus the problem of control of fissiparous tendencies became crucial to the Esperantists.

As the first Esperantist, Zamenhof originally had to deal with both organising the members and controlling fissiparous tendencies. Originally Zamenhof merely sought supporters of the idea of Esperanto. The endpapers of the *Unua Libro* contained forms of promise, upon which the reader was to declare 'I, the undersigned, promise to learn the international language proposed by Dr. Esperanto, if it is shown that ten million people have publicly made the same promise.' The reader could also use the forms to collect promises from others. Those wishing to learn Esperanto unconditionally could so indicate, and Zamenhof also invited proposals for change. Zamenhof sent the *Unua Libro* to numerous newspapers, learned organisations, academics, and professional men; the book was also advertised in various foreign newspapers. Zamenhof obtained far greater support from those wishing actually to learn the language, and after the *Unua Libro* he concentrated his attention mostly on attracting those willing to *learn* Esperanto. New Esperantists were invited to translate a short passage into Esperanto and, if successful, were included in Zamenhof's register of Esperantists. Most of the support for Esperanto at this stage came from individuals; however, one learned society, the American Philosophical Society, took a serious interest in the question of international language. It had already set up a committee to consider Volapük but had been highly critical. The committee had considered that there was a natural development in languages away from highly inflected systems, and subscribed to a theory of natural evolution along such lines. Volapük went against this tendency, since it had extensive systems of declension and conjugation. The committee also criticised the unfamiliarity of the vocabulary of Volapük. They argued that it was essential for the international language to be derived from the roots of 'Aryan' languages, since scientific work was written at present in such languages. While Volapük words derived from 'Aryan' roots, they were so deformed as to be unrecognisable. Volapük was thus rejected, but not the whole idea of an international language. Esperanto met with a much more favourable reception as a contribution to the problem. The committee recommended

that the American Philosophical Society should invite the learned
societies of the world to consider this question, with a view
to calling an international congress on the subject of universal
language.[33]

Zamenhof had been encouraged by the response to his *Unua
Libro* sufficiently to produce a second (*Dua Libro*) in 1888, consisting of material entirely in Esperanto.[34] In a supplement to this
he made reference to the American proposal. He welcomed the
initiative, and in view of the forthcoming congress, proposed not
to make any changes in the language: this work could be left to
the congress itself. Yet Zamenhof clearly mistrusted reliance on
bodies of intellectuals. In a supplement to his *Dua Libro* he wrote:

... to link the fate of the international language beforehand with the future
congress would be very imprudent ... the congress could still not take place,
and if it does take place it could still happen that it will give no practical
results.[35]

Zamenhof thus urged supporters to continue their private work
for Esperanto. He proposed that the Esperantists themselves should
call an international congress to put forward their own proposals,
if the congress proposed by the Americans did not take place within five years. Thus right from the start Zamenhof considered that
self-help was necessary; his standpoint on this was confirmed by
the fact that the congress did indeed not take place. The learned
societies of the world had not shown as much interest as the
Americans had expected: while some that did show interest objected to the proposal that the new language should have an 'Aryan'
base, and to the American Philosophical Society committee's
dismissal of Volapük.[36]

At this time Zamenhof was the sole centre of the movement; he
gave supporters individual encouragement, but gave little direct
advice about how Esperanto and the movement should be developed. He simply urged supporters to work hard, but in their own
way; eventually such tactics would lead to success. This would
come by conversion of individuals; 'every sea is created by separate
drops',[37] Zamenhof wrote in the *Dua Libro*. As early as 1888 a
number of small Esperanto circles and groups were formed, on the
initiative of individual supporters. In 1888 Zamenhof published

the first *Adresaro*,[38] listing those who had contacted him and successfully translated the passage already mentioned. This enabled supporters to contact one another. Although Esperanto was an unusual cause in that, by the nature of the idea promoted, mobilisation was to be international rather than national, initial support came mostly from Russia. Particularly well represented were Jewish intellectuals and Tolstoyans. The other main source of support was Germany, where a strong Volapük movement was a source of potential converts. Most noteworthy among these was Leopold Einstein, who had founded in 1885 the *Nürnberger Weltsprach-Verein*. This group had supported Volapük, but in 1888 Einstein received the *Unua* and *Dua Libro* and was sufficiently impressed to transfer his allegiance to Esperanto. He wrote a pamphlet arguing for the superiority of Esperanto, and by the end of 1888 succeeded in influencing the entire club to follow him. Einstein died the following year, but another Nuremberg ex-Volapükist, Chrystian Schmidt, carried on activities and in 1889 began to issue the first-ever periodical in Esperanto, named *La Esperantisto*. Zamenhof collaborated in its production. Initially some articles were in French and German, but it soon became an all-Esperanto periodical. A certain amount of attention was still devoted to criticism of Volapük, but it was mostly concerned with the development of the Esperanto language and movement. The journal was particularly significant as a source of authority for Zamenhof, and in 1890 it was transferred to his personal supervision. Zamenhof found it necessary to subsidise the journal, as there were only 113 paid-up subscribers (mostly Russian).[39] Zamenhof was the *de facto* international leader of Esperanto, and the periodical became a source of influence and authority. Apparently for fear of reprisal from the Tsarist authorities, Zamenhof played down considerably the value-oriented emphasis on Esperanto which he himself supported; but his contributions did emphasise a conversionist,[40] evangelical spirit. He saw as the duty of new recruits themselves to recruit others; the size of the movement would thus increase in geometrical progression, the movement eventually sweeping the world. Zamenhof expected supporters to work hard for Esperanto. He severely reprimanded some supporters who wrote to him asking how Esperanto was progressing. Such persons were asking the wrong question, said Zamenhof; they should ask themselves what *they* were doing to promote Esperanto.[41] At the same time, Zamenhof urged support from the masses rather than the powerful, and suspicion of those with secular power soon became common policy. Zamenhof wrote in 1891:

Some friends wait in vain for the rich, or important persons and societies, or governments to help us, and they in vain think that the prosperity of our cause depends on such help; no, on the contrary, *their help depends on the prosperity of our cause*, we must never forget this, and therefore we must not sit without doing anything and wait for help from the powerful.[42]

Zamenhof also counselled quietism; he wrote in 1892: 'The true friends of our idea work peacefully and calmly. The fate of our cause in no way depends on peripheral noise and external appearance'.[43] The journal became crucial as a source of Zamenhof's authority in the matter of language. Zamenhof had early suggested that the scheme proposed in the *Unua Libro* was merely provisional, and welcomed changes. When changes were proposed, however, he refused to make any. This was largely due to the fact that potential reformers could not agree on which changes should be made, and the reform proposals often contradicted one another. Yet at the same time the existing structure clearly possessed an important affective significance for Zamenhof, and he intended to avoid change if possible. Zamenhof was willing here to appeal to his own higher authority. He had worked on Esperanto privately for many years before publishing it and had tested it in translation and original composition. He could, and did, often use the argument that proposed changes would not work in practice. He replied in the supplement to the *Dua Libro* in such terms to changes proposed by Henry Phillips of the American Philosophical Society: 'The four changes that Mr. H.P. proposes are theoretically very good, but I already thought of them a few years ago and I found that in practice they were very inappropriate.'[44] Supporters of the existing structure of Esperanto have frequently opposed reform by arguing that Zamenhof had already thought of the proposals but had rejected them before publication.

It is appropriate at this stage to consider the kind of changes that various reformers might propose. There was a reasonable amount of agreement about the weak points of Esperanto, though not usually about what could be put in their place. The alphabet was one source of criticism. Zamenhof had adopted for the orthography of Esperanto the principle of 'one symbol, one sound'; for this purpose he had to introduce a number of extra consonants: ĉ, ĝ, ĥ, ĵ and ŝ. The circumflexed consonants represent the sounds of (respectively) English 'ch' as in 'chip', English 'j' as in 'jam', German 'ch' as in *'Buch'*, French 'j' as in *'jardin'*, and English 'sh' as in 'shop'. These added to the number of letters available, made the language more phonetic, and eliminated digraphs such as 'sh' and 'ch'. Yet they were unique to Esperanto and would have to be specially stocked by printers. A further objection was commonly made to the existence of an accusative case, formed by the addition of the letter -*n*; thus *hundo* dog makes *hundon* in the accusative. The opponents of this pointed out that the accusative mark was absent in French and English, and that Esperanto should be simpler than natural languages, not more difficult. Supporters of the accusative would argue that it permitted greater freedom of word order and eliminated the need for strict rules for this. Another objection was voiced to the concord of adjective and noun in the plural and accusative. In Esperanto *bela floro* [beautiful flower] makes *belan floron* (singular accusative); *belaj floroj* (plural nominative); and *belajn florojn* (plural accusative). Supporters of this practice again appealed to greater freedom of word order, opponents again to the fact that English, for instance, does not possess adjectival concord, so why should Esperanto? Other objections were to the plural ending in -*j*, because of its strange appearance, and to the table of correlative words (see Appendix II). According to some objectors this was a relic of *a priori* languages; they suggested that a system taken from international roots would be preferable, since it would be more immediately comprehensible. Other objections were raised about certain roots chosen in the original vocabulary; it was argued that some of the roots chosen were not as internationally comprehensible as they might have been.

With Zamenhof now in charge of the journal, the future development of Esperanto was in his hands. It was in fact open for anyone to assume a leadership role, but nobody appears to have wished to do so. The social composition of the original supporters of Esperanto is uncertain, but appears to have included many of Zamenhof's early Zionist contacts and adherents of *Haskalah*.[45] These knew Zamenhof personally and saw him as the natural authority figure for Esperanto, since he invented it. Others may have been educated people who had no professional outlet for their talents, and who sought this in Esperanto. As a medical practitioner, Zamenhof had a certain status which reinforced that of the inventor of the language. Yet Zamenhof appears to have retained the leadership role with reluctance, and he made repeated proposals for the formation of a League of Esperantists. His motives for this were apparently varied. Zamenhof evidently suffered financial loss from organising the supporters of Esperanto and could ill afford to do this. He might also have been influenced in a negative direction by the example of Schleyer, who attempted unsuccessfully to exercise dictatorial power. Zamenhof was in addition a retiring personality, and he preferred at least to share the responsibilities of leadership with others. The main topic for discussion at this stage appeared to be the question of reforms. Although Zamenhof had declared that his existing scheme was provisional, he appeared in practice to regard it as entirely satisfactory. He was prepared to abide by majority rule, perhaps confident that his own influence and that of his known personal supporters would be sufficient to outvote the reformists. Yet to settle this issue some formal organisation with a democratic structure would be necessary.

In the third issue of *La Esperantisto*[46] Zamenhof proposed the idea of a League of Esperantists, which could provide an authoritative voice for making changes in Esperanto. Yet problems soon arose as to who had the authority to make the rules of such a League, and some strong supporters of Esperanto were against any kind of formal organisation. Zamenhof's proposal was that the League should consist of a loose federation of local clubs, with a Central Committee (an Academy) of ten persons elected by ballot. No changes were to be made until the Academy was formed. Even this level of institutionalisation met with sufficient opposition for Zamenhof to shelve the project. With the lack of enthusiasm for the League, Zamenhof emphasised the journal as the focal point of Esperanto: 'it is the heart of our cause'.[47] Yet he faced increasing financial difficulty and, in order to ensure continuity for the journal, proposed a shareholding company to provide enough capital for its continued existence. This project was abandoned when the financial question was allayed by a *deus ex machina*. Towards the end of 1891 Wilhelm Heinrich Trompeter,[48] a German underground surveyor (*Markscheider*), offered to guarantee the continued existence of the journal through his financial support. That Trompeter was relatively rich among supporters of Esperanto during this period is some indication of their social composition. One of Trompeter's motives appears to have been to induce Zamenhof to propose reforms; by 1894 he indicated that he would withdraw support if reforms were not introduced.

Discussion of reforms continued, while Zamenhof stressed the need for unity and stability. The number of active users of Esperanto increased and Esperanto began to have an affective significance for others apart from Zamenhof. A small translated literature was being developed, beginning with works of Pushkin and Goethe.

Trompeter continually placed pressure on Zamenhof to introduce reforms, and in January 1893 Zamenhof provided a democratic basis for this by absorbing the idea of a League into the existing collectivity of subscribers to *La Esperantisto*. The League was simply to consist of all subscribers to the journal, and on the issue of reforms a ballot was to take place among subscribers. Zamenhof tried to allay the suspicions of some linguistic conservatives in distinguishing the idea of a League from that of reform:

Some friends do not cease to see in our League a danger for our cause . . . The error consists in the fact that the friends confuse two quite different objects with one another: "League" and "linguistic change". The League was not created for change at all, but to administer and govern in our cause.[49]

Nonetheless, considerable discussion of reform took place. Zamenhof, however, was determined to encourage subscribers to vote for the status quo. In 1893 Zamenhof began a systematic analysis of the grammar and vocabulary with a view to proposing reforms; yet he prefaced the analysis with the remark

. . . many friends have expressed the desire that I should guide the reforms myself. I admit again that, if the matter were to depend on me, I would hold back still all talk of reforms, but because I cannot oppose the flow from a more powerful side, I will willingly try to guide it, to take away its danger and turn the bad into good.[50]

Thus Zamenhof threw the whole weight of his *de facto* authority behind the existing scheme. He emphasised the affective significance of Esperanto in its original form and attached importance to the fact that the present scheme worked in practice; he saw this as far more important than theoretical proposals. But he reluctantly began to suggest areas for possible changes. These included changes in the features already mentioned (the compulsory accusative, the plural, etc.). Zamenhof further suggested replacement of many teutonic and slavonic roots by roots of romance or Latin origin; abolition of the article *la* (difficult for slavonic-speakers); changes in many grammatical affixes, removal of diphthongs; and numerous minor changes. The scheme was presented as a package to the subscribers to *La Esperantisto*. A ballot was to take place in 1894, to be followed by a second ballot if less than a third of the members voted. Before the actual vote Zamenhof canvassed privately for support for the existing scheme. He wrote to the St. Petersburg Esperanto Society, which he knew to be conservative on matters of language, shortly before the ballot, and urged members to become individual subscribers to *La Esperantisto* so that they could vote against reforms.[51] Eventually the ballot provided four alternatives. A second ballot was necessary. The result was as follows: (the four choices are indicated)

1. Should we keep the form of our language unchanged?

2. Should we accept the new form, which I have presented to the members of the League, in its entirety?

3. Should we make other reforms in the language?

4. Should we accept in principle our reform project, but only make a few changes in particular details?

Table 16. *Ballot, 1894*[54]

Choice	August	November
	(No. of positive replies)	
1.	144	157
2.	12	11
3.	2	3
4.	95	93

Although the reformist vote was split, the result can still be interpreted as a vote against reforms, since the total number of votes for all reformist positions was less than the total who wished to keep the language unchanged. Although there is an important centrifugal force among the followers of a constructed language in the form of reformist pressure, this can be counteracted. In the case of Esperanto the centripetal force — the affective value of the existing system, combined with the reluctance of existing users to relearn anything — proved more important. An important factor was the influence of Zamenhof himself, as already noted. It is also significant that appeal had been made during this stage of the development of Esperanto for actual *users*, not merely supporters of the idea of a world language. Zamenhof had soon lost interest in collecting promises to learn, and by now the organisation, such as it was, was concerned with *users* of Esperanto. *La Esperantisto* was by now published almost entirely in Esperanto, and it was on the basis of subscribers to this journal that the vote had been taken. The position was different in France in the early twentieth century, as will be seen: here schismatic tendencies occurred in a situation where recruitment had partly been from those merely wishing to support the idea of Esperanto. In this situation fissiparous tendencies were more successful and led to schism.

As a result of the negative vote on reforms, Trompeter withdrew his financial support for the journal, though continuing to subscribe to it and to remain in contact with Zamenhof till 1901, when Trompeter died. Zamenhof suffered financially from the loss of Trompeter's support, which had included a small remuneration for Zamenhof as editor; yet no other supporter came forward, and Zamenhof again took sole charge of the journal. At this point a significant change of emphasis gradually became evident. Esperanto was important to Zamenhof as a value orientation, not just as scientific innovation. Except in occasional poems such as *La Espero*, Zamenhof had decidedly played down the value-oriented aspect during this period: there were merely occasional references, such as in the *Dua Libro*, to the 'brotherhood of the peoples'.[53] Yet clearly Zamenhof would have preferred to give more attention to idealism but felt under pressure to say little about it. The existence of censorhip of published work in Tsarist Russia was undoubtedly a factor; even if the censorship was erratically and inconsistently applied, the possibility of suppression was too great a risk to take during the early stages of the Esperanto movement. In addition to this, Trompeter was opposed to inclusion in the journal of anything which might have political or religious over-tones;[54] thus nothing of this kind appeared. Now that Zamenhof was free from such pressure, he began to pay more attention to matters previously left to one side. He might also have been influenced by the accession of a new Tsar (Nicholas II) in 1894, sharing a widespread (but unfounded) belief that there might be some liberalisation.[55]

In 1888 Zamenhof sent a copy of the *Unua Libro* to Tolstoy, hoping that he might be sympathetic to Esperanto, but received no reply. However, in 1894, Tolstoy was asked by the journal *Posrednik*, of whose editorial board he was a member, to give his opinion on the subject. Tolstoy expressed a favourable opinion. He argued that the learning of foreign languages was a peculiarly appropriate activity for a Christian, and that Esperanto was a desirable cause since it helped to promote understanding between peoples.[56] In *La Esperantisto* for 1895 (No. 92)[57] Zamenhof drew attention to this and made approving reference to the ideological position of *Posrednik*. Zamenhof remarked that this journal frequently used religious language, but that this should not be confused with the external forms of religion: the religiosity of *Posrednik* was a pan-human philosophical religion. He indicated that this standpoint was worthy of approval by Esperantists: 'Everything which accelerates brotherhood between men, we always greet with joy; everything which sows dispute and hate among men should always keep away from us!'[58]

The value-oriented standpoint still remained a minor undercurrent in *La Esperantisto*, but Zamenhof continued to show interest in Tolstoy's ideas, and in the second issue for 1895 published a translation of a letter by him on 'Reason and belief'.[59] Tolstoy had been suspected by the Tsarist authorities since the early 1880s, when he first began to publish his thoughts on the Christian anarcho-pacifist position to which he had been converted.[60] Some of his work had been suppressed as subversive of Church and State. His contribution to *La Esperantisto* attracted the attention of the censor, and as a result *La Esperantisto* was suppressed. Zamenhof made a short-lived attempt to evade the censor by the use of plain sealed envelopes, but this was discovered and *La Esperantisto* ceased publication in June, 1895. This step threatened the continued development of the Esperanto movement, since over 60% of the subscriptions were Russian. Esperanto publications were not allowed to be issued again in Russia till after the 1905 Revolution. But Zamenhof was still allowed to work on Esperanto individually and to write material which could be published abroad. Also, the St. Petersburg Esperanto Society 'Espero' was allowed to continue its activities, and performed many of the functions of a national Esperanto association until 1908, when the Russian Esperanto League was founded.

These restrictions on Esperanto in Russia were severely damaging to the movement; and had Esperanto been merely Russian-based, the effects would have been even more far-reaching. Yet by its very nature the Esperanto movement recruited on an international basis. Sweden was a country in which Esperanto had found remarkably strong support: indeed, if the criterion of the number of subscriptions to *La Esperantisto* per head of population were to be taken, support for Esperanto would have been stronger in Sweden than in Russia. The *Unua Libro* had been translated into Swedish as early as 1889, and an Esperanto club had existed in Uppsala since 1891. Certain factors in this period of Swedish history contributed to a favourable reception for Esperanto. During the 1880s Sweden was beginning to turn away from her traditional isolationism. This period saw the formation and expansion of new movements that were to influence the direction of industrial Sweden. Socialist, radical, liberal, and rationalist ideas became popular in intellectual circles, and later in the wider society. That the initial basis for support for Esperanto came from the university town of Uppsala suggests some relationship between Esperanto and these currents of opinion.[61] In view of the loss of *La Esperantisto*, the Uppsala Esperanto Club launched in December, 1895, the new journal *Lingvo Internacia*. Sweden had the advantage, in contrast with Tsarist Russia, of a free press, and the new periodical was edited by Paul Nylen, a professional journalist. Trompeter again made a financial contribution, aided by Vladimir Gernet, a research chemist living in Odessa. As with *La Esperantisto*, the new journal served the purpose of linking isolated supporters together: but it was no longer supervised by Zamenhof. Zamenhof's written contributions were infrequent, and Zamenhof thus ceased to be the focal point of the movement. The editorship changed hands a few times. As from 1902 *Lingvo Internacia* began to be edited from Hungary, by Paul de Lengyel, who in 1904 moved to France, where the journal was continued. This journal gradually began to attract attention for literary and cultural contributions, rather than as an important factor in the organisation and cohesion of the Esperantists generally. After 1898, with the foundation of the *Société pour la propagation de l'Espéranto*, and its organ *L'Espérantiste*, Paris rapidly became the focal point of the organised Esperanto movement. The causes and consequences of this will be considered in the next chapter.

The early development of Esperanto in the hostile environment of Tsarist Russia is of considerable significance for the self-conception of the Esperantists. The supporters of Esperanto had intellectual justification for their views but had to come to terms with the dictates of a reactionary and autocratic government. Thus they began to perceive themselves as an enlightened elite. Also, in addition to finding intellectual justification in the Positivist and other currents of ideas, Esperanto evidently had an important affective value for its supporters. This is all the more significant since Zamenhof had decidedly played down the value-oriented interpretation of Esperanto during its development in Russia. Yet an idealistic attitude to Esperanto permeated Russian Esperanto groups through direct contacts. A number of these were formed in Russia in the early period of the development of Esperanto. To a certain extent they were able to attempt a practical application of Zamenhof's proposal to make peace between ethnic groups. Whereas, in many areas of Russia, ethnic groups had little or no harmonious contacts with one another, the Esperanto groups in these areas met on a multi-ethnic basis. After the publication of the *Unua Libro* Zamenhof disseminated his ideas through personal contacts in his own area. He encouraged the development of a shared symbolism in the form of utopian poetry.[62] *La Espero*, written by Zamenhof, is a good example of the content of this work. *La Vojo*[63] is another contribution by Zamenhof to the early poetic literature. Others followed Zamenhof's example, including his brother Felix. An example of this work from outside the Zamenhof family is seen in the following poem by Antoni Grabowski, a polyglot chemical engineer who also devoted much attention to translation into Esperanto;

Tagiĝo

Agordu la brustojn, ho nia fratar'
Por nova, pli vigla jam kanto
Ĝi sonu potence de montoj al mar'
Anoncu al ĉiu dormanto
Tagiĝo, tagiĝo radias en rond'
La ombroj de nokto forkuras el mond'

Post longa migrado, dum dorna la voj'
Minacis nin ondoj de l'maro
Sed venkis ni ilin kaj velas kun ĝoj'
Al verda haveno de l'homar'
Post longa batalo, maldolĉa turment'
La stela standardo jam flirtas en vent'.

Ne venus ankoraŭ ventegoj, batal'
Ni estas jam bone harditaj
Esperon ne venkas la fajro nek ŝtal'
Nek ies perfidoj subitaj
Nenio en mondo elŝiros ĝin for
Ĝi havas radikojn profunde en kor'

Ni velas antaŭen kun kredo, fervor'
Benante la Majstron por verko
Kaj lian anaron, de plej frua hor'
Fidelan al ĝi, ĝis la ĉerko
la mond' aliiĝos, la temp' pasas for
Sed vivos eterne pri ili memor'

La lingvo benata montriĝis al ni
Mirinda donaco ĉiela
Per amo al hejmo, patrujo, naci'
Ni flamas en koro fidela
Kaj same fidelaj al hejma altar'
Ni sentas nin filoj de l'tuta homar'

En ĉiu mondparto, en ĉiu ter-zon'
En koroj de centoj da miloj

Jam vibras por nia saluto rezon'
Do kantas de l'tero ni filoj
Tagiĝo, tagiĝo radias en rond'
La ombroj de nokto forkuras el mond'

Daybreak

Let our chests be attuned, brothers
For a new, yet brisker song
Let it sound powerfully from mountains to sea
And announce to all who sleep
Daybreak, daybreak radiates all round
The shadows of the night run away from the world.

After wandering long on the thorny way
The waves of the sea did threaten us
But we overcame them and sail with joy
To the green harbour of humanity
After a long fight and unpleasant torment
The standard of the star now flutters in the wind.

If gales and battle were again to come
By now we are well hardened
Neither fire nor steel can conquer hope
Nor anyone's sudden treachery
Nothing in the world will tear it asunder
It has roots deep in the heart.

We sail forward with conviction and zeal
Blessing the Master for a work
And his followers — from the earliest hour
Faithful to it, to the grave,
The world will alter, the time passes by
But their memory will live for ever.

The blessed language appeared to us
As a marvellous gift of heaven
Through love for home, fatherland and nation
We flame in a faithful heart
And just as faithful to the home altar
We feel ourselves sons of the whole of humanity.

In each part of the world, in each zone of the earth
In the hearts of hundreds of thousands
By now reason vibrates to salute us
So we sons of the earth do sing
Daybreak, daybreak radiates all round
The shadows of the night run away from the world.[64]

Thus Esperanto became the vehicle for a diffuse millenarian ideal, and literature of this kind, which was published and read among Esperanto-speakers, became the vehicle of its expression. Privat, a historian of Esperanto, makes the following comment on the literature of the period:

National literatures have almost always expressed in the beginning the common hopes or glorious needs of their race. So nothing is more natural than the fact that an international language originally created for itself a literature about humanitarian feelings and aspirations.[65]

Zamenhof was a strong supporter of the development of literary work in Esperanto, both original and translated. In 1894 he began to issue the 'Library of the International Language Esperanto', which could be ordered by subscription. This inclded both original work of the kind just mentioned and translations from various European classics. Of the 'Library' Zamenhof commented: 'If the "Library" flourishes, everything will flourish – if the "Library" falls, everything will fall.'[66] Apart from its role as the vehicle of the distinctive symbolism of Esperanto, Zamenhof attached importance to the 'Library' as an indication to critics that Esperanto worked in practice, and as a bulwark against pressure to reform the structure of the language.

The references in Grabowski's poem to the 'green harbour' (verse 2, line 4) and to the 'standard of the star' (verse 2, line 6) merit explanation. Some early writings of Zamenhof appeared as books in green covers, while some French textbooks appeared with a star on the cover. The green star and green colours generally became the symbol of Esperanto and the value system which Esperanto represents. Many Esperantists still wear a green star as a badge for identification and as an indication of their allegiance.[67]

Thus Esperanto had associated with it an important value-oriented component which is not immediately obvious from the pages of *La Esperantisto*. Popularised through literature and personal contacts, a decidedly 'spiritual' interpretation of the aims of Esperanto developed. It became known as the *Interna Ideo* [inner idea]. The value-oriented interpretation had an important social basis in the situation of strain which Zamenhof had perceived in relations between ethnic groups in Poland. Yet recruitment to Esperanto was international, and many official publications gave scant attention to Esperanto as anything but a language. Thus some recruits to the cause were suspicious of or hostile to the value-oriented component. This applied especially in France, where Esperanto came to terms with bureaucratic and rationalistic pressures. Thus it will be seen that France became the scene for open conflicts in the interpretation of the aims of Esperanto.

NOTES

1. A.L. Guérard, *A Short History of the International Language Movement*, 1922 (Appendix).
2. For discussion of Esperanto literature see I. Lapenna, U. Lins, and T. Carlevaro, *Esperanto en perspektivo* (hereinafter referred to as *Perspektivo*), Ch. 5-7. See also M. Hagler, 'The Esperanto language as a literary medium', Unpublished Ph.D. thesis, University of Indiana, Bloomington, 1971.
3. Reprinted in R. Descartes, *Oeuvres complètes*, 1897, vol. 1, pp.76–82.
4. G. Dalgarno, *Ars signorum, vulgo character universalis et lingua philosophica*, 1661.
5. J. Wilkins, *Essay towards a Real Character and a Philosophical Language*, 1668.
6. G.W. Leibniz, *Dissertatio de Arte Combinatoria* (1666) in *God. Guil. Leibnitii Opera Philosophica*, ed. by J.E. Erdman, 1840, Part I, pp.6–44. For discussion of Leibniz's contribution to the question of international languages see L. Couturat, *La Logique de Leibniz*, 1901, reprinted 1961; L. Couturat, *Opuscules et fragments inédits de Leibniz*, 1903; R.L. Saw, *Leibniz*, 1954.
7. J. Sudre, *Langue musicale et universelle par le moyen de laquelle tous les différents peuples de la terre, les aveugles, les sourds et les muets peuvent se comprendre réciproquement*, 1886. See discussion in L. Couturat and L. Leau, *Histoire de la langue universelle*, 1903, section I, Ch.6; E. Drezen, *Za vseobschim yazykom*, 1928 (more accessible in the Esperanto translation *Historio de la mondolingvo*, third edition 1967). This work will hereinafter be referred to as Drezen, *Historio*.
8. Drezen, *Historio*, pp.98–109; Couturat and Leau, *Histoire de la langue universelle*, *op. cit.*, Section II, Ch.2.
9. J.M. Schleyer, *Volapük, die Weltsprache. Entwurf einer Universalsprache aller Gebildeten der ganzen Erde*, 1880.
10. See A. Ratkai, 'La internacilingva movado kiel kreinto de la Internacia Lingvo', p.169, in *Sociopolitikaj aspektoj de la Esperanto-movado*, ed. by D. Blanke, 1978, pp.166–181.

11. See Couturat and Leau, *Histoire de la langue universelle, op. cit.*, Section II, *passim.*
12. See below, p.57.
13. Reprinted in OV, pp.258–275.
14. A sequel to the disputations with the Volapükists is the fact that the Esperanto equivalent of the proverb 'It is Greek to me' appears as 'It is Volapük to me' (*Ĝi estas al mi volapukaĵo*).
15. Zamenhof, letter to Trompeter, n.d. (c. December 1895 or January 1896), OV, pp.422–425.
16. Drezen, *Historio*, Ch. XI; Guérard, *op. cit.*, Ch. VI, VIII.
17. W. Rosenberger, *Wörterbuch der Neutralsprache*, 1902.
18. For material on the life of Zamenhof see E. Privat, *Vivo de Zamenhof*, 1920; M. Boulton, *Zamenhof, Creator of Esperanto*, 1960; E. Drezen, *Zamenhof*, 1929; M. Ziolkowska, *Doktoro Esperanto/Doktor Esperanto*, 1959; I. Lapenna (ed.), *Memorlibro eldonita okaze de la centjara datreveno de la naskiĝo de D-ro L.L. Zamenhof*, 1960; Zamenhof, letter to Borovko, ?1895, OV, pp.417–422, also in L.L. Zamenhof, *Leteroj de L.L. Zamenhof*, ed. by G. Waringhien, 2 vols., 1948: vol. 1, pp.343–351. In the same work see Zamenhof, letter to A. Michaux, 21/2/05, vol. 1, pp.105–115. This collection of letters of Zamenhof is hereinafter referred to as *Leteroj*. There is further material, in some places highly critical of the earlier biographies, in N.Z. Maimon, *La kaŝita vivo de Zamenhof*, 1978.
19. Often given as *Ludwig Lazarus* or *Ludoviko Lazaro* (Esperanto form). The Yiddish form *Leyzer*, in Cyrillic characters, appeared on his birth certificate. For further details about Zamenhof's name see Maimon, *op. cit.*, pp.47–56.
20. See article 'Bialystok' in *Encyclopaedia Judaica*, 1971, vol. 4, pp.806–811.
21. See article 'Haskalah', *Ibid.*, vol. 7, pp.1,432–1,452; C. Van Kleef, *La Homaranismo de D-ro L.L. Zamenhof*, 1965.
22. Van Kleef, *op. cit*; W.F. Reddaway *et al.*, *The Cambridge History of Poland 1697–1935*, 1951, pp.385ff, 392, 535; R. Dyboski, *Poland*, 1933, p.41 and Ch. IX *passim*.
23. *Perspektivo*, pp.226–229.
24. A. Comte, *Système de politique positive*, 1854, vol. 4, p.75. See also L. Coser, *Masters of Sociological Thought*, 1971, p.11.
25. See *Leteroj*, vol. 2, pp.245–246.
26. 'g' replaces 'h' in accordance with Russian conventions of transliteration. For discussion of the contents of articles in *Razsvet* see A. Holzhaus, *Doktoro kaj lingvo Esperanto, op. cit.*, pp.121–135; also H. Tacuo (ed.), *Hebreo el la geto: de Cionismo al Hilelismo*, 1976, pp.58–95.
27. OV, pp.344–345.
28. Letter to Borovko. The Esperanto here is a primitive version, not to be confused with the final form as published in 1887.
29. Letter to Michaux.
30. See I. Harris, 'Interview with Dr. Zamenhof', *Jewish Chronicle*, 6/9/07, reprinted in Esperanto translation in Maimon, *op. cit.*, pp.161–173.
31. Dr. Esperanto, *Mezhdunarodnyi yazyk: Predislovie i polnyi uchebnik*, 1887. Passages from this work are translated in L.L. Zamenhof, *Fundamenta krestomatio de la lingvo Esperanto*, 1954, first edition 1903, pp.228–239.
32. Letter to Michaux. See also Maimon, *op. cit.*, p.156.
33. See report, 'The scientific value of Volapük', *Nature* 28, 9 August 1888, pp.351–355.
34. L.L. Zamenhof, *Dua libro de l'lingvo internacia*, 1888.

35.   L.L. Zamenhof, *Aldono al la 'Dua libro de l'lingvo internacia'*, 1889, reprinted in OV, p.31.

36.   For the negative reaction of the London Philological Society see A.J. Ellis, 'On the conditions of a universal language', *Transactions of the Philological Society*, 1888, pp.59–98. See also Couturat and Leau, *Histoire de la langue universelle*, *op. cit.*, Section III, Ch. X.

37.   Reprinted in OV, p.29.

38.   L.L. Zamenhof, *Adresaro de la personoj kiuj ellernis la lingvon Esperanto, 1-1000*, *op. cit.*

39.   The significance of control of a movement's publications has been noted for other organisations, such as religious and therapeutic groups. R.K. Jones remarks in 'Some sectarian characteristics of therapeutic groups with special reference to Recovery, Inc. and Neurotics Nomine', in *Sectarianism*, ed. by R. Wallis, 1975, pp.190–210 (p.197), 'Such publications not only determine to a large degree the external image of the movement but they become in turn a source of social control in groups lacking formal leadership roles'. For a comparable situation in the Christadelphians see B.R. Wilson, *Sects and Society*, 1961, p.241. For Esperanto the 'external image' aspect has significance only to the extent of indicating that the group is relatively closed to outsiders, since non-Esperantists cannot read the publications. But as a source of authority the significance of the periodical has been crucial.

40.   This term is taken from B.R. Wilson, 'An analysis of sect development', in Wilson, *Patterns of Sectarianism*, 1967, pp.22–45 (pp.26–27).

41.   See OV, pp.58, 180–181.

42.   *La Esperantisto*, No. 50, (1891), reprinted in OV, p.123.

43.   *La Esperantisto*, No. 51 (1892), reprinted in OV, p.158.

44.   Reprinted in OV, p.31.

45.   See G. Waringhien, 'Historia skizo de la Esperanto-movado', in G. Waringhien, *Lingvo kaj vivo*, 1959, pp.397–423; Maimon, *op. cit.*, pp.79–114.

46.   *La Esperantisto*, No.3 (1889), pp.17–18. Reprinted in OV, pp.59–60.

47.   *La Esperantisto*, No.50 (1891), pp.57–62. Reprinted in OV, pp.126–136.

48.   A. Holzhaus, *Wilhelm Heinrich Trompeter*, 1973.

49.   *La Esperantisto*, No.76 (1893), reprinted in OV, pp.182–184.

50.   *La Esperantisto*, No.77 (1893), reprinted in OV, pp.184–187.

51.   OV, p.512.

52.   *La Esperantisto*, No.88 (1894), reprinted in OV, pp.197–198.

53.   *Dua Libro, op. cit.*, p.3, reprinted in OV, p.21.

54.   See Zamenhof, postcard to Dombrovski, 8 March 1893, reprinted in OV, p.490.

55.   See G. Fischer, *Russian Liberalism from Gentry to Intelligentsia*, 1958, pp.72–76.

56.   For Tolstoy's reaction to Esperanto see E. Privat, *Historio de la lingvo Esperanto* (2 vols.: vol. 1, 1923, vol. 2, 1927) vol. 1, pp.54–55 (hereinafter referred to as Privat, *Historio*); F.I. Kolobanov, *L. Tolstoy i Esperanto*, summarised in I. Lapenna, 'Tolstoj, Zamenhof kaj Esperanto', in *Memorlibro, op. cit.*, ed. by I. Lapenna, pp.37–38; E.J. Simmons, *Leo Tolstoy*, 1960, vol. 2, pp.195–196.

57.   Pp.26–27, reprinted in OV, pp.201–202.

58.   *Ibid.*, p.27 (202).

59.   This is reissued in A. Holzhaus, *Doktoro kaj lingvo Esperanto, op. cit.*, pp.283–285. It does not appear in Tolstoy's collected works, but the existence of the original in the Tolstoy museum in Yasnaya Polyana has been confirmed by Holzhaus.

60.   See A. Maude, *The Life of Tolstoy*, revised edition 1930, vol. 1, pp.145–146.

61. See R.F. Tomasson, *Sweden, Prototype of Modern Society*, 1970, pp.8–13.
62. See E. Privat, *Historio, op. cit.*, vol. 1, Ch. XII.
63. See Appendix II.
64. Reprinted *inter alia* in *Esperanta antologio*, ed. by W. Auld, 1963, pp.42–43.
65. Privat, *Historio, op. cit.*, vol. 2, p.182.
66. *La Esperantisto*, No.93 (1895), reprinted in OV, pp.202–207.
67. This is Zamenhof's explanation of the origin of the Green Star, in *The British Esperantist*, No.86 (1911), p.34, reprinted in OV, p.456.

3

Ideological Conflict in France

It has been noted by observers of social movements that a distinction is frequently drawn between the central figurehead of a movement and the head of bureaucratic organisation. This division of labour is noted by Roche and Sachs's distinction between the 'bureaucrat' and the 'enthusiast':

The bureaucrat, as his name implies, is concerned primarily with the organizational facet of the social movement, with its stability, growth and tactics. To put it another way, he concentrates on the organizational means by which the group implements and consolidates its principles. He will generally be either an officeholder in the organization or interested in holding office. While he may have strong ideological convictions, he will be preoccupied with the reconciliation of diverse elements in order to secure harmony within the organization and maximize its appeal. He seeks communication, not excommunications.

In contrast, the enthusiast, seldom an officeholder, and quite unhappy when in office, concerns himself primarily with what he sees to be the fundamental principles of the organization, the ideals and values which nourish the movement. No reconciler, he will concentrate on the advocacy of these principles at the risk of hard feelings or even of schism. While the bureaucrat tends to regard the organization as an end in itself, to the enthusiast it will always remain an imperfect vehicle for a greater purpose. Whereas the bureaucrat is likely to equate "The Cause" with its organizational expression, the enthusiast, with his fondness for abstraction, identifies it with a corpus of principles.[1]

Although, as Banks[2] points out, these should not necessarily be seen as polar psychological types, they are readily applicable to the Esperanto movement. Zamenhof is best thought of as an 'enthusiast', concerned with articulating the values associated with Esperanto and constantly trying to place the day-to-day running of the movement in the hands of someone else. While the main centre of activity was Russia, Zamenhof made little progress. But by the turn of the century France became the main centre of activity. Initially Esperanto had made only slow progress in that country: there were only ten French subscribers to *La Esperantisto* by December 1892. But as early as 1888 the name of Louis de Beaufront appeared in Zamenhof's *Adresaro*. De Beaufront was soon to have a significant impact on the development of bureaucracy. Privat has already noted this:

In more than one large movement a second person has been evident by the side of the initiator; on account of his energy the former occupies a separate place among the rest, and becomes, as it were, the organisational and legislative chief for a certain period. By the side of Father Schleyer, Volapük had Kerchkoffs. The Reformation in the Sixteenth Century had beside Luther the powerful Calvin. Esperanto once had de Beaufront.[3]

The biography of de Beaufront (1855–1938) is not altogether clear.[4] It is known that he was educated by the Jesuits and that he remained a practising Roman Catholic. He was anti-Dreyfus and generally conservative in politics. Most of the time he was in delicate health. Some of his claims were dubious, and Zamenhof himself was suspicious of them. He maintained that he had renounced a project of his own, called *Adjuvanto*, since he saw that Esperanto was superior. After 1905 he claimed to be a marquis, who on losing his fortune had been forced to seek employment as a private tutor to the family of the Count Chandon de Briailles. His influence on the development of Esperanto at the turn of the century was considerable. He became an active propagandist of Esperanto in France and was able to shape the claims made by the Esperantists in a manner befitting the French environment. An idea originating in Russia and in accordance with Russian conditions was unlikely to make rapid impact on a society with the cultural prestige of France. French cultural influence on Russia was considerable, but the process did not work in reverse.[5] Yet de Beaufront successfully played down the value-oriented emphasis which had arisen in Russia in response to Russian conditions. He preferred to stress the scientific and practical use of Esperanto and was suspicious of the 'inner idea' with its religious and mystical overtones. He feared that

Esperanto would lack official respectability if a value-oriented interpretation were expressed; it might be suspected of association with pacifism and as such would be unpopular with statesmen.

De Beaufront provided the necessary equipment for promoting Esperanto in France. The *Unua Libro* existed in a French version but was not a full textbook; in 1892 de Beaufront provided a comprehensive textbook in French. In 1895 he published a French promotional leaflet. He formed organisations for Esperanto which were international in character but French-dominated. In 1898 he founded the *Société pour la propagation d'Espéranto*, together with a new journal, *L'Espérantiste*. De Beaufront was president of the former and editor of the latter. Secretary of both was René Lemaire, a businessman. Thus de Beaufront formed and directed a central organisation which he was able to shape in accordance with his own ideas. Although founded in France, the new periodical and organisation were used principally to take advantage of the *international* prestige of the French language and culture. *L'Espérantiste* was issued in French or with French and Esperanto parallel texts, rather than entirely in Esperanto in the manner of *La Esperantisto* and *Lingvo Internacia*. In contrast to Zamenhof's recruitment policy, de Beaufront was prepared to accept and encourage those who merely approved of the language, without necessarily being able to speak it. The *Société pour la propagation d'Espéranto* had three categories of members: *approbateurs*, who approved of Esperanto and were prepared to pay a subscription, but who were not willing to learn it; *adeptes*, who had reached an approved standard in the language; and *propagateurs*, who had recruited two *adeptes* or five *approbateurs*.[6] Examinations were set in order to assess standards of competence. De Beaufont was very much concerned to recruit distinguished names to the ranks of the *approbateurs*. He was particularly active in campaigning in French intellectual and scientific circles. Of various efforts in this direction, particularly noteworthy is a lecture (written by Zamenhof) presented by de Beaufront to the Congress of the *Association française pour l'avancement des sciences*, in Paris in 1900.[7] His activities led to the recruitment of a number of intellectuals who shaped the development of Esperanto in France. This was not always in the manner that de Beaufront had wished. A number of different personalities with different ideas were involved in the history of Esperanto at this stage, and the following *dramatis personae* will be of help:[8]

Emile Boirac (1851–1917), philosopher. Became Rector of the University of Grenoble (1898) and Dijon (1902). Wrote his Latin thesis on Leibniz. Recruited to Esperanto in 1900 and became an active member of the French movement, to which he added his intellectual authority. Wrote a textbook on philosophy, and was also interested in psychical research.

Carlo Bourlet (1866–1913), mathematician. Attended the *Ecole Normale Supérieure*, and eventually became Professor of Mechanics at the *Conservatoire des Arts et des Métiers*. Recruited to Esperanto in 1900 by a colleague and became in 1901 President of the newly founded Paris Esperanto Group. Published a number of mathematics textbooks in French for schools and also for architects and engineers. Had a special interest in applied mechanics, with particular reference to the technology of the bicycle. By virtue of this interest had connections with the bicycle industry and the *Touring-Club de France*, and recruited the support of the latter to Esperanto. Organised cycling competitions for the *Touring-Club*. Attracted the attention of the French publishing house Hachette, and after 1906 issued his own periodical *La Revuo*. Conservative in linguistic matters.[9]

Théophile Cart (1855–1931), linguist. Taught French at Uppsala University 1891–1892, then Professor at Lycée Henri IV and the School of Political Science in Paris. Learnt Esperanto in 1904 and immediately became an active propagandist. Cofounder in 1904 of the *Presa Esperantista Societo* (Esperantist Press Company) and in 1907 took charge of *Lingvo Internacia*. Published a number of textbooks of Esperanto, also (in French) an edition of Goethe. Vice-President of the *Société Linguistique de Paris*. Ultraconservative in Esperanto linguistic matters.[10]

Louis Couturat (1868–1914), philosopher and mathematician. Disciple of Leibniz. Numerous philosophical publications, including edition of some of Leibniz's unpublished works. Taught at Caen and other French universities, eventually becoming an independent scholar. Interested in peace movement and international arbitration. Became interested in Esperanto about the turn of the century, but never became a fluent speaker or an active propagandist. Devoted his attention to theoretical studies of international language, and was instrumental in the 1908 schism (see next chapter).[11]

Emile Javal (1839–1907), ophthalmologist. Published substantially on topics in ophthalmology, physiology, and pathology of the eye, including astigmatism. Himself became blind in 1900. Jewish; wealthy; liberal social-democratic outlook, served as a Deputy 1885–1889. Attracted to Esperanto after becoming blind, regarding it as useful for dissemination of Braille literature. Closely linked to Zamenhof through profession and religious sympathies, but advocated reforms in Esperanto.

Alfred Michaux (1859–1937), lawyer in Boulogne. Published a French legal vocabulary. Interested in the welfare of juvenile criminals and of refugees. Originally interested in reformed Latin, to which he eventually returned, but recruited to Esperanto by de Beaufront. Organised the first World Esperanto Congress in Boulogne in 1905.

Hippolyte Sébert (1839–1930), general in French army, retired in 1890. Graduate of the *Ecole Polytechnique*. Extensive publications on military science, member of the French Academy of Sciences, and a world authority on ballistics. Recruited to Esperanto in 1898. President of the French Photographic Society. Interested in the rationalisation and means of dissemination of knowledge. To this end he was concerned with promotion of two innovations – decimal classification of books and Esperanto.

There were others who played an important part in the development of Esperanto in France. Among these were René Lemaire already mentioned; Gaston Moch, an artillery officer turned pacifist, who in 1905 began the Esperantist-pacifist journal *Espero Pacifista*; and Léopold Leau, a professor of mathematics who interested Couturat in theoretical research on international language, and collaborated with him in this work. Also influential was the Belgian Commandant Charles Lemaire, a former colonial officer, who later became interested in reforms in Esperanto and eventually lost interest in international language altogether.

Esperanto thus began to gain popularity among French intellectuals. The Positivist faith in intellectual and social evolution remained influential. In such a milieu the adoption of a language like Esperanto could be seen as a contribution to social evolution and the rationalisation of society. The same situation inevitably gave rise to pressures for scientific scrutiny of the structure of the language as well, but these will be considered in the next chapter. The appeal of Esperanto was not, moreover, confined to intellectual circles. Many Frenchmen might have been anticipating a greater need than before for the learning of foreign languages. Although the international prestige of the French language was still very high, it was not to remain unchallenged as *the* international language. Though France had been first in the field, other national Esperanto societies were formed, and in 1904 the French society changed its name to *Société française pour la propagation d'Espéranto*. By 1907 it had 2,900 members, and there were also 91 local groups, only 11 of which were affiliated to the national association. Some support for Esperanto came from non-Esperanto organisations, and Bourlet was particularly instrumental in forming such links. The *Touring-Club de France* allowed its premises to be used for Esperanto courses, and its periodical contained an Esperanto section. Bourlet also had personal contact with the publishing house Hachette and succeeded in convincing the firm's representative that Esperanto provided a viable publishing proposition. Hachette were unwilling to deal with a Russian directly, and de Beaufront acted as Zamenhof's representative. A controversial publishing contract was for the 'Collection approved by Dr. Zamenhof'. Books in this collection were checked for linguistic accuracy by Zamenhof, who received a small royalty for this task. A number of important works were issued in this collection; they included translations of Shakespeare's *Hamlet* and Molière's *L'Avare*; a translation by Boirac of Leibniz's *Monadology*; and the *Fundamenta Krestomatio* [fundamental chrestomathy], a collection of short stories, articles, and poetry, by various authors including Zamenhof. This latter work was recommended by Zamenhof as a model of Esperanto style. In 1903 Zamenhof transferred the publication of his *Adresaro* to Hachette; with Zamenhof's agreement, it became the world Esperantist yearbook, edited by de Menil. As a result of the contract, Esperanto was promoted by Hachette wherever French was spoken. Yet controversy ensued since Hachette took the contract to mean that they had an exclusive right to publish any Esperanto book. Zamenhof ended the 'Approved Collection' in 1905, though he himself continued to publish through Hachette.[12] The firm lost interest in Esperanto soon after Bourlet's death in 1913.

Thus in various ways Esperanto had secured a firm foothold in France. During the first few years of the twentieth century Esperanto had begun to penetrate England also, and in 1903 a small Anglo-French gathering took place at Le Havre. Michaux, the President of the Boulogne Esperanto group, was sufficiently encouraged by the success of this meeting to call a world Esperanto congress in Boulogne for 1905. In this he obtained the support of the Boulogne and Paris Esperanto societies, the *Touring-Club de France*, and the *Société française pour la propagation d'Espéranto*. Michaux put the proposal to Zamenhof, who responded with enthusiasm and promised to attend himself.[13] Zamenhof suggested that the congress should be able to make authoritative decisions and took the opportunity to suggest a new project for a World Esperantist League.[14] This league was to reflect the previous system whereby all subscribers to *La Esperantisto* were members of a league. In Zamenhof's proposal, an organ of the League was to be issued, and all subscribers would be members automatically. Voting, however, would be on the basis of local groups rather than individuals. A Central Committee would be elected as the governing body of the League; this would be elected at world congresses, which would take place annually. Representation on the Central Committee would be on a national basis, though in proportion to the number of members in each national association. The Central Committee would elect its own president, who would also be president of the League. Groups who were members of the League would send their own delegates to the World Congress; such delegates would approve of or reject the decisions of the Central Committee.

Zamenhof's project also included a number of specialist committees. Such were the Action Committee, responsible for day-to-day practical administration and for the execution of all decisions of the League; the Language Committee, concerned with questions of grammar and vocabulary; the Congress Committee, including both permanent members and members of the group in the town where the Congress was to be held; the Censors' Committee, concerned with official approval of manuscripts 'approved by Dr. Zamenhof'; and the Examiners' Committee, concerned with assessing members' ability to translate into Esperanto.

The League could change its rules at a congress. The Language

Committee had no authority to make changes in the language; changes could be made only by the Central Committee, whose proposals would have to be ratified by a congress, three months' notice having been given.

Zamenhof's proposal for a League, and any other proposal for an authority on matters other than language, was viewed with hostility by the French leaders. Various Frenchmen held important positions in a number of important Esperanto organisations, but none of them emerged as clear leader of them all; de Beaufront had been a pioneer in France, but his academic credentials were overshadowed by those of his converts, and the latter displayed intense personal rivalry among themselves. Zamenhof's authority as inventor of the language was indisputable; the French leaders preferred his authority, or no central authority at all, for fear that the position might go to one of their rivals. The French leaders were, however, prepared to accept an authority on language; some of them were favourable to reforms, and Couturat and Leau had begun their systematic critical study of international languages, which was unlikely to accept the existing structure of Esperanto in every detail.[15] In May, 1905, the committee of the *Société française pour la propagation d'Espéranto* approved unanimously the idea of a strictly linguistic authority.[16] Zamenhof had requested early publication of his project of a League, but neither *Lingvo Internacia* nor *L'Espérantiste* would give it publicity, except critically. De Beaufront argued in *L'Espérantiste* not only that the idea of a League was undesirable, but also that the Boulogne congress had no authority to form one.[17] Before the Boulogne congress he obtained a lawyer's opinion that the congress could only express its wishes and was in no way empowered to make binding decisions. For reasons mentioned in the previous chapter, Zamenhof continued to press for the idea of a League which would take the weight of authority off his hands. He also did not wish the future of Esperanto to depend on himself alone, and Bourlet had already delicately raised the problem of who would approve Hachette's collection after Zamenhof's death.[18] By 1901, too, Zamenhof was beginning to develop a new interest, that of a world religion, and wished to be free to devote his attention to it. The significance of this will soon become apparent.

The Boulogne Congress, which opened on 30 July 1905,[19] was a key factor in the development of the ideology of Esperanto. Outside Russia, few Esperantists had had much opportunity to speak Esperanto, let alone consider in depth its ideological implications. Zamenhof had been pleased at the idea of a congress and evidently wished the congress to strengthen members' affective ties with the language and the social relations of the movement. Writing to Michaux in September, 1904, Zamenhof remarked:

We must ensure that our congresses, by their solemnity and charm, shall become a heart-warming religious centre, which will annually attract the friends of international brotherhood from the whole world.[20]

The Congress itself was an occasion of great emotionalism and excitement. Many Esperantists travelled together between Paris and Boulogne, speaking in Esperanto and putting Esperanto stickers on the train windows. Many of the windows in Boulogne displayed green stars; an exhibition of Esperanto books and posters was held in the local theatre. In all, 688 Esperantists came to the Congress, which was formally opened in the evening of Saturday, 30 July. The officials of the Congress, and Zamenhof, were greeted with thunderous applause. Michaux acted as chairman, and several speeches were made. When finally it was Zamenhof's turn to speak, there was much applause, shouting, and waving of fans and hats. After order had been restored, Zamenhof made a famous speech:

Honoured Ladies and Gentlemen! I greet you, dear fellow-idealists [*samideanoj*], brothers and sisters of the great world human family, who have come together from lands far and near, from the most varied countries of the world, to shake each other's hands fraternally in the name of a great idea which binds us together . . . Today is sacred for us. Our meeting is modest. The outside world does not know much of it, and the words which are spoken in our meeting will not fly by telegraph to all towns and villages of the world; neither heads of state nor ministers have come to change the political map of the world; luxurious clothes and numerous imposing medals do not shine in our hall, cannons do not sound around the modest house in which we are present; but through the air of our hall fly mysterious sounds, very quiet sounds, inaudible for the ear, but palpable for every sensitive soul; it is the sound of something great which is now being born. Mysterious phantoms fly through the air; the eyes do not see them, but the soul feels them; they are images of a future time, a completely new time. The phantoms will fly into the world, will become embodied and powerful, and our sons and grandsons will see them, feel them and enjoy them.

In most distant antiquity, long wiped away from the memory of humankind, about which no history has kept even the smallest document for us, the human family became separated and its members ceased to understand one another. Brothers, all created from one model; brothers who all had the same ideas, and the same God in their hearts; brothers who had to help one another and work together for the happiness and glory of their family — those brothers became quite foreign one to another, and became separated apparently for ever in hostile groups; and eternal war began between them. In the course of many thousands of years, throughout the whole time which human history remembers, those brothers just constantly fought between themselves, and all kinds of understanding between them were absolutely impossible. Prophets and poets dreamt of some very distant nebulous time, in which men would again begin to understand one another and would come together in one family; but this was just a dream. It was spoken of as a pleasant fantasy, but nobody took it seriously, nobody believed in it.

And now for the first time the dream of thousands of years begins to be realised. In this small French seaside town have met men from the most varied countries and nations, and they met each other not as deaf-mutes, but they understand one another and speak one to another as brothers, as members of one nation. Often people of different nations meet and understand one another; but what an enormous difference there is between their mutual understanding and ours! At such meetings only a small proportion of the delegates understand one another, those who have had the opportunity to dedicate a great deal of time and a large amount of money to learn foreign languages — all the rest take part in the meeting only with their bodies, not with their heads; but in our meeting all participants understand one another, everybody who wishes to understand us does understand us easily, and neither poverty nor absence of time closes anyone's ears to our speeches. In other congresses, mutual understanding is attainable through an unnatural method, offensive and unjust, because there a member of one nation is humiliated before a member of another nation, speaks his language, putting his own to shame, stammers and blushes and feels embarrassed in front of his interlocutor, while here he would feel strong and proud; in our meeting there are no strong and weak nations, privileged and disprivileged, nobody is humiliated, nobody is embarrassed, we all stand on a neutral basis [*fundamento*], we all have full and equal rights; we all feel as members of one nation, like members of one family, and for the first time in human history we, members of the most varied peoples, stand beside one another not as foreigners, not as competitors, but as brothers who, not inflicting their own language on one another, understand one another, have no suspicion of one another on account of the darkness which divides them, love one another and shake each other's hand not hypocritically, as one national to another, but sincerely, as man to man. Let us realise fully all the gravity of this day, because today within the hospitable walls of Boulogne-sur-Mer have met not Frenchmen with Englishmen, nor Russians with Poles, but men with men. Blessed is the day: may its consequences be great and glorious!

The speech took a millenarian turn:

. . . . After many thousands of years of being deaf and dumb, and fighting one another, mutual understanding and brotherhood of the members of different peoples of humanity is now, in Boulogne-sur-Mer, really largely beginning; and once begun, it will not stop, but will go forward ever more powerfully, until the last shadows of eternal darkness will disappear for ever. These days, now in Boulogne-sur-Mer, are important indeed, and may they be blessed! . . .
. . . . Soon will begin the work of our congress, dedicated to true brotherhood of man. In this solemn moment my heart is full of something indefinable and mysterious and I feel the desire to lighten my heart with prayer, to turn myself to some force on high and call upon its help and blessing. But just as at the moment I am not a member of any nation, but simply a man, in the same way I feel that at this moment I do not belong to any national or partisan religion, but I am only a man. And at this moment only that high moral force stands before the eyes of my soul, and to this unknown force I turn with my prayer.

Zamenhof concluded his speech with a prayer to God to reunite humanity:

Al Vi, ho potenca senkorpa mistero
Fortego, la mondon reganta,
Al Vi, granda fonto de l'amo kaj vero
Kaj fonto de vivo konstanta,
Al Vi, kiun ĉiuj malsame presentas
Sed ĉiuj egale en koro Vin sentas
Al Vi, kiu kreas, al Vi kiu regas
Hodiaŭ ni preĝas.

Al Vi ni ne venas kun kredo nacia
Kun dogmoj de blinda fervoro
Silentas nun ĉiu disput' religia
Kaj regas nu kredo de koro

Kun ĝi, kiu estas ĉe ĉiuj egala
Kun ĝi, la plej vera, sen trudo batala
Ni staras nun, filoj de l'tuta homaro
Ĉe Via altaro.

Homaron Vi kreis perfekte kaj bele,
Sed ĝi sin dividis batale;
Popolo popolon atakas kruele,
Frat' fraton atakas ŝakale.
Ho, kiu ajn estas Vi, forto mistera
Aŭskultu la voĉon de l'preĝo sincera
Redonu la pacon al la infanaro
De l'granda homaro!

Ni ĵuris labori, ni ĵuris batali,
Por reunuigi l'homaron.
Subtenu nin, Forto, ne lasu nin fali
Sed lasu nin venki la baron;
Donacu Vi benon al nia laboro,
Donacu Vi forton al nia fervoro,
Ke ĉiam ni kontraŭ atakoj sovaĝaj
Nin tenu kuraĝaj.

La verdan standardon tre alte ni tenos;
Ĝi signas la bonon kaj belon,
La Forto mistera de l'mondo nin benos
Kaj nian atingos ni celon.
Ni inter popoloj la murojn detruos,
Kaj ili ekkrakos kaj ili ekbruos
Kaj falos por ĉiam, kaj amo kaj vero
Ekregos sur tero.

Translation:

To thee, O powerful incorporeal mystery
Great force, ruling the world,
To thee, great source of love and truth,
And everlasting source of life,
To thee, whom all men present differently,
Yet sense alike in their hearts

To thee, who createst, to thee, who rulest,
We pray today.

To thee we do not come with a national creed
With dogmas of blind fervour:
All religious dispute is now silent
And only belief of the heart rules.
With this, in which all are equal,
With this, the truest, without compulsion of war
We stand now, sons of the whole of humanity
At thy altar.

Thou didst create humanity in perfect beauty
But it divided itself in battle;
People attack people cruelly,
Brother attacks brother like a jackal.
O whoever thou art, mysterious force,
Hark to the voice of sincere prayer,
Give back peace to the children
Of this vast humanity.

We have sworn to work, we have sworn to fight,
To reunite humanity.
Support us, O Force, do not let us fall,
But let us surmount the barrier;
Give thy blessing to our work,
Give thy strength to our fervour,
So that always, against savage attacks
We shall bear ourselves with courage.

We shall hold the green standard on high;
It stands for the good and beautiful.
The mysterious force of the world will bless us,
And we shall achieve our aim.
We shall destroy the walls between peoples,
They will begin to make a cracking sound
And will be fallen for ever, and love and truth
Will begin to rule on earth.[21]

The speech was greeted with long applause, and cries of 'Long
live Zamenhof! — long live Esperanto!' Zamenhof had reason to be

encouraged by the members of the Congress. The speech is widely reproduced in Esperanto literature. Many historians of Esperanto have perpetrated the myth that he had never spoken in public before, but more reliable sources point out that he made speeches at Zionist meetings during his student years. Zamenhof was, however, a retiring person and not at ease when making speeches.[22]

The rank-and-file Esperantists were enthusiastic, but a conflict had already begun between Zamenhof and the French *leaders* over the religious idealism put forward. Zamenhof had sent the text to Michaux before the Congress, and Michaux had shown it to Cart, Javal, Boirac, Bourlet, and Sébert. These appear to have been anti-clerical without exception (de Beaufront, a Roman Catholic, was peripheral to the Boulogne Congress: he was unable to attend, ostensibly through illness). They had objected to expressions such as 'mysterious phantoms' and especially the prayer. In Boulogne the French leaders painstakingly attempted to persuade Zamenhof to omit the prayer, at least ('We will be ruined by ridicule', Sébert had remarked).[23] Zamenhof agreed only to omit the last verse of the prayer, which was to have been:

Kuniĝu la fratoj, plektiĝu la manoj,
Antaŭen kun pacaj armiloj!
Kristanoj, hebreoj aŭ mahometanoj
Ni ĉiuj de Di' estas filoj.
Ni ĉiam memoru pri bon' de l'homaro
Kaj malgraŭ malhelpoj, sen halto kaj staro
Al frata la celo ni iru obstine
Antaŭen, senfine!

Translation:

Together brothers, join hands,
Forward with peaceful armour!
Christians, Jews or Mahometans
We are all children of God.
Let us always be mindful of the good of humanity
And despite obstacles, without standing still
Let us pursue tenaciously the goal of brotherhood
Forward, without end![24]

In 1905 French opinion was still divided by the controversial *affaire Dreyfus*: xenophobic and anti-Semitic forces had considerable influence. Accordingly the French leaders had taken care to conceal the fact that Zamenhof was a Jew.[25] It would have been undiplomatic to speak of anything which might suggest Jewish idealism. Thus Zamenhof agreed to delete the last verse; but the religious ideas were of considerable importance to him, and he insisted on retaining them. In the event, the Congress was a great success; participants reported enthusiastically on it to their local groups and societies. Allusions were made to the myths of the Tower of Babel and the Pentecostal gift of tongues.

There were other activities apart from formal occasions at Boulogne. These included concerts, recitations, religious services, a banquet and a ball, excursions (including one by ship to Folkestone and Dover), and a presentation in Esperanto of Molière's play *Le Mariage Forcé*. Members were excited at the success with which the language could be used for all these activities. A number of national variations in pronunciation were, however, apparent, and at one meeting Zamenhof answered participants' queries on pronunciation and demonstrated the correct usage.

Apart from the introductory speech by Zamenhof, the other important feature of the Congress was the discussion of the idea of a League of Esperantists. Zamenhof had already presented his own suggestions, while other members had prepared other projects. For the Congress itself, Zamenhof expressed the wish only to be honorary president; he proposed Boirac as *de facto* president of the Congress. The questions of a League of Esperantists and of an authority on matters of language were taken as separate issues. The various proposals for a League were discussed, but a significant element among the participants was hostile to any kind of formal organisation (the *Société française pour la propagation d'Espéranto* had already indicated its opposition). Eventually Cart proposed a neutral motion expressing a wish for closer relations between the various national Esperanto associations, which was accepted. The idea of forming a federation of national associations was to be deferred to the next congress. It was agreed that there would be a second world congress the following year, and this had to be organised. This task was entrusted to the *ad hoc* chairmen of the various meetings during the Boulogne Congress: these included

Boirac, Michaux and Sébert, the latter being president of the new committee. The lack of any more formal organisation enabled Sébert, who was wealthy, to take effective charge of the committee and transform it into a more powerful body than was intended. To this end he founded the Central Office (*Centra Oficejo*, CO) in Paris in 1906. This will be considered in more detail in Chapter 5.

The third important decision made at the Boulogne Congress was the acceptance of the 'Declaration of Boulogne'. Zamenhof had prepared a document, which he wished to get accepted by the Congress, on the 'Essence of Esperantism'. The aim of the document was principally to assure outsiders of the aims of Esperanto, though it evidently served this purpose for insiders as well. Zamenhof had already discussed the contents of the document with Bourlet and the Paris Esperanto Club, and the Declaration was finally presented in the handbook of the Boulogne Congress.[26] Some amendments were made to the Declaration during the Congress, though these were not substantial. The final text, accepted unanimously with enthusiasm, was as follows:

Since many have a very false idea about the essence of Esperantism, accordingly we, the undersigned, representatives of Esperantism in various countries of the world, having come together to the international Esperantist Congress in Boulogne-sur-Mer, have found it necessary according to the proposal of the author of the language Esperanto to give the following explanation:

1. Esperantism is an endeavour to disseminate in the whole world the use of a neutrally human language which, "not imposing itself in the inner life of the peoples and not at all aiming to displace existing national languages", would give men of different nations the possibility of understanding between one another, which could serve as a peace-keeping language of public institutions in those countries where various nations fight one another on account of language, and in which could be published those works which have equal interest for all peoples. Every other idea or hope which any Esperantist links with Esperantism is his purely private affair, for which Esperantism is not responsible.

2. Because at present no investigator in the world doubts by now that an international language can be anything but an *artificial* language, and because all the numerous attempts made in the duration of the last two centuries have presented only theoretical projects, and only one single language, Esperanto, has been shown as effectively finished, thoroughly tested in all aspects, perfectly viable and in all respects most suitable, accordingly the friends of the

idea of an international language, conscious that theoretical disputation will lead to nowhere and that the goal can be attained only by practical work, have for a long time all grouped together around the sole language *Esperanto* and work for its dissemination and enrichment of its literature.

3. Because the author of the language Esperanto refused once and for all, right at the beginning, all personal rights and privileges in relation to that language, accordingly Esperanto is "nobody's property" either in material or in moral respects.

The material master of this language is the whole world and anyone who wishes can publish in or about this language all works that he wishes, and can make use of the language for every possible kind of aim. As spiritual masters of this language will always be regarded those persons who are acknowledged by the Esperantist world as the best and most talented authors in this language.

4. Esperanto has no personal legislator and depends on no particular man. All opinions and works of the creator of Esperanto have, like the opinions and works of every other Esperantist, an absolutely *private* character, compulsory for nobody. The only foundation, compulsory for all Esperantists, once and for all, is the booklet *Fundamento de Esperanto*, in which nobody has the right to make change. If anyone strays from the rules and models given in the said work, he can never justify himself by the words "the author of Esperanto so advises or wishes". Any idea which cannot be conveniently expressed by that material which is found in the *Fundamento de Esperanto* any Esperantist has the right to express in such manner as he thinks fit, in the same way as is done in any other language. But for the sake of full unity of the language for all Esperantists it is recommended to imitate that style which is found in the works of the creator of Esperanto, who has worked most for and in Esperanto and knows its spirit best.

5. An Esperantist is every person who knows and uses the language Esperanto, irrespective of what kind of goals he uses it for. Membership of an active Esperantist society is recommended for every Esperantist, but not compulsory.[27]

Much of the Declaration was concerned with linguistic matters, particularly the question of the basic definition of the structure of Esperanto. The decisions taken on this topic were of great significance in the history of Esperanto, but this matter will be deferred to the next chapter. But on matters not directly connected with the structure of the language the Declaration recorded important characteristics of the ideology of the Esperanto movement. It stressed the unique loyalty of Esperantists to Esperanto; it clarified the role of Zamenhof as the most experienced Esperantist; and it affirmed the purely linguistic mobilisation of the movement. Clause 3 of the Declaration was designed to clear up misunderstanding about the contract with Hachette. Zamenhof also announced at one of the meetings in Boulogne that he proposed to end the 'collection approved by Dr. Zamenhof' and that he would in future have only a personal contract with the firm. A Polish poet, Leo Belmont, expressed a reservation about the Declaration, since it made no mention of the promotion of world peace. It was however decided not to include this as such a mention might be inexpedient for official recognition.[28]

Thus, if the Declaration of Boulogne and Zamenhof's opening speech were taken together, the religious idealism of Zamenhof could be treated as merely his private opinion. Yet this presented certain difficulties, as Zamenhof was the founder and leader of Esperanto, not just an ordinary member. Zamenhof himself was encouraged by the enthusiastic reaction to his speech; his metaphysical ideas seemed acceptable to the participants generally, even if not to the French leaders. Zamenhof took the Congress at Boulogne as a proof of the fact that 'absolute justice, equality and fraternity between the peoples is fully possible.'[29] He saw the Congress as a turning point in history, and wrote

Kion disigis ne unu miljaro
Tion kunigis Bulonjo ĉe l'Maro.

Translation:

What not merely one millennium set apart
Boulogne-sur-Mer brought together.[30]

Thus he was encouraged by the success of the Congress to develop ideas for a world religion. He had already presented some of his religious ideas in 1901, in a Russian pamphlet published pseudonymously.[31] Zamenhof called his religious ideas 'Hillelism'. The Rabbi Hillel[32] (The Elder) a scholar and saint of the first century B.C., and of Babylonian origin, had been influential as a liberal interpreter of the scriptures. He was well known for his exposition of hermeneutic principles. According to tradition, he had summarised Jewish law to a proselyte as follows: 'What is hateful to you do not to your fellow: that is the whole Law; all the rest is explanation: go and learn.'[33]

In his 1901 pamphlet Zamenhof stressed the importance of Hillel's teaching in the solution of the Jewish question. He was particularly concerned with the question of how the Jews should relate to the rest of humanity. He urged that, following Hillel, the teachings of Moses should be interpreted in the spirit rather than in the letter. He also advocated the use of Esperanto among the Jews and the setting up of a colony where the language and Hillelism could be cultivated.

The success of the Boulogne Congress encouraged Zamenhof to broaden the scope of his ideas. Among the French leaders, Zamenhof was able to discuss his religious ideas only with his fellow-Jew Javal; Javal was not unsympathetic but saw little hope for their realisation in the French environment, where the population was mostly Catholic or atheist: neither of these sections of the population would be favourable to the idea of a world religion.[34] Yet Zamenhof saw his ideas as conquering the world slowly, and after a further series of pogroms in Russia felt moved to give his ideas further publicity. In 1906 he published his ideas anonymously in an article, *Dogmoj de Hilelismo*, in the first number of *Ruslanda Esperantisto* for that year.[35] (Esperanto periodicals had been legalised in Russia again following the 1905 revolution.) Building on Hillel's work, Zamenhof set out to provide a positive response to the racial and religious strife in Russia. The article pointed to the Boulogne Congress as a demonstration of the feasibility of its aims, though it stressed that the new religious principles were to be distinguished from Esperanto. The dogmas set out to propose a neutral religion of humanity. They suggested that Hillelism was not intended to take men away from their native land, language, or religion, but rather that it was intended to serve as a 'neutrally human basis' (*fundamento neŭtrale-homa*) for communication between men of all languages and religions. The ultimate aim would be to bind human beings into one 'neutrally human' people, on the basis of a neutral language and neutral religious principles and morals.

A Hillelist was to be a humanist and to regard all peoples as of equal worth. He would regard every country as belonging equally to all its inhabitants, not just to one ethnic, religious, or linguistic group. If a country had an 'ethnic' name it was to be replaced, at least among Hillelists, by a name consisting of the capital city plus the suffix *lando* (e.g. *Varsovilando* 'Poland' from *Varsovio* 'Warsaw'). Ethnically neutral names of countries were acceptable (e.g. *Svisujo* 'Switzerland'). A Hillelist was to be a patriot only in the sense of serving all his fellow-countrymen equally, not in the sense of serving the ethnic, religious, or linguistic majority in his country. Equalisation of all languages and religions would, according to the Dogmas, eliminate the cause of all war and unrest between peoples, and the Hillelist could not condone the persecution of a minority. A Hillelist could refer to his nation as the sum of all people inhabiting his native country, but he was always to add the word 'Hillelist' to the name of his country to show that he was not a national in any chauvinistic sense. Likewise the Hillelist was to speak of his 'family' rather than his 'national' language. A Hillelist was also to add the word 'Hillelist' to the name of his religion. The basic teaching of Hillelism which related specifically to religion was

By the name of "God" I understand the incomprehensible highest Force which rules the world, and whose essence I have the right to clarify to myself as my wisdom and heart dictate. As a fundamental law of my religion I regard the rule "do unto others as you would have done unto you, and always listen to the voice of your conscience". Everything else in my religion I regard only as legends or as religious *customs*, which are introduced by men, to bring into life a defined programme and spiritual warmth, and whose fulfilment or otherwise depends on my personal desire.[36]

The Dogmas pointed out that men belong to traditional religions through birth, not because they best corresponded to their own personal convictions. Thus one should not praise or condemn anyone for his traditional religion. However, religious customs could cause religious hatred, and it was to be hoped that they would eventually be replaced by common, neutrally human customs. In due course, Hillelist temples would be established, where Hillelist principles and festivals could be developed, and the religious philosophies of the great thinkers could be listened to. Until such temples were established, Hillelists were to meet privately.

A fuller version of the Dogmas was published as a separate,

anonymous pamphlet in Russian and Esperanto, in St. Petersburg in 1906. This time, the cult was named 'Homaranismo' (an Esperanto word whose rough translation would be 'the philosophy of membership of humanity'). This name removed any specifically Jewish connotations from the proposals.[37]

Publication of the Dogmas provoked unfavourable reactions from Roman Catholic sources. The first objector was de Beaufront. De Beaufront had in 1906 already argued forcefully that there was no place for politics and religion in Esperanto activities:

. . . . politics or religion should never, never be mentioned in the meetings of our groups . . . . Let us leave our parties, religions and politics at the door of the group . . . . May they never cross its threshold: Esperanto alone should be allowed through.[38]

De Beaufront intensified his campaign with the appearance of Homaranismo. He insisted that Esperanto was merely a language, and that the publication of this document would be damaging to the Esperanto cause.[39] Also in a later article, he urged that too much should not be made of the Boulogne Congress.[40]

A further objection came in an article by Father Alexander Dombrovski in *Ruslanda Esperantisto*.[41] This was more sympathetic but suggested that language and religion were pretexts rather than causes of strife, and that the implications of Homaranismo turned out to be antireligious. De Beaufront took up Dombrovski's criticisms and expressed contempt for the new idea as follows:

No doubt soon we shall be told who are the initiators, prophets or priests of this new theosophy, whose liturgical language is, so we are told, Esperanto. While we await the opening of the temples (Homaranist temples!) which the brochure mentions, we could perform the rites beneath the green of the forests, in green robes covered in gold or silver stars. Very poetic, isn't it?[42]

Zamenhof replied pseudonymously to both these critics. To Dombrovski, Zamenhof replied that Homaranismo was not antireligious and was intended merely as a bridge between religions.[43] To de Beaufront he argued that Homaranists were entitled to pursue their own private ideas. He remarked that the Esperanto cause was dear to the Homaranist, who would not wish to jeopardise it;

and that if de Beaufront was still worried about the possibility of adverse publicity he could quote the Declaration of Boulogne.[44]

Homaranismo continued to be of great personal importance to Zamenhof. As early as 1901 he had written in a private letter that 'the idea of a neutral language will never be truly realised without Hillelism';[45] and Zamenhof seemed to continue to hold this view, although in fact Homaranismo did not meet with much success. In Russia its potential supporters, notably Jews, saw equality between ethnic groups as a precondition for its success: other social movements, notably socialism and Zionism, offered more realistic solutions. In France Homaranismo seemed to resemble outmoded ideas such as Comte's Religion of Humanity (which itself almost certainly influenced Zamenhof's proposals). Javal asked Jaurès for his opinion and received the reply that Homaranismo had no chance in socialist circles.[46] Hostility to Homaranismo grew among French Esperantists, and it appeared to be an open secret that Zamenhof was the author of the scheme. Concern grew about the possibility that Zamenhof might speak about Homaranismo in the forthcoming second World Esperanto Congress, planned for Geneva at the end of August 1906. Javal originally discouraged Zamenhof from attending; Zamenhof eventually decided to attend, but deleted any reference to Homaranismo from his opening speech.[47]

Zamenhof's speech at Geneva was a further revelation of how the author of Esperanto interpreted the ideology associated with it;[48] Zamenhof began by referring to political oppression in Poland:

I come to you from a country where many millions of men are now fighting with difficulty for their freedom, for the rights of man. I would not, however, speak to you about this; perhaps all of you follow this difficult struggle in this large country of many millions, as *private individuals*; however as *Esperantists* this struggle cannot touch you, and our Congress has nothing in common with political matters. But besides the purely political struggle in the said country, something is now being done which we cannot not touch as Esperantists: we see in that country a cruel battle between *ethnic groups*. There it is not a matter of a man from one country attacking men of another country on account of political national interests — there the natural sons of the same country throw themselves like cruel beasts against the same natural sons of that same country just because they belong to another ethnic group . . . .[49]

Zamenhof went on to stress that this was not due to inherent cruelty on the part of any of the ethnic groups concerned, since the people themselves were peaceful. He suggested that the cause lay in the corrupt leaders of the peoples:

We now know perfectly well that a group of disreputable criminals is to blame, who by various most ignoble means, by widely distributed lies and conspiracies, have artificially created terrible hate between some ethnic groups and others. But would the biggest lies and conspiracies be able to bear such terrible fruit, if the ethnic groups knew each other better, if tall, thick walls did not stand between them, such as to prevent them from communicating freely and seeing that the members of other ethnic groups are just the same kind of people as the members of our own ethnic group; that their literature does not preach any terrible crime, but has just the same ethic and just the same ideals as our own? Let us break down the walls between the peoples, and give them the possibility of free knowledge and communication on a neutral basis; only then can disappear such bestiality as we now see in various places.

We are not as naive as some people think we are: we do not believe that a neutral basis will make men into angels; we know very well that bad men will remain bad afterwards; but we believe that communication and knowledge on a neutral basis will get rid of at least the great bulk of such bestiality and crime, which is caused not by ill-will, but simply by lack of knowledge of one another, and forcible coercion.

Now, when in various places of the world the struggle between the ethnic groups has become so cruel, we Esperantists must work more energetically than ever. But for our work to be fruitful, we must first of all clarify to ourselves the inner idea of Esperantism. We all often refer unconsciously to this idea in our speeches and writings, but we have never spoken of it any more clearly. It is now time for us to speak more clearly and precisely.

From the Declaration unanimously accepted in the Boulogne Congress we all know what Esperantism is in practical relations; from this declaration we also know that "an Esperantist is every person who knows and uses the language Esperanto, irrespective of what kind of goals he uses it for." An Esperantist is consequently not only a person who dreams of reuniting humanity through Esperanto, an Esperantist is also a person who uses Esperanto exclusively for practical purposes, an Esperantist is also a person who uses Esperanto to make money through it, an Esperantist is a person who uses Esperanto just for amusement, an Esperantist is finally even a person who uses Esperanto for the most ignoble and anti-humanitarian aims. But apart from the practical side, compulsory for all, and shown in the Declaration,

Esperantism has still another side, not compulsory but much more important, an idealistic side. This side different Esperantists can clarify for themselves in many different ways and degrees. Accordingly, to avoid any unrest, the Esperantists have decided to leave everyone full liberty to accept the inner idea of Esperantism in whichever form and degree they may wish, or, if desired, even not to accept any idea at all for Esperantism.[50]

Zamenhof stressed that these ideas accorded with the Declaration of Boulogne and distinguished between the correct interpretation, that association of ideals with Esperanto was a private matter and the incorrect interpretation, that association of Esperanto with other ideals was forbidden. He declared himself forcefully against a purely norm-oriented interpretation of Esperanto:

.... we all have to tear out of our hearts that part of Esperantism which is the most important, the most sacred, that idea which is the chief goal of the cause of Esperanto, which is the star which has always guided all warriors for Esperanto. No, no, never! We throw this demand aside with energetic protest. If we, the first warriors for Esperanto were to be compelled to avoid anything idealistic in our action, we would indignantly tear apart and burn everything we have written for Esperanto, we would nullify with grief the work and sacrifices of our whole life, we would cast asunder the green star from our chest, and we would cry out in abomination: "With *such* Esperanto, which has to serve exclusively the goals of commerce and practical utility, we want to have nothing in common".[51]

Thus although suggesting that the idealistic interpretation of Esperanto was optional, Zamenhof gave strongly worded support for it. He was able to define the 'inner idea' eventually as 'fraternity and justice between all peoples'.[52] This was the driving force for Zamenhof and other pioneer Esperantists and was what made for the success of the Boulogne Congress:

Everyone had a high regard for Esperanto, not because it brings men's bodies together, even not because it bring men's brains together, but only because it brings their hearts together.[53]

In his closing words, Zamenhof suggested that the idealistic interpretation of Esperanto was appropriate to congresses:

For the indifferent world Esperanto can only be a matter of practical utility. Everybody who uses Esperanto or works for it is an Esperantist, and every Esperantist has full right to see in Esperanto just a language, a simple, cold tool of international comprehension, like shipping signals only more perfect. Such Esperantists will most likely not come to our congresses or will come to them only for the purpose of research or practice, or for cold discussion of purely academic and linguistic matters, and they will not take part in our joy and enthusiasm, which will perhaps seem to them naive and childish. But those Esperantists who belong to our cause not with their head, but with their heart will before everything feel and like in Esperanto its inner ideas; they will not be afraid that the world will mockingly name them utopians and that national chauvinists will even attack their ideals as if they were a crime; they will be proud of being called utopians. Every new congress of ours will strengthen in them love for the inner idea of Esperantism, and little by little our annual congresses will become a permanent feast of humanity and human brotherhood.[54]

Thus Zamenhof no longer appealed to religious idealism but expressed his strong support for a secular idealistic interpretation of Esperanto. He also began in Geneva to draw attention to a distinction between the public and exoteric view of Esperanto, appropriate for the world at large, and the private and esoteric interpretation which would be accepted by the active member. He indicated that Esperanto congresses would give preference to the 'inner idea'. The proper limits of influence of the inner idea concerned relations between ethnic groups; this was to be distinguished from 'politics', which was not the proper business of an Esperanto congress. This raised a problem which has been fundamental to the Esperanto movement throughout its history, and still is: the question of neutrality about politics and religion. Zamenhof took the view that relations between ethnic groups, which he did not count as 'politics', could be discussed, but that political questions must be avoided. At the beginning of the Geneva Congress Sébert succeeded in obtaining support from the participants for a 'Declaration on the Neutrality of Esperanto Congresses'. This suggested that while, in the long term, Esperanto if accepted would have 'important and very fruitful consequences for the life of the peoples in political, religious, and social fields', these could be interpreted in many different ways. Thus in the programme of the Congress itself there should be no discussion of political, religious, and social questions. Anyone speaking about such matters would be called to order by the Congress president.[55] This principle still survives. At the same Congress, however, specialist meetings were permitted for various subgroups, which could be ideologically based, and rooms were made available for them. The specialisms represented at Geneva were journalists, educationists, socialists, Freemasons, Catholics, Protestants, pacifists, seamen, officers, Red Cross, lawyers, businessmen, teetotallers, doctors and pharmacists, musicians, chess players, stenographers, scientists.

Thus it was agreed at Geneva that a secular value-oriented interpretation of Esperanto might be appropriate at congresses, but that this should be distinguished from politics and religion: the latter could be dealt with only at specialist meetings. Those who saw Esperanto merely as a practical instrument, Zamenhof suggested, would be less interested in attending congresses. It was agreed that the third World Congress of Esperanto would be held in Cambridge, and in his speech to this Congress Zamenhof consolidated these ideas.[56] He saw the growing success of Esperanto in Britain as an indication of the fact that British Esperantists were idealistic; this meant

. . . . that men see in Esperantism not just a matter of egoistic opportunism, but an important idea of justice and fraternity between ethnic groups, and men of good will from all peoples, whether strong or weak, wish to serve this idea, whether justice between ethnic groups is profitable for them or not.[57]

Zamenhof went on to discuss the 'essence and purpose of our congresses'. He stressed that what he said was only his personal opinion, but considered that most Esperantists would agree that

We are organising an exhibition and propaganda for Esperantism not on account of any utility which all of us personally may derive from it, but on account of the very great significance that Esperantism has for the whole of humanity, for the pan-human purpose which attracts us active Esperantists to Esperanto; we meet annually from all parts of the world, to have the joy of seeing fellow-idealists, to shake their hands, to warm within us, by meeting together and living together, love and enthusiasm for the idea that Esperantism contains within it. Just as the ancient Hebrews met three times a year in Jerusalem, to invigorate in themselves love for the monotheistic idea, in the same way we meet every year in the capital of Esperanto-land [*Esperantujo*], in order to invigorate in ourselves love for the Esperantistic idea. *And this is the chief essence and the chief purpose of our congresses.*[58]

Zamenhof thus reiterated the distinction between Esperanto as a language for all, for the masses, which as such could be used even by misanthropes and ignoble criminals; and the private and esoteric, enlightened elitist interpretation of Esperanto, the 'inner idea'. This served as the distinctive binding force of the movement, and reached its fullest expression in congresses. Zamenhof recognised the diffuseness of this ideology:

In Esperanto-land rules not only the language Esperanto, but also the inner idea of Esperantism; in Esperanto-land not only official, general Esperantism holds sway; something else rules there as well, something still not precisely formulated up to now, but felt very well by all Esperantists — there rules the *green standard.*[59]

He elaborated the notion of the green standard:

We wish to create a neutral basis, on which the different human ethnic groups could communicate peacefully and fraternally, not enforcing on one another their ethnic peculiarities.[60]

The experience of annual Esperanto congresses would help to clarify this idea. Yet Esperanto congresses were neutral. Zamenhof accepted this, pointing out that neutrality was not so much an absence of ideology, or agreement not to talk about contentious issues, as a distinctive component of the ideology of the Esperanto movement:

You have often heard of the neutrality of our congresses. Yes, neutrality is the chief principle of our congresses; but one must understand exactly the sense of this neutrality. Neutrality exists in all international congresses; but while there neutrality is simply a matter of *tact*, for us it is the chief principle, for us neutrality, or rather the neutralisation of relations between ethnic groups, is the whole content, the whole aim of our work. Thus we must never speak in our congresses about purely political matters, which belong to the diplomats, or about purely religious matters, which belong to churchmen and philosophers — because the green standard prevents us from doing anything which might offend any ethnic or religious group; but everything which, offending nobody, can create a peaceful *bridge* between the peoples, must not only not be timidly avoided at congresses, but on the contrary, must be the very *essence* of our congresses, because it belongs to the green standard.[61]

In conclusion Zamenhof stressed that these were his own purely private opinions; yet he stressed that the diffuse idealism proposed would be felt by everyone:

I do not doubt that in the depth of your hearts you all *feel* the green standard: you all feel that it is something more than just the symbol of a language. And the more we take part in our annual congresses, the more we will become brothers to one another and the more will the principles of the green standard penetrate into our souls. Many people join Esperantism through mere curiosity, for a hobby or possibly even for some hoped-for profit; but from the moment when they make their first visit to Esperanto-land, in spite of their own wishes they are more and more drawn to and submit to the laws of this country. Little by little Esperanto-land will become a school for future brotherly humanity, and in this will consist the most important merits of our congresses.

Long live Esperanto, but above all long live the goal and inner idea of Esperantism, long live the brotherhood of the peoples, long live everything which breaks down the walls between ethnic groups; may the green standard live, grow and flourish![62]

The idea of Esperanto-land, seeing the Esperantists according to the analogy of a nation-state, is significant and will appear again.[63]

Zamenhof made a further speech[64] in England after the Cambridge Congress. He was invited by the Lord Mayor and corporation of London to an official reception in the Guildhall. The speech was translated into English for the mostly non-Esperantist audience. Among the points which Zamenhof made was a reply to the criticism that Esperantists are bad patriots. He protested strongly at this suggestion and outlined what he saw as the proper relationship between Esperanto and patriotism:

Esperantism which preaches love and such patriotism which also preaches love can never be hostile one to another. Anyone can speak of any kind of love, and we will listen to him with thanks; but when chauvinists speak about love for the fatherland . . . we turn away with great indignation.[65]

Thus Zamenhof chose the occasion to reply to possible criticisms from outsiders (in fact the Lord Mayor, Sir Vesey Strong, was a known sympathiser with Esperanto). He outlined here the idea of unity in diversity, that the Esperantists merely sought to create a bridge between the nations and did not seek to interfere with their inner lives. This standpoint was consistent with the line of thinking evident in the Dogmas of Hillelism, for instance, which were concerned with providing a neutral religious system which would link ethnic groups. But there was now a subtle change in emphasis when Zamenhof presented his ideas in a Western European rather than a Russian context. The emphasis was now on peaceful relations between nation-states rather than between ethnic groups within the same nation-state.

Esperanto world congresses continued to be an annual event, and Zamenhof continued to make the opening speech till 1912.[66] He did not, however, add significantly to the ideology that he had already outlined but concerned himself mostly with linguistic, administrative, and tactical questions. After resigning from formal leadership of the movement in 1912, Zamenhof was able to devote attention again to Homaranismo, which had been the main area of conflict between himself and the Esperanto movement generally. In 1913 he published a pamphlet similar to the anonymous 1906 publication, this time under his own name.[67] He also introduced some changes, broadening the basis of the ideology so as to allow freethinkers to associate themselves with it, and removing references to Homaranist temples.

Zamenhof also made two further written contributions to the question of ethnicity. In 1911, in London, a Universal Races Congress (non-Esperantist) took place. The aim of this Congress was to discuss general relations between white and coloured peoples, in order to promote understanding, friendly feelings, and cooperation. A wide range of academic and political leaders supported the venture.[68] Zamenhof contributed a paper on 'Ethnic groups and international language'.[69] The paper argued that political and economic factors were not as such responsible for hatred between peoples; likewise, geographical, physical, and psychological factors were not responsible. The true cause, according to Zamenhof, lay in the diversity of languages and religions. He made only brief and cautious reference to the question of a world religion, but suggested that a world language was necessary to eliminate hatred between the peoples.

Zamenhof continued to work privately for the idea of a world religion. He originally intended to discuss the question at a private meeting at the World Esperanto Congress planned for 1914 in Paris. The Paris organisers dissuaded him from doing this: they argued that the chauvinism around the Congress would be so great that it would be very bad publicity for the author of Esperanto to be associated with such a project, even unofficially and privately. Zamenhof intended to attend, however, hoping to be able to discuss in private the possibility of arranging a congress of Homaranismo with some known sympathisers. Yet this was of no avail, since the First World War broke out while Zamenhof was on his way to the World Esperanto Congress. The Congress could not take place, and delegates were forced to return home; Zamenhof reached Warsaw by a roundabout route. The war strengthened Zamenhof's commitment to Homaranismo; he repeatedly attempted to organise a Homaranist congress in Switzerland but continually had to defer the date as the war continued.[70] In 1915 he published in three Esperanto periodicals an article[71] advising governments what to do after the war. In this article, entitled 'After the Great War: an appeal to the diplomats', he applied the ethical principles that he had previously reiterated. He argued that it would be no use just to rearrange the map of Europe: it would have to be officially declared that every country belonged morally and materially to all its inhabitants. He stressed that all inhabitants of a country should have the right to speak their preferred language and practise their preferred religion. After the war a European Tribunal should be established by agreement between the states of Europe, which could pass judgement upon any injustices. He again suggested that countries should have neutral geographical names, not those of any ethnic group. Zamenhof died in 1917, seriously ill and seeing little hope for the realisation of his ideals.

Zamenhof's speeches have become an important source for the ideology of the Esperanto movement. They displayed a change of emphasis with each congress. His first (Boulogne) speech was religious and inspirational, but bureaucratic checks were swiftly imposed on his enthusiasm by the French leaders. Yet there otherwise appears to have been strong support for Zamenhof's value-oriented interpretation of the aims of the movement. The value-oriented emphasis on Esperanto had already found a firm foundation towards the end of the nineteenth century in Russia. This was expressed notably in original Esperanto literature, as pointed out in the previous chapter. As this was written in Esperanto it was addressed to a world audience, and could thus exert its influence in a context different from that in which it had originated. This transposition of the ideology of Esperanto into a different political context, in France, led to the development of a particularly diffuse and nebulous value system.[72] Zamenhof encouraged the idea of perceiving this in an intuitive manner, and emphasised the right of individual members to their own interpretation of it. This made for popularity of the ideas put forward, since they were so unspecific that few could actively disagree with them.

Yet in France the strategy employed by the pioneers of Esperanto, particularly de Beaufront, was different. Whereas the Russian pioneers had been suspicious of government, the French leaders could hope for better treatment, as progressive currents of opinion were not totally excluded from government in France. De Beaufront had adopted the policy of seeking support from the influential, and looking for official recognition. This necessitated a 'respectable' image for Esperanto. In such a milieu, too, formal organisations were developed, and the clash between the bureaucrats and Zamenhof, the enthusiastic founder–ideologue, was evident behind the scenes of the first two world congresses.

Yet Zamenhof was in a strong position to influence the ideology of Esperanto. Despite de Beaufront's insistence that Esperanto was merely a language, active supporters of Esperanto tended to favour some sort of value-oriented standpoint, and, as already noted, this was sufficiently nebulous as to offend only a few. Zamenhof was influential by virture of his authorship of the language, yet this could not alone account for his popularity. Although after Boulogne no mention was made of God or other nonempirical entities, there appeared to prevail at congresses a decidedly 'religious' atmosphere. If Durkheim's notion of religion as an anonymous and diffuse force, social in origin, is considered applicable, it could be said to have been represented at congresses by certain symbols, notably the green star and the green standard. Boulogne represented the first attempt of the speakers of Esperanto to participate in a communal 'ritual' on a non-national basis. Excitement was generated by the anticipation of this, and its success was widely reported and formed part of the tradition of the movement.[73]

The basis of the legitimacy of Zamenhof's authority will be considered further in Chapter 5. More generally, Sapir points out that diffuse sentiments arise from consciousness of a common speech:

The mere fact of a common speech serves as a peculiarly potent symbol of the social solidarity of those who speak the language. The psychological significance of this goes far beyond the association of particular languages with nationalities, political entities, or smaller local groups.[74]

Thus with Esperanto, sentiments of internationalism arise from an international language in the way that sentiments of nationalism arise from a national language. But internationalism can be defined in various ways, and this question has remained a preoccupation of the Esperanto movement. In this context, too, the question of the definition of 'neutrality' arises. Both Zamenhof and Sébert raised the question of neutrality of Esperanto congresses, but both interpreted it in different ways. Sébert, a leading French bureaucrat, proposed a Declaration of Neutrality of Esperanto congresses: but for him neutrality represented an agreement not to discuss potentially contentious issues, notable politics and religion. De Beaufront had supported an even stronger version of this idea. However, Zamenhof's own interpretation of the idea of neutrality was that of a new ideology in its own right. He referred to 'neutralisation', a new common international value system, providing a rhetoric of interaction in an international milieu. As Esperanto would sweep the world, this would be extended to the world generally. The appropriate expression of this 'neutral' value system, for the movement, was to be found in the social relations of the Esperanto movement, particularly in world congresses. The idea developed in Zamenhof's speeches of Esperanto as a second nationality for members of the movement. The idea, not merely of Esperanto, but of Esperantism, was mentioned as early as 1905, and in 1907 the idea of Esperanto-land with the Congress as its capital was suggested by Zamenhof. The Congress came to be seen as a microcosm of a utopian vision of a future world society.

Zamenhof stressed that his own interpretation was 'private', but he stressed the importance of a value-oriented interpretation of Esperanto during his opening speech and could hardly have been unaware of his own influence. The norm — the Esperanto language — was compulsory for all, whereas the value — the inner idea — was 'not compulsory, but much more important'. Thus anyone could subscribe to the idea of Esperanto as a language, whilst the 'inner idea' was the province of a more enlightened elite. Recruitment to Esperanto was through propaganda documents which would merely stress the practical value of Esperanto, while the congresses were the expression of the idealistic interpretation of the movement's goals.

Zamenhof succeeded in popularising a secular value-oriented interpretation of Esperanto, but his religious proposals met with little enthusiasm and some outright hostility. Religion was personally important to Zamenhof, yet he saw it, like language, as one of the vertical pillars which can divide a society.[75] Yet not all would so readily provide the same kind of solution to both religious and linguistic conflicts. Various solutions might be suggested for the problem of linguistic diversity, but nobody would seriously suggest that the solution would be to dispense with language altogether. In the case of religion, however, whilst some would maintain that religion was necessary to society, others would suggest that the conflicts of religion could best be solved by dispensing with religion altogether. Though it was true that some of the French leaders were influenced by a Positivist tradition which was by no means hostile to all religion, this same tradition would regard a secular value orientation as an adequate religious surrogate. It was this latter tendency that prevailed within the Esperanto movement as such.

Yet Zamenhof still pursued his idea of a universal religion. Zamenhof's ideas appear to have come to him as a result of vivid impressions in childhood; he had developed them against strong opposition at an early age, and it appeared that he was determined to promote them no matter how difficult it was to obtain supporters. Esperanto had considerable success; the same was not true of Homaranismo, but Zamenhof continued to promote it. Nor has there been substantial support for the idea as a separately organised movement after Zamenhof's death. Yet the idea of religion as being of worldwide rather than purely sectarian scope has been popular among Esperantists. Many have been liberals within more churchly religions, and ecumenical ideas were popular among Esperantists before they gained popularity in the wider society.[76] Esperantists appear overrepresented too in Baha'i (with similar aspirations to Homaranismo, and explicitly advocating an international language: this became the faith of Zamenhof's daughter Lidja). Other groups which have gained particular support from Esperantists have been the Quakers, and Oomoto (a Japanese-based cult with aspirations roughly similar to those of Homaranismo).[77]

Zamenhof's speeches had an important influence at the time that they were given; interest in them has continued since they have been published in contemporary periodicals, then in Zamenhof's collected works, and in histories of Esperanto and biographies of Zamenhof. These are widely read. In 1968, 73% of members of the British Esperanto Association were acquainted with such writings.[78] The main focus of ideological change in the Esperanto movement has come from outside — from the wider complex of international relations — rather than from the internal dynamics of the organised movement. The establishment of peace in Europe in the interwar and post-1945 periods has led to the growing international respectability of internationalist ideologies, and the formation of first the League of Nations, then the United Nations. The Esperanto movement, as will be seen, began to associate itself closely with such governmental bodies.

NOTES

1. J.P. Roche and S. Sachs, 'The bureaucrat and the enthusiast: and explanation of the leadership of social movements', *Western Political Quarterly*, 1955, pp.248–261 (pp.249–250).
2. *Op. cit.*, pp.37–38.
3. Privat, *Historio*, vol. 1, p.63.
4. For de Beaufront see Boulton, *op. cit.*; Privat, *Historio*; Drezen, *Historio*, pp.151, 157, 181, 184, 198, 199; *Leteroj*, vol. 1, p.5.
5. See, for instance, P. Burney, *Les Langues internationales*, 1962, p.14.
6. Explained in *L'Espérantiste* 1(1), January 1898, p.7.
7. Text 'Esenco kaj estonteco de la ideo de lingvo internacia' in L.L. Zamenhof, *Fundamenta krestomatio de la lingvo Esperanto* (1903 [1954]), pp.253–297.
8. General sources for biographies of the French leaders are: *Catalogue général des livres imprimés de la Bibliothèque Nationale*, 1897–   ; J. Baltea et al. (eds.), *Dictionnaire de biographie française*, 1933–   ; Boulton, *op. cit; Leteroj*, vol. 1, pp.1–13; *Perspektivo*, Ch. 14 and *passim*.
9. For Bourlet see also L.L. Zamenhof, 'Parolado super la tombo de Carlo Bourlet',

La Revuo 8, 1913–1914, pp.4–5, reprinted in OV, pp.412–414; I.G. Braga (ed.), *Monumento de Carlo Bourlet*, 1940; Paris, Grupo Esperantista, *Carlo Bourlet*, 1914.

10. A collection of Cart's writings is found in *Vortoj de Profesoro Th. Cart*, ed. by S. Grenkamp and R. de Lajarte, 1927.
11. See L. Benaerts et al., *Louis Couturat*, n.d.
12. For documents on the Hachette contract see *Leteroj*, vol. 1, pp.17–88.
13. Zamenhof, letter to Michaux, ?/9/04, *Leteroj*, vol. 1, p.84.
14. Final text published in *Lingvo Internacia* 10, 1905, pp.295–301, reprinted in OV, pp.230–235.
15. See L. Couturat and L. Leau, *op. cit.*
16. *L'Espérantiste*, 1905, pp.97–100. Summary in *Leteroj*, vol. 1, p.156.
17. *L'Espérantiste*, 1905, pp.106–107.
18. *Leteroj*, vol. 1, pp.49–50.
19. The Congress receives detailed treatment in all standard histories of Esperanto. See also P. Boulet, *Boulogne 1905: Testo kaj triumfo*, 1965.
20. *Leteroj*, vol. 1, p.175.
21. Text in OV, pp.360–365 (prayer pp.589–590).
22. See N.Z. Maimon, 'Ĥibat-Cion', in Maimon, *op. cit.*, pp.85–111.
23. *Leteroj*, vol. 1, p.175.
24. OV, p.360.
25. Javal, letter to Zamenhof, 15/10/05, *Leteroj*, vol. 1, pp.209–210.
26. P. Boulet, *Unua universala kongreso de Esperanto: kongresa libro*, pp.81–86.
27. Text in OV, pp.237–239 (showing also changes from provisional text).
28. Boulet, *Boulogne 1905, op. cit.*, p.32.
29. L.L. Zamenhof, 'Dogmoj de Hilelismo', OV, pp.313–321 (pp.314–315).
30. Boulet, *Boulogne 1905, op. cit.*, p.5.
31. 'Gomo sum', *Gillelizm: Proyekt resheniya yevreiskago voprosa*, 1901. Esperanto translation in Zamenhof, *Hebreo el la geto*, ed. by Tacuo, pp.359–442.
32. For general discussion of Zamenhof's religious proposals see C. Van Kleef, *Homaranismo*, 1965; Maimon, *op. cit.*, pp.175–191. For Hillel see J. Goldin, 'Hillel the elder', *Journal of Religion*, 1946, pp.263–277; L. Roth, *Judaism: A Portrait*, 1960.
33. Roth, *op. cit.*, p.79.
34. Javal, letter to Zamenhof, 15/10/05, *Leteroj*, vol. 1, pp.209–210.
35. *Ruslanda Esperantisto* 2(1), 1906, pp.1–11; 2(2), pp.27–28; reprinted in OV, pp.313–322.
36. OV, p.320.
37. *Homaranismo* (anon.), 1906, reprinted in OV, pp.324–328.
38. *L'Espérantiste*, 1906, p.3.
39. *L'Espérantiste*, 1906, pp.65–67.
40. *L'Espérantiste*, 1906, pp.98–100.
41. *Ruslanda Esperantisto*, No. 3 (1906), pp.49–50.
42. *L'Espérantiste*, April 1906, reprinted in *Leteroj*, vol. 1, p.262.
43. *Ruslanda Esperantisto*, May 1906, reprinted in OV, pp.329–336.
44. *Ruslanda Esperantisto*, June–July 1906, reprinted in OV, pp.336–338.
45. Zamenhof, letter to Kofman, 28/5/01, *Leteroj*, vol. 1, p.19.
46. *Leteroj*, vol. 1, p.265.
47. *Leteroj*, vol. 1, pp.279–286.
48. Text of speech in OV, pp.368–374.
49. OV, p.369.
50. OV, p.371.

51.   OV, p.372.
52.   OV, p.372.
53.   OV, p.373.
54.   *Ibid.*
55.   *Leteroj*, vol. 1, pp.287–288.
56.   Text of speech in OV, pp.374–381.
57.   OV, p.375.
58.   OV, p.377.
59.   OV, p.378.
60.   OV, pp.378–379.
61.   OV, p.380.
62.   OV, pp.380–381.
63.   See also P.G. Forster, 'La ideologio de Esperanto kaj la koncepto de superŝtato', *Eŭropa Esperanto-Revuo*, No.7 (1975), pp.2–3.
64.   Text in OV, pp.381–383.
65.   OV, p.383.
66.   Texts in OV, pp.384–392, 393–400, 403–412.
67.   Zamenhof, *Homaranismo*, 1913, reprinted in OV, pp.338–343.
68.   For general details of the Congress see G. Spiller (ed.), *Papers on Inter-Racial Problems*, 1914. See also M.D. Biddiss, 'The Universal Races Congress of 1911', *Race* 13(1), July 1971, pp.37–46.
69.   Submitted in Esperanto and French. English translation in G. Spiller, *op. cit.*, pp.425–432; Esperanto text in OV, pp.345–353.
70.   Privat, *Vivo de Zamenhof, op. cit.*, p.126.
71.   Reprinted in OV, pp.353–358.
72.   For a comparable situation in a different organisation (Baha'i) see P. Berger, 'Motif messianique et processus social dans le Bahaïsme', *Archives de Sociologie des Religions* 4, July–December 1957, pp.93–107.
73.   The position of Zamenhof in the movement resembled that of 'civilising heroes' discussed by Durkheim. See discussion in *The Elementary Forms of the Religious Life*, 1915, pp.284–285.
74.   E. Sapir, 'Language', in *Selected Writings of Edward Sapir: Language, Culture and Personality*, ed. by D. Mandelbaum, pp.7–32 (p.10).
75.   For the notion of 'vertical pluralism' see *inter alia* J.P. Kruijt, 'The influence of denominationalism in social life and organisation patterns', *Archives de Sociologie des Religions* 8, July–December, pp.105–110.
76.   For a history of the Christian Esperanto movement see H.A. de Hoog, *Nia historio*, 1964.
77.   For Oomoto see *Perspektivo*, pp.531–532.
78.   Result of my own survey; see Chapter 12.

4

The Ido Schism

The growth of interest in Esperanto in France towards the end of the nineteenth century has already been noted in the previous chapter. Yet it has been observed that, whilst Esperanto could gain recognition as being in accord with the Positivistic faith in intellectual and social evolution, it was not likely in such a milieu to receive uncritical acclaim. Although the Positivist scientific tradition had begun to wane in France in the beginning of the twentieth century, it remained of key importance in academic circles; and the French emphasis on systematisation of thought showed no sign of diminishing.[1]

This tradition was to have considerable influence in the organised Esperanto movement. It was not unchallenged, by virtue of the international character of Esperanto, but its influence remained considerable because of the strength of Esperanto in France. The implications of this situation, as a potential source of ideological conflict, have already been considered in the previous chapter. It must be recalled that the very structure of the language advocated for international use can be seen as part of the ideology of the movement which promotes it. Linguistic change would be ideological change. It was thus necessary for the Esperanto movement to come to terms with the problem of reform proposals, and to exercise some control over fissiparous tendencies. This had been one reason why Zamenhof had constantly advocated the formation of a League of Esperantists. The Boulogne Congress, mentioned in the last chapter, provided a suitable opportunity for clarifying various aspects of ideology and organisation. The movement had reached the stage where, as King[2] suggests,

Original goals are reappraised: some are now defined as ultimate rather than immediate possibilities, others discarded altogether in favour of quite different objectives. Since values and goals from the incipient phase are mainly of a general kind, they are now supplemented by more specific aims and values — especially if efforts at conversion have not been fruitful.

The relevant document, the Declaration of Boulogne, has been quoted in the previous chapter.[3] In this, the second and fourth paragraphs are significant for the question of language. Paragraph 2 emphasises the fact that Esperanto, and only Esperanto, is the only feasible project for international language. Paragraph 4 goes on to define more clearly the basis of Esperanto (*Fundamento de Esperanto*). The book[4] of that name cannot be changed in any way. The *Fundamento de Esperanto* consists of the *Gramatiko*,[5] the grammatical part of the *Unua Libro* (the alphabet and the Sixteen Rules); the *Universala Vortaro*, a basic vocabulary with translations into French, English, German, Russian, and Polish (first published 1894);[6] and the *Ekzercaro*,[7] a set of elementary exercises in Esperanto, published in 1894. The *Fundamento* was published as a whole before the Boulogne Congress in 1905, together with a foreword (*Antaŭparolo*) explaining its significance. Here Zamenhof argued that to ensure unity of the language, a clearly defined, untouchable, and unchangeable foundation was necessary. He referred to the possibility of future change, in a passage widely known and quoted:

When our language has been officially accepted by the *governments* of the most important nations and such nations by a special *law* guarantee to Esperanto certain life and use, and full safety against all personal whims or disputes, then an authoritative committee, elected by agreement by such governments, will have the right to make, once and for all, all changes desired in the foundation of the language, *if* such changes show themselves to be necessary; but *until this time* the foundation of Esperanto must most strictly remain absolutely unchanged, because severe untouchability of our foundation is the most important cause of our progress up to now, and the most important condition for our regular and peaceful future progress.[8]

The principle was thus established that changes could only be made after the general acceptance of Esperanto by the major governments of the world (this was one of the rare occasions when

Zamenhof considered the possibility of acceptance of Esperanto by governments). The *Fundamento* is untouchable, 'even with its errors'.[9] Neologisms, as opposed to structural changes, are acceptable. Zamenhof also allowed the introduction of improvements (*plibonigoj*). For this purpose Zamenhof accepted the idea of an 'authoritative central institution' of Esperantists; this organisation would not be able to remove or change any existing form in the language; it could, however, propose a new form, recommending its use parallel to the old. Thus gradually, as in any natural language, the old form would become an archaism and the new would take its place. In such a manner Esperanto would change: by archaism and neologism,[10] by evolution, not revolution. In the Declaration (paragraph 4) Zamenhof had suggested that his own style should be imitated, for the sake of unity of the language. As a model of Esperanto style, Zamenhof had already recommended the Fundamental Chrestomathy (*Fundamenta Krestomatio*).[11]

In order to provide machinery for making changes of the kind permitted by the *Fundamento*, a Language Committee (*Lingva Komitato*) was set up at the Boulogne Congress. This was formed on a provisional basis, with 68 members; its members were chosen in a rather haphazard fashion from among well-known Esperantists, including editors of periodicals and presidents of national associations. No attempt was made to select them according to proficiency either in Esperanto or in linguistic matters generally, Nor does democratic procedure appear to have been rigorously observed: when the list was proposed, names were added from the Congress floor, and after the Congress had finished, Zamenhof nominated new members to ensure that certain linguistic groups were properly represented.[12] Two persons elected were later found to be already dead. Thus the authority of the Language Committee was afterwards called into question; for that matter, too, the Boulogne Congress had no *de jure* official status.[13]

Such was the machinery with which the Esperanto movement had to deal, with outside pressures for change originating from French intellectual circles. As already noted, de Beaufront in particular aimed at attracting support among intellectuals and scientists; his campaign in such circles had met with some success, and de Beaufront was soon overshadowed in prestige by his converts. Also in 1900, the Paris Exposition was held, and a growing number of international congresses gained popularity for the idea of a world language. In this context Leopold Leau, a professor of mathematics, showed interest in the development of a world language, though he believed that official recognition of such a project was essential to its success. He was a friend of the Leibnizian scholar Louis Couturat, with whom he discussed theoretical considerations to be applied to the question of an international language. Whilst they both recognised the significance of the success of the chief existing project, Esperanto, they were not prepared to treat it uncritically. Couturat and Leau regarded the question as a worthy topic of scientific investigation, and to gain support for this venture cooperated in establishing the *Délégation pour l'adoption d'une langue auxiliaire internationale*. They hoped that this organisation would succeed in obtaining support from the recently formed International Association of Academies, itself the realisation of another idea of Leibniz. A small group of scientists held an inaugural meeting in Paris on 17 January 1901, and produced a declaration of the aims of the Delegation. The programme stipulated that the language would be auxiliary and international, and not one of the national languages. It would be suitable for general social relations, for commerce, and for science and philosophy. It would be easily acquired by anyone of moderate elementary education, especially if of European civilisation.[14] The Delegation was to obtain the signatures of scientists and intellectuals generally, and collective support from various organisations who realised the need for a world language. The Delegation hoped to influence the International Association of Academies to decide on the question; if the Association was unwilling to cooperate, the Delegation would itself appoint its own committee. The rules of the Delegation authorised the setting up of a society to promote the language chosen.

Couturat had already paid considerable attention to Leibniz's proposals for a universal language in his work *La Logique de Leibniz* (1901).[15] Together with Leau, he now began extensive research into the various projects for a world language that had been put forward. In the belief that serious study of the question was hindered by the fact that most advocates of a universal language know only one system, they produced a comparative study, *Histoire de la langue universelle*[16] (1903) and its supplement, *Les*

Nouvelles langues internationales (1907).[17] The former work
reviewed Esperanto very favourably, suggesting only a few modifications. Neo-Latin projects were discussed, but were criticised as
too elitist and irregular. The supplementary volume devoted further
attention to Esperanto, since Zamenhof's 1894 reform proposals
had only come to light after the first volume was produced. These
reforms did not receive a favourable review. The supplementary
volume also discussed the history of the Esperanto movement till
1907, and was critical of the Declaration of Boulogne. This was
objected to as it implied that no criticism of Esperanto was acceptable, however friendly. For consideration by the Delegation,
Couturat and Leau prepared a report on the question of international language and made certain recommendations. The report
concluded that, although certain neo-Latin projects, such as Idiom
Neutral, had many desirable characteristics, they lacked the flexi-
bility of Esperanto. Apart from its intrinsic qualities, they argued,
Esperanto had the additional advantage of being widespread in
practice. They did, however, suggest that certain changes could be
made, once and for all. These included changes in orthography,
notably the abolition of circumflexed consonants; abolition of
the table of correlatives; abolition of adjectival concord and of
the compulsory accusative; a change in the plural suffix; revision
of certain roots according to the principle of maximum internationality; and regularisation of the system of derivation.[18]

   Reforms of this kind had mostly been suggested before, but the
last reform suggested, that of the derivation system, assumed
distinctive importance in the disputes that were to follow. For
detailed discussion of this problem the student was referred to
Couturat's *Etude sur la dérivation en Espéranto*.[19] Here Couturat
praised the economy of vocabulary which the Esperanto prefixes
and suffixes allowed, but at the same time argued that the application of them was not systematic. Couturat was generally critical of
the commonsensical, pragmatic approach adopted by Zamenhof
and developed a very systematic and sophisticated philosophical
critique of the manner in which Zamenhof had derived parts of
speech from one another. He pointed out that although the various
parts of speech in Esperanto possessed their own distinctive
grammatical endings (*o* = noun, *i* = verb, *e* = adverb, *a* = adjective),
there were no fixed rules about how to derive verbs, for instance,

from nouns. Such a situation gave rise to certain difficulties. Thus *kroni* means 'to crown', but does *krono* mean 'crown' or 'the act of crowning', 'coronation'? To answer questions of this kind the Esperantists would have to fall back on the principle that each root in the language must be allocated to a particular part of speech, from which other forms are derived. Couturat rejected the principle that roots possessed a grammatical character and pointed out ways in which such a system in Esperanto gave rise to certain anomalies, which added to the difficulty of learning Esperanto. Thus in Esperanto the word *ĝojo* 'joy' is a noun root and forms directly the adjective *ĝoja* 'joyful'; whereas *gaja* is a verb root 'gay', and for 'gaiety' an abstract suffix is necessary, making the word *gajeco*. Couturat argued that these should be dispensed with in a rational grammar, and that all derivatives should be made according to the same analogies.

Couturat wished to apply principles of grammatical logic, ultimately deriving from Leibniz, to the question of word formation. He formulated his famous 'principle of reversibility', which he expressed as follows:

S'il y a correspondance entre la forme et le sens de chaque dérivé, toute dérivation doit être reversible, c'est-à-dire que, si l'on passe d'un mot à un autre d'une même famille en vertu d'une certaine règle, on doit pouvoir passer, à rebours, du second au premier en vertu d'une règle exactement inverse de la précédente. Pour prendre un exemple, si le suffixe *ist* designe la personne qui s'occupe (par métier) de la chose désignée par le radicale, comme le montrent les dérivés *artisto, muzikisto*, le substantif obtenu en supprimant ce suffixe doit désigner la chose dont s'occupe la personne designée par le substantif dérivé (*arto, muziko*). Cette exigence de simple bon sens, qui est une condition indispensable de la régularité des dérivations, nous l'appelons le principe de réversibilité.[20]

The Delegation recruited actively from intellectuals and organisations and succeeded in obtaining support from 310 organisations and 1,250 individual members of academies and university faculties. The support was international in character, though France clearly predominated. Many of the organisations were quite small and of no international significance (such as chambers of commerce of small towns), and many organisations and individuals failed to maintain a sustained interest in the subject. In accordance with its

constitution, the Delegation submitted the idea to the International
Association of Academies at its meeting in Vienna in May, 1907.
This organisation deemed itself incompetent to pronounce on the
matter and suggested that an empiricist rather than a theoretical
approach to the question was appropriate.[21] This refusal authorised
the Delegation to appoint its own committee, according to its
constitution. Couturat and Leau organised a vote among the members of the Delegation, with the proviso that authors of language
projects should not themselves be elected to the Delegation Committee. The following were elected, 253 delegates voting out of 331:

Manuel C. Barrios, Dean of the Faculty of Medicine, University
of Lima, and President of the Peruvian Senate.

J. Baudouin de Courtenay, Professor of Linguistics at the
University of St. Petersburg.

Emile Boirac, Rector of the University of Dijon (see p. 77).

C. Bouchard, Professor at the Faculty of Medicine, Paris, and
member of the Paris Academy of Sciences.

R. Eötvös, member of the Hungarian Academy of Sciences,
President of the Budapest Mathematical and Physical Society.

W. Förster, President of the International Committee for Weights
and Measures, sometime Director of the Berlin Observatory.

G. Harvey, publisher of the *North American Review*, New York.

O. Jespersen, member of the Danish Academy of Sciences,
Professor of Philology at Copenhagen University.

S. Lambros, sometime Rector of the University of Athens.

C. LePaige, Director of the Scientific Section of the Royal Academy of Belgium, Administrator/Inspector, University of Liège.

W. Ostwald, member of the Royal Scientific Society of Saxony,
Emeritus Professor of the University of Leipzig. Nobel Prize-
winning chemist.

H. Schuchardt, member of the Imperial Academy of Sciences of
Vienna, Professor at the University of Graz.

It was also decided that those unable to come could send substitutes, and that the Committee would have the right to co-opt
members. Of those elected only Baudouin de Courtenay, Jespersen,
Ostwald, and Boirac actually attended when the Delegation Committee eventually met; and of these, Boirac could not attend all
the sessions. He was accompanied by Gaston Moch,[22] who also
deputised for him in his absence. The absence of many of the

Committee members who had been elected suggests that their interest was not very great; however, some did send substitutes. Bouchard sent Paul Rodet, of Paris, an Esperantist doctor of medicine. Harvey sent Father Dimnet, a teacher of modern languages in Paris. Eötvös resigned and was replaced by Gustav Rados, member of the Hungarian Academy of Sciences. The Committee co-opted W.T. Stead, publisher of the London *Review of Reviews* (who had given much publicity to Esperanto in Britain):[23] he sent Paul Hugon, a linguist from Letchworth, to represent him. The Committee met in the Collège de France, Paris, between 15 and 24 October, 1907, and held 18 sessions. Professor Guiseppe Peano, who was working on *Latino sine Flexione*, was co-opted as from 16 October, and on 22 October the two secretaries, Couturat and Leau, accepted an invitation to become full members of the Committee. Not all came, and in the final session the following voted: Couturat, Leau, Jespersen, Baudouin de Courtenay, Hugon, Moch, Ostwald, Dimnet, Rodet. Förster, who was unable to attend, was elected Honorary President; Ostwald became President, and Baudouin de Courtenay and Jespersen vice-presidents.

Thus the interest of many of those elected appears to have been limited, and those who remained did not appear to regard a democratic mandate as of great importance. Only three of those elected actually came, the remainder being substitutes or co-opted. Since Couturat and Leau provided the central focus of the Delegation, they had considerable say in proposing candidates; they had also earlier chosen whose support they would enlist for the Delegation. Thus the Delegation Committee was largely shaped according to the wishes of Couturat and Leau.

During the same period in which the Delegation was being constituted, the organised Esperanto movement had been gaining strength, particularly in France. A substantial body of Esperantists was being established, many of whom were perfectly content with the existing linguistic scheme. The Boulogne Congress in 1905 had proved that Esperanto in its present form could be used in practice without difficulty: the emotionalism of the Congress also strengthened the affective commitment of many members to Esperanto as it already existed. The Boulogne Congress had expressed allegiance to the *Fundamento*, thus making proposals for radical change much more difficult to accept. Yet though support for the linguistic conservatism of Boulogne was widespread, it was by no means unanimous. Before the Delegation had met, reform proposals continued to be discussed. Zamenhof was affected by reformist pressures through his close friendship with Javal, who was also a fellow-Jew and an oculist. Shortly after the Boulogne Congress, Zamenhof had indicated to Javal that he would be willing to introduce certain reforms by way of neologisms. These would exist parallel to the fundamental forms and would thus not conflict with the *Fundamento*: the forms already appearing in the *Fundamento* would simply become archaisms.[24] Javal did, however, favour more sweeping reforms than Zamenhof was prepared to accept. In particular, Javal subscribed to a theory that accented letters caused eyestrain and thus wished to press for their abolition. In December 1905 Javal wrote to Zamenhof chiding him for not having introduced reforms in 1894: the Jewish symbolism is noteworthy:

In my opinion it is a great misfortune that your reforms of 1894 were not adopted at that time, and, even at the risk of displeasing you, I shall say that it was your fault, *tua maxima culpa*, that it happened. Put that on the top line of the *al khet* so that you can beat your chest next Yom Kippur.[25]

Javal went further, and in January 1906 reissued in a limited edition the relevant sections of *La Esperantisto* which discussed the reform proposals of 1894, thus enabling them to be reviewed in Couturat and Leau's *Les Nouvelles langues internationales*. Zamenhof corresponded extensively with Javal about reforms and did not display outright hostility. He was prepared to distinguish between the 'Period of Propaganda' (1887–1906), when the future of Esperanto was uncertain and any small change or addition to the complication of learning the language could discourage adherents; and the 'Period of Practical Use', after 1906, when the future of Esperanto was assured and the matter of convenience for existing users was to be considered. Zamenhof felt that the second period had by then been reached, since Esperanto had become a spoken as well as a written language.[26] This suggested to Zamenhof that certain improvements (*plibonigoj*) would be appropriate (though not radical structural changes). He regarded only a few changes as genuine and important improvements. He indicated a number of such areas. Some compound words made homonyms with other root words, and these could be changed: some changes in spelling could be made, eleminating diacritical marks. The rules for adjectival concord could be eased, the table of correlatives modified, and the sound *ĥ* eliminated (together with numerous minor changes). Javal attempted to persuade Zamenhof that reforms should be introduced since the French educational authorities were beginning to look favourably on Esperanto, but this argument failed to persuade Zamenhof: he would only be willing to introduce reforms if Esperanto became a compulsory subject in French schools. Javal also generously financed Sébert's Central Office, with the motive of providing a sound organisational base if Zamenhof were to introduce reforms. In 1906 Javal and his fellow-reformer Commandant Charles Lemaire provided a direct financial incentive to Zamenhof to introduce reforms. During the Geneva Esperanto Congress in that year, they privately offered Zamenhof 250,000 francs on condition that he introduced reforms. This would have enabled Zamenhof to retire from his medical practice and devote all his time to Esperanto. Zamenhof doubted the desirability of such a step, by which he would lose his moral independence, but agreed to visit Brussels and Paris in October 1906 to discuss the matter with Javal and Lemaire. They failed to reach agreement about reforms. This matter was concluded when Zamenhof submitted some reforms, which he had already discussed with Javal, to Boirac as president of the Language Committee.[27] Boirac disapproved, and succeeded in dissuading Zamenhof from circulating them. He doubted Zamenhof's assertion that the Period of Propaganda had now ended; he also doubted the possibility of counting grammatical changes such as abolition of adjectival concord simply as neologisms. Boirac also argued that discussion of reforms would not remain secret and would eventually have a bad effect on publicity. He suggested rather waiting for reform proposals from the governments, the International Association of Academies, or possibly the Delegation.[28] As a result of this, Zamenhof wrote to Javal saying that on second thoughts the time was not yet ripe for changes.[29] Lemaire began to use the periodical *La Belga Sonorilo* [the Belgian Bell], of which he was now editor, as an organ of reform propaganda. Javal died in 1907; other reformers turned increasingly to the Delegation to realise their aims.

The attitude of even orthodox Esperantists had never been hostile to the Delegation. Writing in September 1906, Zamenhof assured Couturat of his approval of the Delegation, though remarking that he did not wish to associate himself publicly with it.[30] Yet by December of that year he began to express doubts as to how authoritative the Delegation was. Yet he was willing to agree with whatever the Delegation did, provided only that it was sufficiently authoritative. He even suggested that he approved of the idea of reforms submitted by an outside body and expressed regret at having submitted his own proposals to the Language Committee.[31] Boirac, too, had delayed consideration of Zamenhof's reform proposals in view of the imminence of the meeting of the Delegation Committee. He regarded the Delegation as significant, though he was not prepared to regard its voice as decisive. He did agree to be a member of the Delegation Committee himself, in his capacity as President of the Language Committee.

At the Cambridge World Esperanto Congress, the members were prepared to regard the Delegation as of sufficient importance to elect a committee to discuss it (though this committee seems not to have had any part to play in the subsequent negotiations). Nonetheless, the question of the authority possessed by the Delegation continued to be of concern to the Esperantists. Zamenhof urged that Esperantists should support the Delegation not collectively, but only in a private capacity. There was also unease about the possibility that the Delegation Committee might propose reforms. Two leading French ultrafundamentalists, Bourlet and Cart, expressed disquiet. Each of them was associated with ventures in Esperanto publishing (respectively Hachette and the Esperanto Press Society [*Presa Esperantista Societo*] and grew uneasy about the economic dangers of reforms. Bourlet contrasted the strength of the Esperanto movement, as would be seen in the Cambridge Congress, with the weakness of the Delegation, which would probably not receive the support of the International Association of Academies. The Delegation, he argued, 'could give birth to dangerous discussions about *reforms*!'[32] He was later critical of the changes suggested in Couturat's *Etude sur la dérivation en Espéranto*, suggesting that Esperanto would be unwieldy if it were too precise.[33] Cart began his unwavering, forthright opposition to any reforms. At the Cambridge Congress he illustrated his standpoint by a French fable about a digging competition. In this, two competitors

argued about the suitability of their spades, whilst the third got on
with the work of digging his furrow, and won. The phrase 'let us
dig our furrow' (*ni fosu nian sulkon*) became the rallying cry of
antireformists.[34] Cart's general position was that unity, rather
than perfection, was the most important factor.[35] He displayed a
strong affective link with the existing scheme (the dear language,
kara lingvo).[36] In any case, he argued, Zamenhof would have no
right to agree to reforms, since the *Fundamento* was a contract
between Zamenhof and the supporters of Esperanto.[37]

A split between conservatives and reformers was already beginning on the matter of support for the activities of the Delegation.
Writing on its behalf, Couturat repeatedly tried to reassure Zamenhof, Boirac, and the Esperanto movement generally. In January 1907
Couturat wrote to Zamenhof[38] to the effect that Esperanto had
nothing to fear from the Delegation. He argued that it was incon-
ceivable that any other language but Esperanto would be adopted;
the only issue arising would be whether Esperanto would be adopted
en bloc or with some improvements. Couturat indicated his approval of the idea of making improvements through neologisms
and expressed his willingness to present any such proposals to
Zamenhof in the first instance. Such assurances appeared to satisfy
Zamenhof; it was on Zamenhof's advice that Boirac agreed to join
the Delegation Committee. The assurance did appear to be satisfactory to the Esperantists, and it appeared that any reforms proposed could be dealt with in accordance with the arrangements
made at Boulogne. Esperanto was bound to be accepted in principle.
It had already been favourably reviewed in Couturat and Leau's
Histoire. The only serious criticism of Esperanto on Couturat's
part had appeared in the *Etude sur la dérivation*: it is significant
that Zamenhof urged Couturat to keep this volume secret for as
long as possible.[39] One question which was not raised in negotiations
between the Delegation and the Esperantists was that of rival projects which might have stood a chance, notably neo-Latin projects
such as Idiom Neutral. This was no disadvantage to the Esperantists,
but the neo-Latinists could legitimately complain that the Delegation had been rigged in favour of Esperanto from the start and
that other projects never had a chance.[40]

As already noted, the Delegation Committee met in October
1907. The proceedings were mostly conducted in French: Baudouin

de Courtenay sometimes preferred to speak German, and the whole of the proceedings were conducted in German while discussing one project, *Parla*, at the author's request.[41] Peano occasionally spoke in his own project, *Latino sine Flexione*. The committee had access to Couturat and Leau's extensive documentation and also received a considerable volume of written evidence. The Committee found all *a priori* projects unsatisfactory. Neo-Latin projects were discussed at length but were finally rejected, chiefly in view of the number of irregularities they would entail. Much attention was paid to the critical study of Esperanto.

Zamenhof chose Louis de Beaufront as his representative before the Delegation Committee. Their relations had been strained over the question of Homaranismo, and Zamenhof's motives for choosing him were uncertain. One factor was probably de Beaufront's linguistic conservatism: de Beaufront had for long shown himself capable of applying skills of casuistry derived from his Jesuitical training to defend every detail of Esperanto. De Beaufront performed his duty of expounding orthodox Esperanto and answered questions on matters of detail which the Committee members put forward. Couturat then continued the discussion of Esperanto by putting forward his theories of derivation in Esperanto, and engaged in a long discussion with Boirac on this subject. At this point attention was drawn to an anonymous set of documents about a new project, Ido. This was clearly based on Esperanto, but had modified orthodox Esperanto so as to take into account the standard criticisms (adjectival concord, the compulsory accusative, the circumflexed consonants, the correlatives, and the system of derivation). Although some criticisms of certain details of Ido were made by Committee members, the new scheme met with general approval, since it met most of the criticisms that had previously been made of Esperanto.

Moch presented the only words of dissent. At the beginning of the discussion of Esperanto, he presented to the Committee, through Boirac, a note 'in the name of a group of Esperantists', saying that the Committee had only the right to choose an existing language project, not to make modifications or create a new one. After discussion it was agreed unamimously (including Boirac) simply to take note of this petition and to proceed as the Committee thought fit. This enabled the Committee to be free to come to the conclusion which it later reached. At the last session, at which Boirac was absent, the Committee delared theoretical discussion closed and appointed a Permanent Commission '*dont le premier devoir sera d'étudier et de fixer les détails de la langue qui sera adoptée*'. Ostwald, Baudouin de Courtenay, Jespersen, Couturat, and Leau were appointed to this; later de Beaufront was co-opted '*en raison de sa compétence spéciale*'. The Committee agreed to accept Esperanto in principle in view of its 'relative perfection' and its widespread application in practice: the Permanent Commission was, however, to propose certain modifications on the lines of Ido and the proposals of Couturat and Leau, hopefully in agreement with the Esperantist Language Committee.[42]

The Permanent Commission met once only, on 25 October, deciding to continue its business by correspondence. Thus it was not easy to obtain a collective view when negotiations later took place with the Esperantists. Ostwald communicated the conclusion of the deliberations of the Delegation to Boirac on 26 October, and on the same day Couturat communicated the decision to Zamenhof. In neither case was the reaction favourable. Zamenhof thought that the decision was 'unwise',[43] while Boirac objected to the Delegation's willingness to decide in advance what the changes in Esperanto should be. He thought that such a decision could only be made after a longer period of research. Zamenhof again began to show his distrust of intellectuals and theory, and reaffirmed the value of the practice of a world language. He also invoked the idea of loyalty to the 'Esperantist people'; writing to Moch on 28 October, Zamenhof said:

You should not have betrayed the Esperantist people by submitting many thousands of people, who have worked so much, for so long, and so laboriously, and who have achieved a great deal, by submitting this whole people to the orders of a few persons who perhaps have a very imposing exterior and very glorious names, but who have no right or competence to give orders in matters of international language and who have done nothing, but who come to a ready-made cause.[44]

Zamenhof said very little in print about the decision, but his views are evident from his correspondence with Sébert. Sébert had close contact with the Delegation through Moch, who was then an employee of the Central Office. Zamenhof expressed to Sébert his

view that the conclusion of the Delegation was offensive, but that
the matter of neologisms was still to be considered. These he
intended to propose himself, and they would be dealt with in
accordance with the arrangements made in Boulogne. By November
1907 Zamenhof was saying to Sébert that even the Language
Committee could not negotiate on radical and fundamental reforms
without special permission of an Esperanto congress.[45] He regarded
the only legitimate course of action as being for the Permanent
Commission of the Delegation to join the Language Committee and
negotiate the reforms from within the institutions of the Esperanto
movement. Couturat replied to this suggestion in an abrupt and
hostile manner. During this same period the ultraconservatives
were heavily critical of the Delegation. The periodical *Lingvo
Internacia*, edited by Cart, had previously been mainly literary in
content, but now frequently contained articles critical of the
Delegation and the possibility of reforms. Cart frequently quoted
his slogan *ni fosu nian sulkon*. He repeatedly argued that Esperanto
was artifically created, but was now a living language. It should
thus evolve naturally, without theoretical, foreign reforms.

A key question began to emerge as to who had authority from
Zamenhof, which he could withdraw at any time? What was the
correct interpretation of the Declaration of Boulogne? Was an
outside body in any sense authoritative? The Esperantists were
convinced that the latter was not the case; while some members
of the Delegation were equally convinced that academically unau-
thenticated institutions of the Esperanto movement were not authoritative, while a body of scientists was. The question of the
authority of Zamenhof, the Language Committee, and the Congress
was much disputed within the Esperanto movement. Ostwald
suggested to Zamenhof that it would be better if Zamenhof were
to act in a dictatorial manner, then at least the ground would be
clear for both sides. Zamenhof agreed that eventually he should do
this.[46] In all events, Zamenhof was looked to as the person who
could declare who had legitimate authority in the movement. In a
circular to Esperanto groups he made his disapproval of the conclusions of the Delegation Committee plain. He saw the Delegation
as an advisory body only and did not see it as authoritative in any
sense:[47] he tended to regard those who saw it as authoritative as
'traitors'.

Meanwhile, the Language Committee had been considering the proposals of the Delegation Committee, and January 1908 the votes were counted. On the matter of negotiation with the Delegation Committee, the 61 replies were divided as follows:

8 did not feel themselves well enough informed or did not express their opinion clearly;

8 approved entirely of the Delegation and its reforms;

11 wanted small changes, the product of mature consideration by the Language Committee and made in agreement with the Delegation Committee;

34 did not wish to negotiate with the Delegation Committee and disapproved of all kinds of reform proposals.[48]

Thus over half the Language Committee were unwilling to consider any change or negotiation of change, and only eight approved of the Delegation Committee's findings. Relations between the Delegation Committee and the Esperanto movement suffered considerable strain. Yet the Committee gained the support of a minority of leading Esperantists. De Beaufront was apparently dramatically converted to the reformist cause at the end of the proceedings of the Delegation Committee (hence his membership of the Permanent Commission), and even wrote to Zamenhof saying that Esperanto would soon be only a memory.[49] Commandant Lemaire, always a reformist sympathiser, gave greater publicity to his reformist views than did de Beaufront. He put the point of view of the Delegation Committee and reform in his periodical *La Belga Sonorilo*.

Boirac attempted to keep the discussion open. He corresponded with Ostwald, President of the Delegation Committee, whose scientific integrity he respected: he also felt some obligation towards working through the Delegation Committee, since he had previously urged Zamenhof to withdraw some proposals for consideration by the Language Committee on the grounds that the Delegation Committee would soon be meeting. Zamenhof expressed willingness to submit a new reform scheme to Ostwald, though this was less far-reaching than some of his earlier suggestions. Zamenhof's attitude to reforms remained negative: his view tended to be that, even if changes were unnecessary, some should be made, so that the final form of Esperanto could be fixed.[50] Zamenhof's proposal to Ostwald[51] eliminated adjectival concord and the compulsory accusative but made very few changes in vocabulary. There was also no special reform scheme proposed for the alphabet: Zamenhof merely pointed out that the *Fundamento* already permitted the use of *h* after a letter instead of the circumflex. Zamenhof also made no mention of the system of derivation. Ostwald was initially not unsympathetic to Zamenhof's suggestions, though this was before he had seen the full proposals, which he found too limited. Ostwald eventually rejected both the linguistic proposals and the procedure which gave the Language Committee the final say in the matter.

There thus appeared to be no possibility of further negotiation. Zamenhof finally acted in a dictatorial manner as Ostwald had suggested, and declared negotiations to be at an end. On 18 January 1908 Zamenhof wrote to Ostwald regretting that agreement was impossible but hoping that Ostwald would return to the fold when he saw his mistakes.[52] On the same day, Boirac wrote to Ostwald[53] regretting the end of negotiations. Himself an academic of high standing, Boirac was able to reply to the Delegation in the same Positivist terms with which they were familiar themselves:

Conditions of agreement between the Permanent Commission of the Delegation Committee and the Language Committee do not exist . . . . The duty of solidarity and linguistic loyalty are, to us, a direct consequence of the very idea of language. What would we think of a Frenchman who presumed to speak to Germans in their language, but reserving the right to change the German language according to his linguistic preferences, and who was amazed that he did not meet with unconditional approval from his interlocutors? But this comparison in itself reveals the main cause of our difference of opinion. According to us, Esperanto is an already existing language, living, similar in this respect to natural and national languages, English, French, German etc.; consequently it is like them a *fact*, even a social fact, which will evolve, like all social facts, by the action of humanity for the most part on its own initiative, whose life it makes possible in the same way.[54]

Ostwald was a Positivist in the natural scientific tradition, but Boirac took a more sociological view. His reference to the constraining effects of a social fact suggests Durkheimian influence.[55] As will be seen, this difference in perspective reflects one of the key factors which account for the eventual schism.

On the same day Zamenhof wrote and had published in some leading Esperanto journals a circular letter to all Esperantists, announcing the breaking off of negotiations.[56] Only the Esperantists are entitled to make changes, argued Zamenhof; unity is essential; and the Delegation Committee presented its conclusions in an offensive way. The scientists who have done this will soon see their error, he continued, but until then we Esperantists will go peacefully on our way.

Thus the Permanent Commission of the Delegation Committee and the organised Esperanto movement broke away from one another. Couturat wrote to Zamenhof on 26 January 1908 regretting the step he had taken, stressing that there were many Esperantists who wished for reforms, and drawing attention to a new periodical, *Progreso*, which the Permanent Commission would be issuing.[57] This would contain a systematic critique of Esperanto. The Permanent Commission expressed regret at the secession, and still urged Zamenhof to introduce reforms; however, they were now free to act independently and to consolidate their own project. The Permanent Commission examined various details of Ido, the anonymous Esperanto reform project which had met with the approval of the Delegation Committee. Detailed linguistic discussions continued in *Progreso*, the new periodical issued by the Permanent Commission. Couturat invoked the mandate of the Delegation to form a promotional society, which was called the Union of Friends of the International Language (*Uniono di l'amiki di la linguo internaciona*). The problem of a name for the language remained. Couturat asked Zamenhof's permission to call the language 'simplified Esperanto', but this was refused. Initially the name was not finally settled: the general term 'international language' was sometimes used, also *Ilo* (*Internaciona Linguo* plus the noun ending, also corresponding to the Esperanto root meaning 'tool' or 'instrument'); *Ildo* (as before, but including the initial of the word for 'Delegation'); *Delego*; and *Ido* (this reflects the initials of *I*nternational and *D*elegation, and is an Esperanto root meaning 'offspring' or 'descendant'). Although the new language was developed considerably from the project of Ido that had been before the Delegation Committee, the name *Ido* was eventually used exclusively.

The lengthy discussion of reforms, and the hostility of fundamentalists to any consideration of such reforms, had its repercussions in the French Esperanto movement. An election was to take place for the Committee of *Société française pour la propagation d'Espéranto* in July 1908, when, according to its constitution, one-third were to retire. These were all standing for re-election and had three months in which to campaign. On the matter of reforms, their allegiances were as follows:

Fundamentalists: Broca, Cart, Evrot, Tarbouriech.

Reformists: Bel, Jamin, Michaux.

Cart expressed loyalty to the *Fundmento* in no uncertain terms; he stood on the following platform:

1. Absolute untouchability of the *Fundamento*, the only possible basis of our unity.

2. Free, natural evolution of the language, under the control only of a constituted Language Committee.[58]

Bourlet, another conservative, urged that all candidates for election should declare their agreement with Cart on this point; but Michaux, a reformist sympathiser, who was eventually converted to Ido, objected and published the following counterdeclaration:

The sole language promoted by the *Société française pour la propagation d'Espéranto* is Esperanto, such as it is defined by the works and Declaration of Zamenhof, to evolve under the direction of a central institution, authorised by the whole body of Esperantists.[59]

Bourlet regarded this as reformist and urged the faithful to vote against Michaux and others suspected of reformist tendencies. The result of the vote was as follows: (number of votes in brackets; maximum possible 1,194):

Elected: Evrot (1,148); Tarbouriech (1,136); Broca (1,131); Not elected: Michaux (432); Bel (386); Jamin (373).[60]

The three new members, Saquet, Noel, and Muffang, were all fundamentalists. The reformists were thus unsuccessful in obtaining support from the membership. Yet de Beaufront was still President of the Society, and did not need to be re-elected in that year. His conversion to Ido had already caused considerable controversy, which was only exacerbated by rumours that he was the *author* of Ido, not merely a convert. De Beaufront indicated his desire to resign from his post in a letter to Zamenhof[61] but did not proceed with this. Further evidence of de Beaufront's authorship of Ido became available. Couturat wrote to de Beaufront and Jespersen the same day, but put the letters in the wrong evelopes. The letter intended for de Beaufront, which Jespersen received, contained what appeared to be evidence of de Beaufront's authorship. Since de Beaufront had been Zamenhof's representative to the Delegation Committee, Jespersen realised that such duplicity would be severely damaging to the Idist cause; he therefore demanded that de Beaufront should be unmasked, otherwise threatening to resign from the Permanent Commission.[62] Meanwhile Cart and Bourlet both campaigned against de Beaufront: Cart challenged him, without quite mentioning his name, in an article in *Lingvo Internacia*,[63] while Bourlet tried to enlist Zamenhof's support.[64] Zamenhof was willing, as before, to criticise 'traitors' and 'wolves in sheep's clothing', but refused to mention any names. The campaign finally succeeded in extracting a confession from de Beaufront, which appeared in *L'Espérantiste*, May (June) 1908:

Declaration by Ido

The time has come not to allow such inaccurate interpretations to circulate about the action and intentions of poor Ido.

Having presented his work, or study on reforms, to the Delegation Committee, Ido wanted danger to Esperanto to be avoided which was so foreseeable that it seemed certain: pure and simple rejection. . . . His formal wish, known to the secretaries of the Delegation, was that this work should be presented as a project of reforms for Esperanto, to be discussed and changed, but never as a competing system. And it was indeed so presented, and further with a pseudonym. . . . A different work does not appear in the thought of Ido, rather Esperanto continued *under the same name* with a few changes. He therefore left to Dr. Zamenhof and the Esperantists all the glory rightly acquired. There was no need to talk about Ido himself. After acceptance of the reform, he intended to disappear completely from the scene. Afterwards, as before, the world was to remain with Esperanto alone. Such was the wish of Ido, such was his realisable dream, *if it had been accepted*.

If his work is now presented to the public separately from primitive Esperanto, the cause is that unfortunately the leaders of the Esperantists generally did not even want to examine the question seriously. Thus in times to come they will certainly be reproached for that. Their sincere conviction excuses them; but the future will force them out of their dream. . . .

IDO

The declaration which has just been read is mine. As can be seen, I have discarded my anonymity.   L. de Beaufront[65]

This claim to authorship is almost certainly bogus, like many others of de Beaufront's claims. Ido was very much a philosopher's work and was heavily stamped by Couturat's ideas.[66] But this declaration polarised the reformists and fundamentalists, and no doubt helped to ensure the victory of the fundamentalist 'party' in the elections for the French Esperanto Society committee. Yet de Beaufront remained its President, and he continued to edit *L'Espérantiste*. This periodical carried the subtitle *Organe propagateur et conservateur de la langue internationale Espéranto*; but in July 1908 *'et conservateur'* was dropped, the periodical having advocated reform for some time. The periodical gradually began to be written in Ido rather than Esperanto, with more material than usual in French during the transitional period. *L'Espérantiste*, now an Idist publication, lasted until the First World War. During this period some French local groups associated with Ido still called themselves 'Esperanto' groups. Thus the view of many French converts to Ido, including de Beaufront, was that there ought not to be polarisation: Ido represented a direct continuity with the Esperanto tradition. However, Zamenhof was critical of de Beaufront after his declaration; in an article published in the *British Esperantist* and in *Lingvo Internacia* he stated that he had received no indication whatever of de Beaufront's intentions.[67] De Beaufront was finally unseated from the presidency of the *Société française pour la propagation d'Espéranto* on 8 September 1908, thus severing the one remaining significant link between the two camps. A new periodical, *Franca Esperantisto*, was begun to replace *L'Espérantiste*. In Belgium, with its issue of 4 October 1908 *La Belga Sonorilo* began to carry the subtitle *Journal bi-mensuel des Espérantistes libres*, and in subsequent issues Ido rather than Esperanto gradually became the language used. The orthodox Belgian Esperantists started the new periodical *Belga Esperantisto*.

Strained relations continued between Esperantists and Idists. A number of Esperantists were converted to Ido: it has been estimated[68] that 20–25% of the *leaders* of the Esperanto movement became Idists: in Belgium, where reformist influence was strong owing to Lemaire, the figure was more like one-third. The rank and file of the movement in most countries was, however, not so interested in linguistic questions. They were particularly interested in the relations of the Esperanto speech community, which had no counterpart of any significance in Ido organisations. It is estimated that only about 3–4% of ordinary Esperantists were converted to Ido. Some Esperantists were converted to Ido immediately after the findings of the Delegation Committee. Others still hoped for a while that properly constituted reforms could be undertaken through authorised Esperanto linguistic institutions but, as the Esperantists refused to consider reforms, drifted into Ido. Michaux allied himself much more strongly to the reformist camp after the elections to the French Esperanto committee, in which he attributed his lack of success to Bourlet's propaganda.[69] De Guesnet, another French Esperantist, reports the following experience (shortly afterwards, he became an Idist):

On the 8th of May in the London Esperanto Club took place an *agreed* discussion on the "Untouchability of Esperanto". As a result of disruption of my reformist speech, a personal matter which I did not wish to insist on, I understood that excommunication without futher discussion is the only fate suitable for the "infidels" who criticise the sacred texts of Esperanto. . . . Today, with regret and nausea, I withdraw from a party to which I have generously sacrificed my time, money and work.

Instead of finding in Esperantists, as I believed, progressive and tolerant people, I recognise more and more that Esperanto is only a stupid religion [*religiaĉo*], with dogmas and priests, which one has to obey blindly, and where it is forbidden to think freely.

Today, the dreams and the illusions flew away; I do not want to accept the slavery which people wish to *impose* on me, and I take back my freedom of opinion and action.[70]

Lingvo Internacia, as already noted, devoted much time to criticising Ido and the Idists but eventually returned to its literary content. Bourlet's *La Revuo* tended to ignore the whole question, a standpoint which was encouraged by Zamenhof. After the publication of the findings of the Delegation Committee, Zamenhof frequently argued that mention of Ido and the Delegation gave the impression that they were more important than was in fact the case. This principle, that the best course of action in relation to

Ido is simply to ignore it, still survives in the movement. It is still official policy to avoid mentioning Ido as much as possible; members are urged to distinguish, if circumstances necessitate mention of Ido, between paper projects and the living *language* Esperanto. Although the Ido movement continues to exist, has held world congresses of its own, and has produced some literature, including very comprehensive dictionaries, Esperantists frequently claim that it is now dead. It is very small indeed in comparison with the Esperanto movement.

The Esperantists argued that a number of irregularities took place in the proceedings of the Delegation Committee. They devoted much attention to the duplicity and moral turpitude of de Beaufront, but other criticisms were raised. Boirac claimed that he was not present at the final session since he did not expect it to be final, and considered that the Committee's decisions were abruptly taken at that time since he was not there to object. He also suggested that the non-Esperantists on the Delegation Committee had met *in camera* during the proceedings: a procedure that he found all the more objectionable since he was not aware that certain members were considered as having an imperative mandate with regard to Esperanto.[71]

The Idists in their own publications, notably *Progreso*, paid considerable attention to criticising Esperanto and the Esperantists. Boirac was criticised for not having submitted the full conclusion of the Delegation Committee to the Language Committee; the Esperantist leaders generally for having made no use of the Committee elected in Cambridge to deal with the Delegation; Zamenhof for refusing permission to use the name 'Esperanto' (since Zamenhof had renounced personal rights in Esperanto); Cart and Bourlet were accused of having a commercial interest in opposing reforms. Particularly, however, the self-conception of the Esperanto movement as a 'people' or 'supernation' was criticised. According to Couturat, the Esperantist people were chauvinistic:

. . . . voilà des "combattants pacifiques" qui se flattent de renverser "les murailles millénaires qui séparent les peuples" . . . ; et ils n'ont rien de plus pressé que de constituer un "peuple" nouveau, une "nation" à part et de s'entourer d'une muraille de Chine, pour préserver leur "chère langue" de toute atteinte de la part des "étrangers"!On ne saurait imaginer une contradiction plus ridicule.[72]

Couturat continued to direct the Ido movement and was known as an authoritarian leader. An Ido Academy was set up to consider improvements in the existing scheme and was very active in this respect. There was, however, a certain amount of opposition to Couturat's autocratic leadership. Guérard remarks: 'He had become that most uncompromising of men: the infallible pope of a small schismatic church.'[73]

Bertrand Russell, who knew Couturat through a common interest in Leibniz and mathematical logic, remarks of him:

In the last years I had lost contact with him, because he became absorbed in the question of an international language. He advocated Ido rather than Esperanto. According to his conversation, no human beings in the whole previous history of the human race had ever been quite so depraved as the Esperantists. He lamented that the word Ido did not lend itself to the formation of a word similar to Esperantist. I suggested "idiot" but he was not quite pleased.[74]

Couturat's leadership of the Idists was abruptly terminated in 1914, when he was killed in a motor accident. He had exercised his authority particularly through the Academy, which was much more highly structured than the Esperanto organisations had been at the beginning. The Academy introduced numerous changes until 1913, when a period of stability was introduced. Intended to last ten years, this was extended to 1926 because of the war. During this time, protestant sectarianism exerted itself among the Idists. Not all were satisfied by the temporary halt on change. Whereas the Esperanto movement was again 'purged' of reformers by the Ido schism, and its control over fissiparous tendencies was now greater than ever, the opposite applied to Ido. As a schismatic movement of reformers, the Idists were themselves fissiparous. The Esperantists reported dissent within the Idist camp with great delight, as proof of the rightness of their own fundamentalism. To a certain extent the Idist organisations controlled this tendency by authoritarianism, but more effectively by taking an ecumenical attitude. The Idists did not display outright hostility to other

projects (apart from Esperanto): since they were striving to produce the most perfect international language, they could accept
within their ranks authors of other projects, which could be seen
as contributions to the debate. Thus the Ido movement attracted a
certain number of 'seekers'[75] for maximum perfection in the matter of international language. Jespersen was active in shaping Ido
after the schism, but in 1928 produced his own project, *Novial*.[76]
Ostwald did not regard the decision of the Delegation Committee
as final, and saw further research as necessary. He remained in the
Ido movement, apart from a spell of chauvinistic fervour in the
First World War when he produced *Weltdeutsch*. He was also a
member of Peano's *Academia pro Interlingua*, an ecumenical body
biased towards neo-Latin projects. Peano had also been a member
of the Delegation Committee, but regarded its conclusion as
merely a contribution to the debate (and had not been present in
its final session). He thus felt free to work for his own *Academia*.
Some Idists formed other projects; de Wahl and Michaux, both
Esperantists converted to Ido, were later to publish their own
projects, *Occidental*[77] and *Romanal*[78] respectively. The *Nürnberger
Weltsprach-Verein*, converted from Volapük to Esperanto, was in
1896 converted from Esperanto to Idiom Neutral, and in 1908
from Idiom Neutral to Ido.

The Idists held their first World Congress in 1921,[79] in Vienna.
Here contempt was expressed for the emotionalism of the Esperantists: the central position of Reason and Science was affirmed,
and, consistently with this attitude, the slogan of this Congress
was 'We have come here to work, not to amuse ourselves'.[80] The
Idists have stressed the role of their language as *auxiliary*: linguistic
discussion has reached a high level of sophistication, but little
interest has been shown in the expressive aspects of the Idist
speech community, or in creative literary writing in Ido. The Idists
gradually began to drop their outright hostility to Esperanto and
began to regard every Esperantist as a potential convert to Ido.
The Idists have also regarded it as an advantage to them that the
Esperanto movement continues to exists, since 'Esperanto' and
'international language' are identical in the minds of the general
public.[81] Value-oriented ideals of world peace and brotherhood
have been much less stressed in Ido than in Esperanto, though
they have by no means been absent. More attention was, however,

paid to the perception of Ido in an instrumental manner, and it was explicitly likened at congresses to enlightened scientific innovations such as the telephone, radio, and aeroplanes, which were also international in character. Couturat has continued to be regarded as the founder-ideologue, and appeal to the authority of the Delegation Committee has continued. The Idists have sometimes regarded themselves as true heirs to the ideas of Dr. Zamenhof and have quoted some of Zamenhof's remarks on his 1894 reform proposals in support of their standpoint. Relations with 'our Esperantist half-brothers' (*nia Esperantista mifrati*) were discussed in the Ido congresses: there was debate as to whether the Esperantists were friends or enemies, since every Esperantist could be seen as a potential convert to Ido. Few Esperantists have shown interest in bringing the Idists back to the fold, and the organised movement has certainly not been prepared to make changes in order to assist this. One Esperantist, René de Saussure, published projects known as *Antido* as possible compromises between Ido and Esperanto.[82] Such activities led him into the reformist camp, and he was eventually expelled from the Esperanto Language Committee. The Esperantists regarded the schism as final: nothing short of unconditional capitulation on the part of the Idists would produce unity. This standpoint has irked the Idists: the Idists have claimed to be willing to re-enter negotiations with the Esperantists at any time[83] and have expressed dislike of the term 'schism', which the Esperantists tend to use to describe this event. Couturat wrote of '*la rupture, que dans l'*église *espérantiste on continue à appeler un* schisme'.[84]

As a result of the schism the Esperantists intensified their existing conservatism on the matter of language. Reformists gradually left for Ido and other projects, but there was a continued suspicion of Idist attempts to poach members, or otherwise to thwart the progress of Esperanto. At the World Esperanto Congress held in Dresden in 1908, Esperantists were suspicious of the presence of Idist spies and fifth columnists. It is still believed by many Esperantists that, when the Esperanto movement adopts policies intended to encourage a favourable attitude to Esperanto on the part of outside authorities, Idists will attempt to sabotage their efforts. Many Esperantists still have furious reactions to the mere mention of Ido — though Esperantists now also widely believe that

Ido is dead. Waringhien makes his position plain in his assessment of Ido:

What, then, now remains of Ido? An embalmed doll, wound in the swaddling-clothes of dogmatic logic — pardon, "di dogmatifanta logikozeso" — and it will never die, because it never began to live. The glorious Paris philosopher was not capable of inspiring into it that animating spirit which the unknown Bialystok student gave to his creation. That proves that one can be an excellent anatomist and a bad midwife, and that neither erudition nor pride are ever a substitute for love.[85]

Sharp condemnation has been expressed by influential Esperantists of those Esperantists who failed to display proper loyalty to the *Fundamento*. Dictionaries published in 1910 and 1932 were criticised on account of Idist tendencies.[86] The election of Cart to the presidency of the Esperanto Language Committee in 1920 indicates that fundamentalism persisted.

The schism delayed a possible minor change, in the suffix used for names of countries. The official suffix for names of countries had always been *-uj-*, following the name of the inhabitant. This worked on the analogy of the use of this suffix for containers, thus: *inko* 'ink', *inkujo* 'inkwell': *Franco* 'a Frenchman', *Francujo* 'France', i.e., container for the French. Zamenhof had appeared uneasy about this suffix because of possible racialist overtones: in his 1894 reform proposals he suggested the use of *-i-* instead. The possibility of generalising this suffix instead of *-uj-* was sympathetically considered by the Language Committee in 1907; a sub-committee was set up to discuss the question, but no definite conclusion emerged. But as part of the linguistic conservatism which developed after the Ido schism, the new suffix began to be condemned as a dangerous Idist heresy. In 1907 a new organisation, the Universal Esperanto Association, had begun to operate on a supernational basis; in 1918 it began to use the *-i-* suffix in its periodical *Esperanto*. This provoked strong condemnation from the Language Committee, and especially from Cart.[87]

In 1925 the Esperantists were asked to consider, in private, a proposal to cooperate with advocates of other projects for certain purposes. In 1924 there had been founded the International Auxiliary Language Association for the purpose of comparative research into the question of an international language. Active in this was Mrs. Alice Morris, a member of the Vanderbilt family with considerable financial resources. At the World Esperanto Congress in Geneva in 1925, she suggested to the representatives of the organised international Esperanto movement that a distinction should be made between research and practice, with Esperanto as the sole language for practical use. This was considered in a secret meeting of the representatives of the international Esperanto movement. It was, however, decided that the distinction which she proposed between theory and practice was unacceptable: the Esperantists argued that the best linguistic research depended on practical use. In 1927, however, this cooperation was supported by Teo Jung, editor of *Heroldo de Esperanto*, a privately produced international newspaper in Esperanto. He began a column, 'Ourselves and the Others'. Here he suggested that Esperanto was worthy of support on tactical rather than absolute grounds, as the most suitable *form* in which to promote the *idea* of an international language. He advocated the suggestion that an agreement should be made between supporters of Esperanto and other projects: practical propaganda would concentrate on Esperanto, but the Esperantists would engage in sincere collaboration for the purpose of theoretical improvement. This proposal provoked certain Esperantists to send 'poisonous letters' to Jung; while the Yugoslavian Esperanto periodical *Konkordo* condemned this suggestion under the heading 'Sacrilege'. As a result of such opposition Jung declared that there was 'something rotten in the state of Esperanto-land', and did not pursue the matter.[88]

In 1930, with the help of Jespersen, Morris called a meeting of linguists interested in the International Auxiliary Language Association. A periodical on the subject of international language was founded. The Esperantists gave this venture no official support, though some were associated with it in a private capacity. The International Auxiliary Language Association eventually produced its own project *Interlingua* in 1952, a neo-Latin system.[89]

The schism remains a highly significant episode in the history of Esperanto and of international language generally. In the course of Esperanto historiography attempts have been made to explain the schism, but explanations given by partisans on either side of the schism tend to be defective. Esperantist sources generally attribute it to the psychological characteristics of the chief actors, or to the morally reprehensible actions of certain leading Idists (more often, some combination of the two). The Esperantists have used the schism as proof of the dangers of allowing intellectuals to tamper with Esperanto. Yet particularly their condemnation has been reserved for de Beaufront, the traitor from within the Esperantist camp. Before the schism, de Beaufront had gained considerable popularity by virtue of his activities in organising the French Esperanto movement. He was also the author of influential French expositions of Esperanto grammar. At the Boulogne Congress, where de Beaufront was absent, there was applause whenever his name was mentioned. Yet his activities and claims had given rise to a certain amount of suspicion. Zamenhof had doubted his claim to be a marquis, he also suspected that it was not true that de Beaufront had renounced his own project *Adjuvanto*, seeing Esperanto to be superior.[90] Zamenhof and de Beaufront had clashed very severely over the question of Homaranismo. De Beaufront's dramatic conversion to Ido, and still more his confession of authorship, made the Esperantists pay attention to the negative aspects of his activities. Subsidiary psychologistic explanations have attributed the schism to personal pride on the part of the leaders of both camps, notably Ostwald, Couturat, Boirac, and Zamenhof.

Idist sources tend to suggest that the Esperantists attached too much weight to the manoeuvres that occurred during the period of secession. They argue that the work of the Delegation Committee was a search for scientific truth, and thus the manner in which the Committee had been set up was irrelevant to the discussion. Couturat argued that '*Le choix de la langue internationale n'a rien d'arbitraire, mais dépend de la science elle-même*',[91] while Jespersen wrote 'our final result absolutely could not have been different, even if Dr. Zamenhof himself had been present in person before us.'[92] In addition, the Idists expressed moral condemnation of the Esperantists. Couturat conducted a systematic campaign against the Esperantists during which he presented various explanations of the schism which might discredit the Esperantists. He suggested that Zamenhof was a traitor himself, since he had proposed reforms without consulting the Language Committee. He particularly singled out for criticism the idea of an 'Esperantist people', as already noted.

The explanations given on either side do not make for an adequate historical or sociological explanation of the schism, but an interesting structural feature of the dispute is suggested by the argument that arrogance or high-handedness was an important factor. Both sides put forward arguments of this kind. This suggests that the key issue involved related to the question of who had legitimate *authority* to make changes. The problem of reform proposals and how the organised movement should react to them is endemic to the whole question of constructed international language. This reflects the potential conflict, with which Positivist philosophy has had to come to terms, between Order and Progress.[93] In the last analysis the Esperantists preferred continuity and stability, therefore *order*, while the Idists gave priority to the search for maximum perfection, or *progress*. The only possible way of resolving this conflict was to provide institutions which could enable progress to be made through orderly methods, hence the significance of the Language Committee. The Esperantists, too, were divided among themselves about the proper justification for their linguistic conservatism. Some possessed a strong affective link with the existing scheme and held that the *Fundamento* was of intrinsic value. Others accepted the untouchability of the *Fundamento* purely out of expediency and in fact had lingering reservations. With the institutionalisation of conservatism in the *Fundamento*, reformers had turned increasingly to the Delegation. Significantly this was an outside body, of those with status outside the movement. An organised body of intellectuals provided the only successful major challenge to the official ideology of the movement. Their authority could be valid insofar as it was thought possible to arrive at objective truth in the matter of choice of an international auxiliary language.

Zamenhof had retained links with reformist pressure through his close association with Javal, but on the latter's death was free of these. Esperanto, in its traditional form, was of great affective and ideological importance to Zamenhof, and he was also able to appeal to fundamentalism on the grounds of expediency: fissiparous tendencies are likely to produce further disputation, and Esperanto in its traditional form had already proved its worth in practice. It will be recalled that Esperanto has been associated with promotion by the plain man, the enthusiastic amateur, rather than by professional linguists and other intellectuals. The source of the conflict becomes clear. The Esperanto movement would welcome intellectuals if they supported Esperanto on the movement's own terms (and many were prepared to do this, such as Boirac, Bourlet, Cart, and Sébert); but any suggestion by intellectuals that change should be implemented in Esperanto would simply prove the point that intellectuals were untrustworthy. The Esperantists' appeal was not to *theory*, but to *practice*. Zamenhof had taken account, in devising Esperanto, of factors such as simplicity of grammar and international comprehensibility: yet his way of arriving at a suitable scheme had been through the serendipity pattern[94] rather than through an attempt to apply abstract logical principles. This system was institutionalised at Boulogne with the adoption of the *Fundamento*. The Language Committee elected at Boulogne reflected the amateurish manner in which Esperanto developed: no serious attempt was made to select its members according to ability in Esperanto and language generally. The Delegation, by reason of its intellectual standing and commitment to Positivist worship of science and reason, was thus not willing to accept the authority of a body of amateur Esperantists devoted to the exegesis of Zamenhof's serendipity pattern. Even for the Esperantists, the authority of the Language Committee was uncertain. Zamenhof was willing to act in a dictatorial manner, knowing that he was sufficiently authoritative to carry the bulk of the Esperantists with him, whatever the official arrangements might be; also, when it suited him, he would argue that major changes were too important to be left to the Language Committee, and that only a Congress could decide on them. There were thus two foci of authority conflict; one lay in the claims of the existing users of the language, opposed to the 'objective' claims of reason and science; the other lay in the normative confusion within the institutions of the Esperanto movement itself.

Esperanto would certainly prove inadequate when measured against the standard of 'rational' grammar and scientific foundations, whilst it was on such criteria that Ido was planned. Whereas Esperanto was based on the 'principle of authority', Ido could appeal to the 'authority of principles'.[95] The Esperantists could justify their stand only by adopting a more sociological conception of language than that adopted by the Idists. The Esperantists could appeal to the importance of continuity and the existence in practice of the Esperanto speech community. Zamenhof appears to have been a Positivist of sorts, and his religious views were almost certainly influenced by Comte; but, unlike the Delegation, he had regarded sociological factors as more important than abstract logical principles, right from the first publication of the language. Boirac shared the same view, drawing the analogy between Esperanto and other living languages, and arguing that Esperanto was a social fact. Couturat made his contempt for this view of Esperanto very plain.

The different assumptions of the contending parties, and the apparent impossibility of reconciling them, made schism inevitable. The Esperantists soon began to pay little attention to Ido, though the schism had its aftermath in the Esperantists' ultraconservatism in linguistic matters. A further significant consequence was the recognition among the Esperantists of the need for authoritative decision-making institutions, so that would be clear in future who had the right to speak for the Esperantists as a whole.

NOTES

1. See J. Guitton, *Regards sur la pensée française*, 1968.
2. C.W. King, *Social Movements in the United States*, 1956, p.32.
3. See p. 89.
4. Published as L.L. Zamenhof, *Fundamento de Esperanto*, 1905.
5. Originally published in Dr. Esperanto, *Mezhdunarodnyi yazyk, op. cit.*
6. L.L. Zamenhof, *Universala Vortaro*, 1894.
7. L.L. Zamenhof, *Ekzercaro de la lingvo internacia Esperanto*, 1894.
8. *Fundamento de Esperanto, op. cit.*, p.43 (1963 edition).
9. *Ibid.*, p.45.
10. There have been disputes about the extent to which the introduction of a large number of new root words (other than technical terms) is desirable. Pressures against neologisms have come especially from non-Romance-speaking Esperantists, for whom the new root words (mostly of Latin origin) present particular difficulties. Such pressures have met with little success. For discussion see G. Waringhien, *Lingvo kaj vivo, op. cit.*, pp.244–256. There has also been discussion on the correct usage of the passive participles, a matter about which Esperanto is ambiguous. This tended to be highly esoteric, and has not had sufficient impact on the bulk of the membership to make it of great sociological significance. For discussion of this question see J. Regulo-Perez (ed.), *La Zamenhofa Esperanto: Simpozio pri ata/ita*, 1961; also G. Waringhien, *Lingvo kaj vivo, op. cit.*, pp.189–205.
11. L.L. Zamenhof, *Fundamenta krestomatio de la lingvo Esperanto*, 1903.

12. Zamenhof, letter to Boirac, *Leteroj*, vol. 1, pp.211-213.

13. De Beaufront had consulted a lawyer to confirm that this was the case. For text see *Leteroj*, pp.173-174.

14. For text see L. Couturat and L. Leau, *Histoire de la langue universelle, op. cit.*, Preface.

15. *Op. cit.*

16. *Op. cit.*

17. L. Couturat and L. Leau, *Les Nouvelles langues internationales*, 1907.

18. L. Couturat and L. Leau, *Conclusions du rapport sur l'état présent de la question de la langue internationale*, 1910.

19. *Etude sur la dérivation en Espéranto*, 1907.

20. *Ibid.*, p.7.

21. '. . . wenn Befriedigung erreicht werden sollte, sie leichter auf dem bisher befolgten empirischen Wege, d.h. durch verständige Versuche und durch sorgfältiges Anpassen an das tatsächliche Bedürfnis zu finden sein werde, als durch theoretische Prüfung'. For full text see *La Belga Sonorilo*, 15 September 1907, pp.14-15.

22. See p.78.

23. See Chapter 9.

24. Zamenhof, letter to Javal, *Leteroj*, vol. 1, pp.196-199.

25. Javal, letter to Zamenhof, *Leteroj*, vol. 1, pp.231-232.

26. Zamenhof, letter to Javal, *Leteroj*, vol. 1, pp.244-253.

27. Zamenhof, letter to Boirac, *Leteroj*, vol 1, pp.299-319.

28. Boirac, letter to Zamenhof, *Leteroj*, vol. 1, pp.322-328.

29. Letter to Javal, *Leteroj*, vol. 1, pp.329-333.

30. Letter to Couturat, *Leteroj*, vol. 1, pp.295-296.

31. Letter to Couturat, *Leteroj*, vol. 1, pp.321-322.

32. *La Revuo*, March 1907, reprinted in *Leteroj*, vol. 2, p.22.

33. *La Revuo*, April 1907, p.374.

34. T. Cart, 'La fosiloj', *Lingvo Internacia*, September 1907; reprinted in T. Cart, *Vortoj, op. cit.*, p.37.

35. *Lingvo Internacia*, May 1907, p.195.

36. *Lingvo Internacia*, November 1908, p.498.

37. *Lingvo Internacia*, May 1907, p.194; July 1907, pp.289-291.

38. OV, pp.464-471; also in *Leteroj*, vol. 2, pp.9-15.

39. Postcard to Couturat, *Leteroj*, vol. 2, pp.33-34.

40. See A. Guérard, *op. cit.*, Ch. VII.

41. For official report of the proceedings see L. Couturat and L. Leau, *Compte rendu des travaux du Comité*, 1910. See also H. Jacob, *Otto Jespersen: His Work for an International Language*, 1943.

42. The conclusion was worded as follows: 'Il (the committee) a décidé qu'aucune des langues soumises à son examen ne peut etre adoptée en bloc et sans modifications. Le Comité a décidé d'adopter en principe l'Espéranto, en raison de sa perfection rélative et des applications nombreuses et variées auxquelles il a déjà donné lieu, sous la réserve de certaines modifications à exécuter par la Commission permanente dans le sens défini par les conclusions du Rapport des secrétaires et par le projet d'Ido, en cherchant à s'entendre avec le Comité linguistique éspérantiste', Couturat and Leau, *Compte rendu, op. cit.*, p.26.

43. Letter to Sébert, *Leteroj*, vol. 2, p.52.

44. Letter to Moch, *Leteroj*, vol. 2, pp.53-54.

45. Letter to Sébert, *Leteroj*, vol. 2, p.77.

46. Letter to Ostwald, *Leteroj*, vol. 2, pp.82–83.
47. 'Cirkulera letero al la esperantistaj grupoj kaj gazetoj', *Leteroj*, vol. 2, pp.87–89.
48. *Leteroj*, vol. 2, pp.94–95.
49. See Zamenhof, letter to Sébert, *Leteroj*, vol. 2, p.52.
50. *Leteroj*, vol. 2, p.111.
51. See *Leteroj*, vol. 2, pp.104–124.
52. Letter to Ostwald, *Leteroj*, vol. 2, pp.137–138.
53. Boirac, letter to Ostwald, *Leteroj*, vol. 2, pp.138–143.
54. *Ibid.*, pp.138–139.
55. E. Durkheim, *The Rules of Sociological Method*, 1964, Ch. I.
56. *Leteroj*, vol. 2, pp.144–149; OV, pp.445–448.
57. Couturat, letter to Zamenhof, *Leteroj*, vol. 2, pp.155–157.
58. *L'Espérantiste*, March 1908, p.71, reprinted in *Leteroj*, vol. 2, p.168.
59. *Paris-Espéranto*, April 1908, reprinted in *Leteroj*, vol. 2, p.190.
60. *Lingvo Internacia*, August 1908, p.363.
61. De Beaufront, letter to Zamenhof, *Leteroj*, vol. 2, p.164.
62. *Cosmoglotta*, August 1937, p.72, reprinted in *Leteroj*, vol. 2, p.167.
63. T. Cart, 'Lastaj, necesaj klarigoj', *Lingvo Internacia*, April 1908, pp.145–149.
64. See Zamenhof, letter to Bourlet, *Leteroj*, vol. 2, pp.189–190.
65. *L'Espérantiste*, May 1908, pp.97–100, reprinted in *Leteroj*, vol. 2, pp.204–205.
66. Couturat had a project in mind, and Lemaire had offered to present it (Lemaire, letter to Couturat, *Leteroj*, vol. 2, p.24). If de Beaufront did in fact write Ido, it was as Couturat's scribe.
67. *Lingvo Internacia*, No. 8 (1908), p.368; *The British Esperantist*, 1908, p.147; reprinted in OV, p.451.
68. Estimates from Privat, *Historio*, vol. 2, p.62; *Perspektivo*, pp.424, 452.
69. *L'Espérantiste*, April 1908, pp.91–92.
70. *L'Espérantiste*, May 1908, pp.117–118.
71. *L'Espérantiste*, October 1908, pp.238–239; *Leteroj*, vol. 2, pp.228–230.
72. L. Couturat, *L'Echec de l'Espéranto devant la Délégation*, 1912, p.43.
73. Guérard, *op. cit.*, p.149.
74. B. Russell, *The Autobiography of Bertrand Russell 1872-1914*, 1967, p.134.
75. This term is employed by analogy with the usage of J. Lofland, *Doomsday Cult*, 1966, pp.44–49.
76. O. Jespersen, *An International Language*, 1928; *Novial Lexike*, 1930.
77. See E. de Wahl, *Occidental, unic natural, vermen neutral e max facil e comprensibil lingue por international relationes. Clef pour Français*, 1922.
78. See A.M. Boningue, *Romanal – Metode de international lingue*, 1909.
79. For report see *Oficiala raporto di la unesma internaciona kongreso por la Linguo Internaciona Ido*, Wien, 6a til 10a agosto, 1921.
80. *Ibid.*, p.3.
81. See L.H. Dyer, *The Problem of an International Auxiliary Language and Its Solution in Ido*, 1923.
82. R. de Saussure, *Elementala gramatiko de la lingwo internaciona kun exercaro di Antido*, 1907; and *Teoria ekzamenado de la lingvo Esperanto kun fonetika internacia alfabeto, sistemo Antido n-o 2*, 1910.
83. See, for instance, H. Jacob, *Internacia lernolibro por Esperantistoj*, 1934, pp.26–27.
84. L. Couturat, *L'Echec de l'Espéranto devant la Délégation, op. cit.*, p.45. There are certain parallels with the standpoint of the United Original Secession Church of Scotland in its relation to the Church of Scotland. This body regarded itself as a

part of the Established Church *in a state of secession,* hoping for reunification (which eventually took place). This position was accepted bilaterally in the case of the Scottish churches, however, a situation which was not true of the Esperantist/ Idist division. For details of the Scottish secession see J. Highet, *The Churches in Scotland Today*, 1950.

85. *Leteroj*, vol. 2, p.151.

86. E. Grosjean-Maupin, *Kompleta vortaro Esperanto-franca*, 1910; K. Kalocsay and G. Waringhien, *Parnasa gvidlibro*, 1932.

87. For history of this question see Waringhien, *Lingvo kaj vivo, op. cit.*, pp.174–188.

88. For the controversy see *Heroldo de Esperanto*, 9 September 1927, p.2; 30 September 1927, p.3; 23 December 1927, p.2; 30 December 1927, p.1; *Konkordo*, September–October 1927, pp.43–44; November–December 1927, pp.51–54.

89. For history see L. Courtinat, *Historio de Esperanto*, 1964, vol. 2, pp.583–584.

90. Letter to Sébert, *Leteroj*, vol. 2, p.174.

91. L. Couturat, *Le Choix d'une langue internationale*, 1909, p.12.

92. O. Jespersen, 'History of our language', in H. Jacob, *Otto Jespersen: His Work for an International Auxiliary Language*, pp.16–29 (p.26).

93. For discussion of this question see chapter on 'Auguste Comte' in L. Coser, *Masters of Sociological Thought*, 1971, pp.2–41.

94. This concept is derived from R.K. Merton, 'The bearing of empirical research on sociological theory', in Merton, *Social Theory and Social Structure*, 1968, pp.156–184.

95. See E. Hureau, *Le Problème de la langue internationale*, 1920.

5

International Organisation, 1905–1922

In the early twentieth century, formal organisation of Esperanto on a *national* basis began to be firmly established, especially in France. At the same time, difficulties arose about the extent to which international organisation was possible or desirable. The Boulogne Congress had considered various proposals for a League of Esperantists, but no formal, centralised official authority found acceptance except in the matter of language. Although Sébert's Central Office frequently used the designation 'official', it had no authority to do so, being merely a private institution. Yet while there was opposition to the development of formal organisations, there was no sustained opposition to the ultimate authority of Zamenhof. Until any formal organisations were developed, Zamenhof was seen universally as the person who had the right to designate any institution in the movement as 'official'. Even in the matter of language, for which the Language Committee had been formed, it was uncertain who had the final say in matters such as authority for changes. Indeed, it was particularly the ambiguities surrounding such an important question as this which provided an important stimulus for the formation of properly authorised linguistic institutions. Thus the Ido schism hastened the reorganisation of the Language Committee. This did not turn out to be a controversial issue, though considerable controversy surrounded the question of the formation of formal organisations for any other purpose. Thus a formal international organisation of Esperantists was not established until 1922, and even this ultimately proved unstable.

Thus for a considerable period discussion constantly took place on the matter of organisation. Until such matters were finally decided, moreover, authority remained with Zamenhof. Zamenhof's

influence remained considerable until his death, though he resigned
from formal leadership of the movement in 1912. Hence the
question of charismatic leadership inevitably arises in this context.
As Worsley[1] points out, the concept of charisma can obscure many
vital differences between social situations, and the popularisation
of the term has done nothing to clarify it. Yet, be that as it may,
one can hardly deny the significance of the personal authority of
Zamenhof in the Esperanto movement. The extent of such personal authority is sociologically highly significant and must be
recognised whether it is to be called 'charismatic' or not. Thus
in consideration of the transition of authority from Zamenhof
to bureaucratic, formal organisations, Weber's discussion of the
routinisation of charisma proves useful.[2] Two theoretical points
should first be stressed, however. In the first place, no suggestion
is here being made that Zamenhof's personal leadership *caused*
the Esperanto movement to develop in the way it did. The international character of the movement had the effect of mediating
the leader/follower relationship so that most members did not see
him in person unless they attended world congresses. In spite of
this, Zamenhof was highly influential while alive, and his life and
work continue to be venerated among Esperantists since his death,
and such matters are worthy of further examination. For the purpose of the present discussion it suffices to recognise that the
personal authority of a leader may be highly significant within a
group which is neither very large nor noticeably successful. Such
was the situation with Zamenhof's leadership of the Esperantists.

The relation between the early Esperanto movement and conditions in Russian Poland has already been considered. Zamenhof
had already gained some recognition in the Zionist movement and
was able to use contacts obtained in this way in the formation of
the Esperanto movement in Russia. Among Russian followers of
Esperanto during this period he was already referred to as the
Master (*La Majstro*). This may have been merely a reflection of the
Jewish usage whereby 'rabbi' (meaning 'master') can be applied to
any learned man:[3] since Zamenhof invented Esperanto he was
bound to be more learned in it than anyone else. The Russian
movement remained small: in December 1894 *La Esperantisto* had
merely 373 subscribers. Yet the early Russian movement was
remarkably cohesive: the significance of the early literature in

Esperanto in providing a shared symbolism has already been noted. There are other factors during this period relevant to Zamenhof's position as a leader. He early wished to transfer his personal authority to a League of Esperantists. This appears to have been due to financial and personality reasons. Yet he was aware of his influence on the matter of language and was prepared to use his position to influence members to vote against reforms, once some kind of voting machinery (the subscribers to the periodical) had been established. Zamenhof evidently displayed an emotive attachment to the existing scheme and did not wish for change. Yet he had before him the example of the dictatorial behaviour of Schleyer, which eventually resulted in a schism in which only a minority supported the orthodox line.

Weber defines charisma as follows:

The term "charisma" will be applied to a certain quality of an individual personality by virtue of which he is set apart from ordinary men and treated as endowed with supernatural, superhuman, or at least specifically exceptional powers or qualities. They are such as are not accessible to the ordinary person, but are regarded as of divine origin or as exemplary, and on the basis of them the individual concerned is treated as a leader.[4]

Unlike Schleyer, Zamenhof made no claim to *divine* authority; yet he had a unique position as the inventor of Esperanto. The experience of creating Esperanto from the elements of the natural languages was not available to others: likewise nobody else could claim to have experimented with alternative forms, but to have dispensed with them as unsatisfactory. It is clear that as far as language was concerned, Zamenhof possessed exceptional powers which were later to be successfully institutionalised in the movement. More generally, a certain saintly character has been attributed to him especially since his death. He has been depicted as a dedicated scholar, a gifted linguist, and hard-working; yet always modest, kind to all including his opponents, and generous to his poor patients.[5]

As such, though, Zamenhof's 'exceptional powers' derived from his authorship of the language and could be appealed to particularly in relation to linguistic matters. A distinction can therefore be drawn between two problems. On the one hand, Zamenhof's authority on language was transferred to a Language Committee which had as its basis primarily traditional authority (in Weber's terms); on the other hand, Zamenhof's authority in other spheres was transferred to organisations based on rational-legal authority.[6] The former was closely supervised by Zamenhof, while the latter was only slowly and unenthusiastically engaged in, partly at Zamenhof's insistence.

For Weber, authority is *traditional* when it is seen as 'resting on an established belief in the sanctity of immemorial traditions and the legitimacy of the status of those exercising authority under them'.[7] This bears some similarity to the basis of support for orthodox Esperanto: yet tradition in Esperanto was something created, not given. It was necessary for the traditional form of the language to be sanctioned by some legal underpinnings. This led to the creation of the linguistic institutions, in the first instance the Language Committee. In Boulogne the Committee was drawn from officials of the leading Esperanto periodicals and societies and, ambiguously, from the 'best known Esperantists'. This represented a delicate compromise between democratic election and direct nomination by Zamenhof. Even this procedure was haphazardly and unsystematically applied. The Committee had no legal standing; it was described as 'provisional', and Zamenhof privately expressed the view to Javal that it was too large.[8] In 1906, in the Geneva Congress, the Language Committee became 'definite'. Zamenhof remained nominal president, though the effective president was Boirac. In his report on the work of the Committee, during this Congress, Boirac remarked that

The Language Committee received its entire power from the hands of Dr. Zamenhof himself: thus it does not legislate at all, but only presents its opinion to the Master (*Majstro*) who alone decides.[9]

Zamenhof was inclined to see the Language Committee as authoritative, though he was willing to exercise his influence over the movement by virtue of his personal authority as the inventor of Esperanto.

The consequences of the lack of effective formalisation of linguistic institutions were not serious while there was no attack from without, but the formation of the Delegation brought the Language Committee and its shortcomings into the limelight. Its haphazard organisation did not enhance its academic status in the eyes of the Delegation Committee, and even within the Esperantist camp its authority was uncertain, as already noted. Thus, as a result of the schism, the Esperantists were virtually unanimous in seeing reorganisation of the Language Committee as an urgent priority. Early in 1908, before the final break with the Delegation Committee, Boirac expressed his intention to propose reorganisation of the Language Committee, and by March of that year he was corresponding with Zamenhof about a proposal to form an Academy (*Akademio*), which would be a higher commission of the Language Committee.[10] Zamenhof agreed to this eventually, and elections were held in time for the results to be declared before the fourth World Esperanto Congress, held in Dresden in August 1908. The members of the Language Committee elected the Academy from among themselves: nine members were elected, and a further three were later added. At the Congress itself, Boirac reported on the action of the Language Committee and proposed that the question of reforms could be investigated by the reorganised Language Committee at its leisure. This proposal was accepted, and four permanent commissions of the Committee were established to look into particular areas of interest (Grammar, General Vocabulary, Technical Vocabulary, and Internal Affairs). In October 1908 the Language Committee issued a Declaration, stating that its task was to conserve the fundamental principles of the language and to control its evolution.[11] Thus reforms were not excluded in theory, but in practice no radical change was ever introduced by the Language Committee.

With the formation of the Academy, Zamenhof decided to relinquish one area of charismatic authority that he had retained in the matter of language. Since 1906 Zamenhof had published his *Lingvaj Respondoj*[12] [Linguistic Replies] in Bourlet's periodical *La Revuo*. These were answers to such grammatical questions as had been a source of puzzlement to the Esperantists; Zamenhof provided authoritative statements on them. After the reconstitution of the Language Committee, Zamenhof considered that it would be appropriate to abolish this remnant of charismatic authority, and the *Lingvaj Respondoj* ceased to appear. Nonetheless, they were revived in 1910, though at the request of the Language Committee.

In his Congress speech at Dresden, Zamenhof stressed the importance of the linguistic institutions.

The newly constituted Language Committee soon disposed of
the question of radical changes. Boirac circularised the Academy
summarising the changes proposed so far; these were considered in
1909, at the World Congress for that year in Barcelona. The rules
for acceptance of changes were strict, requiring a two-thirds majority of the members of the Academy in favour of a change; in
the end, the only courses of action accepted by the Academy were
proposals to set up rules for the choice of new roots, and rules of
derivation.[13] Such conclusions were reported at the Barcelona
Congress and as such represented the end of serious consideration,
within the Esperantist camp, of radical changes.

Thus the Academy began to consider the question of rules of
derivation. It was in this area, more than elsewhere, that Idist criticisms of 'illogicalities' in Esperanto possessed a certain amount of
validity. The newly constituted Academy was now of sufficient academic status to set about systematic presentation of the Esperantist
case. The ground was thus set for the development of Esperanto
'apologetics'. An influential figure in this exercise was René de
Saussure, himself a member of the Academy. De Saussure disagreed
with the Idist principle that it was necessary to express through
affixes the entire relationship between a root and its derivative. On
the contrary, he suggested, Esperanto works on the principle of
sufficiency; only those affixes needed to suggest the idea involved
in the derivation are required. Thus, according to de Saussure,
Esperanto quite properly derives the verb *marteli* 'to hammer' from
martelo 'hammer' (noun), on the principle that a verbal action
derived from the noun 'hammer' can only be 'to hammer'. The
Idist practice of requiring the exact nature of the derivation to be
spelt out (in Ido *martelo* 'hammer' [noun] makes *martelagar* 'to
act with a hammer') corresponds in de Saussure's theory to the
principle of necessity, which is alien to the structure of Esperanto.
De Saussure published various reports on this subject, and these
met with general approval.[14] He also considered a related question,
that of the grammatical character of Esperanto roots. This centred
around the issue of whether a root such as *martel* 'hammer' was
intrinsically a noun or a verb, or neither. This issue proved more
controversial, though de Saussure's theory that roots *did* possess a

grammatical character was eventually accepted by the Academy. Another member of the Academy, Fruictier, also published an exposition of this theory.[15] This decision that Esperanto roots had a grammatical character was in opposition to the theories of Couturat,[16] which had also, on this issue, gained a certain measure of support from some Esperantists.

These esoteric discussions did provide a basis for the claim that the Esperantists were being just as logical and scientific as the Idists. They were, however, of little consequence for the bulk of the membership. René de Saussure was highly regarded for his work: at the World Esperanto Congress at Berne in 1913 he acted as Congress President, Zamenhof having ceased to exercise this function. The Academy and the Language Committee engaged in other activities. The Committee considered particularly the question of official sanction for new words and lists of words used by Zamenhof, and concordances of certain of Zamenhof's works were compiled by a number of Esperantists.[17] Commentary on the *Universala Vortaro* (part of the *Fundamento*) was produced, incorporating some corrections of the translations of the vocabulary into the national languages.[18] Certain words, already in use in practice, were officially sanctioned and included in addenda (*Aldonoj*) to the *Universala Vortaro*. Consideration was given to the possibility of issuing an official condemnation of Grosjean-Maupin's dictionary, mentioned in the last chapter, but it was eventually decided just to ignore it. Members of the Academy who showed any attachment to other projects were swiftly disciplined. Moch was expelled from the Academy in 1912, having joined the Ido movement (still wishing to remain an Esperantist). And despite his prestige, de Saussure himself was expelled from the Academy in 1921, after publishing his own project *Esperantido* as a possible compromise between the two competing schemes.[19] Thus rules against Idist encroachment were rigorously enforced, and this was taken to include any attempt at compromise with the Idists.

Yet once the new arrangements for the Language Committee and Academy had been established, linguistic institutions ceased to be an area of controversy. Zamenhof resigned formal leadership of the international Esperanto movement in 1912 and died in 1917, but these events had no repercussions on the linguistic institutions, which had become firmly established. The First World War merely had the effect of suspending the business of the Language Committee, and the linguistic institutions were incorporated unchanged into the general international organisation of the Esperantists established in 1922.

Considerable controversy arose, however, over attempts to form a world organisation of Esperantists for matters other than language, even though Zamenhof encouraged the idea. Zamenhof's early attempts during the Russian period to form a League were not really successful, and in Boulogne, too, the matter of a league of Esperantists was deferred. Zamenhof persistently pressed the idea of a general organisation of Esperantists. He made his position plain at the 1909 World Congress in Barcelona, saying in his opening speech that he did not like being seen by the outside world as the representative of Esperanto.[20] He was clearly seen as such by insiders as well. Whenever there was no official authority on any subject, Zamenhof was appealed to in practice as the leader; no faction which remained within the Esperanto movement seems ever to have engaged in a systematic campaign against him. He was seen sometimes as an arbiter: there was intense personal rivalry among the French leaders, who would write to Zamenhof to complain about each other. They all supported the idea of Zamenhof's leadership, partly for fear that such a coveted position might go to a rival. Faced with such pressures Zamenhof continually pressed the case for formal organisation. He prepared a document for discussion on the matter of organisation for the World Esperanto Congress to be held in Antwerp in 1911,[21] and urged the Congress to make arrangements for collective decision making before it closed. Zamenhof finally forced the issue in 1912, when the World Esperanto Congress was held in Cracow; here he resigned from formal leadership, and asked the Congress:

I ask you to liberate me from that role which I, for natural causes, have occupied in our cause for twenty-five years. I ask you, from now on to cease to see in me a Master (*Majstro*) and that you cease to honour me with that title.[22]

He again pointed out that he did not wish the movement to have too personal a character, and that he did not wish his private ideals to be thought of as being those of the movement as a whole.

Thus another factor in Zamenhof's resignation was that he wished to continue to pursue Homaranismo. In discussion of organisation, he was more concerned that some kind of formal body should be formed than with urging any particular kind of structure. He simply urged the Esperantists to work in harmony and to abide by majority rule.

Thus Zamenhof was able to influence the movement directly by his public pronouncements. He also led the movement to more bureaucratic forms of organisation by working through Sébert and his Central Office. The semi-official status of this organisation was significant in itself. Sébert was a strong supporter of bureaucracy, more so than Zamenhof and most other Esperantists. He was concerned in his activities outside Esperanto with rationalisation and systematisation (such as international bibliography), and having retired from a career as a general continued to think in terms of centralised authority. He was in a position to shape the Central Office in accordance with his own wishes since he was one of its main sources of financial support (the other was Javal). The lack of formal organisation elsewhere enabled him to use words like 'central' and 'official' for institutions which, strictly speaking, had no legal right to such titles. Decisions of the various semi-official Esperanto organisations, such as the Language Committee and the congresses, were reported in Sébert's periodical *Oficiala Gazeto* [official gazette], which he began in 1908. The Central Office was also strengthened in importance by virtue of being the secretariat of the Language Committee, and also of the Permanent Congress Committee, deriving from an *ad hoc* committee set up in Boulogne to supervise the work of organising future congresses. This was modified in Geneva in 1906, when it became a permanent institution. It consisted of an international committee elected by the Congress; the Central Office run by its professional secretary; and a local organisational committee, set up by the national association which had invited the congress concerned. Sébert, elected as President, was the only effective centre of such a body and had effective control. In addition to serving as a secretariat, the Central Office engaged in an extensive programme of documentation of Esperanto.

Writing to Sébert in October 1910, Zamenhof expressed regret that comprehensive projects of organisation of the Esperantists had so far failed and proposed a scheme for 'parliamentary orga-

nisation' for the world congresses.[23] This consisted of a proposal
for 'authorised delegates', which was later to produce much heated
controversy. The details were published in various periodicals, including the *Oficiala Gazeto* for 1911.[24] According to this scheme,
decisions would be binding, but only on official Esperantist organisations. Anyone who paid a subscription would be entitled to
take part in the world congresses, but only the elected delegates of
Esperanto groups or societies would be permitted to vote. Every
Esperanto group would have the right to elect one delegate for
every 25 of its members. The new regulations also allowed the
president of the Permanent Congress Committee to determine
what appeared on the agenda of the congress (in consultation with
its other members), thus giving Sébert additional power. If an item
was refused a place on the agenda it could be reinstated at the congress provided that 100 delegates supported it.

The proposal was eventually discussed at the World Congress in
Antwerp in 1911, but before the discussion took place a number
of other complications had arisen in the whole discussion of organisation. There was considerable opposition in certain quarters to
the idea of an organisation for anything other than language; Cart,
in particular, feared that a formal organisation might usurp some
of the functions of the Language Committee. Bourlet was in favour
of the scheme. Both Cart and Bourlet, however, were at this time
mostly preoccupied with Grosjean-Maupin's heretical dictionary,
and their opposed views on organisation received less publicity
than they might otherwise have done in their respective periodicals.
Zamenhof no longer had his own periodical in which to put forward his views.

The main complicating factor, however, was the formation in
1907 of a new organisation, the Universal Esperanto Association
(*Universala Esperanto-Asocio*, UEA). At the 1906 Geneva World
Congress, a certain A. Carles had proposed the establishment of
Esperanto consuls, who could help travellers and provide commercial and other information. A related proposal by T. Rousseau
advocated the establishment of Esperanto offices in various towns.
The Congress recommended that societies and groups should put
this into practice wherever possible; but a number of young Swiss
Esperanto enthusiasts, notably Hector Hodler (1887–1920),[25]
wished to put this proposal on a firmer footing. Hodler acquired

the year-old Swiss periodical *Esperanto* and turned it into the official organ of proposals of this nature. Details of Esperanto offices and consulates were printed in the journal, and Rousseau and Carles cooperated. By the 1907 Cambridge World Congress there were already 200 consuls in existence. Hodler began to advocate the development of a formal organisation of the Esperantists of the world; he perceived that the conflicts surrounding the decision of the Delegation Committee related to the source of legitimate authority in the movement, and put this point of view in *Esperanto* for December 1907.[26] Here he advocated a scheme whereby groups and specialist organisations would elect delegates who would meet together before or during world congresses. He did not make detailed proposals, but it was clear that he had in mind a development of the already existing consular system. Hodler campaigned by circular letters to individuals and groups for recruits to an 'International Esperanto Organisation' aiming at practical application of Esperanto through international services; and at creating a link of solidarity among members. In the spring of 1908 the name of this organisation became the Universal Esperanto Association. Eleven groups had already elected delegates, and a provisional committee and set of rules was established, to be ratified at a special UEA meeting during the 1908 Dresden World Congress. UEA received an encouraging letter of support from Zamenhof, who agreed to be present at the inaugural meeting. The rules of the new Association approved at Dresden, were as follows:

(a) The goal of the Association is the facilitation of relations of all kinds between speakers of different languages and the creation of a strong link of solidarity between the members.

(b) UEA is neutral in relation to religion, politics, and nationality.

(c) The sole official language is Esperanto, such as it is defined by its literary and scientific vocabulary.

(d) The members are individuals, i.e., a member joins the Association directly, and not through his local group or national society.

(e) In places where this is possible, one of the members is a delegate (his address appears in the Yearbook) and he voluntarily fulfils various practical services for the members who turn to him.[27]

UEA was thus not merely mobilised for practical purposes but also displayed considerable continuity with the 'inner idea' as expounded by Zamenhof. The constitution emphasised solidarity of members and affirmed neutrality on contentious issues. Significantly, it differed from existing organisations in that it recruited internationally; it was a supernational Association of individuals. This system bypassed nation-states and was thus in accord with the nonpolitical internationalism associated with the 'inner idea'. It provided an alternative and potentially conflicting tendency to the ideas already proposed for a federation of national Esperanto associations. UEA continued to receive Zamenhof's approval, and in 1909 he addressed a special meeting of UEA during the Barcelona World Congress; he saw in UEA a practical expression of his idealism:

UEA unites therefore not all Esperantists, but all allegiants of Esperantism (*Esperantismanoj*), that is to say, all those men who consider not only Esperanto in its external linguistic form, but also its inner idea. . . . It is everywhere understood that UEA provides a suitable neutral basis for all inter-human relations and services, and from this reciprocal self-help will result more friendship and respect between ethnic groups, and the barriers which hinder their peaceful communication will disappear. In this principle lies the chief importance of your association.[28]

Zamenhof had earlier expressed the view that, by virtue of its traditional political neutrality, Switzerland would provide a natural permanent centre of the Esperantists. UEA proved a highly successful organisation, and by 1910 it had succeeded in recruiting over 8,000 individual members and 850 delegates (the designation 'delegate' (*delegito*) replacing the earlier 'consul'). UEA met during the annual world congresses as a specialist organisation, except in 1910, when the general Congress took place in Washington, D.C. In that year UEA held a working conference in Augsburg, Bavaria. UEA thus grew rapidly and became a strong contender for official status as the general organisation of the world Esperanto movement. Thus UEA took part in the discussion of organisation in Antwerp in 1911.

Zamenhof spoke in favour of the idea of formal organisation of the Esperantists in his opening speech in Antwerp.[29] The principle of 'authorised delegates' was already in existence *de facto* by then, since Sébert had already arranged that such delegates be elected

after Zamenhof proposed the scheme. At the Congress, the principle
of authorised delegates was approved: since it was the authorised
delegates themselves who voted on the principle, this result was
hardly surprising! A large proportion of Congress members appeared
to be authorised delegates; out of 1,800 members of the Congress,
1,081 took part in the vote. Zamenhof's proposed rules for the
conduct of congresses were accepted; the authorised delegates
then ratified the decisions of previous congresses. This degree of
bureaucratisation provoked hardly any opposition; but conflicts
arose between the bureaucrats and the antibureaucrats, and among
the bureaucrats themselves, as soon as more ambitious schemes of
organisation were proposed. Initially three proposals were before
the Antwerp Congress.

The first proposal, by a group probably influenced by Cart, was
to the effect that the Esperantist people did not wish for a general
organisation. The second proposal, by Harold Bolingbroke Mudie
(President of UEA) was to the effect that UEA would offer its
services to the Esperantists as a whole, and would liquidate itself
in order to facilitate the creation of a new, truly universal association. The third and most ambitious proposal was by Michaux.
Michaux advocated the creation of a single 'International Committee' which would replace all existing organisations and would
become the sole authority for the Esperantists on all questions.
Against all these, however, Bourlet put a further proposal that
the authorised delegates should set up a commission to study the
question and present a practical plan at the following year's congress. Michaux protested, rightly as it turned out, that this was
simply a delaying tactic and that nothing would emerge: nonetheless, the delegates accepted Bourlet's proposal almost unanimously.
This proposal left the Central Office untouched; on this matter, it
was simply decided to form an Administrative Committee, elected
by national Esperanto societies who agreed to support the Central
Office financially, and which would supervise its action and its
budget.

During the following year, between the 1911 Antwerp and the
1912 Cracow World Congress, Cart repeatedly expressed his mis-
givings about the new organisational proposals, in various articles
in *Lingvo Internacia*.[30] He feared that such proposals might interfere with linguistic matters. Zamenhof replied to such criticisms in

a letter to *Pola Esperantisto*; Cart reprinted the article in *Lingvo Internacia*,[31] but commented that authorised delegates would not be representative and in any case could decide nothing. Progress on the formation of anything more ambitious on the matter of organisation was indeed slow. At the Cracow Congress it was reported that the Commission on organisation set up in Antwerp had not yet reached a conclusion, and the matter was deferred for a further year. This Congress also considered a simpler solution, that of a union of national societies. It was decided that this was a matter for the societies concerned, but that such societies should study the report of the Congress and consult with one another. The Commission on organisation was directed to present a report at least three months before the Congress in the following year.

As already noted, Zamenhof resigned at the beginning of the Cracow Congress, and this precipitated attempts to find a solution to the organisational question. The matter was much discussed, though little was achieved and many areas of confusion remained. Thus in the 1913 World Congress at Berne, the principle of voting from the Congress floor, abandoned in Antwerp, was reintroduced to ratify the decisions of the authorised delegates. René de Saussure was Congress President on this occasion, and Zamenhof merely sat in the audience. De Saussure stressed the importance of organisation and advocated the establishment of a new International Esperanto Association for propaganda purposes, to be formed out of existing propaganda organisations. The belated report of the Organisational Commission supported the weak proposal of voluntary collaboration of Esperanto societies, to be coordinated by the Central Office. UEA was left outside the direction of the affairs of the Esperantists, remaining simply an 'applied' organisation.

Attention has so far been concentrated on the internal dynamics of organisational development within the movement. During this period of history it had been possible for congresses to be held undisturbed, and internal development of bureaucracy could continue relatively unaffected by the wider society. Obviously, the situation changed overnight with the outbreak of the First World War. In August 1914 visitors to the World Congress, intended to take place in Paris, were greeted with general mobilisation. Since it was no longer possible for the primarily European-based international Esperanto movement to function effectively, discussion of organisation had to be suspended. Yet the war provided an opportunity for revival of the value-oriented emphasis on Esperanto. The proposed Paris Congress was closed immediately after opening, by Gabriel Chavet, professional secretary of the Central Office, with the words 'In spite of everything, long live the inner idea of Esperanto'. Those Esperantists who had enjoyed peaceful international relations with fellow-Esperantists could look to the restoration of peace. UEA had a particular role to play in this respect; it had been mobilised on a value-oriented basis, it recruited without regard to national frontiers, and its headquarters could remain open in neutral Switzerland. Its periodical *Esperanto* was suspended for six months following the outbreak of war, but it reappeared in January 1915. Hodler immediately proposed a scheme by which Esperantists could put into practice their idealism in a way which would be helpful to those outside the movement. He proposed a service for the forwarding of family correspondence between hostile countries. Letters, in national languages, could be sent open to UEA in Geneva. UEA would send them to the country concerned and would translate the letter into the appropriate language if necessary. No reference to political and military matters was permitted. This service was advertised in the non-Esperanto press and was highly successful: over 200,000 letters were forwarded in this way during the war. Hodler was determined to keep alive the idealistic aspirations of members of UEA. In the revived periodical he wrote an important article *Super* [Above]:

Now is not a suitable time to make sheep-bleats for peace. The powerful of the world wished (did they really wish or did the circumstances make them wish?) that the cannon should speak. If in the meantime it were to help to bring humanity to its senses, we would only be able to bless it.

But do we Esperantists, who for years have sung that "the peoples will form in agreement one great family circle" . . . not have, apart from duties to our native land, other special duties not to be put to one side?

We have the duty *not to forget*.

Not to forget the elementary truth, which the majority of our contemporaries — educated or not — are no longer heeding and have never heeded well.

Namely, that Europeans (I use that word to indicate the representatives of the countries belligerent at the moment) are and remain *human beings*. For us Esperantists such men do not live on a distant planet or in newspaper articles. We have seen them, we have made contact with them. . . .

Just because men behave like wolves, is it fit that we also should join with the wolves and cry? . . .

Apart from our sympathies, we have duties which our position as Esperantists enjoins on us. In fulfilling them, we will as far as we can work for peace — not the kind of peace which diplomats write in ephemeral treaties, but that peace which is engraved on the heart of men and forms the basis of any subsequent rapprochment.

The duty to believe that no people has the monopoly of civilisation, culture or humanity. Our civilisation is indebted to thinkers belonging to widely different races, some of which have long disappeared from history; it develops thanks to the continuous work of all peoples. . . .

Let us not set national cultures against one another and let us not try to set up a hierarchy among them. All of them are merely parts of this common world civilisation, the fruits of all men who have thought and acted. If we do not understand these national cultures to the same degree, instead of excommunicating, at least let us tolerate them for the sake of the love that millions of men have for them.

The duty to believe that no people has the monopoly of barbarity, treachery or stupidity. Only individuals and war are responsible. In our everyday life, in our own country, we meet certain men whom we judge as barbarous, treacherous or stupid. Even the same man at some moments in his life appears barbarous, treacherous or stupid, just as at other moments he is good, humane and prudent. Add to this that war uncovers and exacerbates all primitive instincts which social life as far as possible holds in check. . . .

Only war is to blame, and the system which makes it possible, not the men who are merely puppets of chance as soon as social rules and acquired customs no longer rule their instincts. . . .

But it is useful for some individuals to remain reasonable and beware of the excesses of the masses. We Esperantists could have such a role. We can prepare a better future, only if during the crisis we have been sufficiently strong not to lose our convictions.

It is now the cannon's turn to speak, but it will not sound for eternity. When hundreds of thousands of men lie in war graves and the ruins of the vanquished and the victors bear witness more to technical than to moral progress of our civilisation, then people will come to a solution, and then in spite of everything, international relations will be bound together again, since there is nonetheless something above the nations. . . . If we wish to build a new house on the present ruins, we need those workers who are not frightened away by the difficulties of reconstruction. Such workers are the elites of various countries, who, without prejudice and in a spirit of mutual toleration, will cast their gaze above the horizon of national frontiers, and will become conscious of a harmonious civilisation, broad enough to include all national cultures, tolerant enough to consider their diversity as a beneficial necessity. Such workers will not dislike war; they will declare war on prejudice, on crude instincts, on all kinds of guilt which degrade humanity and which will always remain numerous enough for future generations not to fear debilitating inertia.

Let Esperantists be the embryo of those future elites. In order to fulfil our task in a worthy manner, let us retain our ideal and let us not allow ourselves to be suppressed by despair or by regret.

True progress was not made by men who bowed down before all accepted ideas and blindly followed the masses. It was made by men of strong convictions, who knew how to overturn prejudice and transform opinions.[32]

In this and other articles,[33] *Esperanto* served as a source of reassuring words for Esperantists in belligerent countries. Emphasis was placed on the social causes of war and the Esperantists' duty to remember their commitment to love the whole of humanity. This was not, however, seen as subversive of the Esperantists' 'duty' to their native countries; rather these values should be remembered during the war so that they could be put into practice *after* the conflict. Towards the end of the war, and just afterwards, the Esperantists were able to join a progressive current of thought about postwar reconstruction. Attention began to be concentrated more on external affairs than purely on matters internal to the Esperanto movement, and UEA watched with interest proposals for a League of Nations. After the war, concerns of this kind enhanced the prestige of UEA, making it difficult for this organisation to be left out of a proposal for a common international organisation.

During the period of postwar reconstruction, there were more auspicious times for international organisations generally. There was a consciousness among the Esperantists of the need for unity. Hodler attempted to attain unity by proposing the presidency of UEA to Sébert; this proposal was unsuccessful, and in any case Hodler died in 1920. It was also possible in that year to organise a world congress again, despite difficulties caused by travel restrictions. This took place in The Hague, and the successful discussions of organisation suggested widespread support for the idea of a unified organisation. It was decided to form a new organisational commission consisting this time of two representatives of UEA and two from the Central Office, together with three ordinary members. This represented negotiations between two potentially conflicting tendencies – the international, based on the Central Office in Paris; and the supernational, represented by the Swiss-based UEA. This Commission was able to make a proposal for a common organisation to be considered by the 1921 World Congress, held in Prague, though it had some difficulty in deciding between Paris and Geneva as a common centre. Criticisms and discussion of the plan were heard in the Congress, and the Commission was given the task of producing a revised draft for presentation the following year in Helsinki.

Unlike previous organisational committees, this body was effective, though when proposals were published in April 1922 there was much dissatisfaction. However, as a result of direct negotiation between representatives of the Central Office and UEA shortly before the 1922 World Congress, a compromise proposal was reached. This enabled existing organisations to be linked together rather than producing a completely new organisational structure. The text[34] of the proposal was accepted at the 1922 World Congress, held in Helsinki, and was known as the 'Contract of Helsinki'. The text is as follows:

I

1. The *National Societies* shall elect *Permanent Representatives (Konstanta Representantaro*, KR) of the national societies, consisting of one representative from each national society, with a number of votes in proportion to the number of members for which it pays a subscription to the funds of the KR. Such Representatives shall themselves set up internal rules. [KR] will be able to have a President and General Secretary chosen from outside the Representatives. [KR] will take care of reciprocal information and cooperation of the national societies for common aims and of their financial support to the common Institutions of the Esperantists.

2. Individual Esperantists shall group together internationally by joining the *Universal Esperanto Association* (*Universala Esperanto-Asocio*, UEA) which spreads general usage of the language.

3. The specialist (technical and professional) Societies shall group the Esperantists together for propaganda and use in specialist circles.

II

The *Permanent Representatives* of the *National Societies* and *Universal Esperanto Association* shall agree upon the election of an *International Central Committee* (*Internacia Centra Komitato*, ICK) which shall consist of six members, holding office for three years and to be re-elected at the rate of two per year.

This *International Central Committee* will deal with the general interests of the movement. It will set up a Central Fund and will credit this with donations, congress subscriptions, subscriptions of the national societies by way of the *Representatives*, and a subsidy from UEA.

III

The *Language Committee* (*Lingva Komitato*, LK) is independent, but the National Societies, UEA and Specialist Societies may present candidates to it.

IV

The *International Central Committee* will organise the Universal Congresses and shall delegate their organisation to a local organisational committee.

The Universal Congresses shall consist of:
A solemn opening meeting.
Working meetings, in which the official institutions shall present reports and hear the remarks and wishes of the Congress members.
Specialist meetings.
Meetings of the various official committees together or separately.

The institutions designated 'official' are:
The *Language Committee* and its *Academy*;
The *Permanent Representatives* of the National Societies;
The *Universal Esperanto Association* with its committee;
The *International Central Committee*.

V

Apart from the Universal Congresses, official technical congresses may take place, according to the decision of the Central Committee, which however will not deal with conferences of a political or religious nature.

VI

The official communications of the official institutions shall be published through the Esperanto periodicals.

The official documents and reports shall be published under the jurisdiction of the Central Committee in the *Official Documents* according to their present form.

The Contract might be summarised diagrammatically as shown in Figure 1.

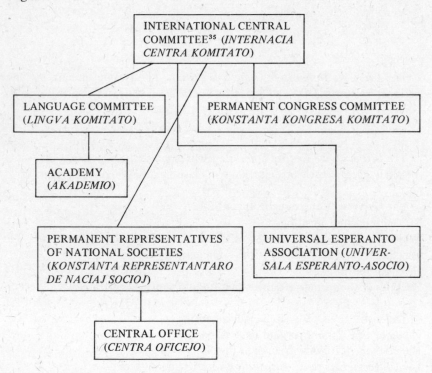

Figure 1.   *Diagrammatic summary of the Contract*

By agreement of the Congress, the existing Permanent Congress Committee became a specialist Commission to which the details of congress organisation were to be delegated by the International Central Committee. The Central Office was given the job of organising the International Central Committee. Sébert became President of the International Central Committee, and Chavet (secretary of the

Central Office) became its secretary. It was agreed that the existing Organisational Committee would form the new International Central Committee until elections were held.

Bureaucratisation was thus relatively swiftly obtained after the resignation and later death of Zamenhof; while the postwar mood of reconstruction made relations with the outside world more significant and there was pressure to settle internal differences as soon as possible.

Internal structural conflicts remained, however, endemic to the rather cumbersome structure proposed in the Contract of Helsinki. The machinery set up incorporated all existing organisations and simply added one other. It represented an attempt to compromise two tendencies which had developed in the existing organisations.[36] The first tendency was internationalism, represented by the national associations promoting an international language, with the Central Office in Paris as a centre for this tendency. This arrangement was effective for promoting Esperanto within a particular country or linguistic group. It was less subversive of national values than supernationalism. This could be seen as an advantage as far as hopes for official recognition were concerned; yet some might consider that it did not fully realise the idealistic potential of Esperanto. With the formation of the League of Nations, this too seemed to have some hopes of official recognition, if only in theory. UEA was important for the realisation of the second tendency, that of supernationalism or cosmopolitanism. This tendency emanated from Switzerland, in accordance with that country's tradition of political neutrality. The possible tension between internationalism and supernationalism remained endemic in the international associations of the Esperantists, and the structure devised in the Contract of Helsinki soon proved unstable. Yet future proposals for alternatives had still to reconcile this structural conflict. But although it proved unstable, the new structure did have the effect of providing for official recognition of various bodies which had hitherto had only semi-official status. It was thus an important step in the direction of bureaucratisation.

The period under consideration therefore was one in which characteristic processes of bureaucratisation of social movements also went on among the Esperantists. During this period, authority was transferred from Zamenhof to formal organisations. Zamenhof was still alive during a large part of this time span, and in the case of nonlinguistic matters he continually had to persuade his followers to develop formal organisations. Opposition arose less on the matter of linguistic authorities. These represented the institutionalisation of Zamenhof's authority, rather than any threat to it. They were largely concerned with the exegesis of Zamenhof's work, which had already been declared untouchable. The close identification of Zamenhof (Dr. Esperanto) and the language has already been commented upon. Thus the Language Committee and its Academy served to reaffirm Zamenhof's authority. A strong affective tie existed between the Esperantist 'people', their 'founder', and their language. A corresponding negative affective reaction was displayed towards schismatics.

The affective attitude which followers possessed towards Zamenhof was thus no hindrance and probably some advantage to proposals to provide formal organisations for linguistic purposes. Yet such an attitude could work against proposals for formal organisation of the Esperantists at an international level: such an organisation might be a threat to Zamenhof's personal authority. Some would also see a loose federation of national associations as sufficient bureaucratisation on an international level. Though Zamenhof continually urged his followers to allow him to relinquish formal leadership, his followers often acted in opposition to the idea. In Antwerp, Zamenhof had just succeeded in obtaining approval for the idea of authorised delegates; yet during the same Congress, a number of English Esperantists, carried away by spontaneous enthusiasm for their leader, unharnessed the horses of Zamenhof's carriage and triumphantly pulled it through the town themselves. The tradition of Zamenhof's moral authority for the Esperantists has carried on since his death. His congress speeches have been published, likewise certain very adulatory biographies. Organisations such as UEA, which served more than a strictly international organisation as an embodiment of Zamenhof's ideals, could prove successful. UEA also explicitly received Zamenhof's blessing. There were, however, advantages for more norm-oriented members in having an international organisation of some kind, and the Contract of Helsinki succeeded, for a time, in combining these two tendencies.

NOTES

1. Worsley, *op. cit.*, 'Introduction', pp.ix–liii; Appendix, pp.266–272.
2. See M. Weber, *The Theory of Social and Economic Organisation*, 1947, pp.358–385.
3. See L. Roth, *op. cit.*, p.72.
4. Weber, *op. cit.*, p.72.
5. The following incident from Privat's biography of Zamenhof might serve as an illustration; 'Once, in an American city, after a talk on the work of Zamenhof to young workers, a Jewish boy from Warsaw asked me, "Was that the same Zamenhof as the kind-hearted oculist from Dzika Street?"' (Zamenhof resided in Dzika Street). Privat, *Vivo de Zamenhof, op. cit.*, p.59n.
6. *Ibid.*, pp.324–385 contains Weber's discussion of types of authority.
7. *Ibid.*, p.328.
8. Letter to Javal, *Leteroj*, vol. 2, p.227.
9. *Lingvo Internacia*, 15 October 1906, reprinted in *Leteroj*, vol. 1, p.289.
10. See Zamenhof, letter to Boirac, *Leteroj*, vol. 2, pp.168–170.
11. *Oficiala Gazeto*, October 1908, reprinted in *Leteroj*, vol. 2, p.230.
12. Later published in book form as L.L. Zamenhof, *Lingvaj Respondoj*, 1910 and 1913, complete collection issued 1925.
13. See *Leteroj*, vol. 2, p.249.
14. For de Saussure's theories see R. de Saussure, *Principes logiques de la formation des mots*, 1911. For an opposing view see E. Ĉefeĉ, *La elementoj kaj la vortfarado, gramatiko kaj sintakso en Esperanto*, 1911, and *Pluaj argumentoj por pruvi, ke la teorio, 'La radikoj en Esperanto havas gramatikan karakteron' kontraŭstaras la intencojn de la Fundamento*, 1912.
15. P. Fruictier, *La esperanta vortfarado laŭ la Fundamento*, 1913.
16. *Etude sur la dérivation en Espéranto, op. cit.*
17. See particularly E. Wüster, *Zamenhof-Radikaro*, 1927; E. Wüster, *La oficiala radikaro kun enkonduko kaj notoj*, 1923; A.E. Wackrill, *Konkordanco de 'Ekzercaro' de D-ro L.L. Zamenhof*, 1907; W.A. Gale, *Konkordanco de la 'Sentencoj de Salomono'*, 1910; W.A. Gale, *Konkordanca vortaro de 'Marta'*, unpublished., British Esperanto Association Library, n.d.
18. T. Cart, *Korekto de la eraraj tradukoj en 'Universala Vortaro'*, 1922.
19. R. de Saussure, *Fundamento de la Internacia Lingvo Esperantida*, 1919.
20. Text in OV, pp.389–392.
21. Text in OV, pp.253–255.
22. OV, pp.408–409.
23. Letter to Sébert, *Leteroj*, vol. 2, pp.263–265.
24. *Oficiala Gazeto* 3(8), 1910–1911, pp.281–282. Reprinted in OV, pp.253–255.
25. For further information on Hodler see E. Stettler, *Hector Hodler, lia vivo kaj verko*, 1928.
26. *Esperanto*, 12 December 1907, p.1, partly reprinted in *Leteroj*, vol. 2, pp.97–99.
27. Reprinted in *Perspektivo*, p.424.
28. OV, pp.392–393.
29. OV, pp.403–406.
30. See particularly August–September 1911, pp.337–339; November 1911, pp.445–446; December 1911, pp.493–497; February 1912, pp.41–42, 43–46; May 1912, pp.161–163.

31. *Pola Esperantisto*, July 1912, reprinted in *Lingvo Internacia* 18, 1912, pp.256–262. and in OV, pp.456–462.

32. Text in *Esperanto*, 5 January 1915, reprinted in E. Stettler, *op. cit*., pp.98–104.

33. *Ibid.*, pp.98–168 contains a selection of these.

34. Text appears in Privat, *Historio*, vol. 2, pp.117–118.

35. This was in fact originally named *Centra Esperanto-Komitato* (Central Esperanto Committee) but was shortly afterwards renamed *Internacia Centra Komitato*. As the latter title is the one invariably used in Esperanto histories, it is adopted here.

36. This point is suggested by I. Lapenna in *La internacia lingvo: Faktoj pri Esperanto*, *op. cit*., p.136. The idea is also suggested in more general terms by Shenton: 'Persons from all parts of the world frequently assemble to discuss common interests. These conversations may include no items of politics or government. They may, for instance, deal only with some phase of arts and sciences, or with some specific problem of social welfare. The parties to the conversation meet as individuals, and not as representatives of any governmental organization. When people from all over the world come together thus to confer on matters of general interest, this intercourse takes on the nature of cosmopolitan conversation'. H.N. Shenton, *Cosmopolitan Conversation*, 1933, p.12.

6

External Relations: The League of Nations

Before the First World War there was little expectation among the Esperantists that officialisation of Esperanto could be achieved by a recognised international intergovernmental body. Attention was paid, if at all, entirely to national governments. In the hostile environment of Tsarist Russia no support for Esperanto could be expected on the part of the government. In the case of France, prospects for official recognition were a little more hopeful, but serious official support for Esperanto was still unlikely. Zamenhof had characteristically seen governments as bankrupt institutions as far as promotion of peace was concerned. But by the side of Zamenhof's idealism there was de Beaufront's practical emphasis. This was concerned with official support, and the tactics of a promotional pressure group were adopted. Those with an idealistic attitude to Esperanto tended also to welcome official support and practical application. This has always been one important appeal of Esperanto, and many Esperantists, including Zamenhof, held to the view that the ideals of Esperanto might eventually be realised after it had become more widely used in practice.

Yet such emphasis on official recognition that existed at this time was concentrated strictly on the national level: this included, for instance, support for the idea of making Esperanto a compulsory subject in French schools. The national Esperanto propaganda societies, such as the French, were suitable organisations for promoting Esperanto in this way. It was only a short step from the formation of national promotional associations to the idea of a federation of national associations. The more subversive, cosmopolitan ideal was by no means absent, however, and became the characteristic province of UEA. As the First World War approached and governments became more militaristic, the symbolic importance of this cosmopolitan ideal began to be stressed. The following incident at the 1913 Berne World Congress is a good illustration of this:

The Esperanto World Congress closed with a striking manifestation of international brotherhood. An English delegate, Mr. Harrison Hill, read a letter from Sir Vesey Strong, a former Lord Mayor of London, inviting the Esperantists to help in the international peace movement. The idea met with a warm reception. Dr. Zamenhof himself expressed the thanks of the congress to Sir Vesey Strong and Mr. Harrison Hill for the suggestion. Thereupon an eminent German Esperantist, Herr Schiff, expressed his pleasure over the fact that German, French and English representatives were at the same congress working for the cause of mankind and brotherhood. Instantly the veteran French General Sébert, a member of the Institute, rose and seized Herr Schiff's hand. Then Colonel Pollen,[1] of Westminster, who had played a leading part at the congress, embraced both the German and the Frenchman simultaneously, amid loud applause and cheers.

   Mr. Harrison Hill then sang an Esperanto song of his own composition, *La Vera Frataro* [True Brotherhood], and the whole assembly sang with him.[2]

   As has been seen with the ideas of UEA, emphasis tended to be placed on dual loyalty of Esperantists, to their own country and to the Esperantist people. The second was not to be seen as subversive of the first. Official patronage tended to be welcomed and could be seen as a sign that the profane world might see the error of its ways. A certain amount of such support had in fact been forthcoming. Javal had ready access to French governmental circles, by virtue of his own political activity. He succeeded in obtaining the support of the French Minister of Public Education in 1905, with the result that Zamenhof was made a *Chevalier de la Légion d'Honneur*. Also the King of Spain, Alphonso XIII, was very sympathetic to Esperanto and, during the 1909 Barcelona World Congress, bestowed on Zamenhof the title of Commander of the Order of Isabella the Catholic. Official observation of world Esperanto congresses began at Cambridge, where Belgium was officially represented at the 1906 World Congress. At Dresden in the following year the United States and Japan were represented, also the International Committee of the Red Cross. The Dresden Congress, too, took place under the official patronage of the King of Saxony. King Alphonso XIII was patron of the Barcelona Congress, and

Belgium, Mexico, Norway, and the United States were officially represented. There was official representation of various countries at world Esperanto congresses in Washington in 1910 (12 countries); Antwerp in 1911 (14); Cracow in 1912 (5); and Berne in 1913 (2).[3]

Thus a certain degree of interest, or at least curiosity, was expressed spasmodically by a number of nations individually. But before the First World War there was no significant international organisation which could be approached with a view to establishing Esperanto on behalf of the nations of the world. This situation changed dramatically after the war, with the foundation of the League of Nations. The Esperantists, too, were in a stronger position to approach an international body. The prestige of UEA had grown during the war, and UEA was in a position to form part of an international organisation of the Esperantists as discussed in the last chapter. UEA also saw its ideas as having an important part to play in postwar reconstruction, and welcomed the proposal for a League of Nations. The League could at least in some way be seen as a contribution towards the 'practical idealism' with which UEA was associated. The destructive effects of the war served to reinforce the commitment to peace displayed by the surviving Esperantists. As Privat put it: 'Before the war, Esperantism was a beautiful dream; after the war it has emerged as an urgent necessity.'[4]

A more peace-loving climate was established, in which it was hoped that Esperanto could obtain a more recognised place. Even linguistic conditions had shifted in favour of Esperanto. The French language had lost its monopoly on diplomatic communication at the Treaty of Versailles, owing to Lloyd George's and Wilson's limited command of French. The number of 'official' national languages in Europe increased with the emergence of several small countries as independent nation-states. This was an appropriate opportunity for the Esperantists to turn to the League. The aims of the League, as stated in its Covenant, were, *inter alia*,

... to promote international co-operation and to achieve international peace and security, by the acceptance of obligations not to resort to war, by the prescription of open, just and honourable relations between nations,[5]

and similar sentiments. The League could at least be seen as a small step forward towards the international respectability of the Esperantists' ideology. The Esperantists now concentrated their efforts on demonstrating to the League the practical value of the language. Contacts in the League were made through Edmond Privat, president of UEA, who served as interpreter from French to English in the League. He later became a member of the Persian delegation, agreeing to serve without payment on condition that he could use his position to support Esperanto if the opportunity arose.[6] Spasmodic attempts had already been made in various schools all over the world to introduce Esperanto lessons (usually as an optional activity outside school hours).[7] Attention was drawn to this fact by Lord Robert Cecil, the South African delegate to the League, and ten other member states (Brazil, Belgium, China, Chile, Colombia, India, Haiti, Italy, Persia, and Czechoslovakia), at the first meeting of the League in December 1920. The proposal read out was

The League of Nations, taking note of the language difficulties which prevent direct relations between the peoples, and the urgent necessity to remove such a barrier in order to assist good understanding between the nations,

Follows with interest the attempts at official instruction of the international language Esperanto in the state schools of various member states of the League of Nations;

Hopes that this instruction will become general in the whole world, in order that children of all nations from now on would know at least two languages, their mother tongue and an easy means of international communication;

Requests the Secretary-General to prepare, for the coming meeting, a detailed report on the results obtained in this field.[8]

This proposal was considered by the League's Committee on Technical Affairs, which recommended an official inquiry into the teaching of Esperanto.[9] France opposed this idea, however; the French delegate argued that French was already the universal language and that consideration of this question should be deferred. Helped by procedural confusion, the French proposal was successful. The matter was again considered the following year, and greater preparation was engaged in by the supporters of Esperanto. UEA invited a representative of the League to the 1921 Prague World Congress, and Dr. Inazo Nitobe, the Japanese Vice-Secretary-General of the League, accepted the invitation. He expressed himself in sympathy with Esperanto and the international friendship underlying it. He also noted the degree of interest taken in Esperanto by a number of learned bodies.[10] Lord Robert Cecil drafted a fresh proposal for the second general meeting of the League in September 1921. It was supported by Rumania, Persia, Belgium, Czechoslovakia, Colombia, China, Finland, Albania, Japan, Venezuela, India, and, with some reservations, Poland. The draft was considered by the League's Committee on the Agenda, which reported as follows:

The above-named delegates have proposed the introduction of the international auxiliary language Esperanto in state schools in order to facilitate direct understanding between all peoples in the world.

The Committee is of the opinion that this problem, in which ever more countries are becoming interested, merits detailed study before it can be dealt with by the meeting. It was referred last year to a committee which presented a short report recommending that the Secretary-General should inquire about experiments already made and about effective results attained. The committee proposes that the subject should be written on the agenda of a future meeting, and that the Secretary-General should in the meantime prepare a full and documented report in accordance with the wishes of the signatories, the report of the second committee and the report of the Vice–Secretary–General on his mission to the Prague Congress will be communicated to the members of the League without delay.[11]

This report was accepted, in spite of some opposition from France, and the Secretary-General was instructed to begin inquiries. A circular was sent to governments of member states and to Esperanto societies. In order to help with research on this topic, UEA proposed an international conference on the teaching of Esperanto in schools. This was arranged in conjunction with the *Institut J.J. Rousseau* in Geneva, an international university school of education which had shown interest in Esperanto in schools. The *Institut* agreed to organise this conference, while the League of Nations agreed to allow the use of its Geneva offices. In his speech of welcome the Secretary-General of the League, Sir Eric Drummond, expressed himself favourably disposed to the idealism of Esperanto teachers, which corresponded with the aims of the League.[12] The Conference itself appeared to be attended almost entirely by Esperantists, since Esperanto was the only language used. At the first meeting, delegates reported on existing experiments in Esperanto teaching, and it emerged that in 250 towns throughout the world there was some school instruction in Esperanto. In most cases, however, this had just begun and was run on a voluntary basis. The second meeting pointed out that the teaching of Esperanto had a beneficial effect on schoolchildren's understanding of grammatical principles, semantics, and phonetics. The third meeting considered evidence to the effect that Esperanto was useful as a first foreign language, as a step to learning others. The fourth meeting considered Esperanto in relation to geographical and peace education. It was reported that children's international correspondence in Esperanto helped in bringing the study of geography to life and in developing understanding of other peoples. Practicalities of teaching Esperanto, such as the number of hours and years of study desirable, were also discussed. The fifth and final meeting passed resolutions to the effect that the experiment of teaching Esperanto in schools should be broadened, and that as far as possible instruction should be made compulsory.[13]

It is hardly surprising that a conference of Esperanto teachers should express such approval of the teaching of Esperanto; but observers from the League of Nations secretariat were also impressed. The speed at which the business of the meetings was transacted, without recourse to interpreters, made a favourable impression, as did the fact that, since nobody was allowed to speak his native tongue, everyone was on an equal linguistic footing. The Secretary-General's report was prepared in time for the third general meeting of the League in 1922.

The report, *Esperanto as an International Auxiliary Language*,[14] took a fairly favourable view of Esperanto. It came down decidedly on the side of Esperanto as against any possible competitor, such as Ido, arguing for one auxiliary language, not several, and supporting the stability and long practical use characteristic of Esperanto. It reported on the success of experimental teaching of Esperanto in schools and emphasised the advantageous 'moral' influence Esperanto had on peace education and interest in the League of Nations. Esperanto was considered in the report as a suitable international language; it had a strong practical basis but was much easier to learn than natural languages. The report went on to point out that school time would not be taken up by Esperanto, since a basis in Esperanto made the learning of other languages much easier. It stressed the importance of stability, which for Esperanto would be guaranteed by the Academy. Esperanto appeared to foster a spirit of international solidarity, the report noted, and this was fully in accord with the aims of the League. The authors of the report expressed hope for a continued interest in Esperanto as a school and telegraph language by the League. They were careful not to suggest the use of Esperanto as a diplomatic language or in the business of the League itself — a proposal which would certainly have antagonised the French.

In any case, the report met with a certain amount of opposition when it was discussed by the general meeting of the League. The right-wing French government of the time was strongly opposed to Esperanto, and the French delegate attempted to prevent discussion by a proposal to refer the matter to the League's Committee on Intellectual Cooperation. Sweden and Norway expressed opposition to Esperanto and support for English, while Denmark expressed support for Ido. The Brazilian delegate attacked Esperanto as 'a language of ne'er-do-wells and communists'. On the other hand, delegates from a number of smaller or non-European language communities — Finland, Persia, China, Japan, and Bulgaria — expressed support for Esperanto, as being fairer to their national interests. France expressed concerted opposition and argued that recommendations regarding schoolteaching were inappropriate, since the League was not empowered to interfere in the internal affairs of member states. Eventually the report was accepted apart from the section which approved of the idea of teaching Esperanto in schools. This specific question of teaching Esperanto was referred to the League's Committee on Intellectual Cooperation.

At this stage, therefore, the strongest opposition to Esperanto came from France, whose strongly nationalistic government opposed the internationalist aims of Esperanto. French nationalism was expressed, *inter alia*, in support for the use of French as the international language. Since Versailles, English had threatened the status of French. The League of Nations was officially bilingual, though (with French encouragement) French soon became its dominant language.[15] France was thus hardly likely to favour any kind of threat to the prestige of its language. The Committee on Intellectual Cooperation devoted two meetings during its second session[16] (26 July–2 August 1923), in Geneva, to the question of teaching Esperanto. French pressure against Esperanto was again felt during the proceedings of this Committee. For a start, it was suggested that the successful use of Esperanto in commerce was irrelevant to the Committee's deliberations, since it was concerned with intellectual cooperation. The view was in fact expressed that Esperanto might be suitable for commerce, but that it was quite unsuitable for intellectuals. Discussion eventually centred on the merits of the learning of Esperanto as compared with the learning of foreign national languages. Particularly, the fear was expressed that the use of Esperanto might have the effect of lessening interest in modern national languages. Although some members dissented, such was the majority view, and the chairman, the philosopher Henri Bergson, was reported as having summarised the matter by saying that

There was no doubt that the adoption of an artificial language such as Esperanto might render great services, but there would also be disadvantages. In order to know whether the advantages would counterbalance the disadvantages, free play must be left for the intellectual and moral forces which might operate on one side or the other. . . . The invention would only be desirable if in the long run it imposed itself.

. . . .The object of the League of Nations was to bring nations together, and here there was no question of that purely mechanical requirement which consisted in facilitating communications. The facilities in this direction offered by an artificial language would not, any more than the telegraph or the railway, influence spiritual rapprochement. In order to triumph over the prejudice which stands in the way of understanding and loving another nation two means only are available: either to go into the country in question and for some time live the life of its inhabitants, or else, from far off, to learn the language and to study its literature.

. . . .this method of rapprochement, the most potent perhaps of all, would have to be renounced the moment that an artificial language was universally adopted, since the whole object of an artificial language was to make superfluous in practice the study of living languages. . . . From henceforth the business of the League of Nations and of its Committee on Intellectual Co-operation was to encourage the study of living languages, and not that of an artificial language. This was not to say, he would repeat, that the artificial language might not end by imposing itself, but it was for others, not for the League of Nations, to take up the cause.[17]

A final resolution was adopted to the effect that the Committee did not feel justified in recommending an artificial language for consideration by the League. Instead, the Committee recommended that the League should promote the study of modern languages and foreign literatures. It did, however, note that there might be practical advantages to be derived from adopting an artificial language. Such a resolution, moved from the Chair, was accepted in the Committee by six votes to three, with one abstention. The cautious wording of the conclusions is noteworthy; while Esperanto was not recommended for the League, they suggested that it was appropriate for the Esperantists to continue with their work. It is on record that Bergson had earlier expressed himself in support of Esperanto; he admitted acting under the instructions of Bérard, the then French Minister of Education, to 'drown' Esperanto.[18]

At the fourth general meeting of the League, in September 1923, the French delegate, under instructions by Bérard, attempted to present a resolution recommending the study of foreign languages rather than an artificial one. This resolution was unsuccessful, however; most countries were unwilling to support a resolution *against* Esperanto. The ultimate outcome was that this proposal was withdrawn and that the opinion of the Committee on Intellectual Cooperation was never ratified by a general meeting of the League.[19]

Esperanto was again discussed in the League in 1924, and by this time the French government had dropped its outright hostility to Esperanto. A new proposal, advocating merely that Esperanto should be adopted as a 'clear' language in telegrams, was presented by Persia. This proposal was intended to put Esperanto on a par with national languages; without such recognition, Esperanto would be treated by the telegraph authorities merely as a 'code', for which a higher tariff was payable. This resolution was considered by the Committee on Technical Affairs and met with some opposition, though not from France, who abstained in the final vote. The resolution was accepted by 13 votes to 9, with Austria, Australia, Bulgaria, Czechoslovakia, China, Finland, Hungary, Italy, Japan, The Netherlands, New Zealand, Persia, and Rumania voting in favour. The resolution was then considered by the general meeting of the League in September 1924, and it was resolved unanimously to recommend to member states that Esperanto be acceptable as a 'clear' language in telegrams. This resolution was considered by the Universal Telegraph Union, meeting in Paris in September 1925. UEA and the League of Esperantist Postal and Telegraph Workers had also organised a petition in support of the idea, and had succeeded in attracting 13,000 signatures. The Universal Telegraph Union agreed to accept Esperanto as a clear language unanimously. A Czech proposal to make Ido acceptable as well was rejected and later withdrawn.[20] Although this recognition of Esperanto was of little practical consequence, it was highly significant symbolically for the Esperantists. In one area of international communication, Esperanto was now established as a legitimate language: this made it less likely that the language would be associated merely with deviant value orientations.

Although on the floor of the League of Nations there was some evident opposition to Esperanto, the attitude of members of the League secretariat tended to be favourable. Such a tendency was especially noteworthy in the International Labour Office. Although supported financially by the League, this organisation acted independently. The International Labour Office accepted a proposal by UEA to offer the services of its delegates in making the work of the I.L.O. widely known. The I.L.O. accepted Esperanto as one of the languages in which it could correspond, originally accepting secretarial help from UEA but eventually teaching some of its own staff Esperanto. The I.L.O. had more language difficulties than the League and used languages other than French and English. UEA proposed a report on language difficulties and was invited to speak to the delegates of the third International Labour Conference in 1921. The result of this was a proposal from a Japanese and a French delegate to the effect that the I.L.O. should issue some documents in Esperanto and that its Administrative Council should increase its use of Esperanto as much as possible 'as a practical means of facilitating international relations'. The I.L.O. began to be represented at World Esperanto Congresses and, from 1923 to 1932, issued a regular bulletin in Esperanto.[21]

This period of negotiation between the Esperanto movement and the League of Nations opened a new era in the strategy of the Esperantists. During the League discussions, Esperanto had not met with a great deal of success and had certainly encountered some opposition; yet the very fact that it was taken seriously by representatives of governments was encouraging. The Esperantists took the opportunity to appeal to the practical value of the language. In negotiations with the League of Nations this took the form of emphasising the compatibility of the Esperantists' 'practical idealism' with the aims of the League. But during the entire period in which the League expressed interest in Esperanto, and afterwards, UEA took steps to demonstrate the practical advantages of Esperanto in a number of directions. The conference on Esperanto in schools (1922) has already been noted. This was the first of several 'technical' conferences called by UEA to discuss Esperanto in relation to special areas of application. The second technical conference was the 'International Conference for a Common Commercial Language' held in Venice in 1923. Interest in this subject arose after the Paris Chamber of Commerce had investigated the potential of Esperanto as a commercial language and had reported favourably. UEA suggested initially that the Paris Chamber of Commerce might call the conference itself, but this suggestion was rejected owing to the hostility to Esperanto that existed in France at that time. UEA looked elsewhere for support and was successful with the Italian Chamber of Commerce in Switzerland, which called the conference in Venice.

Over 200 delegates from 23 countries attended, representing chambers of commerce, trade fairs, and industrial, transport, and tourist organisations. Almost all brought favourable reports of the use of Esperanto, and resolutions were passed encouraging the use of Esperanto in commerce and the teaching of Esperanto in commercial colleges (Paris had already begun to offer an optional Esperanto course). Particularly favourable reports on Esperanto were presented by those concerned with the international trade fairs. Some of these, notably Frankfurt and Leipzig, had successfully established Esperanto secretariats and issued literature in Esperanto. Esperanto was clearly seen in certain commercial circles as of importance in postwar reconstruction of world trade. It is noteworthy, however, that the conference largely consisted, like the schools conference, of practitioners who were already supporters of Esperanto (though some of the delegates had learnt Esperanto specially for the conference). The entire proceedings of the conference took place in that language. The successful experiences obtained were also due in some degree to the fact that the services of UEA delegates had been employed for provision of commercial information.[22]

A certain amount of support for Esperanto from outsiders to the movement was evident from the third technical conference. In the early 1920s a significant feature of international cultural re-leations was the spread of radio communication. The multiplicity of languages of broadcasting was a waste of scarce resources and was recognised as problematic. There were, too, other problems of international coordination, on matters such as wavelengths and technical vocabulary. UEA succeeded in collaborating with the Swiss Radio-Electrical Society in calling a 'Preparatory Conference for an International Radio-Telephony Agreement' in Geneva in March 1924. Delegates came from 39 radio companies, societies, stations, and administrations: only one-third of the delegates could speak Esperanto, which was only one of the languages used. None-theless, the conference unanimously accepted a resolution support-ing the idea of an international auxiliary language for international broadcasting. Support was given by the conference for those radio stations which had already begun Esperanto broadcasts, and the provision of a regular weekly Esperanto broadcast and an Esperanto course was commended to all radio stations. The conference also expressed the opinion that Esperanto was clearly audible on radio and therefore particularly suited for this role.[23]

Here was a small but significant area in which Esperanto was established as a legitimate means of communication with the sup-port of non-Esperantists. This success was short-lived, since, with the spread of radio broadcasting, programmes became of national or local significance rather than international. Sufficient material was available in national languages, and linguistic diversity became less problematic. Amateur radio was a different matter, since this remained more of an internationally based hobby. Some Esperan-tists were pioneers in this field, and at a world congress of radio clubs in Paris in 1925, not organised in conjunction with Esperanto bodies, Esperanto had a favourable reception.[24] This conference recommended the use of Esperanto as an auxiliary language for international communications and radiotelephonic transmissions, for summaries of articles, and for the proceedings of congresses. Esperanto was adopted by the congress side by side with English and French. Esperanto this time had to compete with the claims, not so much of national languages, but of Ido. The Idists saw their language as a technical innovation rather than as a vehicle of idealism, and were keen to associate it with other technical innovations of the period. They were thus particularly active in the field of radio.[25]

In 1921 the French Academy of Sciences passed a resolution favourable to Esperanto. This resolution saw the use of Esperanto as a way of extending internationally the intellectual and cultural influence of France. It supported the teaching of Esperanto in conjunction with scientific education; the use of Esperanto as one of the official languages of international scientific conferences with a view to its eventually becoming the sole official language; the use of Esperanto in scientific publications aimed at an international audience; the learning of Esperanto by existing scientific practitioners; and the compilation of specialist vocabularies for the various branches of science. Encouraged by this, UEA called a conference on the use of Esperanto in science and technology, to be held in Paris. This did not take place until 1925, by which time the French government had become more favourably disposed to Esperanto. The Esperantist International Central Committee requested the Esperantist Scientific Association (founded at the 1906 Geneva Congress) to organise it. Delegates came from scientific associations and institutes of 37 countries; not all of these were Esperantists and the status of many was effectively that of observers, since Esperanto was the language of the conference. The proceedings dealt mainly with the implementation of the recommendations made in 1921 by the French Academy of Sciences.[26] In particular, the desirability of Esperanto summaries of scientific articles was stressed; some Japanese periodicals already provided these.

Simultaneously with the scientific conference, a second conference on the use of Esperanto in commerce and industry was held. This took place under the official patronage of the Paris Chamber of Commerce, by agreement between the Esperantist International Central Committee, the French society *Esperanto et Commerce*, and the Paris Fair committee. It was attended by representatives of chambers of commerce, trade fairs, and industrial corporations from 33 countries, and ten governments were represented officially. After reports on Esperanto in commerce, on the lines of the Venice conference, discussion took place on the consolidation of the place of Esperanto in commerce. Much attention was paid to the idea of 'keys' to Esperanto. Zamenhof had advocated the use of these;[27] they consist of an inexpensively produced basic vocabulary, in which grammatical endings and suffixes are also presented as separate roots. They are intended for insertion with a letter in Esperanto to a non-Esperantist, who should be able to decode it with the help of the key. By 1925 a number of such keys had already been produced in the major world languages, on the initiative of H.V. Hoveler (Ĉefeĉ), following up Zamenhof's idea. The conference discussed extension and standardisation of this system. The addition of suitable commercial terms was proposed. The conference consolidated use of Esperanto in commerce further by discussing the suitability of certain new root words in commercial Esperanto. Finally, favourable reports were presented on the teaching of Esperanto as a commercial language.[26]

UEA thus successfully carried out a programme of developing the use of Esperanto in specialised practical spheres. This was still in the spirit of self-help which the movement had long adopted as its policy; but now that there was an international intergovernmental body which might be impressed by this activity, the Esperantists adopted pressure-group tactics in order to attract it. It was clear at this period in history that Esperanto was beginning to be taken seriously outside the organised movement. Yet it did not obtain official recognition by the League, and it is worth investigating the forces in operation which worked against such recognition.

Significant in this connection was the attitude of France, not only to Esperanto but to the general conception of a League of Nations. French foreign policy after the Treaty of Versailles was concerned with taking punitive measures against Germany rather than with promotion of international solidarity. France had a large and well-equipped army and had succeeded in building up a series of military alliances. During the period 1920–1924 she was at the height of her prestige in Europe.[29] Thus although France was only one member of the League she occupied a key position. The right-wing Poincaré government was not enthusiastic about internationalist idealism. This did not, however, prevent French activity in the League, since the central issue of national sovereignty had been left untouched.[30] Thus France was not interested in taking seriously the 'moral reform' in international relations which the League was expected, at least in theory, to represent – and which was in accordance with the international idealism of the Esperantists. France's attitude was also significant in relation to the specific question of language. Linguistic nationalism has always been a facet of French nationalism, and the claims of French were being pressed particularly strongly during this period since French was beginning to lose ground to English. The height of French nationalism coincided with the beginning of the League, and during this period the discussion of Esperanto took place. In any international organisation, the question of official languages is an early administrative matter which has to be settled quickly. Thus it was early in the history of the League that discussion of Esperanto took place.

If all this was not sufficient, further difficulties arose for Esperanto owing to true and imagined connections with left-wing politics. The utopian international idealism of Esperanto was unlikely in any case to be supported by right-wingers; even purely practical use of Esperanto might be felt to weaken national culture. Thus Esperantists generally tended (though not exclusively) to be left of centre. This period also saw explicit association between Esperanto and the class struggle. In the first place (and to make matters worse, in France), the pacifistic tendencies of French socialism had been fertile soil for the development of the World Association of Non-Nationalists (*Sennacieca Asocio Tutmonda*, SAT), which associated Esperanto with the labour movement. Secondly, the revolutionary regime in Russia had begun to take an interest in Esperanto as a vehicle for the spread of world socialism.[31] Thus right-wing French forces were likely to see in Esperanto a Bolshevist threat.

In all events, Esperanto was perceived as a threat to French nationalism, and this was reflected in educational policy. Bérard, the Minister of Education in the Poincaré government, forbade the teaching of Esperanto in French schools. He argued that French would always be the language of civilisation[32] and that Esperanto would have to be opposed, since its aim was to prevent national culture from existing. When, under French pressure, the League Committee on Intellectual Cooperation supported the learning of modern languages rather than Esperanto, there can be little doubt that this was a diplomatic way of saying 'learning French'. The cultural prestige of France was so great that nobody could oppose it effectively. The only other major European power in the League which could give support to Esperanto was Britain; and, while British nationalism was less linguistically based than French, there was no more enthusiasm forthcoming for teaching Esperanto than there was for widespread teaching of languages generally. The English language had just increased in international prestige and it was English, not Esperanto, that was to be encouraged.

In 1924 the French right-wing government was succeeded by a leftist coalition, under the premiership of Herriot. The League began to grow in importance and effectiveness. Foreign ministers began to attend in person instead of sending distinguished, but not powerful, representatives.[33] By this time other arrangements had been made for the languages to be used by the League; and now that the League had greater prestige it had, as it were, more important subjects to discuss than Esperanto. Delegates to the League continued to be responsible for their own national interests. States with little cultural prestige might support Esperanto, but the powerful states that dominated the League could still press for their own cultural interests. The position of the League secretariat was very different. The 1920 Balfour[34] Report stressed that its membership was to be based on merit, but recognised a need to select persons from different nationalities. The basis of its organisation was international:

The members of the secretariat, once appointed, are no longer in the service of their own country, but become for the time being exclusively officials of the League. Their duties are not national but international.[35]

The secretariat owed its position to internationalism; while its sections were divided according to subjects, not according to nationality. Thus its members were dependent for their position upon internationalist sentiments. Service in such a body no doubt attracted many who shared such ideals. Yet Esperanto could not be seen as a 'purely administrative' matter that could be effectively decided upon by the secretariat. Power on issues of this kind remained in the hands of those who wished to pursue national interests. More recently, in other international bodies, a group of administrators whose position depends on the exercise of certain multilingual skills has grown up; thus administrators of some international bodies have often tended to oppose Esperanto, which could be seen as a threat to their position.

The Esperantists' activities in relation to the League had very little success, but were not seen as a failure. Esperanto was not decidedly *condemned* or *rejected*; Bergson had expressed the opinion that one day Esperanto might succeed, but that it was not the purpose of the League to assist such development. The Esperanto movement felt justified in continuing a policy of self-help and practical demonstration of the value of Esperanto. At the same time, the employment of pressure-group tactics helped to consolidate and institutionalise the movement, as was seen in the Contract of Helsinki. Ido, too, was firmly rebuffed; although Idist organisations brought notice of their existence to the League, and Ido was mentioned in its meetings, the decision was always that Esperanto was the sole serious contender. The policy of individual conversion of members was thus continued, but policies concentrated more on directly practical aims such as use of Esperanto in commerce. Esperanto became a specialist organisation in international relations, but never got further. The League of Nations was the only intergovernmental organisation of any stature that might officialise Esperanto, but it refused to do this.

The Esperantists continued to examine the practicalities of the use of Esperanto at a number of conferences. In 1927 a conference was called by the International Central Committee in Prague, on the subject of 'Peace through the School'.[36] President Masaryk acted as Patron, and Beneš gave greetings to the conference. 494 delegates attended from 19 countries, and of these about one-quarter had learnt some Esperanto for the conference, about one-half were already fluent, and the remaining quarter spoke no Esperanto. Esperanto was thus only one of the languages used. Discussions included the psychology of the question, practicalities of teaching, and the removal of chauvinistic bias from history textbooks. A further conference on Esperanto in schools was held in 1934 in Vienna.[37]

After the League had ceased to take an interest in Esperanto, the Esperantists concentrated on spasmodic, piecemeal successes, and there were a number of these. The revolutionary regime in Russia viewed Esperanto favourably until the rise of Stalinism. The non-nationalists (SAT) grew rapidly in strength, and only slightly at the expense of the 'bourgeois' movement. Esperanto was still popular with certain radio stations, particularly in Czechoslovakia and Italy.[38] In the 1938 World Eucharistic Congress, Esperanto was one of the official languages. Many organisations passed resolutions in favour of Esperanto, even if they then did nothing about them. The piecemeal and specialised support for Esperanto during this period can be overrated; a catalogue of support of this nature could be given for the present day. Esperanto began to take its place as a significant, but unofficial and specialised, organisation.

NOTES

1. A former President of the British Esperanto Association, and one of the organisers of the 1907 Cambridge Congress.
2. *The British Esperantist*, October 1913, p.198.
3. See E.D. Durrant, *op. cit.*, p.79.
4. Privat, *Historio*, vol. 2, p.98.
5. League of Nations, *Ten Years of World Cooperation*, Annex I, 'The Covenant of the League of Nations' (pp.417–439), 1930, p.417.
6. E. Privat, *Aventuroj de pioniro*, 1963, pp.83–86.
7. Privat, *Historio*, vol. 2, pp.105–112.
8. *Ibid.*, p.136.
9. For further discussion of the League of Nations and Esperanto see *Perspektivo*, Ch. 22.
10. I. Nitobe, 'The language question and the League of Nations' (Doc. A.72, 1921, xii.), *League of Nations Official Journal*, January–March 1922, pp.295–298.
11. Privat, *Historio*, vol. 2, p.138.
12. *Ibid.*, p.106.
13. *Ibid*, pp.105–122; Internacia Konferenco pri la Instruo de Esperanto en Lernejo, *Resuma raporto*, 1922.
14. League of Nations, *Esperanto as an International Auxiliary Language*, 1922.
15. See H.N. Shenton, *op. cit.*, Ch. X, *passim*.
16. League of Nations, Committee on Intellectual Cooperation, *Minutes of the Second Session*, 1923.
17. *Ibid.*, pp.41–42.
18. For further discussion of opposition to Esperanto in France during the Poincaré government (1922–1924), see Ch. VIII.
19. For a summary of the League debates see Privat, *Historio*, vol. 2, pp.136–151; E.D. Durrant, *op. cit.*, pp.83–91; *Perspektivo*, pp.748–760.
20. For a summary of the discussion see Bureau International de l'Union Télégraphique, *Documents de la Conférence télégraphique internationale de Paris*, 1925, 2 vols., especially vol. 1, pp.72, 74; vol. 2, pp.58, 157–160, 192, 215. See also Privat, *Historio*, vol. 2, pp.149–151, 171–173.
21. See Privat, *Historio*, vol. 2, pp.169–171; E.D. Durrant, *op. cit.*, p.92.
22. For details of this conference see Privat, *Historio*, vol. 2, pp.119–125; E.D. Durrant,

op. cit., p.93; London Chamber of Commerce, *Commercial Conference at Venice, 2 to 5 April, 1923. Report of the Delegate*; A. Bandet, *La conférence internationale de Venise pour l'adoption d'une langue commerciale commune (Rapport adopté par la Chambre de Commerce de Paris, 1923).*

23. See Preliminary Conference for an International Agreement of Wireless Telegraphy, *Report of the Proceedings*, 1924.

24. *Premier Congrès International des Radio-Amateurs*, 1925.

25. For general discussion of Esperanto on radio during this period see E.D. Durrant, *op. cit.*, pp.106–116; Privat, *Historio*, vol. 2, pp.152–159.

26. See Privat, *Historio*, vol. 2, pp.160–164; E.D. Durrant, *op. cit.*, pp.96–97.

27. See L.L. Zamenhof, *Unua Libro, op. cit.*, better accessible in his *Fundamenta krestomatio, op. cit.*, pp.234–239.

28. For report of the conference see Privat, *Historio*, vol. 2, pp.164–168.

29. For discussion of France in this period see E.H. Carr, *International Relations Between the Two World Wars (1919–39)*, 1961, Ch. 1.

30. For discussion of this question see W.E. Rappart, *The Geneva Experiment*, 1931.

31. For the relationship between socialism and Esperanto see next chapter.

32. See U. Lins, *La danĝera lingvo*, 1973, p.7; V. Sadler and U. Lins, 'Regardless of frontiers: a case study in linguistic persecution' in *Man, Language and Society*, ed. by S.K. Ghosh, 1972, pp.206–215.

33. For discussion see Carr, *International Relations Between the Two World Wars, op. cit.*, p.98.

34. See League of Nations, *Ten Years of World Cooperation, op. cit.*, p.15.

35. *Ibid.*, p.16.

36. See L. Courtinat, *op. cit.*, vol. 2, pp.615–616; W. Flusser, *Die internationale Konferenz 'Durch die Schule zum Frieden', Prag, 16-20 April 1927.*

37. L. Courtinat, *op. cit.*, vol. 3, pp.831–832.

38. E.D. Durrant, *op. cit.*, pp.110–115.

7

External Relations: Socialism and Esperanto

Esperantists have traditionally shown a distrust in political action and have tended to concentrate their efforts on recruitment of individuals. However, socialist ideology has been highly compatible with the democratising spirit of Esperanto, and organisations have consequently been formed with the aim of establishing a formal connection between the two ideals. Various areas of compatibility between them have been perceived. Internationalist ideas of the unity of workers of the world have been seen as effectively fostered through Esperanto. Socialism has been associated with the idea of scientific planning of society, and Esperanto has been supported as being compatible with such a scientific spirit. Esperanto has been seen as subversive of national loyalties which themselves support capitalism and militarism. Finally, the practical advantages of Esperanto in workers' education, in the proceedings of international workers' conferences, and generally in the fostering of direct contacts among workers, have also played an important role. Esperanto has been associated with various strains of socialist opinion, and certain disputes have occurred. The term 'socialist' will here be applied to any organisation or state that claims such a title; but in Esperantist socialist circles, as elsewhere, disputes and debates have taken place on the issue of what constitutes 'true socialism'. In particular, Esperanto gained a certain measure of support in the Soviet Union after the Revolution; disputes soon broke out since Soviet Esperantists and their supporters wanted the world Esperantist socialist movement to follow a strictly pro-Moscow line. By 1921 a unified Esperantist socialist movement[1] had been founded, but a major split took place on this issue in 1930.

The beginnings of Esperantist socialism were national rather than international in origin, or even of purely local significance.

An Esperantist workers' club is reported to have been founded in Stockholm in 1903. By 1910 local workers' Esperanto clubs existed in Britain, France, Germany, Hungary, and The Netherlands. These mostly formed the germ of national associations of worker Esperantists. In France particularly Esperanto became popular with socialists. Couturat, who had interests in peace and international arbitration, was socialist in sympathies; he wrote articles for the French socialist journal *L'Humanité* reporting on the 1905 Boulogne World Congress and stressing the value of Esperanto for the workers, who do not have the means for luxuries such as learning foreign languages.[2] A French socialist Esperantist periodical *Le Travailleur Espérantiste* was founded in 1912. In Germany, too, a national Workers' Esperanto Association was founded in 1911, and a year earlier a periodical *Der Arbeiter Esperantist* was established. Zamenhof appears to have had socialist sympathies, though he was cautious for fear that violent revolution might occur.[3] In 1910 he wrote some words of encouragement to the new German periodical:

The field which you have chosen for your work is very important. Perhaps for nobody in the world does our democratic language have such importance as for the workers, and I hope that sooner or later the working class will be the strongest support for our cause. The workers will not only experience the utility of Esperanto, but more than any others they will feel the essence and idea of Esperantism.[4]

Various other national Esperantist workers' movements were formed; in Czechoslovakia, in The Netherlands, and even as far away as China and Japan. Yet of greater significance in the realisation of Esperantist socialism were the attempts at establishment of a worldwide movement. At the 1906 Geneva World Congress a meeting of socialists had taken place, and such meetings continued within the framework of the neutral movement for a number of years. UEA, too, set up a workers' section in 1911, and the idea of workers' Esperanto delegates was suggested. Attempts were also made to found international workers' movements of Esperantists which would operate independently of the neutral movement. In 1906 was founded in Paris the International Peace and Freedom Association (*Internacia Asocio 'Paco-Libereco'*). This was opposed to militarism, capitalism, alcoholism, and all dogmas and prejudices. It aimed to promote Esperanto among internationalists, free-thinkers, socialists, and libertarians; to promote socialism and libertarianism, and to oppose militarism, among the Esperantists. This body combined in 1910 with another small international movement, the Esperantist Working Class (*Esperantista Laboristaro*), to form *Liberiga Stelo* [Emancipation Star]. This body had similar aims to *Paco-Libereco*, except that it declared its opposition to religion rather than to alcoholism. It was not very active, though it had been intended to discuss the question of international organisation in the framework of the 1914 Paris World Congress, which in the event could not take place because of the war. A periodical *Internacia Socia Revuo* was begun in 1907 and lasted till the war.

Though all discussions of international Esperantist socialism had to be suspended because of the war, its ultimate effect was the consolidation of international organisation of worker Esperantists. As was also the case with UEA, the war led to a revival of idealism among Esperantists, and lent support to the desirability of a supernational basis for organisation. Yet, while UEA concentrated its efforts on the internationally recognised League of Nations, the Esperantist socialists developed their ideas in a more subversive direction. A new organisation stemmed directly from the internationalist and revolutionary syndicalist traditions of the French labour movement. Such currents of opinion had been characteristic of French socialism[5] before the First World War; in 1908 the *Confédération Génerale du Travail* had declared that it recognised only economic frontiers between the capitalist and the working class. It took the view that the workers had no native country and that geographical boundaries were arbitrary; accordingly, if war were declared, the trade unions would call a general strike. Yet once general mobilisation had been declared in 1914, this policy was abandoned and many socialists adopted chauvinistic and militaristic sentiments. In Germany, too, although Revolutionary Syndicalism had not played such an important role in the labour movement, the socialist movement had affirmed its solidarity with the French working classes. Yet when the war began, no enthusiasm was shown for war resistance.[6] This situation was perceived by a certain Eugene Adam as representing a failure in non-nationalist education for socialists. Adam (1879–1947) was a self-educated technical teacher, originally trained as a joiner. Having served in an ambulance unit in the First World War, he became convinced of the futility of nationalism. He had already come into contact with anarchist teachings before the war, and during the war he learnt Esperanto. He was active in French socialist circles; he acquired a reputation for disagreement with orthodox wisdom, as he was concerned to develop his own theory of society. He thus acquired the nickname *L'anti* which in an Esperanto form, *Lanti*, became the name by which he was known in left-wing Esperanto circles.[7] After the war he was asked to take over the editorship of *Le Travailleur Espérantiste*, as the organ of *Liberiga Stelo*. He transformed this periodical into *Esperantista Laboristo*, and began to publicise some of his own political ideas. His articles were written under the pseudonym *Sennaciulo*, meaning, literally, 'one who is without a nation'. These articles developed the ideology of a new organisation. Lanti stressed the importance of Esperanto as a key to non-nationalist education. He was influenced not only by anarchism but also by Marxist and Positivist ideas, and saw technological societies as the fruits of reason and progress. He pointed out that, while scientific invention had made distances shorter, linguistic diversity still remained. However, he suggested, thanks to Zamenhof's invention, it was now possible for science to solve the language problem also. Lanti admired not only Zamenhof, but also Hodler. He approved of the 'practical idealism' enshrined in Hodler's UEA, and particularly approved of the way in which UEA was organised: on the basis of individual membership, irrespective of nationality, and not as a federation of national associations. The only fault he saw in UEA was that of political neutrality. He considered that the Esperanto movement generally suffered because of its quasi-religious atmosphere, which had had the effect of clouding the class consciousness of proletarian members. Lanti's articles were eventually republished in a pamphlet with the slogan *For la neŭtralismon*[8] [Away with neutralism] as its title. Lanti suggested that even militarists claimed that their actions were aimed at promotion of peace, so there was no disagreement about ends. However, he pointed out, the means to promote peace were disputed and uncertain. Yet it was clear that there were some forces inimical to peace. Application of the proverb *si vis pacem para bellum* had never produced prolonged peace; also dogmatic religions were powerless to promote human brotherhood, and fanatical religious faith could even cause war. The capitalist system, he continued, was unjust because it produced classes of exploiters and exploited. Because of such injustice, war was latent in capitalism. Socialism, on the other hand, enabled a society to be based on the principle that, among healthy people, only he who worked would eat. This could be contrasted with the capitalist principle that anyone was allowed to eat who had money. Thus Lanti proposed that *Liberiga Stelo* should commit itself to opposing capitalism and should exclude militarists and dogmatic religious people from membership. *Liberiga Stelo*, he argued, should be committed to socialism, but not to any particular party. He saw no need for the Esperantist socialists to choose a particular doctrine, since they did not expect to achieve socialism unaided.

Indeed, Lanti saw the distinctive task of *Liberiga Stelo* as educational rather than political. He urged that citizens should prepare themselves for the time when economic, linguistic, and state boundaries no longer existed. The failure of socialist internationalism in 1914 showed that participants had not sufficiently tried to eliminate nationalistic education. The particular object of attack for *Liberiga Stelo* was *nationalism*. Lanti built on existing ideas of the 'Esperantist people'; Esperantists all spoke the same language, and this could be used to advantage in the formation of a new society. It would be possible to form a 'people without a nationality' (*sennacieca popolo*), which would be organised in the same way as a future world society.

At the end of his article in *Esperantista Laboristo*, November 1920, Lanti called for support for an organisation of the kind he proposed. The inaugural meeting would be held in Prague in 1921, within the framework of the neutral World Congress. In January 1921 Lanti suggested a name for the new organisation: *Sennacieca Asocio Tutmonda* (SAT). This would translate as 'the World Association of Those Without a Nationality', for convenience referred to here as the 'World Association of Non-Nationalists'. By April 1921 an agenda was prepared for the Prague meeting. In June of that year Lanti found it necessary to reply to a Russian Esperantist who suggested that SAT should only follow the way of the Third International. Lanti suggested, however, that

Our association must not be a political organisation, in the narrow sense of the

word. Let it be educational, instructive, helpful and effective; in such a manner it will be more revolutionary than the political parties, which especially
aim at making *partisans*, not conscious revolutionaries, i.e., men in whose
minds old-fashioned ideas have disappeared and into whom have entered
qualities enabling a new social system.[9]

This foreshadowed many further conflicts with Russian members. Lanti wrote to radical politicians and writers, hoping for support; and although he was successful in obtaining approval for his
ideas from some (notably Henri Barbusse and Romain Rolland), he
became disillusioned with this kind of activity; famous men would
not be active in the movement and in particular would not take
the trouble to learn Esperanto. Thus, like Zamenhof, Lanti placed
his trust in the plain man.

The inaugural meeting of SAT took place as a specialist meeting
within the framework of the neutral 1921 World Congress. It was
attended by 79 people from 15 countries. The meeting prepared a
resolution which was to be the guideline for the new organisation.
This emphasised the use of Esperanto in the class struggle and
rejected UEA as inadequate for this role because of its political
neutrality. All class-conscious members of the proletariat were
urged to join SAT and not to cooperate with 'neutral' organisations except on technical matters. Like UEA, SAT aimed at promoting solidarity between members. All members were expected
to carry out functions of the kind that delegates performed in
UEA.[10] In accordance with the non-nationalist aims of the movement, it was organised on a non-national basis. SAT divided the
world according to time zones rather than political frontiers: the
highest authority of SAT, the General Council, was elected by the
entire membership, with representation on this basis.

After 1921 SAT held its own world congresses, independently
of the neutral movement. The second of these was held in Frankfurt, in 1922. It was here decided to forbid simultaneous membership of SAT and a neutral or 'bourgeois' Esperanto organisation,
unless there was no workers' Esperanto group in one's town. This
rule remained till 1924, when a SAT world congress in Brussels
modified it. The matter was henceforth to be left to the individual
conscience for ordinary members, though the SAT Executive still
had to conform to it. At this congress, too, a proposal to modify

the Esperanto-only basis of mobilisation of the movement, making it more like an 'International', was rejected.

SAT appealed to international language and socialism in the name, among other things, of reason and progress. Under such circumstances it was not surprising that a certain amount of competition was felt from supporters of Ido. Even before the formation of SAT, much attention had been paid among French Esperantist socialists to opposing Ido. At the time of the schism, a proposal was discussed and rejected that the *Internacia Socia Revuo* should become an Idist publication. Lanti himself had originally wavered between Esperanto and Ido, finally deciding on Esperanto because of its well-established basis in practice. Not all supporters of international language in socialist circles had been so convinced; in 1921 the Ido supporters founded their own 'Emancipation Star' (*Emancipanta Stelo*), at the first Ido congress in Vienna. A Communist Idist section (*Komunista Ido-Federuro Internaciona* or *Kifintern*) was formed at the same time. The Idists were particularly active in Communist circles: the Comintern had set up a special study commission to consider the question of international language. The secretary of this was an Idist, and in 1921 the three-man commission had voted to approve both Esperanto and Ido, but had suggested that Ido was preferable as more perfect.[11] This decision was never ratified by the Comintern, and soon afterwards the Commission was dissolved without any action being taken. This did not, however, prevent the Communist Idists from staging a counterdemonstration in Kassel in 1923, where the World Ido Congress and the World SAT Congress were held at the same time; posters were put up in the town suggesting that Trotsky favoured Ido, a claim that later proved to be unfounded. Unlike the neutral Esperanto movement, SAT found it worthwhile to oppose Ido directly in its periodical *Sennacieca Revuo*. In 1924 a party of SAT members, including Lanti, attended the Ido World Congress for that year, and held a meeting to promote Esperanto. Lanti attached importance to the existence of Esperanto as a living language and regarded this characteristic as decisive.

Membership of SAT grew rapidly from 390 in 1921 to 6,329 in 1929, the latter being about two-thirds of the figure for the neutral movement (9,113) for that year. From October 1924 the periodical *Sennaciulo*, issued by SAT, became a weekly.

A potential source of conflict existed between SAT and various workers' Esperanto associations, which now existed in a number of countries. There were suggestions that an international structure would be more realistic, and that it was not clear how the work of SAT was to be distinguished from that of the national workers' Esperanto associations. It was eventually agreed at the Gothenburg SAT World Congress in 1928 that, whereas the national workers' associations should work *for* Esperanto, SAT worked *through* Esperanto.

A further problem which proved difficult to resolve was agreement on a common programme for the movement. Apart from constant attempts by Communist members to recruit the whole of the movement to the Third International, many other political disagreements were evident within the movement, which consisted of a loose federation of Communists, social democrats, and anarchists. Already in 1924 a small group of anarchists had split off to form the *Tutmonda Ligo de Esperantistaj Senŝtatanoj* [World League of Stateless Esperantists].[12] This group objected to the fact that its own point of view was inadequately represented in SAT, while Communism was overrepresented. SAT refused, for instance, to criticise the Soviet Union in its publication. The Stateless Esperantists formed a few local groups and from 1925 to 1931 issued an irregular journal *Libera Laboristo* [Free Worker]. SAT set up a commission to consider a common programme in Vienna in 1926 but did not succeed in producing a definite proposal. This problem was discussed annually at SAT world congresses; finally, at Leipzig in 1929 it was decided that such attempts to produce a common programme were futile. Specialist interests have continued to be catered for in SAT by various 'fractions' (*frakcioj*), so called in order to emphasise the basic unity of SAT over and above the different interests. Members of fractions are expected to encourage the use of Esperanto within their own parties. SAT thus emerged as a loose organisation of various socialist interests, with a characteristically cosmopolitan emphasis. Out of the latter Lanti developed his own distinctive ideology, *sennaciismo*.[13] Whereas *sennacieco* would translate as 'the condition of being without a nationality', *sennaciismo* implies rather an *ideology* of being without a nationality. Lanti rejected any suggestion that socialists should capture power within the state in the first instance. Esperanto was of key

significance to Lanti in the emancipation of the proletariat, since
the linguistic unity of the nation-state made for solidarity between
bourgeoisie and proletariat. Thus *immediate* emphasis on solidarity
of workers of the world set *sennaciismo* apart from the various
internationalisms, including the Third International. Lanti was
opposed to all national traits: national languages, national cultures,
customs, and traditions. He saw all of these as barriers to the unification of the proletariat. In contrast to Zamenhof and almost all
exponents of the ideology of the neutral Esperanto movement,
Lanti expected national languages to disappear, except as archaisms,
with the triumph of Esperanto. He would give no more than purely
tactical support to movements of national liberation. *Sennaciismo*
was rationalistic and antimysticism, stressing the benefits of reason
and progress; it aimed at world administration and rational utili-
sation of energy and resources for the benefit of all. *Sennaciismo*
was not the official ideology of SAT, being only one 'fraction' of
the movement; though Lanti saw SAT as a particularly fertile field
in which this ideology could grow.

Apart from political education, SAT had a number of distinctive
literary and linguistic activities. In 1925 appeared the first issue of
Petro, an Esperanto reader for beginners. This was socialist in content and told of the adventures of a young worker.[14] SAT sponsored
the translation of a number of great works of literature into Esperanto, in the belief that appreciation of such works stood above
partisan loyalties and was important for the education of the proletariat. In 1930, SAT issued the first all-Esperanto dictionary,[15]
compiled by sympathetic members of the Esperanto Academy,
although the Academy as a whole believed that the time was not
yet ripe. Two linguistic details are worthy of note. SAT adopted
the policy of writing personal names in the Esperanto alphabet, corresponding as nearly as possible with their sounds, as an anti-elitist
gesture and in anticipation of the time when national languages
would disappear. SAT also took sides on the much-disputed issue
of names of countries. *Liberiga Stelo*, Lanti, and eventually SAT
followed the practice of using the *-i-* suffix; this was considered as
more appropriate to the ideology of non-nationalism; the non-
nationalists preferred to speak of territories rather than nations
and could not approve of a suffix suggesting a 'container' for a certain national group. (In more recent times, Communist countries

have almost invariably used this suffix; but now that the Ido schism has become a matter of past history, it has also gained considerable popularity in the neutral movement.)

During the first ten years of its existence, SAT had constant difficulties in relation to its Russian members and supporters of the Soviet regime. Russian support for SAT was an early feature of the movement, and originally Russian members swelled the ranks of the movement to its advantage. Prerevolutionary Esperantists in Russia tended to be politically left and welcomed the Revolution in 1917.[16] They expected that socialism would be to the advantage of Esperanto: a planned society could be expected to be favourable to a planned language. Esperanto would also be helpful to an international movement, and the idea of workers of the world uniting would help the cause of the language. The new regime was not in fact unfavourable to Esperanto. The Soviet Esperanto Union (SEU) was founded in 1921, intending to use Esperanto particularly to promote revolutionary ideas and the aims of Soviet socialism abroad. There was also the possibility of language planning being taken seriously in the Soviet Union. There were many language problems within the Soviet Union, and Lenin had opposed the enforced 'russification' policy that had been characteristic of Tsarist times. This set the stage for linguistic research being supported by state ideology, and thus helped state interest in planned international languages.

SAT appeared to conform to those currents in Marxism which regarded national boundaries as of no importance and which stressed the common cause of the politically conscious proletarian with his fellow workers of the world. Thus the idea of a socialist international formed an essential component of Marxism. By the time SAT was founded, however, a revolutionary socialist movement had already come into power in one country. Previous 'Internationals' had been loose federations of working-class parties and as such would have been compatible with the non-party basis of SAT. But in 1919 the Comintern had been founded. A large, authoritarian nation-state now imposed discipline on the world working-class movement. The Comintern claimed that Communism was the sole truth and regarded other socialist movements as lackeys of the bourgeoisie. The interests of Soviet Communism were viewed by the Soviet Union as identical with those of Communism everywhere. Soviet Communism, moreover, developed in the authoritarian environment of the Tsarist period and contained none of the libertarian, nonviolent, democratic, and anarchistic strains which had variously characterised socialism in Western Europe. Such factors caused important splits in the labour movement everywhere, not merely in SAT.[17] The fortunes of SAT and those of Esperanto generally in the Soviet Union depended on the extent to which Soviet authorities favoured international contacts. When, after the sixth congress of the Comintern in 1928, all 'bourgeois' political activity, especially social democracy, came under attack from Stalin,[18] tensions within SAT were soon exacerbated and schism resulted.

Already in 1921, as has been noted, Lanti had found it necessary to oppose a suggestion that SAT should follow the Third International. This dispute was the first of many. A Soviet leaflet published in 1923 condemned the political imprecision of SAT. It argued that anarchists and social democrats were more dangerous than the open bourgeoisie and suggested that SAT's neutrality was just as reprehensible as that of the openly neutral movement. Communists were very active and influential in SAT and were not confined to Russia. Communism had become popular, rather than revolutionary syndicalism, among French trade unionists after the First World War. Lanti was himself a French Communist Party member between 1920 and 1928. He had become disillusioned with the lack of success of anarchist teachings in practice on the outbreak of the First World War. The Bolsheviks, in contrast, he saw as displaying the unity of theory and practice. The German Communist Party had also gained in strength after the war. Lanti still wished SAT to remain a broadly based movement, but many other Communist Party members in SAT, especially the Russians, expected it to follow the Moscow line.

A significant figure in controversies following the formation of SEU was Ernest Drezen. A former Tsarist officer, coming from a wealthy Latvian background, Drezen had supported the cause of the Revolution and had then served in the Red Army till 1921, when he became a civil servant (secretary of the nominal head of state, M.I. Kalinin, from 1921–1924; later Director of the Institute of Communication). Drezen was President of the SEU from its foundation and was also very loyal to the Soviet regime. A short study of Zamenhof written by Drezen in 1929[19] paid tribute to him but claimed that his ideology was wrong in not being Marxist. In 1922 Lanti visited the Kremlin, and Drezen expressed regret to him that SAT was not purely Communist. He did not wish to co-operate with anarchists and social democrats, though he joined SAT as 'aspiring member'. Drezen and other Russian members constantly attempted to bring the workers' Esperanto movement under the control of the Third International. SAT refused to accept this pressure but still gave considerable favourable publicity to the Soviet Union. In 1923 the entire text of the constitution of the R.S.F.S.R. appeared in *Sennacieca Revuo*. In 1926 the SAT World Congress was held in Leningrad, and the Soviet government issued two postage stamps to commemorate it, with Esperanto inscriptions. Kalinin wrote the introduction to a SAT publication, *Documents of Communism*, in 1923. Lanti continued to resist Soviet pressures. He had been unfavourably impressed on his visit to Russia in 1922. In May 1925 he withdrew his support from the publication *Sennaciulo* because of the editor's 'Bolshevik bias'. Opposition to the non-party basis of SAT continued from its flourishing Communist 'fraction'. Conflicts frequently arose at SAT world congresses over SAT's failure to give more positive support to the Communist cause. In 1923 Drezen publicly criticised Lanti for holding back party ambitions. Drezen was unsuccessful, and the congress reaffirmed its unwillingness to be divided by matters which divided the labour movement generally. By 1928, at the SAT World Congress in Gothenburg, Drezen began to issue threats. He warned that the Soviet Esperantists might have to leave SAT if the non-Communists did not do so. This again produced a re-affirmation of the goals of SAT, emphasising its nondogmatic, educational character. A similar conflict occurred in Leipzig in the following year, when it was finally decided that SAT could not have a definite programme. The final split between SAT and the Communists began in 1930, at the SAT World Congress in London.

Relations with the Communists had grown progressively worse during 1929. Many members had wished to meet in Moscow in 1930, but Drezen had been unwilling to invite the congress: ostensibly because social democrats in SAT would be refused permission to attend from their own parties. Relations were further strained between Russian members and others owing to an official Soviet clampdown on overseas debts. As a result of this, a serious financial situation occurred in SAT, since payment for SAT publications and subscriptions was not received from the Soviet Union. No Soviet members attended the 1930 SAT World Congress in London (although 45 had registered), but there was still strong support for the Communist cause — shortly before the Congress, the German Workers' Esperanto Association had affirmed its commitment to Bolshevism. The Communists formed an 'opposition' to the SAT executive and a stormy debate between the two groups took place on the congress floor. In the course of the debate, the non-Communists criticised not only the activities of the Soviet members, but also, for the first time, the Soviet sytem itself. Orthodox Communists reacted with indignation. One remarked of the Soviet Union, 'We can allow praise, but let us not tolerate condemnation'.[20]

Schism did not occur immediately, though shortly after the London Congress the SEU began to act independently. It proposed to cooperate with the Communist German Worker Esperantists and to call a congress in Moscow in 1931 to set up a new independent revolutionary organisation. This congress never took place, though by October 1930 a new periodical *Internaciisto* was started in Berlin. Its first issue[21] contained a critique of SAT and especially of Lanti and *sennaciismo*. SAT was now seen by the Communists as merely a competitor to the bourgeois movement.

In the meantime, the supporters of nonpartisanship had obtained some encouragement: the Dutch Workers' Esperanto Association had declared full support for SAT as it stood at the moment. It was therefore decided to hold the 1931 SAT World Congress in Amsterdam. SAT continued to experience further difficulties in the Soviet Union; SEU refused to accept further subscriptions to *Sennaciulo*, and eventually the latter journal was banned from the USSR entirely. However, SEU urged its supporters to attend the Amsterdam Congress and to put the Bolshevik point of view about the existing leadership of SAT. Since the situation had deteriorated further for SAT in the Soviet Union, the opposition met with no success. Towards the end of the Congress, the opposition interrupted the proceedings, reading out their own declaration. They eventually left the congress hall singing the Internationale. When they had left, the supporters of the existing SAT sang the Internationale and the schism became final. The Congress now expressed regret at the schism, hoping that it would not be permanent; the meeting hoped for renewed contact with Soviet comrades and for eventual success of Soviet socialism.

It was in accordance with Soviet policy that the Esperanto movement there would be carefully directed, especially as regards foreign contacts. Esperanto originally received favourable attention from the Soviet government, but always with close official supervision. Thus correspondence between Soviet Esperantists and *Communists* in other countries was always officially encouraged, but other international contacts were viewed with grave suspicion. Drezen was a strong supporter of the policy of official supervision. Drezen was active in organising the SEU but also made theoretical contributions to the problem of international language and strove for greater official recognition. His work in turn was influenced by the linguist V.Y. Marr.[22]

Marr gradually began to receive favourable notice after the Revolution. This helped the Esperanto cause, since his theories were favourable to a certain amount of official support for Esperanto. Initially a specialist in Caucasian languages, Marr developed more all-embracing theories in the twentieth century, both before and after the Revolution. Marr posited a language family known as the 'Japhetic' family (so called after the third son of Noah, whose name had not been allocated to a family of languages). This group became very broad indeed; by 1920 it included not only the Caucasian languages but also a wide range of languages in Asia Minor and the Mediterranean area. Evidence for the connections between the languages was taken from certain common lexical items selected on a somewhat idiosyncratic basis. Marr's theory incorporated the idea of 'layers' — different dialects assignable to different social strata. This idea was, after the Revolution, found to be in accordance with Marxism. In 1923 Marr was working on the problem of the relation of the Indo-European languages of the Mediterranean to the Japhetic family and concluded that such languages were a transformation of the already present Japhetic languages. Significantly, at a time when only a Marxist theory would be viable in the USSR, Marr gave an economic explanation of the phenomenon: he attributed the transformation to a social revolution consequent on the discovery and use of metals. This theory was gradually developed as a 'New Theory of Language'. Citing references to language in Engels's letter to Bloch[23] as justification for a Marxian view of language as part of the superstructure, Marr proceeded to relate evolution of language to its economic base. He supported the idea of sudden linguistic change consequent on social revolutions. He saw class analysis as applicable to language; the people speak a more archaic language than the ruling classes. As the theory developed, Marr argued that it had 'surprisingly' proved Marx right.

Marr's theories were significant for Esperanto in that a linguistic revolution would follow the victory of world socialism. Thus, though never an active Esperantist, Marr supported the Esperanto movement as a progressive force in this direction. In 1928 Marr wrote the preface to Drezen's book in Russian about the history of world language.[24] Marr's support for Esperanto was only conditional: he held that the future world language would be an entirely new system. Drezen[25] concurred with this position, regarding the Esperanto movement's existing policy as too utopian. Esperanto, however, he saw as helping to form the basis on which the new system would grow. It contained the best elements of national language and its progressive role in history was confirmed by wide support from the proletariat.

The significance of these theories for state support for Esperanto lay in the fact that Stalin adopted a position very close to Marr's. In 1930, at the Sixteenth Congress of the Communist Party of the Soviet Union, he declared that the language of the future would be entirely new, arising from the merging of national languages. This was a prediction for the future: during the period of the dictatorship of the proletariat the policy would be to encourage national cultures to flourish. Drezen appeared reluctant to support wholeheartedly a policy which gave Esperanto such a modest role, and even joined a breakaway movement from Marr. This group, composed of young linguists, was known as the *Yazykfront*: it argued that 'mechanistic' tendencies in Japhetidology stood in the way of a truly Marxist linguistics. This group could have been significant for Esperanto, as it might have created a new theoretical basis for Esperanto under the conditions of 'socialism in one country'. However, the group in practice seemed to give little support for Esperanto, suggesting rather that SEU was paying too little attention to problems of the transitional stage; attempts to discuss the future language now were too utopian. This group was in fact short-lived, since Stalin affirmed his support for Marr.

The SEU publicised and supported these views on the role of a world language. After breaking away from SAT, SEU formed part of a new *Internacio de Proletaraj Esperantistoj* [International of Proletarian Esperantists, IPE]. This was strictly pro-Moscow and dominated by the Comintern. It continued to issue the periodical *Internaciisto* until 1933, in which year it was replaced by *Sur Posteno*, published in France. The IPE was mainly active in organising a correspondence service between Soviet Esperantists and Communist Esperantists in capitalist countries. Esperanto remained popular in Soviet circles: in 1934 SEU had some 9,000 members. While SAT expected loyalty to SAT to stand above party loyalties, IPE was Communist first and Esperantist second. Thus its members were able to support state ideology in the USSR which was only moderately pro-Esperanto. By the mid-1930s official support became less and less forthcoming, ostensibly because of economic difficulties. Esperanto was not yet officially condemned in 1937, when some works of Stalin and the 1936 constitution still appeared in Esperanto. In 1937, however, the IPE centre in Moscow was abruptly closed and was set up again in London. Some signs of official disapproval had begun in 1935, when a member of the Central Committee of SEU was sentenced to five years' hard labour. By the time of the Great Purges, beginning in 1937, Esperantists were specially singled out for attention as anti-Soviet elements. Esperantists were suspect by virtue of having contacts abroad. It was also discovered that correspondence between Soviet and Western Esperantists did not merely have a one-way effect of promoting the Soviet cause. Esperanto also enabled critical viewpoints to enter the USSR. In correspondence abroad, members of the SEU were expected to send stereotyped letters favourable to the regime; this was not always observed, and some members sent abroad graphic criticisms of the regime. When this was discovered, Esperanto was viewed with even greater disfavour. Exact figures are unknown, but apparently thousands of Esperantists were executed or given long terms of imprisonment; Drezen himself was shot in 1937.[37] The IPE continued until the war in 1939 as a Western-based organisation: it eventually urged its members to join the neutral movement. *Sur Posteno* survived till 1938, when *Internaciisto* appeared again in London. During the Spanish Civil War an interesting feature of IPE publications was the discussion of the activities of the International Brigades, and appeals for material help were organised partly through this periodical. In the initial stages of the war, some Esperantists had served together.

(The theories of Marr — who died in 1934 of natural causes — were eventually officially condemned by Stalin in 1950.[27] Stalin now saw Russian as the language of the whole of the Soviet sphere of influence, a policy which was by then practised in the USSR itself. Since Stalin's death the Soviet Esperanto movement has enjoyed a limited revival, though only in 1979 was it possible to establish a full-fledged national organisation. This is still very small and enjoys only limited international contacts, especially when compared with the movement in many smaller Communist countries).

The loss of the Soviet membership, and also of the German workers, who had lent their support to the Soviet cause, was a severe blow for SAT and had a number of implications for its future activities. Not the least of these was financial difficulty. SAT became nearly bankrupt through repudiation of debts by the Russians and through loss of Russian and German subscriptions. The German schism was short-lived in any case, since socialist organisations of all kinds were soon to be suppressed by the Nazis. In 1933, in consequence of this policy, the administrative head-quarters of SAT were moved from Leipzig to Paris. A further con-sequence of the schism was the loss of some social democrats, based in Austria. As early as 1923 social democrats had unsuccessfully tried to change the structure of SAT so as to resemble an 'Inter-national'. It was now argued that there was no longer any point in remaining in SAT, since with the loss of the Communists it had ceased to be a movement representing all shades of socialist opinion. Thus in 1933, the *Internacio de Socialistaj Esperantistoj* [Inter-national of Socialist Esperantists] was formed in Vienna. This group was led by Franz Jonas, who in 1965 became President of Austria. This organisation enjoyed little popularity outside Austria, since many socialists preferred the socialist fraction of SAT and were critical of the schism. This movement, too, did not survive Fascism. One effect of this was that Lanti's own ideology (*sennaciismo*) became more influential in the movement, since the remaining members were more likely to be committed to an ideology that was a distinctive feature of SAT. Indeed, in 1933, Lanti resigned from formal leadership of SAT for the same reason that Zamenhof had done in the neutral movement in 1912: he did not wish his own ideology to be confused with that of the movement as a whole. He remained active in the movement till 1935, after which date he devoted his time to writing and travelling round the world. He died in 1947 in Mexico, having committed suicide because of an incurable illness.

After the 1930–1931 schism SAT continued to discuss the problem of the unification of the Esperantist labour movement, though without success. Three principles of the mobilisation of SAT were declared (at the 1935 Paris SAT World Congress) not to be negotiable in dealings with the Communists. These were the principle of *class division* which led to the foundation of SAT; the nonpartisan character of SAT; and the division of labour between work *for* Esperanto, the province of national workers' Esperanto associations, and work *through* Esperanto, the province of SAT. These negotiations met with no satisfactory response from Moscow; the last reply, in 1935, insisted on collective affirmation of the truth of dialectical materialism, condemned anti-Soviet propaganda in SAT publications, and suspected SAT of Trotskyite tendencies. After his resignation from leadership of SAT, Lanti devoted some of his writing activity to criticism of the Soviet Union.[28] Other activities of SAT congresses before the Second World War provoked little controversy. The only internal structural change of note was a proposal, discussed in 1938 and accepted in principle in 1939, for the establishment of a committee of national workers' Esperanto associations. This was to be merely advisory, with no executive powers, and it was eventually decided that such a body was not incompatible with the non-national basis of SAT. In 1937, the constitution was changed to describe SAT as 'not party-political' instead of 'not political'.

The war prevented formal activities of SAT, and *Sennaciulo* was suspended in 1939. SAT passed without notice in France, however, and the Paris office remained open throughout the war. French subscriptions were still received, and from 1943 a duplicated newssheet was issued. A new bulletin began to be issued in January 1946, and by July this became *Sennaciulo* again. One of the first postwar activities was a meeting in Amsterdam in 1946, of Danish, British, Dutch, and Swedish workers' Esperanto associations with the SAT executive, to realise the proposal of 1939. From 1946 to 1951 a characteristic activity was the sending of food and clothing to impoverished Esperantist workers in various countries, from the proceeds of collections in richer countries, notably Denmark and the United States. Annual world congresses were resumed in 1947. A resolution was passed regretting that German members were unable to attend owing to travel restrictions; food and clothing for German comrades were delivered by congress members returning through Germany. Thus, unlike the neutral movement, SAT had no difficulty in reassimilating its German members, though they were unable to be present legally till 1949. Membership grew considerably after the war, in common with other Esperanto organisations (1939: 2,002; 1947: 4,284; 1949: 5,134), but thereafter declined (1950: 4,623).

No ideologue of comparable stature has emerged to replace Lanti.[29] A feature of the postwar movement has been virtual abandonment of efforts to form a united movement which would include members in Communist countries. There are a very small number of SAT members in some other Communist countries (e.g. 13 for the Soviet Union in 1968);[30] but Yugoslavia is the only Communist country where SAT continues to exist to any great extent, and world SAT congresses have twice been held there. Revival of Esperanto activity in Communist countries in the 1950s was called for in a unique open letter to Stalin in 1952, written jointly by SAT and UEA.[31] This objected to the prohibition of Esperanto as 'linguistic imperialism'. Revival of Esperanto in Communist countries has taken place since the death of Stalin, but this has been within the framework of the politically neutral, 'cultural' UEA, not in SAT. Also in 1953 was founded, in Vienna, the *Mondpaca Esperanto-Movado* [MEM, World Peace Esperanto Movement]. This has taken the political line of the Warsaw Pact and has proved particularly popular in Communist countries; in capitalist countries Communists appear to be particularly well represented among its members.[32]

Discussions have taken place within SAT on the question of relations with UEA. SAT has always recognised the Academy: Lanti argued that this no more constituted collaboration than using money implied collaboration with the financiers. In 1949 SAT protested to the Academy that it had ignored SAT's literary output. SAT is now recognised by the Academy and receives its bulletins; in return, SAT provides some financial support.[33] SAT continues to issue the only all-Esperanto dictionary,[34] which in practice is treated by most Esperantists as the supreme authority on linguistic matters. SAT affirmed its independence and unique contribution in 1950. The neutral movement is partly organised on the basis of national representatives, a principle unacceptable to SAT. SAT has reaffirmed its slogan, 'Away with Neutralism!' though it has sometimes been argued that SAT represents the true tradition of neutralism, which has been distorted in UEA. SAT possesses its own emblem, a green star surrounded by a red circle. The question of a SAT hymn has been much discussed, and in 1954 the following proposal was accepted. It can be sung to the tune of Beethoven's 'Ode to Joy':

Laboristoj ĉiulandaj	Workers of all lands
unuiĝu en SAT-rond'!	unite in the circle of SAT!
Malgraŭ mastroj vin komandaj,	In spite of your commanding masters,
unu lingvo unu mond'!	one language, one world!
Solidare kiel bloko	Solidary as a block,
ek al nova mond-soci'!	towards a new world society!
Pri kutimoj nia moko, } bis	Customs are our mockery, } repeat
kontraŭ dogmoj la raci'!	reason against dogmas!
El mallumaj labirintoj	From dark labyrinths
de l' nacia kredokult'	of the national creed
Marŝas miloj da lernintoj	March thousands of the informed
jam liberaj de la stult'!	already free from stupidity!
Ruĝa-verda SAT emblemo	Let the red and green SAT emblem
nin instigu al batal',	urge us on to battle,
Klasa frat' kun toleremo } bis	Class-brother with tolerance } repeat
jen komuna ideal'	Here is a common ideal.
Sama sort' sur sama tero	The same fate on the same earth
Ĉiu homo estas frat!	every man is a brother!
Vivi volas en libero	Wants to live in liberty
Sen katenoj de la ŝtat'!	Without the fetters of the state!
Donu fortojn malavare,	Give strength generously,

kunlaboru por sukces!	work together for success!
Kaj grandnombre ĉiujare ⎱ bis	And in large numbers every year ⎱ repeat[35]
al tutmonda SAT-kongres'! ⎰	to the world SAT congress! ⎰

SAT is socialist in form, but just as significant in its ideology is the conception of the 'Esperantist people'. Esperanto is seen as the language of a nation, and there is a respected tradition for this self-conception in the history of the neutral movement. Zamenhof's speeches — especially in Cambridge — referred to the idea of neutrality, which was to be an ideology in its own right. 'For us neutrality, or rather the neutralisation of relations between ethnic groups, is the whole content, the whole aim of our work',[36] Zamenhof said. Also, early in the First World War Hodler stressed the duty of Esperantists not just to their own country but to their second country, the Esperanto movement. SAT incorporated ideas of this kind but was more overtly political in content: it was more directly a 'social movement' in the traditional sociological sense, arising out of a specific condition of strain. SAT arose directly out of the Franco-German conflict, which revolutionary syndicalist ideas had failed to prevent. Like UEA, SAT was concerned with postwar reconstruction. Instead of supporting internationalism and being interested in organisations like the League of Nations (of which SAT was suspicious) a more radical solution identifying nationalism of any kind as a point of normative failure was called for. The ideology was also anticapitalist; it derived from existing pacifistic ideas of world working-class solidarity in non-Esperantist socialist movements, and aimed to act as an educational movement to make such ideals a reality. In its extreme form, as proposed by Lanti, it meant total rejection of the principle of membership of a state or nation. Lanti refused to consider himself a Frenchman and adopted Esperanto as his home language. It is perhaps symbolic of his lack of national identity that on his retirement in 1935 (at the age of 56, as part of a voluntary redundancy scheme), he embarked on a trip round the world and never returned to France. This standpoint accorded well with ideas in socialism which saw the governments as wrong and the people as right. This idea accords also with the traditional suspicion of governments in the Esperanto movement. It was also Esperanto, not Ido, through which these aims were to be realised. Idists supported ideals of science and progress, as did Lanti, but the emotive commitment to a world people, characteristic of Esperanto, was viewed in Idist circles with suspicion. The Ido movement did have its own 'Emancipation Star' (*Emancipanta Stelo*) with a Communist section, but it did not obtain support comparable to that of SAT. Whereas Esperanto had a sufficiently large speech community to enable separation between bourgeoisie and proletariat, such a luxury was not available to Ido. Idists had to defend their language as such against Esperanto as well as against the outside world, and resources were concentrated on this end.[37] The only hope for success was an attempt to obtain the support of the Comintern; when this failed, the movement lost momentum.

Like the neutral movement, SAT was mobilised on the basis of a very diffuse commitment, yet possessed its own private and esoteric ideology. SAT was presented to the public as a loose body representing all shades of socialist opinion. Yet in its esoteric form, *sennaciismo*, the ideology demanded as much commitment of members to the movement as a nation-state demanded from its members. Thus a tension between the two bases of commitment developed. The social democrats were less committed to non-nationalism; being less radical, they could accept the state pragmatically as a basis within which to work. This element of opinion produced strains within the movement and eventually a separate 'International' was formed, though not supported by all social democrats. A much more far-reaching conflict in SAT was between Communists and other members. Communists perceived of the new Communist nation-state, the Soviet Union, as different from other states and as commanding the allegiance of all socialists the world over. The tendency in SAT to discourage and to strive to weaken national loyalties was anathema to orthodox Soviet Communists. Even the Esperanto language was given only a subordinate part to play in the development of world socialism. In any case, all contacts of its citizens abroad through Esperanto were carefully supervised by the Soviet state. As the idea of 'socialism in one country' gained prominence, the role of Esperanto in international socialism became steadily undermined, and isolationist policies eventually led to total opposition to Esperanto.

SAT was thus fissiparous, but those who remained in it were able to provide continuity of its existence and to hold annual world congresses except when war prevented this. SAT declined in importance when the strain that produced it in the first place, arising out of hostile Franco-German relations, was resolved. SAT has not retained the degree of importance in the Esperanto movement that it possessed in the past. The 'cold war' situation in European politics could not provide a role for SAT, which has been virtually forbidden in most Communist countries. Outside Europe, it is no longer so easy for the left to oppose nationalism, since nationalistic movements are frequently movements of national liberation in colonised countries. Lanti explicitly rejected support for such movements. SAT remains as a loose nondogmatic movement of socialist Esperantists. It is often preferred by its members to UEA, since UEA discusses chiefly the affairs of the Esperanto movement, while SAT gives the opportunity to speak in Esperanto about something else.

NOTES

1. For the history of the Esperantist socialist movement, material has been drawn especially from G.P. de Bruin, *Laborista esperanta movado antaŭ la Mondmilito*, 1936; Plenumkomitato de SAT, *Historio pri la skismo en la laborista Esperanto-movado*, 1935; Sennacieca Asocio Tutmonda, *Historio de S.A.T.*, 1953. See also *Perspektivo*, Ch. 19.
2. *Leteroj*, vol. 1, p.186.
3. See Privat, *Vivo de Zamenhof, op. cit.*, p.127.
4. *Leteroj*, vol. 2, p.263.
5. For French socialism see J. Montreuil, *Histoire du mouvement ouvrier en France des origines à nos jours*, 1946; G. Lefranc, *Le Syndicalisme en France*, 1953.
6. See J. Joll, *Europe since 1870*, 1973, pp.187–189.
7. For biography see E. Borsboom, *Vivo de Lanti*, 1976.
8. E. Lanti, *For la neŭtralismon*, 1922.
9. *Esperantista Laboristo*, June 1921, p.7, reprinted in *Historio de S.A.T., op. cit.*, p.15.
10. The constitution appears in SAT, *Jarlibro*, 1922, pp.8–13.
11. See article 'Komunista internacio' in *Enciklopedio de Esperanto*, ed. by I. Ŝirjaev *et al.*, 1933–1934, vol. 2, p.296.
12. See article 'Senŝtatanoj', *ibid*, vol. 2, p.488.
13. E. Lanti, *Manifesto de la sennaciistoj, kaj dokumentoj pri sennaciismo*, 1931 [1970].
14. SAT, *Petro*, 1925.
15. E. Grosjean-Maupin et al., *Plena vortaro de Esperanto*, 1930.
16. See U. Lins, *La danĝera lingvo, op. cit.*, pp.32–33.

17. See, for instance, G.F. Hudson, *Fifty Years of Communism: Theory and Practice 1917-67*, 1968, Ch. VII.
18. See D.W. Treadgold, *Twentieth Century Russia*, 1959, pp.308-311.
19. E. Drezen, *Zamenhof*, 1929, reprinted in *Socipolitikaj aspektoj de la Esperanto-movado*, ed. by D. Blanke, 1978, pp.125-165.
20. *Historio de S.A.T., op. cit.*, p.59.
21. *Internaciisto*, October 1930.
22. For the Marrist controversy see L. Laurat, *Staline, la linguistique et l'impérialisme russe*, 1951; G.P. Springer, *Early Soviet Theories in Communication*, 1956; L.L. Thomas, 'Some notes on the Marr school', *American Slavic and East European Review*, 16(3), October 1957, pp.338-364; Lins, *La danĝera lingvo, op. cit.*, pp.39-44, 53-56; also in *Perspektivo*, pp.725-729, 737-739.
23. F. Engels, letter to J. Bloch, 1890, in *Marx and Engels: Basic Writings on Politics and Philosophy*, ed. by L.S. Feuer, pp.436-439.
24. E. Drezen, *Za vseobschim yazykom, op. cit.*, pp.3-9.
25. *Ibid.*, p.230 (Esperanto edition).
26. For Esperanto in the Great Purges see Lins, *La danĝera lingvo, op. cit.*, pp.45-49; also in *Perspektivo*, pp.730-734.
27. See Laurat, *op. cit., passim.*
28. See, for instance, E. Lanti and M. Ivon, *Ĉu socialismo konstruiĝas en Sovetio?*, 1935.
29. Among Lanti's works, noteworthy are *La laborista Esperantismo*, 1928; *Naciismo: Studo pri deveno, evoluado kaj sekvoj*, 1930; *Vortoj de kamarado Lanti*, 1931; *Absolutismo*, 1934; *Leteroj de E. Lanti*, 1940.
30. *Perspektivo*, p.656.
31. Text in *Esperanto*, June 1952, pp.163-165.
32. Brief details of this organisation are in *Perspektivo*, pp.529-530.
33. See G. Waringhien (ed.), *Aktoj de la Akademio*, 1967, p.11.
34. Recently enlarged and reissued as *Plena ilustrita vortaro*, ed. by G. Waringhien, 1970.
35. SAT, *Jarlibro*, 1954-1955, pp.32-33.
36. OV, p.379.
37. Drezen, *Historio de la mondolingvo, op. cit.*, p.223.

8

Internal Conflicts and the Rise of Nationalism 1923–1947

The Contract of Helsinki remained a compromise and did not succeed in resolving internal tensions between two principles. Ideas of internationalism could coexist easily with the norm-oriented tendency in the Esperanto movement, which saw Esperanto primarily as a practical instrument. Yet UEA represented a different dimension and had developed as a value-oriented movement with an organisational form which was potentially subversive of national interests. The Contract had attempted to incorporate both this cosmopolitan ideal and the principle of a federation of national organisations. Thus the new proposals in the Contract represented nothing more than an umbrella organisation, where the International Central Committee was added to those organisations already in existence. Yet initially no conflict of interest was felt, and there had, in any case, never been an outright confrontation between internationalist and cosmopolitan tendencies. Many members of national organisations supported the ideals of Zamenhof, and UEA was keen to stress the importance of practical application and practical services. Everyone in the movement had in common the advocacy of Esperanto as a *language*; thus the norm-oriented tendency did not feature as an area of conflict. Yet the value-oriented interpretation of Esperanto, enshrined in UEA, was optional, and an attack on it could be interpreted as an attack on the structure developed at Helsinki. Growth of nationalist sentiments in Europe between the two world wars had the effect of threatening this structure.

There were in fact two sources of the weakening of the value-oriented emphasis on Esperanto within the neutral movement. In the first place, SAT was founded in 1921 and was able to provide a much more radical and cosmopolitan interpretation of the goals of Esperanto than had hitherto been available. If some potential members were discouraged by its political interpretation of the values of Esperanto, many more were encouraged, particularly among workers. Thus SAT expanded rapidly and in some countries exceeded the neutral movement in size. By 1931, the German Workers' Esperanto Association claimed 5,450 members, as against only 2,114 in the neutral German Esperanto Association. Austria, Sweden, and The Netherlands also had more members of workers' associations than of the neutral movement in that year.[1] The growth of the workers' movement occurred only slightly as a result of transfer of membership from the neutral movement: but SAT was an important competitor for new recruits who emphasised the radical message of Esperanto. Its existence also made it possible for antinationalists who found unacceptable the 'neutral' movement's increasing compromise with nationalistic values to transfer their membership. They were thus less likely to show interest in reshaping the neutral movement in accordance with their ideas.[2]

Nationalism soon increased its strength in Europe after the First World War. In the immediate postwar period the Esperantists had been able to profit from the wave of pacifist sentiment which had swept Europe. This trend proved short-lived, or at least began to decline in importance except among certain deviant groups. Resurgence of this nationalist sentiment had the effect of exacerbating the conflict between UEA and the national associations. UEA was committed to supporting the supernational, value-oriented tendency, but national associations tended to seek official recognition by playing down any suggestion that there could be any conflict between Esperanto and nationalism. The 'neutral' national associations found it particularly necessary to 'correct' the impression given by SAT that Esperanto was a subversive tool. Thus French Esperantists, trying to create a favourable impression of Esperanto in a hostile environment, remarked of SAT that anyone can use Esperanto for bad purposes as well as good.[3] Tensions of this kind were present in all national Esperanto associations representing large and powerful nation-states. This was true of the French movement especially during the Poincaré government, but it was nowhere more evident than in Germany, where a conscious attempt was made to avoid offending the Nazi party. Such tendencies had had their first significant impact on the international organised

Esperanto movement in 1932, when at the Paris World Congress the Contract of Helsinki came to an end.

Since its original acceptance, the Contract had undergone only one minor change. At the 1924 Vienna World Congress, the basic principles of the Contract were again discussed but the arrangements were mostly confirmed. The exception was the Permanent Congress Committee: this was considered to have ceased to function and to be unsatisfactory anyway since the International Central Committee should control congress expenditure directly. It was almost unanimously agreed that the Permanent Congress Committee should be abolished. Other arrangements continued, but in 1932 UEA was in serious financial difficulties. These began with a large deficit from the Vienna Congress, but UEA also suffered from the general economic recession and, in particular, the expense of providing its services had steadily increased. Finally, in 1932, UEA reduced its grant to the International Central Committee from 2,500 to 500 Swiss francs. This precipitated open conflict between the permanent representatives of the national associations and UEA. Alternative proposals to Helsinki were already being discussed, and the financial problem aggravated the conflict rather than caused it directly. Finance also had its repercussions on the attitude of the Esperantists generally to the Helsinki structure. Some could no longer afford more than one subscription, and thus the national associations and UEA were in direct competition for members. The French Esperanto society wished to have only one international association, whose members would be the national associations, but which would also issue a yearbook. According to this proposal, delegates would continue to function, but they would now have to be approved by the national association in the country concerned. The French proposal was discussed in Paris at the 1932 World Congress; the final conclusion was that the Contract of Helsinki would definitely be repudiated but that a commission would be set up to study new constitutional arrangements. Of the five national associations voting in favour of the French proposal (Britain, France, Germany, Italy, and Sweden) four were representatives of large nation-states. Representatives of smaller national associations (The Netherlands, Czechoslovakia, and Switzerland) were opposed to the scheme, and so also was UEA. UEA was invited to join the new commission but refused to do so, seeing no place for itself in the new organisation. The Commission reported in November 1932 and proposed a federation of national societies to be called the *Universala Federacio Esperantista* [Universal Esperantist Federation]. The proposed constitution eliminated UEA and made no reference to ideals such as promoting solidarity between members, which appeared in UEA's constitution. Comments were invited from UEA, which refused to discuss the proposal. UEA merely protested that a federation of national associations of the kind proposed was intending to usurp some functions of UEA, such as the Yearbook and the network of delegates. UEA also detected the lack of a value-oriented component, and took the opportunity of reaffirming the ideals of Zamenhof.[4] Stettler, one of the earliest activists of UEA, wrote:

It is the goal of UEA to bring together, under the green standard, all men who believe that humanity forms one great family, who are ready to direct their actions and those of their fellow-nationals according to this belief, which aspires to peaceful mutual understanding through the language and in the spirit of our Master. . . .

We have too much faith in the good sense of the Esperantists to believe that the national principle will really win in the movement. . . . But a great danger threatens the movement through making concessions to contemporary political trends under the flag of nationalism.[5]

The UEA committee saw the idea of a federation of national associations, as had been proposed by the commission, as an inadequate moral basis for organisation. The appropriate basis was seen as supernationalism, already found in the structure of UEA. The conflict was exacerbated by the fact that the 1933 World Congress was to be held in Cologne, now under a Nazi government. Events in Nazi Germany had not been openly discussed in Esperanto periodicals, for fear of transgressing the principle of political neutrality. At this time the German Esperanto Association had succeeded in using arguments for Esperanto which would be acceptable to the Nazi regime.[6] It was argued, for instance, that Esperanto purified the German language by preventing encroachment of foreign words. Esperanto was presented as a way of spreading accurate knowledge of Germany abroad. Hitler had already condemned Esperanto, and the German Esperantists continued to stress that Esperanto was perfectly compatible with Nazism: thus they particulary played down the supernational tendency. Instead, they suggested that internationalism was possible only on the basis of strong and sane nationalism. The independent weekly international newspaper *Heroldo de Esperanto*, published in Germany, had also tended to whitewash the regime. It argued that, apart from a few excesses, the perpetrators of which were punished, the national revolution in Germany was being fulfilled in a very disciplined manner. Arrested Communists and socialists, it was stated, were 'no worse treated than other prisoners'. *Heroldo* proudly pointed out that the Cologne Esperanto group met in the same building as the Brownshirts and that the two groups enjoyed good relations. The general line taken was that reports in the foreign press were misleading, and that Esperanto proved its worth in helping to disseminate the truth about Germany.[7]

Since UEA was excluded from the new arrangements for a federation of national Esperanto associations, it was now independent again. UEA therefore considered itself not obliged to hold a meeting in the same place as the World Congress.[8] It pointed this out to the Local Congress Committee in Cologne: the Cologne committee assured members that there would be no difficulties put in the way of foreign guests, and that the mayor of Cologne had confirmed this. The Declaration of Boulogne was quoted to the effect that Esperanto in no way wished to interfere with the internal life of the peoples.[9]

Eventually UEA agreed to take part in the Cologne Congress and reconsidered the question of participation in a new international association. Before the Congress, negotiations took place between Stettler, President of UEA, and the commission representatives, to work out a plan for an agreement. This formed the basis of the 'Agreement of Cologne', which was accepted during the Congress. In this scheme the *Universala Federacio Esperantista* was abandoned, and the new organisation took the name of UEA. Membership of UEA was now to be through national associations, which could affiliate and pay a small subscription for each member. This entitled members to the services of the delegates. If individual members then wished to become *active* members of UEA, receiving the Yearbook and the periodical *Esperanto*, it was necessary for them to pay a higher subscription. National associations were to encourage members to become active members of UEA. Delegates were now to be nominated by national associations. UEA was to be governed by a committee consisting of representatives of national associations (one, plus one for each commencing 500 members). The committee could co-opt members to up to one-third of its composition. Thus the supreme authority of UEA was now based on national representation: in spite of its previous protestations, UEA was now changed beyond all recognition. The only concession to the previous structure was that the final authority was not the committee, but a general vote of the delegates: but delegates were now to be nominated by national associations.

This proposal appeared to be a sellout for UEA, but it was apparently accepted so as to ease financial difficulties of both UEA and individual Esperantists. The new proposal did at least eliminate the rivalry between UEA and the national associations for subscriptions. A significant feature of the proposals was the arrangement that one-third of the membership of the committee could be co-opted. It was expected that this provision would enable a certain degree of representation on a non-national basis. Elections were held for the committee of the new organisation at the 1934 World Congress in Stockholm. Representatives of the national associations had already been elected, and they proceeded to elect the co-opted members during the Congress. The old UEA had been confident that its leaders would be represented in this capacity; yet Privat came bottom of the poll and Karsch, a long-standing committee member of UEA, was also not elected. The third unsuccessful candidate was Andrei Cseh, an idealist and popular teacher of Esperanto by the direct method. It was clear that the new regime wished for no representation of the ideology of the old UEA; in consequence the remaining members of the old regime, Stettler (President) and Jakob (Director), resigned in protest.[10] A heated discussion took place and it was noted that a shift in ideology away from the supernational tendency had occurred. The value- and norm-oriented division became clear; value-oriented Esperantists reproached the norm-oriented camp for 'not having the inner idea', and in turn were rebuked by the norm-oriented camp for being 'mystics'.[11]

After this 'palace revolution' the defeat of the ideals of the old UEA became evident. In a speech about his resignation Stettler expressed his disillusionment with the new structure, though he admitted that the elections were perfectly legal. Louis Bastien, a French general, was elected as president; as vice-president was elected Anton Vogt, a member of the Nazi party who had opposed the previous structure of UEA, although he had been a delegate. The official organ *Esperanto* had hitherto been the organ of the old UEA and had given sufficient space to the value-oriented tendency; but Privat resigned as editor after the Stockholm Congress and the periodical began to adopt a different standpoint. In its first issue of 1935 Vogt stressed that a shift of ideology had taken place. Under the heading 'A new goal – a new spirit', Vogt emphasised the importance of discipline and the need for strong leadership.[12] This view did not monopolise the pages of the journal, but authoritarianism and nationalism were now acceptable values. The last issue of 1934 had already carried an article on 'The German viewpoint on the racial problem'. This article argued that the Nazis were merely saying that the races were different and that confusion of racial divisions was dangerous. It pointed out that German legislation on the subject of race was not aimed at judging the different races.[13] The 1935 World Congress was held in Rome, in another Fascist country, and Vienna was chosen for 1936.

Meanwhile, the German Esperanto movement had continued to make further concessions to Nazi ideology. The mayor of Cologne had spoken at the 1933 Cologne World Congress and had remarked that 'The National-Socialist Revolution had to come in Germany to guard the world against Bolshevism'. This remark had been greeted with applause.[14] After this Congress, the German Esperanto Association adopted the slogan 'Through Esperanto for Germany'; it urged its members to put the official points of view in letters to overseas correspondents. There were even pamphlets issued in Esperanto mentioning the bad influence of Jews in German public life. In 1935 it expelled its Jewish members and adopted 'dissemination of the National Socialist World-View' as one of its aims. In 1935, also, a more pro-Nazi organisation, the *Neue Deutsche Esperanto-Bewegung*, was formed. This criticised the German Esperanto Association for not being sufficiently pro-Nazi. It pointed out that the German Esperanto Association was prepared to advertise the *Plena Vortaro*, the all-Esperanto dictionary published by SAT, and also books by Jewish authors. The new movement claimed close relations with the Gestapo. It recognised the incompatibility between Zamenhof's ideals and those of National Socialism, and criticised the German Esperanto Association for attempting to reconcile the two ideologies. A proposal to issue a 'German library' in Esperanto, including translations of works by Hitler, never materialised.

The new UEA should not be thought of as a Fascist front organisation. Most European countries were represented among the membership of the committee. Rather UEA became an organisation in which powerful nationalist forces, including but not confined to Fascism, could easily be accommodated. Esperanto was seen more as a technological innovation which made international contact easier, and no attempt was made to develop a value-oriented ideology which could be subversive of chauvinistic ideas. This position was far removed from the ideas of the old UEA; yet many influential pioneers of the old UEA were still active in the Swiss Esperanto movement. Schism was a definite possibility if the opportunity should present itself, and such an opportunity was not long in coming. In March, 1936, it was reported in *Esperanto* [15] that (the new) UEA had decided to move its headquarters from Geneva to London, so as to benefit from the cheaper cost of living in Britain. This decision was made by a majority vote on the committee, but a group of Swiss Esperantists, who became known as the *Svisaj Protestantoj* [Swiss Protesters], objected. They argued that this decision was unconstitutional, since the constitution required the headquarters of UEA to be in Switzerland: thus the Swiss group took the matter to court. The court ruled that the move was indeed unconstitutional. Constitutional changes were, however, possible by a vote of the delegates, and UEA organised a postal ballot. This resulted in an 80% majority in favour of the move to London, and removal began. [16] Yet the Swiss group succeeded in finding formal errors in the procedure, and the Swiss courts still held that the move was illegal. Rather than engage in further lawsuits, the existing committee of UEA proceeded to form a new organisation, called the *Internacia Esperanto-Ligo* [International Esperanto League, IEL], and urged all existing members, delegates, and national associations to leave UEA and join the new organisation. This move was successful; by March, 1937, it was reported that all the national associations had joined IEL apart from Spain (in difficulties because

of the Civil War) and Switzerland.[17] The strength of the new organisation was consolidated by the gift of a house in Heronsgate,
Rickmansworth, which served as its new headquarters.

This left the largely Swiss UEA with much-reduced membership.
At the end of 1937 UEA had only 1,300 members, as opposed to
IEL's 13,500. It should be remembered, however, that only 3,000
of the latter were *individual* members, the remainder being associ-
ates through their national association.[18] Yet a committee was set
up, and in November, 1936, UEA began to issue its own periodical
Esperanto. It began to reaffirm the value-oriented tendency which
had been stifled in the post-Cologne organisation. Articles were
written urging a return to the *interna ideo* and stressing the importance of the Zamehofan ideal. The Swiss UEA obtained the
support of Lidja Zamenhof, daughter of the founder.[19] The journal
began to speak out against Nazi Germany and the position of
Esperanto there. By the end of 1937 a front-page article by Privat
went so far as to suggest that there indeed *was* incompatibility
between fighting for one's country and the ideals of Esperanto:

Youth of the whole world, will you be prepared tomorrow to destroy peaceful towns and slaughter women and children?
    ....The voice of Zamenhof is asking and calling you — not of one man
lying in a tomb, but of that humanitarian feeling which he expresses through
the whole of his life and work.....[20]

This standpoint contrasts with the usual value-oriented position
in the Esperanto movement, which has tended to emphasise a dual
loyalty, to one's country and to the ideals of Esperantism.[21] Characteristically the second has been seen as something to be suspended,
though not forgotten, during war, and to be put into practice
in postwar reconstruction. The Swiss UEA also began to provide
certain services, started before war had actually broken out. In
June, 1938, *Esperanto* began to accept advertisements from people
wanting to emigrate, usually from countries where Jews were
persecuted. During the war UEA and IEL both took part in a
scheme to help the Zamenhof family, and by the end of the war
advertising for missing Esperantists became an important activity.

If UEA became a more decidedly value-oriented movement, it
did not follow that IEL became correspondingly more norm-

oriented. Though the schism had reflected such a division of orientation within the movement, the difference was not absolute. External factors were decisive in preventing this division, since German Esperantists' attempts to placate the Nazi regime eventually proved unsuccessful. To understand this question it is necessary to consider the Nazi attitude to Esperanto in more detail. Esperanto, after all, had been devised by a Jew, and German Fascism had long been opposed to Esperanto. Hitler criticised the internationalism of Esperanto as early as 1922, in a speech in Munich.[22] In *Mein Kampf* (1925) he condemned Esperanto as part of a plot for Jewish domination of the world:

As long as the Jew has not become the master of the other peoples, he must speak their languages whether he likes it or not, but as soon as they become his slaves, they would all have to learn a universal language (Esperanto, for instance!) so that by this additional means the Jews could more easily dominate them.[23]

Esperanto was generally attacked in right-wing German milieus, as a tool of cosmopolitanism and Communism. Inevitably, the socialist Esperanto movements were the first to suffer from Fascism, and in 1933 the German workers' Esperanto movements were disbanded. The neutral movement, as already noted, continued to exist and attempted to placate the regime, though it remained under suspicion. Yet neither the neutral movement nor the *Neue Deutsche Esperanto-Bewegung* succeeded in making Esperanto respectable in Nazi Germany. In 1935 the Education Minister Bernhart Rust condemned Esperanto as weakening the essential value of national characters[24] and forbade teaching it. In February 1936 Nazi party members were banned from joining Esperanto organisations, and by July of that year the Esperanto movement was made illegal.

In many other countries where Hitler extended his domination, Esperanto was also made illegal. The Austrian Esperanto movement was liquidated in 1938, the Polish in 1939, the Czech in 1940, and the Dutch, Yugoslavian, and Belgian in 1941. In some cases, particularly in Belgium, activity continued underground. Suppression of Esperanto was not universally practised in Nazi-dominated countries: the Danish and Norwegian movements were allowed to continue, and there was no *systematic* prohibition of Esperanto in France, where even SAT continued some of its activities. In the case of Poland, a particularly unpleasant feature of the Nazi occupation for the Esperantists was the arrest of the Zamenhof family. Not only were they Jewish, but among Jews they were particularly singled out for arrest. Zamenhof's son and two daughters perished in concentration camps; his son's wife and her son escaped from a train and survived. In many countries occupied by Hitler, Esperanto books were burnt, though some were confiscated for preservation in Nazi dossiers.

Esperanto was opposed, though not to the same extent, in some countries allied to Nazi Germany. In Fascist Italy, radio broadcasts in Esperanto continued, though in 1936 the Italian Esperanto Federation found it necessary to make pro-regime remarks and to urge support of Esperantists for the Italians in the war in Abyssinia. In 1939 it expelled its Jewish members and during the war the Italian movement disappeared completely. In Japan the socialist Esperanto movements came under suspicion: the Japanese Proletarian Esperanto Union was made illegal in 1939. The neutral Japanese movement was allowed to continue, though suspect, until 1944. In Bulgaria, Radio Sofia ceased broadcasting in Esperanto in 1942.

These tendencies were already gaining momentum as the schism between UEA and IEL took place. IEL began to issue its own monthly *Esperanto Internacia* after the schism, and also signed a contract with *Heroldo de Esperanto* whereby this periodical became an official weekly organ of IEL. The editor of both of these, Teo Jung, had previously been editor of *Heroldo* while it was an independent weekly, and had tended to whitewash the Nazi regime. A definite change of emphasis appeared in these periodicals. Jung had himself found it necessary to transfer the publication of *Heroldo* from Germany to The Netherlands in 1936, as a result of Nazi harassment. A more 'radical' position was now taken. Already in November 1936 *Esperanto Internacia* said that it was a mistake to condemn all 'revolutionary ideas' out of hand, since they were the source of human progress.[25] Esperanto organisations and periodicals no longer felt able to tolerate simply any kind of regime, whatever might have been the traditional commitment to neutrality.

Thus the ideological basis of the schism tended to appear far less profound than it had been at its inception.

The attitude of both organisations was in fact to regret the schism, and various proposals were made for unity. IEL began to use the slogan *Unueco estas forto* [unity is strength]. UEA did not organise separate world congresses of its own, though separate issues of the Yearbook appeared. An attempt was made at the 1937 Warsaw World Congress to unify the movement. This attempt was a popular measure; at the beginning of the Congress there were calls from rank-and-file members for unification. UEA and IEL had reached agreement with the Warsaw Local Congress Committee to the effect that the Congress was valid for both organisations. A committee consisting of three representatives from each organisation was set up to negotiate agreement. To encourage consensus, appeal was made to the tradition of the movement. The Congress was being held in Poland to commemorate the fiftieth anniversary of the publication of Esperanto. The meetings of the committee which attempted reconciliation took place in Zamenhof's old study, and Dr. Adam Zamenhof, son of the founder, was chairman. No agreement was reached, however, the main contentious issue being the site of the headquarters. UEA wished the headquarters to be in Switzerland, with a branch in Britain, while IEL proposed the opposite.[26] A further attempt to promote unity failed at the 1939 Berne World Congress, despite the pressure to unity that the threat of war might have supplied.[27] A continued contentious issue was that UEA, arguing that IEL was using UEA's money for its own ends, conducted a personal lawsuit in the French courts against General Bastien, which continued until after the war.

Both organisations continued to function throughout the war. UEA was situated in neutral Switzerland; IEL was situated in Britain which, though belligerent, was never occupied. Both organisations issued periodicals, though *Esperanto* (Geneva) was suspended after June 1942, reappearing in January 1946, a broadsheet *Informa Bulteno* being produced during the intervening period. IEL continued to issue *Esperanto Internacia* and a Yearbook, though *Heroldo* was suspended. Although UEA forwarded some correspondence, this was on a much smaller scale than in the First World War. UEA was now a much weaker organisation after the schism, and Esperanto was in any case banned or discouraged in many Nazi-dominated countries. After the war, ideas of postwar reconstruction again put pressures for unification of the movement, and this time negotiations were successful. In 1946, representatives of the two organisations reached an agreement and planned a new organisation, which would take the old name UEA. According to this proposal, *both* national associations *and* individual members would be able to join UEA. The Committee would consist of one set of members elected by the national associations, according to their number of members; a second group of members elected by the delegates; and co-opted members elected by the rest of the committee. Thus a compromise was reached between the two principles of mobilisation. On the internal Anglo-Swiss dispute about the headquarters, a compromise was reached by having two offices. The British office was to deal with general and financial administration, relations with national associations, and congresses, while the Swiss office would deal with services, delegates, and the official journal. The committee would be ruled by an Executive of nine members. A contract was signed between the two organisations on this basis in April 1947.[28]

This contract contained no definite commitment to a norm- or value-oriented position, though there was much ongoing discussion of this matter. This question was originally couched in the framework of relations with Esperantists in Germany. The extent to which the pro-Nazi sentiments of some German Esperantists were genuinely held cannot be established with certainty. Some adopted pro-Nazi standpoints as part of a last-ditch attempt to placate the regime: yet there were also some active Nazis among the German Esperantists. The final suppression of the Esperanto movement by the Nazis showed that organised Esperanto and Fascism were completely incompatible (technically, the *language* was never made illegal). The Esperanto movement's international connections developed in its members, in however small a degree, certain beliefs about the unity of humanity which were unlikely to be viewed with favour by a Fascist government. The problem arose in the new UEA of how to react to these facts of history. Esperanto had been made illegal in Germany, Esperantists persecuted, and the Zamenhof family sent to concentration camps. Hans Jakob, writing in *Esperanto* (Geneva) in 1946,[29] called for acceptance of a new ideology which would support everything which made for friendship between ethnic groups. But the negative side of the question also asserted itself. From some quarters came suggestions that the whole German people bore collective responsibility for the Nazi tyranny. One article referred to

. . .the German Esperantists, who for me and for many Esperantists will only be speakers of the same language, with whom we will avoid having relations of fellow-idealists.[30]

The problem of reassimilating German members reasserted itself when, in 1947, the Esperantists in the Western zones of Germany formed a new German Esperanto Association. The neutral and workers' movements joined forces to form an organisation which, while neutral about politics, race, and religion, was to be 'decidedly anti-fascist, and pacifist'. Former activists in Nazi parties and organisations were to be barred from membership.[31] A few Germans attended the first postwar World Congress, held in 1947 in Berne. One offered to greet the Congress in the name of the German Esperantists, but withdrew his offer when Yugoslavian, Polish, and Jewish Esperantists threatened to walk out in protest.[32] More attention was paid at Berne to a proposal to condemn Fascism. This came from the Esperanto associations of Bulgaria, Yugoslavia, Rumania, Austria, Czechoslovakia, Hungary, Palestine, and Poland. It was proposed by Dr. Ivo Lapenna, who before the war was a member of a group of Yugoslavian Esperantists who contributed to the journal *La Suda Stelo*, to the effect that the Esperanto movement was unable to tolerate Fascism. Lapenna had received acclaim as the representative of Yugoslavian Esperantists, when he condemned Fascism as responsible for the war when he greeted the Congress. The motion condemned aggression and the threat of further war, regarding the international language as an instrument of friendship. It condemned Nazi and Fascist crimes and urged immediate severe punishment of those guilty of them; called for vigilance in opposition to the remains of Fascism; and urged the United Nations, international organisations, and all progressive forces to pay attention to Esperanto as a powerful means of world solidarity. This particular motion was rejected, only slightly more than one-fifth present voting in favour. Some who took part in the discussion objected on the basic principle of neutrality, while others disagreed with part of the resolution, though not all. An important source of opposition came, however, from those who felt acceptance of this motion would involve taking sides in the coming cold war situation. This fear was confirmed by one Polish member who suggested that, if Fascism was to be condemned, then capitalism should be condemned as well. Thus there were incipient conflicts between Communist and capitalist interpretations of the ideology of Esperanto. The existing concepts of democracy and neutrality had been much criticised since the war in the periodical *Internacia Kulturo* originating from the Balkan states, and some members feared that a motion of this kind would be pro-Communist.[33]

Yet although the motion proposed by Lapenna was not accepted, the anti-Fascist sentiment proved popular. After the prohibition of Esperanto in the Third Reich the Esperantists had begun to recognise the limits of neutrality; though the question was complicated by the problem of admission of Germans to UEA again. It was finally decided to permit membership of Germans, provided that they had not associated themselves with the Nazi party. In 1949 a German greeted the Bournemouth World Congress, and in 1951 the World Congress was held in Munich. By 1955 the German Esperanto Association was again admitted to UEA, and the coalition between neutral and worker Esperantists in Germany was ended. Finally, no direct reference to opposition to Fascism was accepted for inclusion in the UEA constitution; in its place a positive commitment to human rights was adopted. Thus, while continuing to express its neutrality on matters of politics and religion, the 1947 constitution of UEA contained the corollary that 'the respect for human rights is an essential condition for its work'.[34] This foreshadowed the great significance that was to be attached to the Declaration of Human Rights, United Nations, and UNESCO in the postwar ideology of the movement.

The norm-oriented and value-oriented interpretation had been conflicting interpretations of the goals of Esperanto in the interwar period – though the division into the two opposing camps was never an absolute one. Although at the 1947 Berne World Congress there was some disagreement about the wording of the constitution, there was little support for the view that Esperanto should be seen merely as a language. The disastrous consequences of accepting Fascism as a legitimate ideology to be associated with Esperanto, the persecution of Esperantists, and the fate of the Zamenhof family made a totally norm-oriented position difficult to defend. Thus discussion centred rather on the kind of value orientation to be adopted. The Esperanto movement had long been fraught with schismatic tendencies over the ideals to be associated with Esperanto. Originally tensions had arisen on the matter of religious neutrality. SAT had raised the question of political neutrality, but had in the end recruited mostly newcomers to Esperanto rather than suggesting that UEA should take sides on political matters. In any case, there were many instances of overlapping membership of UEA and SAT. After the Second World War it was impossible for UEA to avoid discussion of politics. Zamenhof had regarded politics as an inappropriate subject to be discussed at Esperanto meetings; yet discussion of conflicts between ethnic groups was admissible, and, when Fascism was under consideration, it was scarcely possible to distinguish between ethnic and political problems. Thus although the tradition of the movement made for hesitation in broaching the subject, once the barrier had been overcome it was found that the anti-Fascist viewpoint was greeted with enthusiasm. However, the tradition of the movement contributed a preference for a more positive commitment to human rights, rather than a negative commitment against Fascism, when it came to the wording of the constitution.

The limits of naivety of the traditional ideology of Esperanto were therefore recognised. The traditional 'functionalist' view of international relations which stressed the validity of national belief systems within their own cultural context was no longer totally acceptable: Esperanto could not be used to help foreigners to remove their prejudices and 'understand' Fascism. A new factor in the international situation complicated the move away from absolute political neutrality: Esperanto was strong in some European countries which had become Communist after the Second World War. Communist ideology accepts the fundamental principles of the 'inner idea' of Esperanto — peace, justice, and world brotherhood. Yet it regards political revolution as the only true road to the effective realisation of these ideals. Communism is not averse to the use of force to achieve such a revolution, and can be interpreted as a justification for forcible intervention in the political developments of foreign countries. The specific experience of UEA with the Soviet Union had given grounds for suspicion of Communism. Soviet Esperantists were first assimilated only into a socialist world movement, then into a Communist-only movement; and finally the Soviet Esperanto movement had been outlawed entirely. UEA had never had its ranks swelled from the Soviet Union, and was thus liable to view the new representation of Communist countries with suspicion. There were some Communist sympathisers and even party members among UEA members in capitalist countries, but these were only a small minority. Most other Esperantists had entirely different solutions to the problem of international strife. Thus the threat of Communist influence was a further complication in the discussion of political neutrality.

While the incipient 'cold war' situation was an important centrifugal force, there existed a countervailing centripetal force. Ideas of postwar reconstruction made for renewed support for international organisations supporting peaceful international relations. Of necessity these organisations were nonpolitical in the sense of not being able to commit themselves to a particular political ideology. They also stood for values such as peace, justice, and international cultural relations. These were values which the Esperanto movement had always upheld, and they were also expressed within the framework of political neutrality. Organisations such as the United Nations were more firmly based than the League of Nations and were more articulate in support of the values to which the Esperantists had always subscribed. Thus changes in 'international society' made the values of Esperanto closer to dominant values. By 1947 the Esperanto movement had already begun to articulate this connection; the process of consolidation of the link was to take over two decades.

NOTES

1. See *Esperanto*, October 1932, p.147.
2. For this suggestion see U. Lins, 'Esperanto dum la Tria Regno', in *Socipolitikaj aspektoj de la Esperanto-movado*, ed. by D. Blanke, *op. cit.*, pp.84–122 (p.95).
3. See, for instance, A. Bandet, *La Conférence internationale de Venise, op. cit.*, p.2: 'La langue, même internationale, peut être à la fois la meilleure et la pire des choses: La meilleure, si l'on s'en sert pour augmenter l'expansion commerciale, scientifique, ou intellectuelle; la pire, si on l'utilise a accroître des propagandes néfastes dans tous les domaines où elles peuvent s'exercer'.

4.   See *Esperanto*, August–September 1932, pp.121–124.
5.   *Esperanto*, December 1932, p.185.
6.   For a full analysis of the position of Esperanto in the Third Reich see U. Lins, 'Esperanto dum la Tria Regno' in Blanke, *op. cit.*; also his *La dangera lingvo*, *op. cit.*, pp.9–20, reissued in *Perspektivo*, pp.702–710; also Sadler and Lins, 'Regardless of frontiers', *op. cit.*
7.   *Heroldo de Esperanto*, 9 April 1933, pp.1–2.
8.   *Esperanto*, May–June 1933, p.98.
9.   *Heroldo de Esperanto*, 16 July 1933, p.1.
10. For details see *Heroldo de Esperanto*, 19 August 1934, pp.5–6; *Esperanto*, August–September 1934, pp.132, 137–138.
11. See, for instance, *Esperanto*, October 1934, p.141.
12. *Esperanto*, January 1935, p.3.
13. *Esperanto*, December 1934, p.169.
14. *Germana Esperantisto*, 1933, p.99.
15. *Esperanto*, March 1936, p.35.
16. *Esperanto*, May 1936, p.67; June 1936, pp.83–85; July 1936, p.97. For a general discussion of the schism see *Perspektivo*, pp.439–442.
17. *Esperanto Internacia*, March 1937, p.41.
18. *Esperanto Internacia*, February 1938, p.24.
19. *Esperanto* (hereinafter referred to as *Esperanto* [Geneva] to distinguish it from the IEL publication), November 1936, p.115.
20. *Esperanto* (Geneva), December 1937, p.89.
21. See, for instance, Hodler's article *Super* (quoted in Ch. 5).
22. Lins, *La dangera lingvo, op. cit.*, p.9, reissued in *Perspektivo*, p.702.
23. A. Hitler, *Mein Kampf* (English translation), 1943, p.307.
24. 'Die Pflege künstlich geschaffener Welthilfssprachen wie der Esperanto-Sprache hat im nationalsozialistischen Staate keinen Raum. Ihr Gebrauch führt dazu, wesentliche Werte völkischer Eigenart zu schwächen'. Quoted in Sadler and Lins, *op. cit.*, p.209.
25. *Esperanto Internacia*, November 1936, p.11.
26. *Esperanto Internacia*, October 1937, pp.146–149.
27. *Esperanto* (Geneva), August–September 1939, p.29.
28. *Perspektivo*, p.442; *Esperanto Internacia*, September 1946, p.129.
29. *Esperanto* (Geneva), March–April 1946, p.11.
30. *Esperanto Internacia*, February 1947, p.27.
31. *Esperanto Internacia*, June 1947, p.83. See also Lins in Blanke, *op. cit.*, p.116.
32. Lins, *loc. cit.*
33. Lins, *loc. cit.; Esperanto Internacia*, September 1947, pp.128, 132; *Perspektivo*, pp.443–444.
34. *Perspektivo*, pp.443–444.

9

The Postwar 'Prestige' Policy

It has been observed that the value-oriented interpretation of Esperanto had declined steadily in the interwar period, even to the extent of compromise with Fascism. Yet the limitations of the norm-oriented stance became evident; neutrality in relation to Fascism was no longer a realistic possibility, if only because under Fascism the very language had been made illegal. Changes in the wider complex of international relations, first the war itself, then postwar reconstruction, gave the opportunity for a 'spirititual revival'. On the basis of the traditional values of Esperanto, what had been a highly diffuse ideology underwent a certain measure of clarification. The traditional view of the 'inner idea' had been one of an intuitive, almost mystical perception of the significance of Esperanto in promoting world solidarity. The emphasis on the solidarity of those with a common speech was clearest in SAT, though in UEA too there was a strong element of this.

In the postwar period, the history of the Esperanto movement has been marked by a tendency towards institutionalisation of the 'inner idea' and bureaucratisation of structure. The establishment of organisations such as the United Nations and UNESCO, on a firmer basis than the League of Nations, presented the opportunity to bring the ideology of Esperanto nearer to certain values which had now at least in theory begun to be taken seriously in international relations. This involved some shedding of the traditional mysticism of the 'inner idea'; it also represented a shift away from the traditional neglect by Esperantists of political leaders. International governmental organisations could now be seen as having goals equivalent to the values of Esperanto. The Esperantists now aimed to encourage organisations of this kind to use the language officially, as well as subscribing to aims similar to those of Esperanto.

There was a precedent for such a policy in relation to the League of Nations; but United Nations bodies became the focal point of the Esperantists' campaign, to a far greater extent than was true of the League.

The problem arose of the articulation of the connection between such goals and Esperanto. The diffuseness of the 'inner idea' had led to many possible ways of interpreting it. In the past, a sophisticated exponent of this ideology had been able to exercise considerable influence. The influence of Zamenhof's congress speeches has already been commented upon. Lanti put forward his own socialist interpretation of Esperanto, though as a consequence he took his supporters outside the ranks of the neutral movement altogether. Hodler had considerable influence in the formation and development of UEA on a supernational basis. The diffuse nature of the ideology of Esperanto enabled a sophisticated exponent to articulate his own distinctive version. To be successful in obtaining support from rank-and-file members, such an exponent had to possess a relevant message to the followers.[1] This can be distinguished from 'relevance' to the outside world, though the latter is to be taken into account as well. Since the Esperanto movement seeks international recognition, developments of the ideology can be justified in terms of the way in which they might encourage such acceptance. An exponent of such developments has also to possess sufficient authority to ascertain that his interpretation would have sufficient influence. This authority can derive from a variety of sources. In Zamenhof's case, it evidently stemmed from his unique position as inventor of the language; this was helped by some of his personal qualities, though oratorical talent was not one of them. Authority can also derive from positions outside the movement and personal skills possessed by the exponent. In the postwar period UEA possessed a new ideologue in the person of Dr. (later Professor) Ivo Lapenna, mentioned in the previous chapter. Lapenna was to have a considerable influence on the shaping of the ideology of Esperanto. Eventually, in 1964, he became President of UEA, though his influence has been felt through the whole of the postwar period in the Esperanto movement. Unlike Zamenhof, who was both retiring and undogmatic (on most subjects), Lapenna is an accomplished orator and also somewhat averse to criticism of his own standpoint. Lapenna possesses many personal qualifications in matters other than Esperanto, and these have helped him to exert his influence in UEA. He was born in Yugoslavia in 1909;[2] he studied law at the university of Zagreb, receiving his doctorate in 1933. During the war, he served in the Yugoslavian army of national liberation. After 1945 he was active both as an academic lawyer and as a representative of Yugoslavia in international circles. He became Professor of International Law and Relations at Zagreb University. He served as expert adviser on international law at the Paris Peace Conference in 1946, and in 1947 was Counsel-Advocate at the International Court of Justice at The Hague. However, in 1949 he became disillusioned with the Yugoslavian regime and left for Paris. In Paris he engaged in research at the *Centre National de la Recherche Scientifique* until 1953. In 1956 he began an academic career in Britain, at the London School of Economics, rising from Research Fellow in 1956 to Professor of Soviet and East European Law in 1973. He is an accepted authority on international and East European law and has published widely in languages other than Esperanto.[3] He is fluent in several languages. He displays the sophistication of the cultured cosmopolitan. He has distinguished himself as a sportsman and a musician.

Lapenna has taken an anti-Fascist position for a long period within Esperanto circles as well as outside. Together with other contributors to the Yugoslavian periodical *La Suda Stelo* he had been critical of the traditional concept of political neutrality, which could permit Fascism.[4] He has developed his oratorical talents in Esperanto, and in 1950 published a book in Esperanto on rhetoric.[5] Qualities such as Lapenna's are unusual in the Esperanto movement, at least among those who are prepared to be very active. Lapenna's own commitment to the cause of Esperanto stems from an education in Yugoslavia overcharged with the learning of languages, followed later in life by finding his own Serbo-Croatian language useless in international communication. He has thus appealed to Esperanto as a means of promoting the rights of minority language groups. He has opposed 'language discrimination' in international conferences and organisations which recognise only a few languages as official. Lapenna's specialism in international law accords closely with the ideas of peace and internationalism associated with Esperanto.

It was to be expected that a person such as Lapenna would, if active, wish for changes in the movement. Lapenna originally joined the IEL Executive in 1938, but became best known through the Balkan periodical *Internacia Kulturo* and at the 1947 Berne World Congress. Lapenna had been severely critical of the neutrality of the newly constituted UEA, for fear that Fascism might not be condemned. He was supported in this view by the Balkan Esperantists. He had also expressed criticisms of the basis of the new constitution, which he did not see as democratic.[6] The most significant criticisms were made by Lapenna about the Berne World Congress. In a long article in *Internacia Kulturo*, Lapenna criticised the failure of the Congress to support his motion on Fascism, as mentioned in the previous chapter. He was also critical of the kind of orientation which a number of members present associated with Esperanto:

Among those present [at Berne] were only a few workers, and a similarly small number of intellectuals. As far as I know there was not a single peasant present. Thus in social composition the congress was largely petty-bourgeois with a strong and accented religious-mystical-spiritualistic colour, with a mass of naivities and frivolities, which only compromise the cause of the International Language.

· *Proofs*: in the official congress programme, as *separate points in the programme*, there are mentioned altogether thirteen religious services. . . .

. . . .Further, as *specialist meetings* are mentioned in the official congress programme, among others, meetings of Christians, Barrier-Breakers, stamp-collectors, Rotarians, To Abundance, Spiritualists, Oxford Group, Baha'i, Christians again, spiritualists again, etc. According to *Plena Vortaro* a specialism (*fako*) is a separate branch of science, art, industry, etc. . . . I have yet to hear that there exist, for instance, specialists on Spiritualism!

. . . .Would it not be possible to prevent such "specialist meetings" during our congress, *or at least eliminate them from the official programme*? Do people still not understand that one of the most serious hindrances to the dissemination of Esperanto among serious people is exactly that strange mysticism which incessantly encircles the movement? In the eyes of the masses we make a laughing-stock of ourselves and the cause of International Language by such frivolities.

. . . .Finally, there was certainly no shortage of cranks (*stranguloj*). On the contrary, they were abundant. One woman with green stockings explained to me that every lady Esperantist should wear only green stockings for propaganda purposes. One came to the ball in a dress, like a nightdress, with masses of green stars, large, medium and small. I saw a loud yellow tie with an even louder green star woven into it. In general, one could see stars everywhere; on the chest, in the hair, on belts, rings, etc.

People will say again that everyone has the right to dress as he wishes. Certainly; but could we not kindly request such cranks not to hinder the spread of Esperanto by their standpoint and external appearance? If that does not work, have we not at least the right to make a mockery of them, since they make a mockery of Esperanto?

. . . .[On proposals for promotion of Esperanto] Among the many "proposals", a remarkable one came from Vilĉjo Verda [Will Green] (England). His prescription is: at the beginning of the propaganda season all Esperantists gather together in the town church, where they take part in a service. Afterwards they should go in procession through the town with the green insignia and carry green flags.[7]

As a linguistic movement, Esperanto has been attached to a wide range of different ideologies and activities. As early as the Second World Congress in Geneva special arrangements were made for meetings of subgroups of this kind. There has, too, been since Zamenhof's time a stress on individual effort, which has meant that any activity for Esperanto in any direction has been seen as worthy of approval. Members have thus promoted Esperanto in any manner which accorded with their conscience and abilities, and with the opportunities which presented themselves. Thus, over a period of time, many individual Esperantists have associated Esperanto with a wide range of causes, not all of which have prestige in the wider society. Religious, quasi-religious, and other mystical aspirations have been particularly popular. The Esperanto movement had generally tended to be apolitical, concentrating on the conversion of individuals and through them the world. This, together with certain millenarian tendencies about the final victory of Esperanto, has made Esperanto compatible with a wide range of religious aspirations. Esperantists frequently display a quasi-religious fervour in their support for Esperanto and wish to indicate this in personal adornment. Though only a minority may deviate to this extent from orthodox conventions, those that do so tend to attract public attention and thus Esperanto is associated with 'crankiness'.[8] An important feature of postwar policy of UEA became the promotion of Esperanto in newly formed intergovernmental organisations, such as the United Nations and particularly UNESCO. Emphasis was placed on the respectability and prestige of Esperanto as a language of cultural exchange. A constant threat to this policy were certain 'cranks' who would not comply with official directives that Esperanto should appear respectable.

A related point of conflict with more traditional attitudes in the movement was the new conception of the organisation of UEA. The new contract between UEA and IEL was a much closer and more stable link between the conflicting perceptions of organisation than previous arrangements had been. Helsinki had merely seen the formation of a confederation of organisations that already existed. Cologne represented a more monolithic structure, but was too one-sided to remain stable. The new contract between IEL and UEA incorporated a balance between different interpretations. A constitutional document on the basis of the principles of the agreement between UEA and IEL was accepted in 1948.[9] In 1955 certain changes were introduced, of which one involved the much-disputed question of the site of UEA headquarters. The 1948 constitution had provided for two offices, the Central Office and the Geneva Office. The former was concerned with administrative matters and propaganda, while the latter dealt with publications, archives, and the delegate service. In 1955 the revised constitution merely provided for a 'service centre' in Geneva.[10] This change was accepted by UEA members at the time, and by Hans Jakob, administrator of the Geneva Office. But in 1965 Jakob claimed that certain details of the UEA–IEL agreement were not being properly observed and that UEA was misusing certain capital left to it. This dispute eventually involved litigation; but Jakob obtained hardly any support for his stand and the dispute terminated with his death in 1967. In 1958 UEA was accepted in the law of The Netherlands as a legal entity in its own right, enabling it to be sued directly instead of through its officials. The 1958 structure of the committee allowed national representation *and* representation of the delegates. The committee was formed of Committee Members *A*, elected by affiliated organisations (mostly national, but neutral specialist organisations, such as the Railwaymens' Esperantists, could also elect a Committee Member *A*); Committee Members *B*, elected by the delegates (the delegates themselves being chosen in consultation with the national associations, where one was affiliated); and Committee Members *C*, elected by Committee Members *A* and *B*. The committee was responsible for electing an Executive of approximately eight members, including the President.[11]

In this scheme, national representation and representation of the delegates were combined. Members of an affiliated national association automatically became 'associate members' of the new UEA; a higher subscription was payable for full membership, entitling the member to UEA publications and to service on the committee. It was not essential for a full member of UEA to be a member of his national association. Since 1948 there has been a strong emphasis on UEA as the sole representative of the neutral Esperanto movement, symbolised in the motto 'Unity is strength'. In the 1958 Mainz World Congress, the President, Professor Giorgio Canuto, stressed that the Esperanto movement and UEA were now identical.[12] Together with the emphasis on UEA as sole representative of the neutral Esperantists there has been a stress on the importance of democracy. Ideas of this kind have been articulated particularly by Lapenna who, although not President till 1964, was chosen to make an address at most world congresses since 1950. Lapenna has pointed out that decisions must be democratically arrived at, but that after the decision has been accepted all must abide by majority rule. At Mainz in 1958 his speech included the following words:

If we are unified, even if not very numerous, we can impose our standpoint on the world. We need still greater unity of conviction as to the rightness of our way, unity of action on that right way, and unity in the observation of decisions taken. That does not mean to say that everyone must have the same opinion. On the contrary, this means to say that all of us should freely give our opinion on the methods to be applied, that we should discuss widely and profoundly, even at length, all aspects of our action, but after those discussions and after we make decisions in the most democratic manner, we should all observe them and help in their realisation with all our strength. Only in such a manner will we go forward. Only such is the true meaning of our internal democracy, which is not imaginable without self-discipline.[13]

The committee of UEA advocated the idea of a monolithic structure with all policy decisions made through the central organs. Disciplined adherence to official policies has been expected of members. There has also been a specific attempt to formulate appropriate policies for the action of UEA. This policy was consolidated in the acceptance of the First Basic Work Programme of UEA in 1955,[14] and the Second Basic Work Plan in 1962.[15] Both of these stressed the unified nature of UEA policy. They indicated the necessity for parallel action along all lines suggested for the plans to succeed. The work plans spelt out in considerable detail the kind of action appropriate for UEA. Some felt that such policies left little room for individual initiative and questioned their desirability. Arising from discussion of the 1962 Work Plan, Lapenna replied as follows to such criticisms, at the 1962 Copenhagen World Congress:

During the discussion some raised the question of whether the Work Plan had a compulsory character for all, including the organisations and individual members which made up UEA, or whether it was compulsory only for the central organs of the Association. If we are to understand the word "compulsory" in the sense of forcible imposition with the help of constables, then obviously the Work Plan is compulsory for nobody. But if we are to conceive correctly the causes, goals and methods of organised work in its entirety, then the Work Plan, accepted by the committee according to the constitution, and after exhaustive discussion, is morally compulsory for all: at least to the same degree as the constitution and rules of the Association.[16]

Though some resentment was evident about the high degree of centralisation, there was much support for UEA's policies. Results of the postwar policies have been impressive, not least in the growth of membership figures. The membership of UEA, including associate members, grew from 17,707 in 1948 to 32,202 in 1964 (since when it has tended to level off). The new period also saw a marked expansion of activities of UEA. In 1949 Lapenna was commissioned to engage in a lecture tour through a number of European countries, and this gave him the opportunity to familiarise himself with the Esperanto organisations in many countries. He was also able to encourage support for the policies of UEA. There has further been a concerted attempt to raise the intellectual and cultural level of the movement. Since 1925 a series of lectures on academic subjects, known as the 'International Summer University', had been a feature of world congresses, but there had been no systematic rules for ascertaining appropriate academic standards for the speakers. In 1949 rules were set up requiring the lectures to be given, generally speaking, by university teachers.[17] A new development (though with some spasmodic counterparts in the past) was the Fine Art Competition, for which rules were drawn up and the first competition held at the 1950 Paris World Congress. The rules provide for sections in prose, drama, and poetry (original and translated).[18] Theatrical presentations had been a feature of Esperanto congresses ever since Boulogne, but after 1957 attempts were made to raise the standard of performances. A further development (though again not totally new) was the 'Oratory Competition for Youth' held annually between 1949 and 1974. This development, designed to produce better public speakers of Esperanto, has been particularly strongly supported by Lapenna, who drafted the rules[19] and in 1960 presented a silver cup, the 'Ivo Lapenna Cup', on which the name of the winner was inscribed each year.

UEA generally and Lapenna in particular stressed the gravity of raising the cultural level of Esperanto. Among other things this involved the production of good works of literature in Esperanto. At the 1954 Haarlem World Congress, Lapenna made the subject of his inaugural address 'The cultural value of the international language'. He observed that

Languages in the true sense of the word are ordinarily born firstly as spoken languages and only afterwards, over their long period of evolution, are they also transformed into written, literary languages. The International Language can jump this long evolutionary process and, using the cultural heritage of the richest national languages, it can begin life immediately as a literary language. Dr. Zamenhof understood very well that a language without its own literature cannot have cultural value nor can it play the role of a general instrument of communication and thought in all spheres of international life.[20]

He remarked that all literary work in Esperanto enriched the language and filled it with comprehensive, high-quality cultural content. As a subject for attack he chose those who would reject the idea of Esperanto as a cultural language:

. . . .there still exist people, even those of high standing in the cultural hierarchy, who with a superior arrogance characteristic of all important people, assert, light-heartedly and without embarrassment, that Esperanto is not a cultural language. They do not understand that as such cultural and noncultural languages do not exist, but that the cultural character of any language depends exclusively on the cultural values created in it. They sing odes to their own national languages and even more so to those of the great peoples and completely forget that what we now admire in those languages was once considered a very simple primitive matter. . . .

But let us leave this! What is important above all for us is the undoubted fact that Esperanto is a social reality and that, besides, it has already become a cultural language.[21]

He concluded stressing the importance of development of Esperanto culture and of paying more attention to cultural activities. At subsequent congresses Lapenna returned to this theme.

In order to promote Esperanto more successfully, systematic documentation was begun. In 1952, at Lapenna's suggestion, was founded the Research and Documentation Centre (with its office in Lapenna's house, Lapenna as Honorary Director, and Lapenna's wife as professional secretary). The Centre has been concerned with encouragement of research into matters relating to Esperanto, collection of important documents and statistics, and, on the basis of this information, provision of a wide range of documents in languages other than Esperanto, mostly English. Such documents are then circulated to international organisations and other institutions where Esperanto is promoted. The Centre has also published books[22] giving information on aspects of Esperanto, and in 1969 it began to issue *La Monda Lingvo-Problemo* (later *Lingvaj Problemoj kaj Lingvo-Planado*), an academic journal on language problems which publishes articles in the major national languages with summaries in Esperanto. This periodical accepts contributions from non-Esperantists. Apart from the Research and Documentation Centre, other evidence of planned action has been apparent. This includes the provision of a press service at every world congress since 1949, and the establishment in 1963 of an Institute for Esperanto in Commerce and Industry, a separate body from UEA but with interlocking membership of its executive and that of UEA.[23] Commissions and Commissioners have been established for a wide range of other activities.

On a more abstract level, UEA policy during this period has been devoted to raising the prestige of Esperanto and the movement. Such was the ultimate aim of the basic work plans. An important facet of this policy has been to encourage the election of persons of high prestige in the outside world to the guiding positions in the movement. Lapenna remarked in his speech at the 1958 Mainz World Congress:

We can be proud that at the top of UEA where at one time we had our eminent Professor Privat, today we have our eminent Professor Canuto, an important specialist in his subject, known not only in Italy, but also in the world, who has just received the highest honour of the Italian government for his merits in the educational field. It is superfluous to say that persons in such high social positions contribute to the raising of the prestige both of UEA and Esperanto. What I have said about UEA applies in the same way to our national associations and other organisations. The more prestigious people are found in positions of authority in our organisations, the higher prestige our move-ment enjoys.[24]

In what represents a break from the tradition of the movement, which had put its trust in the plain man, Lapenna went on to stress the importance of support for Esperanto from those in public life. A corollary of this policy has been the avoidance of any suggestion that Esperanto might be subversive of certain established values. According to the Constitution, the goals of UEA are to be realised only by legally permitted means, wherever UEA operates. Attention has also been paid to the splitting off of administrative roles from policy making. In 1955 a distinction was drawn between the gen-eral administration of the Central Office on the one hand and public relations on the other. The former task was put in charge of a full-time employee, the latter being the duty of a 'Secretary-General' who was chosen from the Executive. Lapenna was the first Secretary-General. In the early 1950s, doubts had been expressed about the desirability of having UEA headquarters in Heronsgate, rather remote from the public view. Other factors such as the difficulty of finding employees were taken into account, but one factor was prestige. Thus, after attempts to transfer the head-quarters to London had failed owing to the high cost of property there, the Central Office was transferred in 1955 to Rotterdam. At the world congresses the prestige of UEA has been reflected in the kind of buildings in which some chief meetings have been held. At the 1971 London World Congress, the inauguration was held in the Royal Festival Hall and the ball in the Lyceum Ballroom.

Apart from a general suspicion of 'cranks', certain specific criticisms were made by the leaders of UEA when it was considered that the dictates of general policy were not being properly observed. In 1956 a radio broadcast on Esperanto, in Britain, was criticised for not being properly aimed at intellectuals, and for failing to stress the importance of UNESCO, world peace, science, and culture.[25] General guidelines for promoting Esperanto were drawn up in the 'Fundamental principles of information about the international language', accepted at a meeting of representatives of information departments of various national Esperanto associations at Frostavallen, Sweden. These principles, known as the 'Principles of Frostavallen', received wide publicity, and were printed in UEA's rule book. Apart from discussing the organisation of promotional activity for Esperanto, there is a section relating to the quality of such information:

Chief errors:
    (a) Calling the language artificial, auxiliary, green, etc.;
    (b) Unnecessarily mentioning various projects for a common language.
    (c) Not distinguishing clearly between Esperanto as a living language and those projects, if circumstances necessitate speaking about them.
    (d) Using Esperanto expressions in texts in national languages, e.g. *samideano, Majstro, verdstelanoj* [followers of the green star] , etc.
    (e) Writing about Esperanto in incorrect national language.
    (f) Calling information about Esperanto 'propaganda'.
    (g) Giving the Esperanto movement a sectarian character (too many stars and flags, singing of the Hymn and other songs at unsuitable times and places, eccentricities in dress during congresses and other public meetings, etc.). *Errors in information have turned tens of thousands of people away from Esperanto and have greatly jeopardised the movement in many milieus.*
    (h) In order to raise quality it is necessary to accept everything which shows the cultural and practical value of the language: literature, scientific work, the International Summer University, Fine Art Competitions, the Network of Delegates, especially help in travelling and in professional work. *The dignity of all public arrangements should reflect the respect which the Esperantists themselves have for the international language.*

Esperantists are also urged by the Principles to have the courage of their convictions and to speak out in support of Esperanto and against erroneous impressions. They should always wear the green star, but only one.[26]

Lapenna in particular stressed the importance of the Principles. UEA's centralised work observed them closely, but the same did not necessarily apply to national associations, local groups, or individuals. In 1965 a series of articles appeared in *Esperanto* on the role of the local groups in the realisation of the Work Plan of UEA. In an article contributed to this series by Lapenna, he stressed that the 'errors' in promoting Esperanto had been considerably diminished but not eliminated.[27] Similarly in 1967 he pointed out that the Principles had not been fully observed, particularly in the matter of making Esperanto seem like a religious cult.[28]

If there was some resistance to the prestige policy, it also achieved important results. Particular attention was paid throughout this period to the relationship with UNESCO, though in the first instance attention was drawn to the United Nations generally.[29] A petition, urging the UN to take Esperanto seriously and encourage its spread, was begun after the war, and by the end of 1949 it had been signed by 895,432 individuals and 492 organisations with a combined total of 15,454,780 members. Signatories included Vincent Auriol, ex-President of France, and the prime ministers of The Netherlands, Austria, Poland, and Czechoslovakia. The petition was transferred to the UN Secretariat in 1950, who in turn referred it to UNESCO as the competent body to deal with such questions. Eventually, in 1952, the UNESCO Secretariat suggested as part of the proceedings of the General Conference for 1953 and 1954 that the Director-General be authorised to study the language problem and means of solving it. A document was produced on the subject and made reference to the petition, but was noncommittal in its approach.[30] However, two observers from UEA were permitted to attend the 1952 General Conference of UNESCO. One of these was Lapenna. A special document was sent by the Research and Documentation Centre to all delegates to this conference. During the proceedings of the programme commission Lapenna was able to speak to the matter, suggesting a resolution including the section 'UNESCO has every reason to give its attention to the results realised by the language Esperanto for the progress of intellectual and moral relations between the peoples'. The Swiss delegation supported a similar resolution at the General Conference, though the final res-

olution accepted merely authorised the Director-General to communicate the petition to member states and to undertake preparatory work to enable the next General Conference to decide what
action should be taken.

Preparation for the next UNESCO General Conference, in 1954,
made for great activity in UEA and particularly its Research and
Documentation Centre. Detailed advice on appropriate strategies
was circulated to national Esperanto organisations. A comprehensive dossier on the history of Esperanto in the world was compiled
and delivered to the UNESCO Secretariat, at its request. Prep-
arations were made for an Esperanto exhibition in Montevideo,
where the meeting was to be held. UNESCO sent an observer to the
1953 World Esperanto Congress in Zagreb. At the 1954 Haarlem
World Congress the general theme was 'The international language
before UNESCO'. Just before the Montevideo conference the Research and Documentation Centre produced a special document
showing how Esperanto could contribute to the goals and activities
of UNESCO. This was distributed to all delegates at the conference.
The UNESCO Secretariat had produced its own report on the
petition, including replies from member states.[31] The petition had
a mixed reception. UEA was again invited to send an observer to
the conference, and Lapenna was chosen. Apart from the petition,
UNESCO had also to consider an application from UEA for the
status of an organisation in consultative relations. After discussion
in the UNESCO Executive this particular proposal was accepted
unanimously by its Committee on Administration and eventually
by the General Conference as a whole.

On the matter of the petition, the efforts of UEA had succeeded
in impressing a Mexican delegate; at a meeting of the Committee
on the Programme and Budget, Mexico proposed a resolution
favourable to Esperanto. The proposal was opposed by Professor
Andreas Blinkenberg, a Danish linguist, who ridiculed the language
and declared it lacking in cultural value. Although Lapenna quickly
replied to such criticisms,[32] the vote went against the Mexican
resolution. However, important procedural errors were discovered
in the meeting, and Mexico was nonetheless able to present a resolution in the final Plenary Session. The text of the resolution read:

The General Conference, having discussed the Report of the Director-General on the international petition in favour of Esperanto.

1. Takes note of the results attained by Esperanto in the field of international intellectual relations and in the rapprochement of the peoples of the world.

2. Recognises that these results correspond with the aims and ideals of UNESCO;

3. Authorises the Director-General to follow current development in the use of Esperanto in education, science and culture, and, to this end, to co-operate with the Universal Esperanto Association in matters concerning both organisations;

4. Takes note that several Member States have announced their readiness to introduce or expand the teaching of Esperanto in their schools and higher educational establishments, and requests the Member States to keep the Director-General informed of the results attained in this field.[33]

The resolution and the granting of consultative relations were greeted with jubilation by the Esperantists. *Esperanto* in 1955 carried many enthusiastic articles. Lapenna described the decision as indicating that for the first time the educational, scientific, and cultural value of Esperanto had been officially recognised.[34] Hans Jakob, editor of *Esperanto*, regarded it as 'the beginning of a new epoch'.[35] The decision was even described as 'victory' (*la venko*), implying that UEA had achieved its aims. Meanwhile there was much eulogising of Lapenna for his role in this success; he was described as the 'hero of Montevideo'. The Basic Work Plan presented by Lapenna to the UEA Executive saw the decision of UNESCO as the beginning of a new stage of official recognition. The 1955 Bologna World Congress expressed satisfaction with the UNESCO resolution and suggested that steps to bring the peoples nearer to one another could not ignore Esperanto.

The status of being in consultative relations involves reciprocal information and the right to representation at conferences. It meant that UEA had the right to be consulted in matters relating to its own particular areas of competence. In return, UEA had the responsibility to promote the aims of UNESCO and to report on its own activities. UEA took promotion of the aims of UNESCO very seriously and presented them as identical with the values enshrined in Esperanto. This provided a politically neutral subject which could be freely written about in the official international publications of UEA. Even certain aspects of UEA's presentation of itself appear to have been modelled on UNESCO or the UN. The office of Secretary-General, established in 1955, is reminiscent of such a position in the UN. The documents issued by the Research Documentation Centre of UEA are similar in appearance to UNESCO documents; and, after the Montevideo decision, the appearance of the periodical *Esperanto* began increasingly to resemble that of the *UNESCO Courier*. UEA was in fact regarded in some circles as promoting not only its own aims, but the ideology of UNESCO (*Uneskismo*, 'UNESCO-ism').[36] In 1960 UNESCO divided up organisations in consultative relations into three categories, A, B, and C. Only a small number of organisations achieved the A status, but UEA succeeded in obtaining a position in category B. There was occasional discussion of Esperanto in the *UNESCO Courier*.[37] In collaboration with a UNESCO project UEA issued a series of books entitled 'East/West'. These contained translations of classical works of Eastern and Western culture.[38] UEA had also participated in occasions such as Human Rights Year and International Cooperation Year (and, more recently, in International Women's Year and the International Year of the Child). In 1959, the centenary of his birth, Zamenhof was named by UNESCO as one of the 'great personalities of humanity'.

The success obtained with UNESCO encouraged UEA to try again to influence the UN. The 1964 Hague World Congress pledged support for the UN's work for peace but drew attention to language difficulties as an obstacle to international cooperation. This Congress passed a resolution on the subject, and this became the text of a new proposal, which in 1965 was circulated to members and others on a sheet with spaces for signatures. These were collected over a period of two years. By 25 January 1967, 925,034 individual signatures had been collected, together with 3,846 organisations with a total of 72,892,000 members. Signatories included the President of Austria, the prime ministers of Denmark, Iceland, and Norway, and others with diverse claims for distinction in public life, ranging from the author Upton Sinclair to the Patriarch of the Bulgarian Orthodox Church. A delegation to the UN, led by Lapenna, presented the proposal to the Secretariat in New York on 6 October 1966. With the petition were presented a memorandum in support of the proposal, various documents of the Research and

Documentation Centre, and some examples of Esperanto literature. However, the proposal was never communicated by the Secretariat to member states. Despite sustained and highly sophisticated pressure put on the UN Secretariat by UEA, it appears that certain members of the Secretariat prevented the proposal from going any further.

UEA had continued to relate its own ideology to that of the UN and UNESCO. In 1968, Human Rights Year, UEA issued a seal for letters inscribed in Esperanto 'For the International Language – Against Language Discrimination – Year of Human Rights'. The concept of opposition to language discrimination was particularly emphasised in activities of the Esperanto movement. The Declaration of Human Rights is opposed to discrimination on the grounds of language, and it is argued that the practice of having official and working languages in the UN and related bodies is contrary to human rights.[39] This practice discriminates in favour of those who can speak their own language and against those who must work in a foreign language. At the same time, the number of official and working languages in the UN and its subsidiary organisations has steadily increased.[40] Thus for both idealistic and practical reasons UEA had hoped for acceptance of Esperanto by the UN, believing that Esperanto is the only feasible solution to the problem.

During the development of this policy, Lapenna was well known as the chief architect of the postwar strategy of UEA, and he communicated his ideas at world congresses through his imposing oratory. As early as 1950 it was observed of his address to the Paris World Congress that 'everyone became conscious that we had found a new star of the oratorical firmament'.[41] Lapenna gave the opening address at most world congresses, though only in 1964 did he become President of UEA. Lapenna showed tireless and sophisticated activity in the Research and Documentation Centre, the work plans, and in promoting Esperanto in the UN. He became a very popular figure, acclaimed from the congress floor whenever he entered the hall.

Lapenna obtained a further mandate for certain policies at the 1968 Madrid World Congress. Here he initially resigned but, after pressure to continue in office, agreed to do so provided that certain fundamental theses were accepted as the basis for the future work of UEA. These theses stressed the importance of conviction, not

defeatism, and pointed out that the evolutionary process was leading to Esperanto as the answer to the world language problem.
They indicated that unity was essential; this would involve linguistic discipline, constitutional action, and diligent effort through
UEA. These theses were approved of with applause, and Lapenna
had a mandate to continue and strengthen the policies with which
he had been previously associated.

Support for UNESCO in this way did not represent a sharp
break with tradition in the movement. The constitution of UEA
expressed support for human rights; as well as directly aiming at
spreading the use of Esperanto, the constitution stated that UEA
aimed 'to facilitate all kinds of spiritual and material relations
between men, without regard to nationality, race, religion, politics,
or language'. As a means of attaining such aims, the 1955 constitution outlines creation of a link of solidarity between members;
developing understanding and respect for foreign peoples; common
action of Esperanto organisations; creating international services;
calling world congresses; and any other legal means.[42] These aims
were left substantially intact after the revision of the constitution
in 1979. The aims for which UEA stands compare very closely
indeed with those of UNESCO, whose policy it is to

... contribute to peace and security by promoting collaboration among the
nations through education, science and culture in order to further universal
respect for justice, for the rule of law, and for human rights and fundamental
freedoms which are affirmed for the peoples of the world without distinction
of race, sex, language and religion, by the Charter of the United Nations.[43]

Thus the diffuse goals of the movement were such as to be
able to accommodate 'UNESCO-ism' without difficulty. Lapenna
articulated the link between the goals of UEA and UNESCO, and
this link was very widely accepted. There were, however, some
elements of dissent. Some would take issue with the policy of
making the aims of Esperanto accord with internationally accepted
values, believing that it had a more radical message. Others would
object to the amount of attention paid to UNESCO; others objected
to the centralised, monolithic, *dirigiste* conception of UEA which
had characterised Lapenna's pronouncements: Lapenna's close
association with the latter and his stress on a disciplined approach,

together with his oratorical abilities, led to accusations of dictatorship and a personality cult. Many had felt that a wider range of
options should be open to members: *A tout seigneur tout honneur*,
but another point of view would be welcome. Thus at various times
conflicts have arisen between usually small groups, or even individuals, and Lapenna and his supporters.

By far the most important of these have been the 'cranks'.
Lapenna had been very critical of 'crankiness' since the 1947
Berne World Congress, and had continued throughout the postwar years to criticise eccentricities in clothing and anything that
gave the impression of a closed, sectarian organisation. At the 1966
Budapest World Congress Lapenna still found it necessary to remark
that

What we need today is. . . not a sect of cranks in unusual clothes, but a cultural movement enjoying prestige and esteem. Fortunately we have attained
this almost one hundred per cent. But unfortunately there still exists this
"almost" which jeopardises the seriousness of our work, belittles the attain-
ments, hinders new steps and puts a brake on progress.[44]

Thus the relentless anticrank campaign did not have total success. This was noticeable earlier in the period under consideration.
A long-standing custom in world congresses has been for many members to appear at the Congress Ball in national costumes. This was
discouraged after the war, but by the early 1950s was beginning to
revive. Cranks, moreover, can answer back. They will have a strong
conviction of the rightness of their own deviant outlook. In particular, when confronted with arguments that their activities can
jeopardise negotiations with UNESCO and governmental organisations, they reply suggesting that support from these organisations is of little importance and might even be dangerous. They
are also impervious to any suggestion that smacks of 'party discipline'. Notable among representatives of such a point of view is
Verdiro (pseudonym meaning 'Telltruth', in fact John Leslie, professional secretary of the British Esperanto Association, 1951–1967).
Verdiro expressed his views regularly in the weekly Esperanto
section of *The Socialist Leader*, organ of the Independent Labour
Party. Verdiro was not in fact a socialist, but rather a supporter of
social credit, and was also described as an 'anarchist, freethinking,

patriotic Scot'. His articles criticised a variety of positions taken by Lapenna. He objected to supporting UNESCO, regarding it as a bulwark of financial capitalism. He appealed to the higher value of political neutrality of UEA in support of this standpoint. He also opposed formality in dress and defended deviations. He was critical of oratory, reminding readers that Hitler too was an orator. He praised the informal equality among Esperantists of all walks of life and criticised the importance attached to attracting those famous in other spheres.[45]

Not all members of the UEA Executive shared Lapenna's views. Hans Jakob, who had a mouthpiece for his views by virtue of being editor of *Esperanto*, expressed his own disagreements. Jakob stressed the importance of the value-oriented interpretation of Esperanto but was less specific than Lapenna on the means of attaining this ideal. He merely expressed the hope that the ease of personal contact and service through Esperanto would help mutual understanding on the level of ideas.[46] He suggested that there was a mystique, an atmosphere at congresses, which even rationalists notice.[47] In particular Jakob suggested that cranks are well intentioned and enthusiastic; he considered it the Esperantists' duty to be indulgent and educate them rather than condemn them.[48]

In 1966 appeared the first issue of the periodical[49] of the *Instituto por Oficialigo de Esperanto* [IOE, Institute for Officialisation of Esperanto]. This organisation, which survived till 1972, acted as a 'ginger group' to UEA. It particularly aimed to bring Esperanto to the notice of the outside world, and to break the 'green curtain' which it saw as surrounding Esperanto. The publications of this organisation were not however polemical in content.

Conflicts with Lapenna also came from different sources. E.L.M. Wensing, a Dutch industrialist and member of the UEA Executive, came into serious conflict with Lapenna about the values to be associated with the language. He advocated a much more norm-oriented approach, seeing the value-oriented standpoint as really part of the past history of Esperanto. He also disagreed with Lapenna about the importance of 'cultural content' in Esperanto, suggesting, for instance, that businessmen were more favourably impressed by the fact that certain firms (e.g. Philips, Fiat) produce advertising material in Esperanto than by translations of the Koran.[50]

He came into serious dispute with Lapenna on such issues and eventually left the Executive, returning on the resignation of Lapenna.

A further source of conflict was the Youth Movement. This organisation, *Tutmonda Esperantista Junulara Organizo* [TEJO, World Esperantist Youth Organisation], has origins dating to 1938, though only in 1956 did it become the official youth section of UEA. Since then, UEA members under 25 have automatically also been members of TEJO. In 1963 TEJO began to issue *Kontakto*, a quarterly periodical containing articles of wider interest rather than merely about the activities of the Esperanto movement. TEJO received much financial and moral support from UEA, which had long been concerned with its aging membership in many countries. TEJO holds its own world congresses; these are held immediately before or after the UEA congress, usually in the same or a neighbouring country, enabling TEJO members to attend both if they wish.[51]

Influenced by 1968 student activities, which were also international in character, at its congress in Tyresö (Sweden) TEJO produced in 1969 the 'Declaration of Tyresö'. This drew on ideologies popular among student movements at the time. It noted the consciousness of youth that the free development of the individual was endangered by established systems of order, which had an overstandardised view of man and allowed technology to dominate the individual. It saw language as intimately linked to other social and political phenomena. Accordingly, it saw all linguistic and cultural discrimination as something to be opposed, and pledged that TEJO would work towards such ends.[52] After the declaration, *Kontakto* began to express radical views on education, sex, the Third World, and other issues.[53] This was somewhat curbed after 1970 when, at the TEJO World Congress in Graz, two Italian Maoists continually interrupted the proceedings, calling for a 'revolutionary Esperanto movement' and at one point dropped two small incendiary devices.[54] Yet a certain radical tendency prevailed, and in particular TEJO gave its support to the struggles of minority language communities. *Kontakto* was still published by UEA, and conflict arose between UEA and TEJO about a possible threat to political neutrality; for a short time opposing definitions of neutrality were articulated, and conflict arose with Lapenna as representative of UEA. There have even been suggestions by Lapenna that the Declaration of Tyresö paved the way to a Communist takeover of TEJO and UEA.[55] It is true that in 1971 TEJO signed a contract with the World Federation of Democratic Youth, an anti-imperialist organisation based in Eastern Europe, for exchange of information.[56] Although Communists would approve of the anti-imperialist sentiments expressed by articles in *Kontakto*, this appears to have been only one of a number of forces operating. As a result of conflict with Lapenna on such issues, TEJO became a forum in which critical views of Lapenna could be expressed.

Other criticisms were expressed of Lapenna and the existing policies of UEA. *Esperanto*, the official organ of UEA, would conceal certain controversial issues, but the newspaper *Heroldo de Esperanto*, independent again in the postwar period, was under no obligation to do so. Objections from Wensing, TEJO, and other sources, together with editorial criticism, were presented in this periodical. Later, beginning in April 1973, articles in *The British Esperantist* began to express critical views; there were varying reactions, but many were prepared to defend the right to make such criticisms.

By 1974, when it was constitutionally necessary to re-elect the president of UEA, concerted opposition to Lapenna had been built up. It was planned to contest his re-election at the Hamburg World Congress, but in the event this was unnecessary as Lapenna resigned from all offices in UEA at the beginning of that Congress. Those elected to the Executive in Hamburg included Wensing and two former presidents of TEJO. After the elections Lapenna described the events as a 'putsch' which had involved the takeover of UEA by Communists and fellow travellers.[57] He formed a short-lived breakaway movement from UEA, officially describing itself as a continuation of the neutral movement. Nearly all its members soon returned to UEA. There has been no evidence for the view that UEA was set to follow a Communist line, although recruitment from Communist countries has continued to increase. Any tensions arising from this have been managed by maintaining strict neutrality in the world movement, but allowing national Esperanto organisations a considerable degree of leeway.

Nor has there been any tendency to repudiate Lapenna's contribution to the development of the movement, and the links between

UEA and UNESCO have been strengthened. This was particularly evident at the 1977 Reykjavik World Congress; in that year the Icelandic government had invited the Director-General of UNESCO, Amadou Mahtar M'Bow, on an official visit. UEA succeeded in persuading the Icelandic authorities to let this visit coincide with their World Congress. M'Bow visited the Congress and said encouraging words. UEA officials also succeeded in holding a private meeting with M'Bow in Paris in 1980, and were given to believe that his support was based on more than mere politeness. Lobbying of the UN has also continued at its secretariat in New York.

There has, however, been a broadening in the scope of activities of UEA. In particular, UEA has become conscious of its overwhelmingly European base, and attempts have been made to correct the imbalance. At the 1976 Athens World Congress a fund was set up to help the spread of Esperanto in the Third World. Lecture tours have been held by UEA officers to non-European countries, to encourage the movement where it exists. This activity has been most successful in South America, where the number of Esperantists is not insignificant. In 1978 the first international congress of Latin American Esperantists was held in Brazil, and Brasília has been chosen as the venue for the 1981 World Congress. Political factors have also helped Esperanto in certain non-European countries. In China, the movement has revived following the demise of the 'Gang of Four', while shortly before the overthrow of the Shah there was a sudden vogue for Esperanto in Iran. Reforms have been made in the organisation of UEA so as to encourage non-European members. These have included the use of airmail for sending the periodical *Esperanto* to non-European destinations; reduced subscriptions for members in poorer countries; and abolition of the constitutional provision that Executive members should preferably not live too far from the Rotterdam Central Office.

There have also been changes in the organisation of UEA. Economies have been made in staff salaries by instituting a 'volunteer service' akin to Voluntary Service Overseas, where members can give a year's service to the movement in return for living expenses and a small allowance. Not all volunteers are based in Rotterdam, thus making it possible for 'Esperanto Centres' to be established elsewhere. There has, however, also been a tendency to establish branch offices outside The Netherlands, staffed by full-time employees, though often supported by local voluntary assistance. The Antwerp Printing Centre was established in 1977, dealing with printing and distribution of the movement's literature, but also bringing in revenue by accepting outside orders. Also in 1977 a 'European Esperanto Centre' was set up in Brussels, concerned especially with lobbying the European Common Market. Lobbying the UN was finally professionalised by a decision in 1979 to open an office in New York, and a further branch is planned for Budapest.

Certain constitutional changes were implemented at the 1979 Lucerne World Congress, notably in the direction of greater democratisation. In future, Committee Members B will be elected by UEA members as a whole, and not just by the delegates. Proposals have also been accepted to restrict the power and period of office of the president. It has also been agreed to allow a maximum number of committee members per country.

There has also been a tendency to a more pragmatic outlook, an acceptance of the fact that Esperanto, even if officially accepted, would not provide a solution to *all* language problems overnight. It has even been permitted in the periodical *Esperanto* to insert advertisements for details of proposals to reform Esperanto orthography, provided that they are inserted in the small advertisements columns and not on full pages.

In summary it can be said that the postwar policies of UEA, associated with Lapenna, have been concerned to relate the values of the 'inner idea' to internationally acceptable values. Esperanto is worldwide, but its particular strength has lain in Europe, and peace in Europe has been a significant step on the road to establishment of the values of Esperanto. At least in theory, if not in practice, the UN represents a commitment to common values, including peace, world friendship, and human rights:

The first purpose of the United Nations is declared to be the maintenance of international peace and security. No government would publicly dissociate itself from the principle that the maintenance of international peace and security is desirable and that to this end individual states should refrain from the use of force. It is significant that even the opposing parties in the "cold war" profess fervently their loyalty to peace, protest that they have no aggressive intentions, and justify their armaments solely on the grounds of self-defence.[58]

Although there are parallels between UEA's action towards the League of Nations and the United Nations, UEA has placed much more confidence in the latter than the former. UEA supported interest taken in Esperanto by the League, but never incorporated the League's values into its own ideology. With the more firmly based United Nations, UEA has been able to express explicit support for the organisation without feeling that it would go against political neutrality. The current of opinion in support of postwar reconstruction encouraged the efforts of the Esperantists, but the Esperanto movement too had to reconstruct itself, having previously attempted to compromise with Fascism. This situation gave the opportunity for a new ideologue to present himself, and Lapenna filled this role. Zamenhof had previously been influential as a moral leader of the Esperantists, but his position rested on his charisma as creator of the language. Lapenna, by contrast, depended for his legitimacy more on his personal charisma. He also successfully built on the value-oriented position adopted by Zamenhof, but related this diffuse ideology to more specific organisations and institutions characteristic of the postwar period. Yet there was always a latent opposition. Esperanto is for everyone, the Boulogne Declaration states, and Esperantists are free to interpret the 'inner idea' as they wish, Zamenhof later went on to point out. Characteristically, members of Esperanto organisations have tended to emphasise the intrinsic satisfactions derived from participation in the movement. The movement has often been seen as expressive rather than instrumental, and the efforts of individuals have been valued rather than support for established institutions. UNESCO was particularly seen as the official intergovernmental organisation with aims compatible with Esperanto. UNESCO was indeed prepared to support the ideals of the Esperanto movement: but it was inclined to support the expressive functions of Esperanto, as a contribution towards its own aims, rather than going further and using the language itself. Both before and after the decision of Montevideo, UEA adopted the tactics of a pressure group. As such this was likely to require a disciplined approach of the kind proposed by Lapenna: yet it was always open for dissidents to appeal to the tradition of the movement to legitimise their own point of view. Thus the specific point of conflict arose between 'cranks' and those seeking international respectability.

POSTSCRIPT TO CHAPTER 9: ESPERANTO AND THE 'COLD WAR'

A suggestion at the 1947 Berne World Congress that capitalism should be condemned as well as Fascism made for fears that UEA would become aligned to one side or the other in the coming 'cold war'. In *Esperanto* for November 1947, Jakob urged members not to take sides.[59] Esperanto often met with considerable success in countries where Communism was established after the Second World War. Frequently in such countries Esperanto had been associated with radical currents of opinion in the recent past, and particularly with opposition to Fascism. In all smaller Communist countries (except the German Democratic Republic, Albania, and Rumania), Esperanto gained considerable ground after the war. A new source of Communist support was China. Here too Esperanto had been associated with revolutionary ideas, and Esperantists had previously been active in denouncing Japanese imperialism in their publications.[60] Mao Tse-Tung in 1939 expressed approval for Esperanto provided that it was associated with internationalism and revolution. In Yugoslavia Tito was able to speak some Esperanto. Various periodicals began to be published in the new Communist countries, notably *El Popola Ĉinio* [From People's China] and *Nuntempa Bulgario* [Bulgaria Today], illustrated propaganda magazines begun in 1950 and 1957 respectively. The people's democracies in Europe suffered from the fact that there was no flourishing Esperanto movement in the Soviet Union; thus at varous times Esperanto was discouraged or forbidden, though Poland and Yugoslavia succeeded in maintaining an Esperanto movement with a continued existence. It was not always possible for Esperantists in Communist countries to be members of UEA and, apart from politics, exchange control has continued to make full participation difficult.

On the other side of the 'cold war', support for Esperanto by Communist countries was viewed with considerable suspicion.[61] This was first noted in 1949 when an American source began circulating anonymous pamphlets against Lapenna. By 1951 this campaign appeared in print, and the growth of Esperanto in Communist countries was viewed with disfavour in articles in the *American Esperanto Magazine*. One article suggested that it was not surprising that Esperanto was illegal in the Soviet Union since it can 'punch holes in the Iron Curtain'. Although Esperanto is neutral, it continued, it is also democratic, enabling people to speak directly to one another, and thus is a threat to totalitarianism.[62] In the same issue the point was put more forcibly: 'We declare to the world that we cannot be "neutral" between good and bad, democracy and absolutism, freedom and slavery, America and the Soviet Union'.

This article, written by G.A. Connor,[63] went on to quote Zamenhof's favourable impressions of the United States, which he visited for the 1910 Washington World Congress.[64] The campaign soon became widened to a full-scale attack on 'Communist infiltration', particularly in UEA. Although Lapenna had left Yugoslavia, disillusioned, he was nonetheless accused of taking a Communist stand on the UEA committee; likewise other Yugoslavian members. Connor acted as secretary of the Esperanto Association of North America (EANA) which was viewed with suspicion by UEA for making such attacks and for transgressing the principle of political neutrality. As this organisation had succumbed to McCarthyite pressure, a new organisation, the *Esperanto-Ligo por Norda Ameriko* [Esperanto League for North America] was founded, and was recognised by UEA in 1953. This was continually denounced by EANA as Communist. UEA imposed sanctions on EANA, such as refusing to deal with its publications, and directed member states to do the same. EANA stepped up its propaganda against Lapenna and the UEA committee, the latter being regarded as a Communist front by virtue of the presence of a number of Yugoslavians.

The final break with UEA came in 1956, when EANA resolved at a business meeting to view the growth of interest in Esperanto in Communist countries with concern. It further pointed out that Communist partisans dominate the official Esperanto movement and threaten its foundations. The resolution also gave support for the stand against this development taken by the *American Esperanto Magazine*, and urged the UEA committee to be aware of the situation. The meeting further adopted an amendment to the constitution, which would now refuse membership to Communists and to 'those who believe in the overthrow of the government of the United States by force and violence'.[65]

At the 1956 Copenhagen World Congress, UEA reacted by condemning the attacks by the *American Esperanto Magazine* on

UEA and particularly Lapenna, with whom it expressed sympathy and solidarity. Rigorous neutrality was reaffirmed. A committee was set up to consider the question, and its outcome was that Connor was expelled from UEA, in accordance with the disciplinary procedure outlined in the constitution. The rules allow expulsion, after an inquiry, of those who 'evidently work against the goals of UEA'. This is the only time that the rule has ever been invoked. Machinery was set in motion to expel EANA, but this proved unnecessary since the organisation resigned from UEA in any case. Action against UEA continued for a short period but declined with the falling off of McCarthyism.

In Communist countries, there are now affiliated Esperanto movements in Bulgaria, Czechoslovakia, the German Democratic Republic, Hungary, Poland, and Yugoslavia. There are a small number of individual members of UEA in the Soviet Union, where the large number of unaffiliated organisations have recently succeeded in forming a national association. A Soviet Esperantist Youth Movement was formed in 1969, and the Association of Soviet Esperantists in 1979. In Rumania, Esperanto has been little developed because linguists who advised on official policy have viewed Esperanto unfavourably, but the situation has changed recently. Finally, in Cuba the national Esperanto association obtained official recognition in 1979, though before that Esperanto had been widely used as a means of communication between Cubans and Bulgarian and Czechoslovakian technical advisers.

In Communist countries Esperanto depends for its fortunes very much on the extent of state support. If support is strong, as in Bulgaria, facilities and subsidies will be provided, but if there is official indifference or hostility the Esperantists have difficulty in organising themselves independently. China has long used Esperanto for external propaganda, and an internal movement was allowed to exist until the Cultural Revolution. After the Cultural Revolution internal activities were checked, and some leading Esperantists were imprisoned. Internal activities have now been resumed.

UEA maintains a policy of political neutrality, but accepts that certain statements can be neutral from the point of view of one country but not from another's. Publications of affiliated movements in Communist countries are allowed to praise their own achievements but not to attack either the principle of neutrality of

UEA or the policies of other countries.[66] The view usually taken by Communist Esperantists is that the 'inner idea' is a noble aim but can only be fully realised under Communism.[67] The main conflict that has arisen is in relation to the pro-Moscow *Mondpaca Esperanto-Movado*, which had passed political motions, especially against American action in Vietnam, at its meetings within the framework of world congresses, and which has also expressed opposition to the principle of neutrality adopted by UEA. This organisation has now ceased to be an affiliated member of UEA.

NOTES

1. For matters relating to the sociological concept of charisma see Chapter 5.
2. For Lapenna's biography see *The Academic Who's Who*, 1973–1974, p.265; U. Lins, 'La juna Lapenna', *Kontakto* 2(1), 1974, pp.15–17.
3. His works include *Conceptions soviétiques de droit international public*, 1954; *State and Law: Soviet and Yugoslav Theory*, 1963; *Soviet Penal Policy*, 1968.
4. See U. Lins, *La dangĝera lingvo, op. cit.*, p.22, reissued in *Perspektivo*, pp.712–713.
5. I. Lapenna, *Retoriko*, 1950.
6. For some of Lapenna's chief contributions see *Internacia Kulturo*, November 1946, pp.3–5; February–March 1947, pp.3–4; May 1947, p.3; June 1947, p.13.
7. *Internacia Kulturo*, September–October 1947, pp.4–5, 15.
8. The concept of 'crankiness' is considered in more detail in the conclusion.
9. The 1948 constitution appears in UEA, *Jarlibro*, 1948, *dua parto*, pp.25–41.
10. The 1955 constitution appears in UEA, *Jarlibro*, 1955, *dua parto*, pp.51–65.
11. The 1958 constitution is issued as 'Statuto de Universala Esperanto-Asocio', *Statuto kaj regularoj de Universala Esperanto-Asocio*, pp.3–20, 1968.
12. Courtinat, *op. cit.*, vol. 3, p.1,215.
13. Lapenna, *Elektitaj paroladoj kaj prelegoj*, 1966, p.62.
14. *Revuo Esperanto Internacia*, June 1955, pp.186–187.
15. 'Dua baza laborplano de UEA', *Statuto kaj regularoj de Universala Esperanto-Asocio, op. cit.*, pp.47–57.
16. *Esperanto*, October 1962, p.171.
17. *Statuto kaj regularoj, op. cit.*, pp.33–34.
18. *Ibid.*, pp.35–37.
19. *Ibid.*, pp.45–46.
20. Lapenna, *Elektitaj paroladoj kaj prelegoj, op. cit.*, p.30.
21. *Ibid.*
22. *Perspektivo* is based on extensive research and documentation engaged in by the Centre since its inception.
23. *Perspektivo*, pp.687–691.
24. Lapenna, *Elektitaj paroladoj kaj prelegoj, op. cit.*, p.60.
25. *Esperanto*, February 1956, p.21.
26. 'Fundamenta principaro de informado pri la Internacia Lingvo', *Statuto kaj regularoj, op. cit.*, pp.58–62.

27. *Esperanto*, February 1965, pp.22–24.
28. *Esperanto*, November 1967, p.150.
29. Full details of these activities are to be found in *Perspektivo*, pp.760–792.
30. UNESCO Document 7C/PRG/11.
31. UNESCO Document 8C/PRG/3.
32. Lapenna, *Elektitaj paroladoj kaj prelegoj*, pp.33–37.
33. English text appears in *The British Esperantist*, March/April 1955, p.17.
34. *Esperanto*, February 1955, p.36.
35. *Esperanto*, April 1955, p.105.
36. See, for instance, Verdiro (pseudonym), *Elingita glavo*, 1962, pp.28–29, 35–40, 43–45, 82–83.
37. A debate on Esperanto appeared from time to time in the correspondence columns; see particularly *UNESCO Courier*, March 1963, p.33; May 1963, p.33; June 1963, pp.31–32 (contribution by Lapenna).
38. Including translations of Tagore, the Koran, Sartre's *La nausée*, Dante's *La Divina Commedia*, and the Finnish epic *Kalevala*.
39. See Article 2, paragraph 1 of United Nations Declaration of Human Rights: 'Everyone is entitled to all the rights and freedoms set forth in this Declaration, without distinction of any kind, such as race, colour, sex, language, religion, political or other opinion, national or social origin, property, birth or other status', *Yearbook of the United Nations*, 1948–1949, p.535.
40. See I. Lapenna, 'La Situation juridique des "langues officielles" sous le régime des Nations Unies', *La Monda Lingvo-Problemo*, May 1969, pp.87–106.
41. Courtinat, *op. cit.*, vol. 3, p.1,077.
42. *Statuto kaj regularoj, op. cit.*, p.3.
43. *Yearbook of the United Nations*, 1946–1947, p.713.
44. Lapenna, *Elektitaj paroladoj kaj prelegoj, op. cit.*, p.109.
45. Many of Verdiro's articles are reprinted in *Elingita glavo, op. cit.*
46. *Esperanto*, June 1951, p.161.
47. *Esperanto*, December 1953, pp.345–346.
48. *Esperanto*, March 1954, pp.65–66.
49. *IOE-Gazeto*, after 1968 *Esperanto-Gazeto*.
50. *Esperanto*, January 1972, p.7. For Lapenna's reply see *Esperanto*, March 1972, pp.47–49.
51. For history of TEJO see *Perspektivo*, pp.534–547.
52. *Kontakto* 6(3), 1969, pp.3–4.
53. *Kontakto* 7, 1970, *passim*.
54. *Kontakto* 7(3), 1970, pp.8–9.
55. Lapenna's version of the dispute is contained in I. Lapenna, *Hamburgo en retrospektivo*, 1975, Ch. 4.
56. *Kontakto* 8 (3), p.5.
57. Lapenna, *Hamburgo en retrospektivo, op. cit., passim*.
58. L.M. Goodrich, *The United Nations*, 1960, p.66.
59. *Esperanto Internacia*, November 1947, p.157.
60. For brief histories of the various national Esperanto movements see *Perspektivo*, pp.447–507.
61. For the history of this dispute see Courtinat, *op. cit.*, vol. 3, pp.1,160–1,167; *Perspektivo*, pp.582–584, 719; Lapenna, *Elektitaj paroladoj kaj prelegoj, op. cit.*, p.38n.

62.   W. Solzbacher, 'Esperanto and the Iron Curtain', *American Esperanto Magazine*, September/October 1951, pp.75–77.

63.   *American Esperanto Magazine*, September/October 1951, p.82.

64.   The opening words of Zamenhof's congress speech at the 1910 Washington World Congress had been 'Land of freedom, land of the future, I greet you! . . . Realm of men which belongs not to a particular race or church, but to all its honest sons, I kneel before you, and I am happy to see you and breathe at least for a short while your free air, monopolised by nobody'. Text in OV, p.393.

65.   *American Esperanto Magazine*, July/August 1956, p.108.

66.   See Lapenna, *Hamburgo en retrospektivo, op. cit.*, p.24.

67.   See, for instance, D. Blanke, 'Pri la interna ideo de Esperanto', in D. Blanke, *op. cit.*, p.195.

PART II

Esperanto in Britain

Introductory Note

The Esperanto movement presents certain distinctive problems by virtue of being an international organisation. In practice this has meant 'international within the European context' to a large extent, but even this context is wider than that in which a social movement is normally investigated. In examining UEA, attention has been paid particularly to the internal dynamics of organisational development, though with due notice taken of the context of European relations in which this occurred. In many respects, this would seem an adequate treatment of Esperanto. The aims of Esperanto can only be truly realised in an international context. The language is intended to be international, and the social relations of the movement involve the recognition of important shared symbols: the language itself, the green star, literature and songs, periodicals, and particularly the affirmation of cohesion of the Esperanto speech community reflected in the world congresses.

Yet it is appropriate to consider a further dimension. As well as the interpretation of Esperanto expounded by powerful, influential, and articulate leaders, there remains the attitude of the rank-and-file member. A distinction can be drawn between the 'great' and the 'little' tradition in a manner akin to Redfield's distinction for peasant societies. As Redfield suggests,

In a civilization there is a great tradition of the reflective few, and there is a little tradition of the largely unreflective many. The great tradition is cultivated in schools or temples; the little tradition works itself out and keeps itself going in the lives of the unlettered in their village communities. The tradition of the philosopher, theologian and literary man is a tradition consciously cultivated and handed down; that of the little people is for the most part taken for granted and not submitted to much scrutiny or considered refinement and improvement.[1]

Although it would scarcely be possible for the Esperanto movement to have illiterate members, it can still be demonstrated that the gap between elite and mass culture among Esperantists is considerable. Investigation of the linguistic and philosophical underpinnings of Esperanto has reached a high level of sophistication. Esperanto has been in competition with alternative projects, and it has been necessary to provide the appropriate theoretical backing for Esperanto 'apologetics'. Yet the extent to which it has been possible for the Esperantists to appeal to intellectual linguists and philosophers has been limited. There has been a certain suspicion of the allegiance of such persons, who might prove to be innovators. Esperanto has rather appealed to those only moderately well educated, or self-educated. The problem of a universal language, considered by Wilkins, Dalgarno, and Leibniz, and later by those such as Ostwald, Peano, and Couturat, has through Esperanto penetrated to groups with relatively little philosophical sophistication. Thus the problem of the relation between the great and the little tradition assumes considerable significance.

The concept of 'culture' is worthy of consideration in this connection. In an anthropological, Tylorian sense, Esperanto has no culture in that it is not normally passed on within a given society from generation to generation. Yet the idea of the Esperantist 'people' has assumed some importance, as already noted, and attempts have been made to create a culture in an anthropological sense. Some Esperanto-speaking parents have brought up their children bilingually with Esperanto. Some international marriages have taken place as a result of contacts initially made within the movement and in such cases Esperanto has become the couple's home language. A register of 'native' speakers of Esperanto (*denaskaj Esperantistoj*, 'Esperantists from birth') is maintained by UEA; many of them, however, are no longer active in or specially interested in the movement. Schemes have also been proposed to form Esperanto-speaking colonies, where eventually it might be possible for learners of Esperanto to receive expert advice from native speakers. These have mostly not achieved any stable existence, and some would disapprove of such a proposal, since Esperanto aims to put everyone on an equal linguistic footing and thus should have no native speakers.

Esperantists' attempts to create a high *literary* culture have met with greater success. As already noted, original as well as translated literature has been produced, especially poetry, and a number of Esperantist poets have achieved a well-established position. Such activity is known of and approved by the rank-and-file Esperantist, but still tends to be an elite activity. The vocabulary of such poets is often wider than that required for ordinary texts.

In examining relations between elite and mass, attention must also be paid to the way in which the goals of the movement are interpreted. Officially, at any rate, the international leaders of the Esperanto movement have generally looked to the aim of international recognition, and from recognition adoption, of Esperanto. Followers have more often been interested in Esperanto as an international or even merely local club, and have been more concerned with club activities and with the intrinsic satisfactions derived from speaking the language than with official recognition. Thus followers have adopted a more expressive and less instrumental orientation towards Esperanto than have leaders. As Berry suggests, a political party can be considered for many purposes as a voluntary association, when participation at a local level is the focus of attention, and the same is true of Esperanto organisations.[2]

For convenience, problems of this kind will be examined particularly in relation to the Esperanto movement in Great Britain. This will involve many general considerations of the relations between elite and mass. Yet the specific characteristics of British society must also be taken into account, where appropriate. The relation between the Esperanto movement and the dominant values of the societies in which it is to be found must be examined. If 'society' and 'nation-state' are taken as roughly identical, it is evident that national values will have their effect on national organisations to promote Esperanto. In some societies, Esperanto may be supported by dominant values and be perceived to be in accordance with them. This can be seen in Bulgaria, where the national Esperanto association is organised as a section of the ruling Fatherland Front. In Britain, however, Esperanto occupies a decidedly marginal position. There is no systematic information on this question, but it seems a widely held view in Britain that English is the world language anyway. That English is *the* international language is widely asserted, often as an objection to Esperanto. What is exactly involved by this assertion is rarely made clear. It is not specified, for instance, whether it is anticipated that English will completely replace foreign languages; whether English will be a second language for all, or only for certain groups or for certain purposes; and if so, for which groups or purposes. But given that the idea of the internationality of English is widely believed in, such a belief will constitute an obstacle to recruitment to the Esperanto movement. This belief will of course hinder recruitment anywhere, and not merely in Britain; it is, however, suggested that the belief in the internationality of English will present distinctive difficulties for Esperanto in English-speaking countries. It might thus make for a tendency for recruitment of English-speakers to be particularly prevalent among certain deviant groups. Those who support Esperanto in Britain tend to be deviant in certain other respects: a deviance syndrome is evident. It is thus necessary to examine relations between Esperanto and not only dominant values, but deviant values as well. It is found that Esperanto tends not to be associated with groups opposed to dominant values to the extent of wanting to overthrow the existing social structure by political revolution. Rather there exist, linked with Esperanto, a number of individualistic forms of deviation, such as vegetarianism, which are labelled by the wider society as 'cranky'. Such orientations will be examined more closely when the social composition of the Esperanto movement is looked at in greater detail.

Yet such groups do not even form a majority of members. They remain a conspicuous minority, and it has been noted that Lapenna's anticrank campaign was directed against them. Yet Esperanto is not solely associated with 'cranks', even in Britain. Britain possesses a geographical situation which makes for consciousness of linguistic differences. This is less true of Britain than of most other European countries, since Britain is an island, but it remains the case that societies speaking a language other than English are fairly easily accessible. This contrasts with the United States, for instance. English has fewer native speakers in Europe than German. English has also competed with French in the League of Nations and more recently in the European Common Market, with French usually taking slight precedence over English. Shenton points to the fact that pressure to change the practice of using French exclusively at international gatherings has come in the twentieth century not so much from British delegates as from those from non-European English-speaking countries.[3]

At the same time, Britain's position as an island and as a major imperial power has led to a certain marginality to events in Europe. She has ranked as a great power within Europe, and during the existence of the Esperanto movement has been belligerent in two world wars. Yet at no time in living memory has Britain been occupied by a foreign power. A situation of this kind has enabled pacifistic ideas to flourish more easily. It has also been the case that wartime disruption of the British Esperanto movement has been relatively slight.

These factors will be seen to be of significance in the study of the British movement, together with more specific historical events which will be noted when relevant.

NOTES

1. R. Redfield, *Peasant Society and Culture*, 1956, p.70.
2. D. Berry, *The Sociology of Grass Roots Politics*, 1970.
3. Shenton, *op. cit.*, p.300.

10

The Development of Esperanto in Britain

Esperanto is intended to reduce the need for learning of foreign languages, thus the availability of textbooks in a wide range of languages is important for its spread. Zamenhof himself prepared the Russian, French, German, and Polish texts of the *Unua Libro*, but his command of English was too limited for such a task. He arranged for an English translation to be made, and this appeared in 1888. The translator clearly knew little more English than did Zamenhof; the text began:

The reader will undoubtedly take with mistrust that opuscule in hand, supposing, that I am speaking about an irrealizable utopy; therefore I must before all pray the reader to leave off prejudice and treat seriously and critically the question I bring forth. . . .[1]

and continued in similar vein. The book was reviewed by the periodical *The Office* (devoted to general commercial matters, including modern languages) in 1888. It received favourable mention, though much attention was paid to the peculiar English. Likewise a review in *Languages* for 1894[2] paid more attention to the style than to the content. But intellectuals and linguists could approach Esperanto through the other texts, especially the French. Proficiency in French is notable in the biography of many British pioneers of Esperanto. The first-ever mention of Esperanto in the British press appears to have been in the *St. James's Gazette*, 24 November 1887. This aroused the interest of a Bristol solicitor, who inquired to Zamenhof, writing in Latin. He received a copy of the German textbook but took no further interest in it. He passed the text to his friend Richard Geoghegan, a linguist of Irish birth, who soon became a strong supporter of the language. He translated the *Unua Libro* into respectable English and also translated some French and German textbooks. Geoghegan made texts available but did not become an active propagandist, and towards the end of the nineteenth century he emigrated to North America. Britain thus had no counterpart to de Beaufront in France. Britain also lacked a strong Volapük movement[3] from which converts might be drawn such as was the case in Germany. All things considered, the initial progress of Esperanto in Britain was very slow. Zamenhof's first list of addresses, for 1889, listed only nine Esperantists in Britain and Ireland.

The beginnings of an organised movement did not come till the twentieth century.[4] Joseph Rhodes (1856–1920), a Keighley journalist, was associated with this development. Concerned with self-improvement through evening classes, Rhodes studied first stenography, then French. His French teacher, a native Frenchman, was also an Esperantist. He introduced Rhodes to Esperanto, and Rhodes showed interest as soon as his command of French was sufficient to read the textbooks. Rhodes was already active in charitable and church affairs and saw fit to organise an Esperanto society. Thus the first-ever Esperanto society in the United Kingdom was founded in Keighley in November 1902; it met in the Temperance Institute and the annual subscription was five shillings.

Much wider publicity to Esperanto in Britain was given by W.T. Stead's periodical the *Review of Reviews*. Stead (1849–1912) had long been active in promotion of various liberal causes and programmes through his publishing activities. He achieved greatest notoriety in 1889. In that year, in order to demonstrate how easily this could be done, he procured a girl for prostitution. As a result he received three months' imprisonment. He was active in a wide range of other causes, and by the beginning of the twentieth century showed particular interest in the promotion of peace through international arbitration.[5] Such interests led him to favour Esperanto. He also expressed preference for Esperanto over an alternative proposal for English with simplified spelling. In 1902 the *Review of Reviews* began to make favourable reference to Esperanto;[6] as a result of this Rhodes made contact with Stead and, encouraged by the success of Esperanto in Keighley, Stead suggested the formation of a London Esperanto society.[7] A notice was placed in the *Daily Mail* as well as the *Review of Reviews*, while Stead made the latter's premises available for the inaugural meeting on 16 January 1903.[8] Seventy inquirers attended the meeting and many joined; Stead himself became treasurer, and Miss E.A. Lawrence, Stead's private secretary, became secretary of the Esperanto society. As president was elected Felix Moscheles, an artist, godson of Felix Mendelssohn.[9] Moscheles was also chairman of the International Arbitration and Peace Association, and associated Esperanto with this concern. A periodical *The Esperantist* was issued, for which Stead gave a financial guarantee.[10] On the first birthday of the London club, Zamenhof sent a recorded message of appreciation for the work done in the past year.[11] At first the London club had a national membership, but provincial clubs began to be formed apart from Keighley: Plymouth and Edinburgh were early in the field. In 1905 the British Esperanto Association (BEA) was founded, its rules being finalised by 8 June. This organisation began the periodical *The British Esperantist*, which still survives: *The Esperantist* was incorporated into it in 1906. A formal structure of the organisation was early in evidence. A governing body, the Council, was democratically elected. The BEA was registered as an incorporated company, with its memorandum and articles of association. A paid secretary was appointed, and the BEA has always had at least one full-time employee. Provision was made for examinations in Esperanto and also, in the initial period, for a Censor Committee to approve the language of members' manuscripts. Annual British Esperanto congresses began in 1908. Income has always been derived from subscriptions and book sales, any deficit being made up from members' bequests, donations, and guarantees. Stead continued to show some interest, but was active in promoting many other causes and could best be regarded as an initiator of the British movement, rather than an activist. He never learned to speak Esperanto fluently. All his activities were abruptly terminated in 1912 with his death in the *Titanic* disaster.

The British Esperantists early took part in the activities of the international movement. In 1903 British Esperantists took part in the first organised international Esperantist gathering. An invitation from Esperantists in Le Havre was publicised in the *Review of Reviews*,[12] and in July, in response to this, a small party crossed to France. Participation in such early gatherings was characterised by great enthusiasm and emotionalism; the *Review of Reviews* reported that 'each English Esperantist was received as even the nearest relations rarely are'.[13] The expressive and value-oriented interpretation of Esperanto was affirmed even more strongly by British participation in the first World Congress in the accessible town of Boulogne. Enthusiastic reports were published, commitment to the cause sometimes appearing fanatical. A BEA member criticised this development:

I feel that it is time to call the attention of Esperantists in general to a very grave matter, which will, if not seriously considered, do much towards defeating our own ends. I mean the spirit of intolerance which is gradually creeping in among our enthusiasts. . . . While at the Congress one person was in a great state of indignation about an article in *The Times*, which he said was against us. . . and communicated his indignation to all those to whom he spoke about it. On my return home, I looked up that article, and found to my surprise that it was quite temperate and sensible, and in no way antagonistic in the real sense of the word.[14]

This letter went on to quote other similar examples and suggested that such fanaticism was damaging to the cause. Like Zamenhof, the editor of the *British Esperantist* advocated quietism:

What is required is a serious body of fellow-thinkers, a bond of pioneers pleased to work, to fight, even to suffer, without wasting their breath in futile shouting.[15]

Zamenhofan idealism came directly to Britain in 1907, when the World Congress was held in Cambridge. It was organised by the popular *ad hoc Trio por la Tria* [trio for the third], consisting of George Cunningham, a doctor of medicine; John Pollen, a lieutenant-colonel, also a doctor of law, retired from the Indian Civil Service; and Harold Bolingbroke Mudie, a stockbroker. Pollen was president of the BEA, a post which Mudie was later to occupy. Mudie was a member of the editorial committee of the *British Esperantist*. Publicity was given in the Esperanto press to the value-oriented interpretation of Esperanto and the importance of attendance at the Cambridge Congress to realise these aims was stressed. One article by John Ellis, a Keighley pioneer, gave Esperanto a quasi-religious interpretation. It was entitled 'The transcendental essences of Esperanto' and likened Zamenhof to 'a patriarch blessing the race'.[16] During the Cambridge Congress itself, Zamenhof stressed the idealism of the British Esperantists, who had little material benefit to derive from Esperanto since English was already widely disseminated.[17]

A significant problem in considering the development of Esperanto in Britain again emerges as the relationship between norm- and value-oriented interpretations. The extent to which Esperanto is seen to accord with dominant values in British society is also worthy of examination. These two issues are related but not identical. Esperanto supports the principle of 'unity in diversity' and it has been declared that Esperanto is not intended to interfere with the internal lives of the peoples. Ideals of world peace, which might not accord with the actual behaviour of a state at any given moment, can be reserved as long-term objectives. The aims of Esperanto attracted the attention of Sir Vesey Strong, Lord Mayor of London, in whose presence Zamenhof's well-known speech in the Guildhall was made. Strong was interested in moral training, world peace, and international arbitration. At the same time he occupied a respectable position in the established value system of British society. The BEA has continually expressed loyalty to the reigning monarch and, on the death of King Edward VII, expressed 'appreciation of the pacific policy so consistently exercised during his reign'.[18] On the voyage of a P. & O. liner between England and India, Pollen had succeeded in attracting the interest of the Duke of Connaught, who acted as patron of a number of congresses of British Esperantists. Esperanto, too, has always been associated with practical advantages, and the value of Esperanto in commerce became an important point in Esperanto propaganda. Esperanto could be seen as simply a practical commercial aid such as short-hand or the typewriter. Esperanto was introduced into Britain during an era of growing prosperity, free trade, and travel – yet at the same time the effect of business competition from abroad was being felt. Thus widening horizons favoured promotion of Esperanto in commerce. Commerce could also be used to promote Esperanto: an Esperanto brand of cigarette was offered for sale from 1905.

According to a survey of BEA records in 1912, 42.5% of members had 'professional' occupations, including 15% teachers.[19] Yet during this period Esperanto began to be associated with certain deviant value orientations. A group of self-confessed 'cranks', meeting regularly in a vegetarian restaurant in London, produced a digest of their thoughts called *The Crank*. From 1904 this had a regular page in Esperanto. The periodical was continued in 1907 as *The Open Road*: the influence of Tolstoyan ideas was evident, though less attention was now paid to Esperanto. In various ways, more respectable kinds of progressive thought were associated by various individuals with Esperanto. The Esperantist founder of Letchworth Garden City, Ebenezer Howard, made a speech to excursionists from the 1907 Cambridge World Congress: he concluded that 'Esperanto and the Garden City are two leaders towards newer and brighter conditions of peace and goodwill'.[20] Shortly before the First World War, Bedales, the progressive school, began instruction in Esperanto.

Since Esperanto aims at world peace, the extent of likely tension with dominant values is best observed during wartime. Before the First World War broke out, an article in 1912 stressed love for foreign Esperantists, especially Germans, at this difficult time. British Esperantists showed appreciation of the festive evening at the Berne Casino during the 1913 World Congress. Yet the value system of Esperanto has always enabled compromise. World peace can be seen as a long-term objective, and support for national values can be seen as necessary during the interim period: indeed, it might even be declared to be desirable for propaganda purposes. A distinction can also be drawn between individual and collective responsibility. Announcing war in the *British Esperantist*, September 1914, the editor drew such a distinction:

Firstly we must remember that the people of any country are not at all responsible for the hostile actions of their country. Also the soldier who aims a gun at you or sticks his lance into you is not doing that through hatred: we are all parts of a cruel, insensitive machine, the militaristic system, which brings no true good to anyone, but crushes and ruins innumerable millions of well-meaning and blameless men in all countries.[21]

Individual responsibility in the situation was not ruled out: but it was declared that the duty of such individuals was to study the causes of the militaristic system and, through international movements such as Esperanto, to prevent it from surviving. The Quaker Esperantist, Montagu C. Butler, who in 1916 became honorary secretary of the BEA, was unusual in making a forthright declaration of refusal to fight, during a sermon at a religious service in Esperanto in London. The *British Esperantist* generally took the line of preparation for future peace. From October 1914 a section was headed 'In time of war, prepare for peace'. The problem of appropriate action for the BEA during the war was raised. An influential opinion was expressed in a letter:

Our first motherland needs all our strength, and I feel that as Esperantists we have special duties to perform. . . . If our movement does not rise on the wave of patriotism now sweeping the land, it will go under, and when will it emerge?[22]

This contributor suggested making clothes for the Red Cross. Another opinion expressed was that help should be given equally to friend and foe. Eventually a proposal was put forward which all members could find acceptable: a fund to collect £400 was set up to purchase an ambulance for the Red Cross. This proved so successful that over £800 was raised, enabling two ambulances to be bought. These were delivered to the Belgian Red Cross; Harold Clegg, professional secretary of the BEA, was initially driver of one of them. Conflict arose during the war about the willingness of the BEA to conform to the exigencies of the wartime situation. The BEA regularly held an annual congress and continued to do so during the war. In 1915, at the eighth British Esperanto Congress in Bath, a proposal was made that the Congress should send its greetings to fellow idealists in other countries, even enemy. This proposal was rejected on the grounds that it would be detrimental to the movement to relate to the enemy at the moment. It was argued that fellow idealists in enemy countries would know that the British Esperantists had faith in them in any case.[23] Remarks in the *British Esperantist* tended to favour the idea of patriotic duty; a BEA Council resolution expressed regret at the death of the son of Emile Boirac, wishing to 'place on record their admiration for the noble death he died on the battlefield'.[24] By the end of 1915 a resignation was received from a member who objected to expressions used by the BEA about the war, and about the failure of the Bath BEA Congress to send greetings to Esperantists in enemy countries.[25] It appears therefore that only a minority of BEA members held that Esperanto was subversive of 'patriotic' war-time values; others were more concerned with reforms within the national value system when the war was over. To balance this picture, it must be added that the *British Esperantist* contained none of the denunciations of the 'Hun' or vituperations against conscientious objectors that characterised most of the British press of the period. Eventually, as the war progressed, emphasis was placed on noncontroversial linguistic topics. As the war drew to a close, interest in postwar reconstruction was evident, and particularly in the proposal for a League of Nations. As early as 1916 a resolution was sent to Lloyd George urging the importance of Esperanto in the inquiry into education after the war; while in 1918 a memorial was sent to Lloyd George and Balfour approving of the idea of a League of Nations and advocating Esperanto as its language. Parliamentary activity was continued the following year.

As in the international movement, the post-1918 era was one of confidence for the BEA. Much attention was paid to League of Nations activity, and local groups and regional federations were urged to pay attention to this work. The dismissal of Ido and other projects in the League of Nations report on international language was greeted with acclamation. The British Association for the Advancement of Science took an interest in the idea of international language and reported favourably on an artificial language as the solution.[26] It could not, however, make up its mind between Esperanto and Ido. When the report was presented at the British Association conference in 1921, a dispute broke out between Esperantists and Idists present;[27] as a result of the unfavourable impression that this created, nothing further was done about it. There was still great confidence during this period; in 1922 an editorial was poetic in its enthusiasm:

There is a feeling of hope in the air! .... Life is yet LIFE: hope is on the wing, the folds of *La Verda Standardo* [the green standard] are stirred as by the winnowings of invisible plumes: and we remember that we are *esperantoj*, we hope![28]

The BEA had early attracted the support of the music-hall singer
Harrison Hill, who composed a number of songs for Esperanto. In
1922 he composed a millenarian song with the following chorus,
in honour of the BEA Congress:

Kantu, kantu kamaradoj!	Sing, sing comrades!
Gloran estontecon havas vi!	You have a glorious future!
Estas hela la ĉiel', ĉiam	The sky is bright, our
brilas nia stel',	star always shines,
La fluanta tajdo estas nun	The flowing tide is now
ĉe ni!	with us![29]

This song is still sung, but more as a matter of faith than of real
conviction. There were at this period numerous other suggestions
that the final triumph was almost in sight. In order to encourage
the development of Esperanto as a mass movement, the subscription to the BEA was reduced from ten to five shillings in 1927. A
new periodical, named *International Language*, was issued between
1924 and 1931. For propaganda purposes, this was in English and
could be bought from a newsagent's. There was encouraging progress of Esperanto in the Labour colleges, and the *Daily Herald*
contained regular articles in Esperanto. *World Radio* began to
publicise Esperanto after 1929. There were two world congresses
of Esperanto in Britain in quick succession – Edinburgh (1926)
and Oxford (1930). In 1930, too, SAT held its World Congress in
London. In order to improve its publicity, in 1929 the BEA purchased a motor car, and continued to own a car until the Second
World War.

During this period, Esperanto was presented to the general public in a wide range of situations. The BEA was proud of the fact
that not only cranks now supported Esperanto. A wide variety of
specialised journals, such as the *LNER Magazine* and the *Good
Templar* now had pages in Esperanto. Despite financial difficulties
within the BEA, consequent on the general British economic situation, an optimistic outlook prevailed in the early 1930s, and in
1931 membership of the BEA passed the 2,000 mark for the first
time. Attempts were made to provide mass advertising of Esperanto,
and there were some successes; Messrs. Dean and Dawson, the
travel agents, made their branch windows available for exhibitions
of Esperanto in 1933.

Although membership of the BEA reached over 2,000 again in 1934 and 1935, optimism began to flag about this period. It still persisted, but was more cautious and based on faith. There was still evidence of support, sometimes in unexpected quarters. In 1938 the World Congress was held in London. In an article advising those travelling to London for this congress, the BEA secretary mentioned the high fares of London taxis. This comment produced a vigorous rejoinder from the 30-strong London taxi drivers' Esperanto group.[30] But general membership of the BEA fell towards the close of the 1930s; and Esperanto lost establishment support. A Welsh Esperantist prepared a broadcast talk for the BBC in 1937, about his travels, which incidentally made reference to Esperanto. He was instructed by the BBC to delete mention of Esperanto in the talk. The BEA challenged this and received the following reply from the BBC:

You probably know that for many years the BBC has felt bound to take the view that it could not accept suggestions for broadcasts in Esperanto or broadcasts pressing the claims of Esperanto as an international language.[31]

Thus the BEA increasingly looked to success abroad, feeling that Esperanto had lost credibility in the eyes of the general public. Already in 1936 the question 'Is Esperanto still alive? I never hear about it' is suggested as commonplace. Otherwise the BEA relied on a small band of devoted followers, which included some 'cranks'. The following letter is a good example of the latter:

Dear Sirs — We should like to pay tribute to the *British Esperantist* as an advertising medium. We have used it to bring our medically commended preparation, Cinubi Dentifrice, to the notice of your readers and also to draw attention to our Esperanto cafe-lounge in Ipswich. We have no hesitation in saying that from an advertising point of view the *British Esperantist* holds its own with the other periodicals we have used and we hope to see again this summer the Esperantists from all over England who visited our cafe-lounge last year in response to our advertisement in your pages. You may make any use you like of this letter.
  Yours truly,
  W.E. SCOTT,
  Secretary, "Regnego"[32]

(*Regnego*, meaning approximately 'large realm' in Esperanto, is a rather obscure world government organisation believing in the fatherhood of God and the brotherhood of man, and advocating the rule of law in all existing societies but also free immigration and emigration everywhere. It officially supports Esperanto.)

The BEA had to deal with competition as well as flagging interest at this time. Occidental was objected to, but the particular competitor was Basic English. Various articles appeared in the late thirties in the *British Esperantist* criticising this project. Yet a revival of interest took place as a result of the 1939–1945 war. 1939 had already shown a small increase of members, and in the same year the BEA purchased a house in London as its permanent headquarters. During the war, the finances of the Association were stable. BEA moved to Heronsgate with IEL and effected some economy by sharing staff. The BEA did not display a 'patriotic' bias during the war; nor did it provide help comparable to the ambulance fund in 1914–1918. The slogan 'in time of war, prepare for peace' was reaffirmed. During the war, attention was paid to the problems of future peace, which would include the language question. Parliamentary action was again engaged in, with a petition to the government in 1942. Widespread public interest was again shown: popular and educated support for discussion of the subject was evident. Other solutions had to be opposed, such as Anglo-French bilingualism; and particular attention was again paid by the BEA to Basic English. This was significant enough to have received governmental attention. The Prime Minister appointed a committee on the subject in 1943, though it never reported. The BEA welcomed discussion of Basic English since it gave the opportunity for general discussion of language problems. Many articles critical of this project appeared in *The British Esperantist* until after the war, and critical attention was also paid to proposals for English with simplified spelling as a world language. Discussion of competing projects did in fact help the spread of Esperanto. Such controversies, together with discussions of postwar reconstruction, including a proposal for a firmly organised intergovernmental body, encouraged support for the BEA. During the war a large increase in enrolment for the BEA's elementary course in Esperanto took place. There was also a large increase in membership, and the record figure of 3,039 was reported for 1945.

The growth of membership and interest proved to be short-lived. Membership declined after 1945; by 1952 it was less than 2,000 again and has never reached the 2,000 mark since. Much more modest progress was reported in the 1950s, and the BEA became more inward-looking. An attempt to arrest this development was made in 1956, by an advertising campaign in mass-circulation periodicals. Advertisements were placed in *Everybody's*, *Illustrated*, and *John Bull*. This had some success but no lasting impact. The BEA became conscious of an aging membership, and a preoccupation with methods of attracting young people was evident. To this end a Youth Section was founded in 1960: this had some success, but depended for its viability on groups of activists to run it, preferably in the same place (such as the same university). As the turnover of these is high, the fortunes of the Youth Section have been varied. There were also some private initiatives in this direction, such as the naming of a set of games for learning vocabulary 'Teenage Esperanto'. At the BEA Congress in 1966 a foundation known as the *Norwich Jubilee Esperanto Foundation* was set up, with the aim of promoting education for international understanding by awarding travelships and prizes to young students and encouraging research in schools, colleges and universities. It was initiated by a donation by Alderman E.F. Dean of Norwich, where the BEA Congress was held in 1966, and is supplemented by members' donations.

Yet the BEA made little lasting impact in the wider society, and a certain inward-looking tendency continued. It was preferred to urge members to order books directly from the BEA so as to obtain profits from them. This meant that ordinary bookshops would be unlikely to stock Esperanto books, giving the impression that none existed. Two books were published on Esperanto by outside publishers in Britain. These were Boulton's *Zamenhof, Creator of Esperanto* (1960) and Cresswell and Hartley's *Teach Yourself Esperanto* [33] (1957). This was followed in 1969 by Wells's *E.U.P. Concise Esperanto and English Dictionary*. [34] The latter two books contain the address of the BEA for those seeking further information. The *Teach Yourself* course had a considerable impact on recruitment to the BEA: 26% of all members recruited between 1957 and 1968 had first heard of the Esperanto movement from this book. [35] Continued encouragement for members was possible through events in the international movement. During this period consultative relations between UEA and UNESCO had been achieved, and the growth in membership of UEA had been considerable. Thus British Esperantists could obtain some encouragement from the success of Esperanto abroad.

A few attempts were made to improve the respectability of Esperanto in relation to dominant values, but these proved unsuccessful. There was an attempt to have Esperanto approved as a G.C.E. subject,[36] but this was rejected. Some C.S.E. boards accept Esperanto, however, and in a few schools Esperanto is a well-established subject. Harold Wilson had learnt Esperanto while in the Boy Scouts and had taken part in a Scouts' Esperanto Camp in The Netherlands in 1930.[37] Attempts were made to remind him of this allegiance, but a reply was received to the effect that language was 'not one of the most serious obstacles to international cooperation'.[38] In 1967 the BBC actually started some overseas broadcasts in Esperanto, but after the third broadcast these were suppressed by higher authority. The BEA became conscious of a period of stagnation and little support in the wider society. Some changes have recently taken place in an attempt to modernise the image of Esperanto. The opportunity presented itself as the existing professional secretary approached retirement. John Leslie, appointed in 1951, had been associated with a number of causes regarded as 'cranky' by the wider society. He had in 1923 been foreign editor of a short-lived revival of *The Open Road*, which explicitly had as one of its aims the airing of 'cranky' views.[39] His appointment as secretary of the BEA had also been on the condition that he did not use his position to promote the Social Credit party among BEA members. The new secretary, Herbert Platt, was appointed in 1967; significantly, he was appointed from outside the movement, on grounds of personality and administrative ability. Since his appointment a modernisation programme has been actively pursued, including complete re-equipment of the London office, whose decrepit appearance had certainly given the impression of a dying organisation. During this period the balance of power within the BEA began to shift. The need for a new policy appeared obvious since the marginality of the BEA to societal values was evident and had shown no sign of diminishing. The elderly middle-class social composition, together with an apparent lack of immediate hope for official recognition, led the BEA to concentrate on expressive rather than instrumental activities: it resembled a club for genteel old people. Yet some members had a strong commitment to Esperanto and its aims, but not to the existing activities of the BEA. Many members now took the opportunity to suggest new activities and policies. A broader interest in language problems was encouraged by the *British Esperantist*, which began to contain many articles on linguistic minorities and language problems generally. The periodical also began to have a higher literary content. Certain contributions were fairly obviously intended to shock some of the traditional members; sexual matters began to be more openly discussed and provocative suggestions put forward, such as the formation of a group for Esperantist homosexuals. Side by side with the *British Esperantist*, from 1971 a broadsheet *Esperanto Contact* (later *Esperanto News*) was also produced, mostly in English and containing more traditional material, such as details of club activities.

BEA activities generally took a more political turn, partly as a result of Pompidou's suggestion that French should still remain the working language of the Common Market after British entry. A demonstration in favour of Esperanto was subsequently staged in London outside a Common Market meeting. There is now sustained parliamentary activity in the form of the Esperanto parliamentary group. This developed from an 'Esperanto lobby' founded in 1972 at the BEA Congress in Brighton. By 1980 this had a membership of over 100 MPs, of all parties but mostly Labour. Again it seems that language problems in the Common Market have been an important factor in stimulating parliamentarians' interest.

BEA AND REFORMS IN ESPERANTO

The enthusiasm of early recruits to Esperanto in Britain, especially about the early world congresses, has already been noted. A corollary of this has been a tendency to see the existing structure of the language as sacred: British Esperantists have tended to support the untouchability of the *Fundamento*. No important critical tradition has ever developed outside the Esperanto movement, though small movements exist in Britain for other projects. Few of the projects of the past, as discussed by Couturat and Leau, were designed by British people. In the twentieth century, proposed reforms in Esperanto have been discussed mainly in France, and in French, and have not greatly penetrated the British movement. During the Ido schism, a few conversions to Ido took place among British members, schisms arising in local groups in London, Carlisle, Birmingham, Manchester, and Newcastle.[40] The cause of the schism was usually the conversion of an influential member. Only in the case of Newcastle did the schism present a serious threat to the group, and in no case at all does an Ido group still survive. In 1977 the British Ido society had approximately 30 members. Since the schism, strict allegiance to the *Fundamento* has continued. Ido was hardly discussed in the British Esperanto press after the report of the Delegation. Ido is still discussed by British Esperantists and usually dismissed. At times some of the most gentle, peace-loving Esperantists can be stirred into paroxysms of hate by the mere mention of Ido. The BEA stood for rigorous enforcement of the *Fundamento* in the international movement. Unease was expressed at UEA's use of the *-io* suffix in names of countries, and a resolution condemning this was passed at the BEA Congress in 1919. At the same Congress a resolution was also passed condemning René de Saussure's activities with his project *Esperantido* and demanding his retirement from the Academy.[41] At the 1924 BEA Congress, the arrangements for the Contract of Helsinki were approved but concern was expressed at UEA's continued use of the *-io* suffix. BEA delayed signing a contract with UEA until a satisfactory undertaking on this matter had been given.

BEA AND UEA RELATIONS

Enthusiastic participation in world congresses early made for strong interest in the international movement. Mudie became President of UEA in 1907. Since then, Britain has provided a number of activists in the international movement. These include John Merchant, President of the International Central Committee from 1923–1928. More recently, Ivo Lapenna has taught in London since 1956. His successor after the 1974 Hamburg World Congress, Humphrey Tonkin, is British-born and was formerly active in British Esperanto circles, though he now resides in the United States. World congresses have been held in Britain on a number of occasions (in Cambridge, Oxford, Edinburgh, London (2), Bournemouth, and Harrogate). British enthusiasts identified closely with the emotionalism of Boulogne and were hostile to the proposal at the 1911 Antwerp World Congress for bureaucratisation by the creation of 'authorised delegates'. This was objected to by BEA congresses in the first instance, though in the end the British Esperantists accepted the majority opinion. Support for the expressive and supernational tendency of UEA was tempered by the fact that BEA was a large national organisation. Thus BEA took the side of those large national associations which approved of the Cologne agreement in 1933, which effectively removed the previous conception of UEA from the international movement. Some British members objected to this to the extent that an Extraordinary Meeting had to be called in April 1933. The motion, which objected to the use of the word 'Universal' in the title of the new federation of national associations, and which disapproved of the proposal of the new federation to usurp UEA's functions by issuing a yearbook and creating delegates, was in the end unsuccessful. When the schism between UEA and IEL took place, support for IEL's side was overwhelming among BEA members. The *British Esperantist* put IEL's case entirely, and during the war there was, as already noted, much cooperation in shared premises and staff.

The main area of dispute between BEA and UEA has been relatively recent. This arose out of the postwar policy of centralisation effected by UEA. BEA is a large organisation with a long continued existence as a formal structure; while the consolidation of UEA as a formal organisation has been much more recent. With such centralisation and bureaucratisation of the international movement the possiblity of tension arose. Originally UEA was pleased with BEA: Lapenna visited the British movement in 1950 and was favourably impressed by its organisation. Conflict began, however, over the question of the legitimate loyalties of UEA committee members who represented BEA. It was resolved in 1956 that BEA representatives should vote in accordance with BEA policy save under exceptional circumstances, which should be reported to the BEA committee.[42] This matter became of some significance when BEA and UEA entered into dispute over UEA's policy towards the *Esperanto-Asocio de Norda Ameriko* (EANA). Originally, BEA objected to UEA's withholding of certain information about the conduct of this matter; while the issue was further complicated by a personal dispute between John Leslie, secretary of BEA, and Ivo Lapenna. In the early stages of the conflict, a conflict-avoiding mechanism was resorted to by suggesting that such disputes were 'contrary to the spirit of Dr. Zamenhof'.[43] This caused only slight delay to more overt conflict on the issue of whether BEA had the duty to carry out UEA policy. At a meeting of the BEA Council for 12 October 1957, it was reported that UEA had adopted the policy of breaking off relations with EANA, and that it was expected that member states would impose similar sanctions.[44] This was discussed at a later meeting (7 December 1957) and it was decided that, while BEA in no way approved of certain articles in the *American Esperanto Magazine*, it did not wish to take part in the boycott. This conclusion was arrived at only after much discussion, and a resolution on the matter was finally passed by 28 votes to 10.[45] The reaction of UEA leaders to this decision was hostile. Canuto (President) and Lapenna (Secretary-General) wrote to the BEA in December 1957, pointing out that 'decisions made by the committee of UEA were compulsory on BEA as an affiliated national association'.[46] This was clarified in a further letter from the same source in January 1958. This pointed out 'that the committee does not issue orders to national associations, but that the latter must fulfil the decisions of the committee'.[47] Lapenna and Canuto continued their campaign by writing individually to British full members of UEA, putting the latter's point of view.[48] In its annual report to the general meeting at the 1958 BEA Congress, the Council pointed out that the whole matter

. . . raised in a very definite form the question of whether national associations are to lose their independence, and submit themselves to the discipline of a small committee which meets once a year for a few days during the busy congress week, and whose personnel is liable to considerable change from year to year.[49]

Considerable discussion continued within BEA on the principle of whether UEA had the right to issue directives to national associations. In 1958 BEA placed a motion before the UEA committee at the Mainz World Congress to the effect

That the Committee of UEA recognises the fact that an affiliated national association or specialist association is a freewill collaborator which by joining indicates the desire to support the work of UEA and the decisions of its Committee.

However, the Committee recognises that membership in no way implies that a national association or specialist association is an inferior body in relation to UEA, or that decisions of UEA are compulsory for a national or specialist association.[50]

UEA rejected this proposal by 31 votes to 3. The matter continued to cause widespread controversy within the BEA, neither party to the dispute moving from its original position. The matter ceased to be controversial when the cause of the original dispute, McCarthyism, ceased to be a significant problem.

BEA had thus asserted its independence of UEA. The conflict arose after the policy of centralisation developed in the international movement. There has not been any antagonism in principle to UEA: on the contrary, British Esperantists have attached particular importance to it. National associations tend to be promotional in orientation; the expressive satisfactions of speaking Esperanto are much more successfully realised in an international context. Yet there has been a decline in effective opportunities for promoting Esperanto in Britain since the 1950s. British Esperantists have continued to derive satisfaction from the social relations of the international movement. Attention has thus been paid to world congresses, Esperanto holidays, correspondence, and literature; and to UEA as representative of the international movement. BEA has given much publicity to UEA activities. At the same time BEA has a long history as an independent organisation, and conflict has arisen on the principle of centralisation of decision making.

THE WORKERS' ESPERANTO MOVEMENT IN BRITAIN

In 1907[51] a British League of Esperantist Socialists was founded, and set up a few local groups. It soon became dormant but was revived in 1920, with approximately 30 members. By 1927 SAT had been founded, and in that year the British socialist Esperantists changed their name to *Brita Laborista Esperanto-Asocio* (BLEA) [British Workers' Esperanto Association]. The National Council of Labour Colleges showed some interest, and its organ *Plebs* contained regular notes on or in Esperanto. The split between IPE and SAT had the effect of sharply dividing the British socialist Esperantists. In 1932 the annual meeting of BLEA voted to affiliate to IPE rather than SAT. Support had previously been mobilised to this end among British Communists. The *Daily Worker* urged Communists to join the BLEA 'to keep out the reactionaries'.[52] Communists, by no means all Esperantists, packed the BLEA meeting and secured the affiliation to IPE. As a result of this, the remaining SAT supporters among British Esperantists formed a new organisation, *SAT en Britio* (SATEB) [SAT in Britain]. Those who remained in this organisation were mostly Labour Party supporters, with a sprinkling of anarchists and representatives of smaller groups (SPGB and ILP).[53] The ILP's periodical contained a regular column in Esperanto right up until 1970. In that year it was ended by the party's National Administrative Council, as 'they did not see it as being relevant to the ILP's political perspective'.[54]

The organ of SATEB, *The Worker Esperantist*, continues to appear bimonthly. Membership of SATEB has never been high: it has fairly consistently remained around the 100–150 mark. The present-day membership suffers from a lack of young recruits to an even greater extent than the neutral movement in Britain. The British Workers' Esperanto Movement has thus never rivalled or outstripped the neutral movement in strength. It appears to have been associated primarily with workers' education (a goal fully in accordance with the original aims of SAT). This may relate to the tendency of British socialists to expect that their aims can be achieved within the framework of established political institutions. Thus socialist Esperantists have found no difficulty in accommodating themselves in the neutral movement in Britain. This situation was consolidated at the 1977 Hastings BEA Congress by the formation of a Trade Union and Cooperative Esperanto Group. This has obtained the support of a number of well-known trade union leaders; moreover, in 1980, in retirement, Sir Harold Wilson agreed to serve as Vice-President.

In many other European countries such ease of accommodation of socialists into the neutral movement has not been evident. In some countries, too, the 'neutral' movement has tended to display an overtly bourgeois orientation, and polarisation between the workers and the 'neutral' Esperantists has accordingly been greater.

THE 'GREAT' AND THE 'LITTLE' TRADITION WITHIN THE BEA

Members of the BEA vary widely in their degree of sophistication about the traditions and policy of the Esperanto movement. This is obviously true of all national Esperanto movements. While a national Esperanto movement reflects the national culture in some degree, it also reflects certain characteristics common to Esperanto organisations generally. In particular, the shared symbolism – the green star; the Hymn and various other songs – belongs to Esperantists the world over. Thus some of the characteristics here indicated for the British Esperanto Association may be found in other national movements as well, though certain distinctive characteristics of the relation of Esperanto to British dominant values have already been noted and will exert their influence.

The BEA as a whole meets only once a year, at the annual BEA Congress; otherwise members conduct most of their activities for Esperanto within local organisations. The BEA is governed[55] by a Council. This has long consisted of both national officers and representatives of local, regional, and specialist groups affiliated to the BEA. The Council generally meets four times per year, once during the BEA Congress, otherwise mostly though not always in London. Effective policy making is done by the Executive of the Council, which meets more regularly in London. This consists of 13 members, while the Council as a whole may have over 70 or even 100 members. Local groups have always been able to affiliate to the BEA, and in due course the idea developed of federating certain groups within the same area. This is now done over most of the country, and both federations and groups have traditionally been entitled to representation on the BEA Council. However, as a result of recent reorganisation of the BEA, groups are now represented only through federations.

Esperanto groups tend to be created by local initiative. Anyone can form an Esperanto group, and there is no obligation to affiliate to the BEA. Usually a group in its early stages will be independent, affiliating later as it grows in strength. New groups consisting of beginners may be a course rather than a group or club. The language in which proceedings of Esperanto organisations should be conducted (except in an international context) has been much debated. Some well-established groups conduct every meeting entirely in Esperanto, including official business. Even in such established groups, however, it is common for conversation to change to English when, for instance, coffee is served after a meeting; though sometimes, to impress a visitor, conversation in Esperanto will be continued. There are also some very dedicated Esperantists who always speak Esperanto to fellow Esperantists and are spoken to in Esperanto in return. Other groups conduct meetings normally in Esperanto, though they hold business meetings in English or bilingually. Groups which contain mostly beginners will speak English most of the time, while trying to extend the use of Esperanto. The regional federations characteristically conduct their entire proceedings in Esperanto, including official business. The BEA is constituted as a company limited by guarantee and is required to conduct its business in a language comprehensible to all. It is an organisation of supporters of Esperanto: there is no requirement to be able to speak the language to join the BEA. Thus the Annual General Meeting of the BEA is conducted in English. The same applies to the Council and the Executive, though some attempts have been made to change this. It was eventually decided that Council and Executive should continue to conduct business in English since there were some enthusiastic members who had joined later in life and who were too old to master the language.

At all levels the characteristic symbolism of the movement is evident. Flags with the green star will be draped on walls and tables during congresses, and at local and regional meetings as well on occasion; there may also be a bust or photograph of Zamenhof. The BEA annual Congress contains the business meeting, which consists mainly of examination of the content of the Annual Report of the Council, which will have been previously circulated. Advance notice is required to introduce other matters of substance. Otherwise the annual Congress provides for talks, slide shows, singing, dancing, a dinner with speeches, sketches, excursions, and religious services. On all these occasions the language used will be Esperanto. It is customary for the BEA to invite distinguished foreign Esperantists as its guests. The BEA Congress is only held once annually, but most Esperantists in centres of population are members of local groups or regional federations. A separate subscription is required for these. The constitution of such organisations will usually say that the aim of the group is the promotion of Esperanto. Neutrality on matters of politics and religion is generally provided for. The constitution is drawn up independently by each group. The usual method of promoting Esperanto adopted is the provision of a beginners' class. This will be advertised in the local press, in shop windows, and through other methods such as local exhibitions and distribution of leaflets. The attention of local dignitaries will be drawn to Esperanto, and campaigns will be set up for matters such as the naming of a local street after Esperanto or Zamenhof, or for encouragement of teaching Esperanto in schools. Members may be requested to sell ball-point pens with 'Esperanto' marked on them. The local library will be encouraged to stock Esperanto books. A sustained campaign is built up towards the autumn, when the classes begin. A small group is usually recruited and is instructed in the language, often in the ideals of Esperanto as well, and in activities possible through it. Course members are often encouraged to take part in activities of the Esperanto group, and on completion of the course some may become members. (Some elderly groups suffer from the problem of the 'perpetual beginner', who has begun to learn Esperanto late in life and enrols in the course year after year.) New members of the BEA who have learnt Esperanto by other means, such as correspondence courses or 'Teach Yourself', are put in touch with the local group.

Such are the instrumental activities of the local groups. The groups also provide expressive activities for their members, who will wish at least to have the chance to practise speaking the language. Club meetings consist of talks, slide shows of holidays and especially world congresses, panel and party games, dances and parties, singing in Esperanto, study of literature and language, and country walks. There is much variation according to the composition and abilities of the group. Federations offer similar activities, though the programmes are usually more thoroughly prepared since members come to these meetings from a longer distance. In certain

towns (at present London, Manchester, Bristol, and Bournemouth)
it is possible to attend a monthly interdenominational religious
service in Esperanto, but in conformity with the policy of strict
religious neutrality this is organised as a separate group. Groups
may make reciprocal arrangements with a foreign group for the
exchange of letters and tapes. Many groups and federations arrange
the meeting nearest Zamenhof's birthday (December 15) as a
Zamenhof festival. This will include an address on Zamenhof's life
and work. At the conclusion of this and other important meetings,
the group will stand and sing *La Espero*. Group reports are sent for
inclusion in *Esperanto News* from time to time. These used to
appear in the *British Esperantist*. The editor of the latter has occasionally had cause to express concern at the quality of these
reports. The following item has been quoted as an example of what
not to write:[56]

What to avoid

The weekly meeting of our Esperanto class, which will perhaps some day
affiliate to the BEA, was held last Tuesday as usual, in the house of the friend
of one of our *membroj*, Miss Jonkins, who kindly lent her cosy drawingroom
por la okazo, but did not commence punctually as announced, as members
struggled in late owing to the rain, though 6 *samideanoj* were present, including a visitor, who was much impressed (he is a local bookseller); and the
smallness of numbers was compensated by the enthusiasm of those who had
braved the elements. The chair was taken by our energetic secretary, *Fraŭlino*
Tupton, who is also the *kasisto* and librarian of the *Grupo*, and after her opening remarks, in which she explained that *la kara* is an international language
designed to help and not to hinder the spread of the national languages,
invented by Dr. Zamehof, the *kunveno* was commenced by Miss *Ĝonz*, who
though she had learnt Esperanto only 3 weeks and 2 days was tastefully clad
in green *crêpe de chine*, and sang with great feeling and perfect pronunciation
the international anthem *La Espero* to the music of Menil, gracefully accompanied by her charming *fianĉo* Mr. Smyth Robinson (the leaves of the
music being most carefully turned by their mutual friend *Sinjoro* Brown) and
responded to a hearty encore by repeating the last verse, in the last line of
which all present in the room joined, and went home hoping to have the
pleasure of hearing the talented *fraŭlino* again at a no distant date, after which
the meeting closed at the usual hour.

During periods of stagnation of recruitment, such as have been characteristic of recent years, attempts have been made to retain the presence in the eyes of the general public that Esperanto already possesses. Members were urged to enter examinations in Esperanto which were still set by the Royal Society of Arts, so that this body would continue to examine in Esperanto. In the event this campaign failed, since such examinations were discontinued in 1976. Members have been urged to borrow Esperanto books from their public library (even if they do not read them) so that the books will not be put in the stacks. There has been a certain amount of formal support for Esperanto from local authorities. The mayor or his deputy can often be brought to a federation meeting, at least, and produce appropriate platitudes about the desirability of world peace and harmonious race relations, and the value of Esperanto in achieving such ends. These can take a bizarre form, such as the suggestion, in support of Esperanto, that 'in our paper-shop, some of our nicest customers are immigrants', made by the mayoress of a small Yorkshire town. A few Esperantists are employed by local authorities, or are members of local political parties. By having access to local councillors they can try to ensure that Esperanto in schools is at least not disapproved of, and might encourage attention to Esperanto on local radio, or the use of the name 'Esperanto Street'.

The BEA has recently attempted to improve the quality of local group activities; it has been felt that many present activities might constitute an obstacle to recruitment and be negative propaganda (*malpropagando*). Certain lectures at BEA congresses have been devoted to better propaganda methods. It has, for instance, been stressed that 'a speaker at a public meeting should be well dressed and look like an intellectual', and that 'the propagandist for Esperanto must not appear on television like a crank'. Also, 'we should not use old-fashioned leaflets, since it is obvious that if we use them we don't sell them very often'. Changes of this kind seem to have stemmed partly from UEA policy, partly from internal changes within the BEA.

Finally, a few snippets of conversation and other observations might help to clarify and amplify some of these points:

Propaganda. 'When I lost my Esperanto pen I thought it wasn't too bad: it's all propaganda'. (Overheard at BEA Congress, Owen's Park, Manchester, Easter 1968.)

Idealism. Member to driver of excursion coach, while waiting for members to re-assemble after the visit: 'Though we are all idealists, somebody fiddled a book token on the bookstall yesterday.' (Excursion to Jodrell Bank during 1968 Manchester BEA Congress.)

Neutrality. During a slide show at a federation meeting of a member's trip round the world (i.e. round Esperantists of the world), the member commented in support of the political neutrality of Esperanto: 'A lady we stayed with in Hungary was a very active Communist and had obtained a prize from the government for her work. In spite of that, she never mentioned politics once during the week we stayed there.'

Songs. Shortly after the excursion coach had set off to Jodrell Bank during the 1968 Manchester BEA Congress, one member began to lead the passengers in Esperanto songs. This was continued on the return trip. Not all joined in. Some songs were printed in the Congress programme. Here are examples of Esperanto songs:

Al la Esperantistaro	To the Esperantists
Tie ĉi kaj trans la maro	Here and overseas
Nia samideanaro	Our band of fellow idealists
Turnas sin kun am',	Turn themselves with love,
Malprosperu ĝi nenie,	Nowhere let it fail to prosper
Dio donu ke ĝi plie	May it by God's gift
Kresku dum la jaroj	Everywhere grow further through the
ĉie	years
Ĝis grandega fam'.	Up to tremendous fame.
Kiel familioj vivu la nacioj,	Let the nations live like families,
Kresku frata amikeco, ĉesu la	Let brotherly friendship grow and
envioj;	envies cease;
Baldaŭ homa militado	Soon human warfare
Kaj ĝisnuna malamado	And hate that has existed till now
Pro la interkomprenado	Owing to mutual understanding
Malaperas jam.	Disappear.
Altidea pacamanto,	High-idea'd peace-lover,

Patro li de Esperanto,	Father of Esperanto,
Ĉiam estu la gvidanto	May Zamenhof always be
Zamenhof al ni.	Leader of us.
Ĉien lia lingvo iros,	The language will go everywhere,
Tutan mondon ĝi konkeros	It will conquer the whole world
Naciaron kune tiros	Draw the nations together
Pro la ben' de Di'.	Through the blessing of God.

* * *

Plenigu la glason, ho ĉiu bonul',	Fill your glass, every man of good will,
Vivu la Verda Stel'!	Long live the green star!
Kaj kantu la homoj el ĉiu angul'	And may men sing from every corner
Vivu la Verda Stel'!	Long live the green star!
Vivu la, vivu la, vivu la Stel' (3)	Long, long, long live the star!
Vivu la Verda Stel'!	Long live the green star!

Plenigu la glason, kaj tostu kun mi	Fill your glass and toast with me
La lingvon kreitan por ĉiu naci'.	To the language created for every nation.

Per voĉoj de nia kunbatalantar'	By the voices of our comrades-in-arms
Resonu la voko sur tero kaj mar'.	May the call sound out on earth and sea.

* * *

Ĉiu, ĉiu, ĉiu, ĉiu	Everyone, everyone, everyone, everyone
Ĉiu homo vidas tuj	Every man sees at once
Ke l'plej bela familio	That the most beautiful family
Troviĝas ĉe ni en Esperantuj'.	Is found among us in Esperanto-land.
Ĉiu, ĉiu, ĉiu, ĉiu	Everyone, everyone, everyone, everyone
Scias ke sub la verda stel'	Knows that under the green star
Nia granda familio	Our great family
Konsistas el sanktuloj de l'ĉiel'	Consists of saints of heaven.
Se iu venas eĉ el Afrik'	If someone comes even from Africa
Vi lin komprenas sen helpo de mimik';	You will understand him without the help of mimicry;
Aŭ se vi iros al Amerik'	Or if you go to America
Tuj iu diros, 'Sidiĝu do, amik''.	Immediately someone will say 'Sit down, friend'.

Ĉiu sinjoro dediĉas sin   Every gentleman dedicates himself
El tuta koro al ĉarma   Wholeheartedly to a charming
    kursanin',   lady member of the course,
Se ŝi hezitas pri l'gramatik'   If she hesitates about her grammar,
Li ŝin invitas volonte al   He willingly invites her to
    praktik'.   practise.
Ni dum kongreso kunvenas por   We meet during the congress to
Konsenti jese kun ĉiu orator'.   Agree with every orator.
Kaj eĉ l'eterna statutbatal'   And even the eternal constitutional quarrel
Finiĝas per la plej harmonia bal'.   Ends with the most harmonious ball.

Numerous songs have also been translated from various national languages. English songs translated into Esperanto include *Clementine* and *On Ilkley Moor baht 'at*.

Mottoes. Some Esperanto groups and federations have mottoes; here are some examples from Britain:

Venko per konvinko [victory through convincement] — Lancashire and Cheshire Esperanto Federation (later North-Western Esperanto Federation).

Antaŭen ĝis la venko [forward to victory] — Yorkshire Esperanto Federation (later Yorkshire and Humberside Esperanto Federation). This motto formerly appeared under the heading of the Federation's bulletin *La blanka rozo*, but at a meeting in Hull in 1967 it was agreed, with hardly a dissenting voice, to delete it 'since this gives the impression that it is a cranky movement'.

Ĉiam antaŭen [ever forward] — Leicester Esperanto Group.

CONCLUSION

The Esperanto movement in general has always had to reconcile conflicting pulls of instrumental and expressive tendencies. The expressive tendency has usually been paramount, owing to the emphasis in the culture system of the movement on conversion of individuals, the movement sweeping the world, and world congresses. The British movement in the 1950s and 1960s had an increasing problem of lack of public attention, the assumption outside the movement being that Esperanto was dying or already dead. This is of some significance for its effect of furthering expressive at the expense of instrumental orientations. Arising from a study of the Townsend Plan (an American movement to provide old-age pensions as a mechanism for alleviating economic dislocation) Messinger observes,

When the movements themselves lose impetus through a shift in the constellation of social forces, their organized aims are deprived of conditions necessary to sustain them in their original form. But organizations are not necessarily dissolved by the abatement of the forces initially conjoining to produce them. They may gain a certain degree of autonomy from their bases and continue to exist. We will expect, however, that the abatement of the particular constellation of social forces giving rise to the movement will have important consequences for the remaining structure. The most general of these is, perhaps, increasing lack of public concern for the organizational mission. . . . Within the organization, the abatement of social forces spells dropping membership and, more serious in the long run, the end of effective recruitment.[57]

Yet there has not exactly been a *decline* of recruitment to the BEA. Esperanto in Britain has stagnated rather than declined. Rather the culture system of the movement tends to be self-preserving and self-perpetuating. The Esperanto movement has had difficulty in recruiting members in the 1950s and 1960s, yet has retained the allegiance of enthusiastic supporters of very long standing; hence the elderly social composition of the movement.[58] Thus the British Esperanto movement has long tended to reflect the culture of the aged genteel. It was as such unlikely to attract any but the most dedicated supporters of Esperanto from other status groups: yet a small but significant number of members has been sufficiently interested in Esperanto to retain their allegiance in spite of the existing membership. Such members eventually began to exert their influence during the modernisation of the BEA, and this process is likely to continue. Many of the long-established members have shown a remarkably favourable response to the modernisation programme.

Esperanto, too, is not a cause which stands in a close one-to-one relationship with other social forces, and it is difficult to see at what point it can be said to have 'lost social relevance'. Rather it is likely to be seen, as by Harold Wilson, as 'not an urgent priority'.

But this lack of successful recruitment for Esperanto in Britain has not been characteristic of other countries. Thus Esperanto does not totally correspond to Zald and Ash's[59] notion of the 'becalmed' movement, although it possesses certain features of that type. The following description could be applied suitably to Esperanto in Britain:

Many MOs [movement organizations] do not represent either successes or failures. They have been able to build and maintain a support base; they have waged the campaigns which have influenced the course of events; and they have gained some positions of power. In short, they have created or found a niche for themselves in the organizational world but their growth has slowed down or ceased. Members do not expect attainment of goals in the near future, and the emotional fervour of the movement is subdued. . . . However, the goals of the MO are still somewhat relevant to society. Thus, the organization is able to maintain purposive commitment and avoids losing all of its purposively oriented members to competing causes.[60]

The greater success of Esperanto in certain other countries has helped to retain new recruits and to encourage existing members. Yet even so, 'success' abroad has tended to mean greater public and official recognition and approval, rather than actual adoption of Esperanto as an auxiliary language. In this situation, expressive rather than instrumental aspects of the movement have still tended to be emphasised. As one Esperanto song puts it: *la verda stelo restas sen fin'* [the green star goes on without end].

NOTES

1. Quoted in *The Office*, 8 December 1888, p.12.
2. *Languages*, 15 May 1894, quoted in *The British Esperantist*, February 1915, pp.36–37.
3. Volapük did have *some* support in Britain; in 1886 there were five Volapük clubs and two British Volapük periodicals. See *Volapükagased* 24, 1959, p.23.
4. For early history of the British Esperanto movement see J. Merchant, *Joseph Rhodes kaj la fruaj tagoj de Esperanto en Anglujo* (n.d.).
5. For biography of Stead see W.S. Smith, *The London Heretics*, 1967.
6. *Review of Reviews* 26, 1902, pp.384–385.
7. *Review of Reviews* 26, 1902, p.625.
8. *Review of Reviews* 27, 1903, p.71.
9. *Review of Reviews* 27, 1903, p.168.

10. *Review of Reviews* 28, 1903, p.392.
11. OV, pp.359–360.
12. *Review of Reviews* 27, 1903, p.77.
13. *Review of Reviews* 28, 1903, p.187.
14. *British Esperantist*, December 1905, p.176. The article (the leader of *The Times* for 8 August 1905 [p.7]) was in fact quite hostile, suggesting that uses of Esperanto were limited and advocating learning of foreign languages instead.
15. *British Esperantist*, August 1906, p.81.
16. *British Esperantist*, January 1906, *Supplement*, p.1.
17. OV, pp.374–375.
18. *British Esperantist*, June 1910, p.118.
19. *British Esperantist*, December 1912, p.233.
20. *British Esperantist*, September 1907, p.174.
21. *British Esperantist* (hereinafter referred to as BE), September 1914, p.161.
22. BE, October 1914, p.185.
23. BE, July 1915, p.125.
24. BE, August 1915, p.160.
25. BE, November 1915, p.212.
26. British Association for the Advancement of Science, *Report of the Eighty-Ninth Meeting*, 1922, pp.390–407.
27. For a report of this incident see BE, May 1922, p.61.
28. BE, March 1922, p.17.
29. BE, May 1922, p.66.
30. BE, March 1938, p.267; May 1938, p.301; June 1938, p.306.
31. BE, September 1937, p.145.
32. BE, July 1936, p.344.
33. J. Cresswell and J. Hartley, *Teach Yourself Esperanto*, 1957.
34. J. Wells, *E.U.P. Concise Esperanto and English Dictionary*, 1969.
35. See survey results, Chs. 11–12.
36. The history of this question is contained in N. Williams, *Application to the Secondary School Examination Council: Esperanto 'O' Level Subject for G.C.E.*, 1963.
37. BE, February 1966, p.293.
38. BE, November 1965, p.215. (Letter from J. Dew, Political Assistant, on behalf of the Prime Minister). But see below, p.286.
39. *The Open Road*, 1923, p.1.
40. L. Courtinat, *op. cit.*, vol. 1, p.228.
41. BE, July 1919, p.87.
42. BE, March 1956, p.48.
43. BE, November 1957, p.160.
44. *Ibid.*
45. BE, January 1958, p.191.
46. BE, March 1958, p.218.
47. *Ibid.*
48. *Ibid.*, p.219.
49. BE, March 1958, p.213.
50. BE, November 1958, p.336.
51. For early history see G.P. de Bruin, *op. cit.*, pp.6–7.
52. Information from circular letter about the split to members of SATEB.
53. Information from Ethel Prent, personal communication.

54.   Information from Pauline Bryan, Assistant Secretary of ILP, personal communication.

55.   See *Articles of Association of the BEA*, revised edition, BE, May 1972, pp.248–257.

56.   BE, May 1926, p.136. Glossary: *membroj*=members; *por la okazo*=for the occasion; *Fraŭlino*=Miss; *kasisto*=treasurer; *Grupo*=group; *la kara*=the dear (language); *kunveno*=meeting; *Ĝonz*=Jones in Esperanto spelling; *fianĉo*=fiancé; *Sinjoro*= Mister.

57.   S. Messinger, 'Organizational transformation: a case study of a declining social movement', *American Sociological Review*, 1955, pp.3–10 (pp.9–10).

58.   With all due reservations about citing fiction literature as evidence, it is impossible to resist quoting from *Flowers on the Grass* by Monica Dickens (1945, pp.53–54). The scene is a seaside boarding-house. 'The winter guests at the Lothian were mostly long-term, although this lot had the air of being there while they waited for something. Mrs. Lewin was waiting with her twelve-year-old son Curtis for her Canadian husband to send for her. Miss Wyllis was waiting for a man. She had been waiting all her life. Old Mr. and Mrs. Parker were waiting for their daughter to ask them to go up north and live with her. Miss Rawlings was waiting for her mother to die in the nursing home round the corner. She went in every day and read *Pilgrim's Progress* to her in Esperanto, but had not killed her yet. Mr. Dangerfield, who was the MC at the Palace Ballroom, was waiting for the summer season, when he could stop giving private lessons and once more be Our Own Dudley Dangerfield in white gloves and tails to the ground, chanting into the microphone for the old-fashioned dances: "Swing your partners and turn *around*. Knees to the middle and bow to the *ground*"'.

59.   M.N. Zald and R. Ash, 'Social movement organizations: growth, decay and change', *Social Forces* 1966, pp.327–341.

60.   *Ibid.*, p.334.

11

Social Composition of the British Esperanto Association

Information drawn upon up to this point has been derived largely from documents, with the addition of some material derived from participant observation. In order to amplify this information and to obtain some statistical data, a questionnaire was sent to members of the British Esperanto Association in 1968. The survey was carried out with the full cooperation and approval – even encouragement – of the Executive of the BEA. Earlier versions of the questionnaire were tested in personal interviews with some Hull members; a later version was tested on a small national sample of members, this time being sent through the post. The BEA Executive approved the wording of the questionnaire, and did not wish for any changes to be made. For the final sampling frame, the membership list of the BEA was taken, with some omissions. These were (a) members in the Irish Republic, recorded in BEA lists in the same alphabetical sequence as United Kingdom members; (b) overseas members, kept in a separate sequence; (c) members who had already taken part in the pilot surveys. A questionnaire was sent to a representative sample of all other members. Ordinary members, junior members, and Councillors, kept in separate lists by the BEA, were separately treated, though the same questionnaire was used for all members. For ordinary members, a sample of 25% was taken. This was technically a quasi-random sample,[1] incorporating every fourth member on the list, though the starting point was chosen by a random method. A 100% survey was made of junior members and Councillors. In the case of junior members, three had already been enumerated in the pilot postal survey; as the questionnaire was hardly changed between the pilot and the final survey, these were absorbed with the main survey results.

The questionnaire was in English (see Appendix VI). The survey was begun in the autumn of 1968. A reminder was sent to those members who had not returned the questionnaire after one month, and the reminder was supported by a notice in *The British Esperantist*.[2] All questionnaires received up to 31 December 1968 were counted, only one in fact being received too late for inclusion. The response rate was as follows:

Ordinary members: 82.5% (235 questionnaires received)
Councillors   88.9% (64 questionnaires received)
Junior members   87.2% (41 questionnaires received, plus 3
                                      from the pilot survey)

This is an excellent rate for a postal questionnaire.[3] In this and the following chapter, the results of the survey will be presented in tabular form. Information derived from sources other than the questionnaire will be included where appropriate. The present chapter will include responses to those questions which did not directly relate to Esperanto. The following chapter will deal with those questions relating to Esperanto, including cross-tabulations with the data reported here. In the present chapter results will be compared, where possible, with statistical data for the United Kingdom, including census material. The nearest census to the survey was the sample census of 1966, and this material has been used extensively. Available sources often exclude Northern Ireland, which the present survey includes; there are, however, so few members of the BEA in Northern Ireland that it is not felt that this will affect accuracy of comparisons made. In all tabulations, percentages are given to the nearest whole number of percentage points. The following abbreviations will be used:

O   Ordinary members   N   Number in any given cell
J   Junior members   M   male
C   Councillors   F   female

Figures are often presented for all members, i.e. the total number in the survey, whether ordinary, junior, or Councillors. In computing such totals the figures for juniors and Councillors are divided by four, so as to correct for the variable sampling fraction. As a result of such procedure, the figures for all members do not always appear as whole numbers.

SEX

The sex composition is shown in Table 17.

Table 17. *Sex composition of the BEA*

	M		F	
	N	%	N	%
Ordinary	154	65	81	35
Junior	39	89	5	11
Councillors	48	75	16	25
All members	175¾	67	86¼	33
U.K. (1969) (000's)	26,984	49	28,550	51

The proportion of women is less than in the population at large but is still substantial.[4] Male domination is increased in the membership of the Council. Evidently very few young females are recruited to the movement. The findings suggest that the BEA, like other social movements not holding aims of particular interest to women, is composed mainly of men.

AGE

Table 18 shows the age distribution of BEA members. Since 'junior' is itself an age category, juniors have been combined with ordinary members, correcting for the variable sampling fraction.

The survey results confirm the fact that the BEA has an aging membership; considering, too, that some members wrote saying that they were unable to fill in the questionnaire because of their age, this might even be an underestimate. It can be seen that 45% of all members are over 60. Generally speaking, the age ranges up to 49 are underrepresented, range 50–59 reflects the national distribution, and age ranges above that are overrepresented. It has been noted that, after a short-lived upsurge in 1945, membership of the BEA has declined and more recently stagnated. During this period, those remaining faithful to the movement will have grown older, while new recruits who have stayed in the movement will

Table 18a. *Age distribution of the BEA: ordinary and junior members*

Age range	M		F		All	
	N	%	N	%	N	%
15–19*	6	4	1	1	7	3
20–29	14¾	9	2¼	3	17	7
30–39	20	12	7	9	27	11
40–49	22	13	16	19	38	15
50–59	27	17	15	18	42	17
60–69	37	23	19	23	56	23
70–79	21	13	16	19	37	15
80–89	12	7	4	5	16	7
90–up	2	1	0	0	2	1
No answer	2	1	2	2	4	2
Total	163¾		82¼		246	

* Three junior members were in fact only 14, but for this and subsequent tabulations they are counted as 15 years old; it would otherwise be difficult to make comparisons with national data.

Table 18b. *Age distribution: Councillors*

Age range	M		F		All	
	N	%	N	%	N	%
15–19	0	0	0	0	0	0
20–29	4	8	0	0	4	6
30–39	2	4	2	13	4	6
40–49	10	21	5	31	15	23
50–59	10	21	4	25	14	22
60–69	10	21	4	25	14	22
70–79	7	15	1	6	8	12
80–89	3	6	0	0	3	5
90–up	0	0	0	0	0	0
No answer	2	4	0	0	2	3
Total	48		16		64	

Table 18c. *Age distribution: all members, showing comparison with U.K. population for 1966*[5]

Age range	M			F			All		
	N	%	U.K. %	N	%	U.K. %	N	%	U.K. %
15–19	6	3	10	1	1	10	7	3	10
20–29	15¾	9	18	2¼	3	16	18	7	17
30–39	20½	12	17	7½	9	15	28	11	16
40–49	24½	14	17	17¼	20	16	41¾	16	17
50–59	29½	17	17	16	19	17	45½	17	17
60–69	39½	22	13	20	23	14	59½	23	13
70–79	22¾	13	6	16¼	19	9	39	15	7
80–89	12¾	7	2	4	5	3	16¾	6	2
90–up	2	1	0	0	0	0	2	1	0
No answer	2½	1		2	2		4½	2	
Total	175¾			86¼			262		

Arithmetic means age (all members) = 55. Standard deviation = 18.
Arithmetic means age (Councillors) = 56. Standard deviation = 12.

have mostly been those who found the existing members congenial, usually members of similar age. Thus the BEA has proved unattractive to young people.

MARITAL STATUS

Table 19 shows the marital status of members: those figures for all members also include comparisons with national data. Junior members are not enumerated separately, since at the time of the survey all were single.

The minimum legal age of marriage is 16, though the total British 'population' here considered is that aged 15 and over. It is not expected that this minor difference will substantially affect accuracy. Likewise, in the BEA survey 'separated' members were counted as divorced, while the population census counts them as married. This discrepancy is also not likely to have significant consequences. The results indicate that a large proportion of the

Table 19. *Marital status of BEA members*

	M			F			All		
	N	%	GB%	N	%	GB%	N	%	GB%
Ordinary and junior members									
Single	37	24		41	51		78	33	
Married	103	67		26	32		129	55	
Widowed	9	6		12	15		21	9	
Divorced	4	3		1	1		5	2	
No answer	1	1		1	1		2	1	
Total	154			81			235		
Councillors									
Single	8	17		12	75		20	31	
Married	33	69		4	25		37	58	
Widowed	5	10		0	0		5	8	
Divorced	1	2		0	0		1	2	
No answer	1	2		0	0		1	2	
Total	48			16			64		
All members, showing comparison with British population in 1966[6]									
Single	48¾	28	26	45¼	52	22	94	36	24
Married	111¼	64	69	27	31	63	138¼	53	66
Widowed	10¼	6	4	12	14	14	22¼	8	9
Divorced	4¼	2	1	1	1	1	5¼	2	1
No answer	1¼	1		1	1		2¼	1	
Total	175¾			86¼			262		

women in the BEA are unmarried. While the marital status of male members of the BEA does not differ substantially from the national figures, over half the women members are single, as opposed to less than a quarter of the total female British population. It has been noted that all junior members are single. This will appear to be a consequence of the fact that junior members are mostly still undergoing full-time education.

FAMILY SIZE

Members ever married were asked if they had any children, and if so, how many. The results were as shown in Table 20.

Table 20.   *Family size of BEA members*

No. of children	O		C		All	
	N	%	N	%	N	%
0	44	28	9	21	46¼	28
1	34	22	5	9	35¼	21
2	46	30	13	30	49¼	30
3	18	12	11	26	20¾	12
4	4	3	3	7	4¾	3
5	4	3	1	2	4¼	3
6	0	0	0	0	0	0
7	0	0	1	2	¼	0
No answer	5	3	0	0	5	3
Total	155		43		165¾	

Arithmetic mean: ordinary members 1.4; councillors 2.0; all members 1.4.

Even allowing for the high social class composition of the BEA (see Table 21), the size of BEA ordinary members' families tends to be small. This is less true of the Councillors, who also tend to be higher in social class than the membership as a whole. Over one-quarter of BEA members ever married have no children at all. In view of the high age structure of the BEA, it should also be noted that these figures will in a large number of cases relate to completed families.

Summarising the data so far, it can be said that the BEA is predominantly male and elderly. Of the women members, a large proportion are unmarried, though this is not true of the men.

Family size tends to be small, and many married members are childless. The explanations for these figures, apart from the age composition, would appear to relate to the general characteristics of social movements rather than Esperanto in particular. Stacey, on the basis of an analysis of 71 associations in Banbury, concludes that 'membership has certain special characteristics: it is predominantly male, middle-aged, and above-average occupational status'.[7] Men preponderate, especially in positions of authority, in associations, in a society where men are expected to take positions of responsibility. Married women are more likely to define their situation as centred around the home, and may thus be less active in a nationally organised movement like the BEA. Those women who are active tend to be unmarried. There does not, it should be noted, appear ever to have been any discrimination against women in the BEA, or the Esperanto movement generally. The families of those married (though not of Councillors) tend to be small or non-existent. Various possible considerations might here be relevant; the predominantly middle-class social composition, the small number of Roman Catholics in the BEA (see Table 36), and possibly (though no data are available) late age of marriage. In addition, those with small families or without children are freer to take part in activities of the movement and are more likely to remain members.

SOCIAL CLASS

'Social class' is here used in the sense employed by the Registrar General, and in strict sociological terms should be 'social status'. Each social class, in the Registrar General's terms, is regarded as homogeneous in relation to the basic criterion of the general standing within the community of the occupations concerned. The five social classes are as follows:

    I   Professional, etc., occupations
    II   Intermediate occupations
    III Skilled occupations
    IV   Partly skilled occupations
    V   Unskilled occupations

It is possible to classify retired persons according to their former occupations, full-time housewives according to their husbands' occupations. Full-time students at schools and colleges, the armed forces, and the unemployed are excluded. The BEA members are distributed between these groupings shown in Table 21, giving comparisons with national data:[8]

Table 21.   *Social class of BEA Members*

| | O | | J | | C | | All | | G.B. | |
	N	%	N	%	N	%	N	%	N ('000s)	%
I	32	14	3	33	12	19	35¾	14	1,428	4
II	115	50	0	0	37	58	124¼	50	6,238	16
III	67	29	6	67	13	20	71¾	29	19,152	48
IV	12	5	0	0	0	0	12	5	8,764	22
V	2	1	0	0	1	2	2¼	1	3,178	8
Not classified	4	2	0	0	1	2	4¼	2	1,019	3
Total	232		9		64		250¼		39,780	

It is clear that BEA members are heavily concentrated in social classes I, II, and III; classes IV and V, consisting mainly of manual workers, are very much underrepresented. Councillors are generally of higher status than ordinary members. The BEA thus reflects the tendency, already noted, for participation in voluntary associations to be predominantly middle-class, with the officials of higher status in the wider society than ordinary members. Bottomore points out for Squirebridge that 'there is a correlation between high occupational status and the exercise of leadership, which involves more *intensive* participation in activities'.[9] Likewise Stacey notes that

...the third special characteristic of voluntary associations is the relatively high social status of their members. Furthermore, the committee tend to have a higher social status than the membership.[10]

Apart from such general factors, it should be added that the Esperanto movement provides satisfaction from membership for those who have learnt the language. This implies a need for verbal facility and an inclination for reading, which in turn strengthens the middle-class social composition of the movement.

It is also possible to compare the proportion of those economically active in the BEA with figures for the general population aged 15 or over.[11] This information is as shown in Table 22.

Table 22.   *Proportion of members economically active*

	O		J		C		All		G.B. ('000s)	
	N	%	N	%	N	%	N	%	N	%
Economically active	127	55	9	20	37	58	138½	53	24,856	62
Retired*	85	37	0	0	24	38	91	35	2,411	6
Students**	1	0	35	80	0	0	9¾	4	1,265	3
Others***	19	8	0	0	3	5	19¾	8	11,508	29
Total	232		44		64		259		40,040	

* Females 60 and over and males 65 and over were presumed in the BEA survey to be retired. It is realised that this will not represent a strictly accurate measure, but many replies were not sufficiently clear on this point for a different indicator to be used.
** I.e. persons over 15 receiving full-time education.
*** Mainly housewives.

The high proportion of retired members is noteworthy: 35% of BEA members as opposed to 6% of the general population. This corresponds to the high age structure already noted.

The Registrar General divides the economically active population into 'occupational orders'. In each of these, the kind of work done and the nature of the operation performed are broadly similar. Table 23 represents a comparison between the British economically active population and that of the BEA. Figures for Great Britain[12] are given in thousands, while all BEA figures relate only to economically active members.

The heavy concentration of members in Order XXV (professional, technical workers, artists) is evident. Clerical workers are also well

Table 23. *Occupational orders of BEA members*

Order		BEA N	BEA %	G.B. N	G.B. %
I	Farmers, foresters, fishermen	0	0	864	3
II	Miners and quarrymen	0	0	373	2
III	Gas, coke, and chemicals makers	0	0	146	1
IV	Glass and ceramics makers	0	0	104	0
V	Furnace, forge, foundry, rolling mill workers	0	0	211	1
VI	Electrical and electronic workers	5¼	4	615	2
VII	Engineering and allied trade workers n.e.c.*	7¼	5	2,769	11
VIII	Woodworkers	1¼	1	468	2
IX	Leather workers	0	0	136	1
X	Textile workers	1	1	405	2
XI	Clothing workers	4	3	468	2
XII	Food, drink, and tobacco workers	¼	0	401	2
XIII	Paper and printing workers	4¼	3	336	1
XIV	Makers of other products	0	0	336	1
XV	Construction workers	1	1	593	2
XVI	Painters and decorators	1	1	322	1
XVII	Drivers of stationary vehicles, cranes, etc.	1	1	319	1
XVIII	Labourers n.e.c.*	0	0	1,291	5
XIX	Transport and communication workers	5¼	4	1,499	6
XX	Warehousemen, storekeepers, packers, bottlers	0	0	862	3
XXI	Clerical workers	20½	15	3,402	14
XXII	Sales workers	5¼	4	2,383	10
XXIII	Service, sport, and recreation workers	7¼	5	2,991	12
XXIV	Administrators and managers	10¼	7	766	3
XXV	Professional, technical workers, artists	58¾	42	2,375	10
XXVI	Armed forces (British and foreign)	0	0	251	1
XXVII	Inadequately described occupations	5	4	170	1
Total		138½		24,856	

* n.e.c. = not elsewhere classified

represented, but not substantially more so than in the rest of the population. Again it can be seen that orders consisting mainly of manual workers are heavily underrepresented, particularly in agricultural, extractive, and heavy industrial occupations. In occupational Order XXV, teachers are particularly well represented (a total for all members of 28 (20%) compared with 2% of the general population. Here the BEA corresponds to a pattern found in many other social movements, in which teachers are frequently seen to be the largest occupational group. This has been found to be the case with the Campaign for Nuclear Disarmament,[13] the Humanists,[14] and no doubt other organisations too.

SOCIAL MOBILITY

Table 24 compares the social class distribution of BEA members with that of their fathers. Figures relate to all categories of members.

Table 24.   *Social mobility of BEA members*

Class	Own class		Father's class	
	N	%	N	%
I	35¾	14	20	8
II	124¼	47	74¼	28
III	71¾	27	119½	45
IV	12	5	16¼	6
V	2¼	1	6	2
Armed forces	0	0	8	3
Students	9¾	4	–	–
Unspecified	2	1	18	7
Total	262		262	

The social mobility profile of the BEA reflects the national pattern. A certain amount of mobility is possible between classes I, II, and III, but very little from classes IV and V.

GEOGRAPHICAL DISTRIBUTION

Using the complete membership list, the location of members' addresses in various geographical areas was ascertained. BEA membership was related to the population of such areas, and figures for over- or underrepresentation were arrived at. In order to ascertain the degree of over- or underrepresentation it was necessary to arrive at an index for average strength of the BEA in the nation as a whole. This presented certain problems, since use was to be made of C.A. Moser and W. Scott's classification of British towns,[15] which was based on 1951 figures; while for larger geographical areas more recent figures were taken. The index was based on the observation that about 1 in 50,000 of the British population is a member of the BEA. This is approximately the case since, in recent years, the British population has been somewhat more than 50 millions, the BEA membership somewhat more than 1,000. Investigation proved that BEA members were not at all evenly distributed between the various national divisions of the United Kingdom. Table 25 shows the distribution of BEA members between the national divisions. The column e (expected number of Esperantists) is based on the assumption that 1 in 50,000 of the British population are members of the BEA.[16] Column o indicates the observed number of Esperantists, as derived from the BEA membership list.

Table 25.   *National distribution of BEA members*

	e	o	o/e
England	868.8	1,141	1.3
Wales	52.8	41	0.8
Scotland	109.0	79	0.7
Northern Ireland	38.5	9	0.2
Isle of Man	1.0	1	1.0
Channel Islands	2.2	0	0.0
Total	1,072.3	1,271	1.2

The BEA is thus stronger in England than in Scotland, Wales, or Northern Ireland. These figures, it should be noted, relate to BEA members and not to organised Esperantists generally. In the case of Scotland, it is strongly suspected that many Esperantists see the Scottish Esperanto Federation as their national association. Members in Northern Ireland might sometimes prefer to join the Irish

Esperanto Association. No comparable association exists for Wales: it is, however, possible that here and perhaps in other Celtic-speaking areas those interested in language support Celtic language movements rather than Esperanto.

For England, the index of 1.3 can be taken as the norm. In any area in England, the BEA can be said to be over- or underrepresented insofar as it deviates from the score o/e = 1.3. An examination of English local authority areas containing over 50,000 population (before reorganisation of local government) was made, using the classification of Moser and Scott in *British Towns*. On the basis of the national figure of one BEA member per 50,000 population, it could be expected that every 'town' considered by Moser and Scott would have at least one member. Moser and Scott divide English towns into 14 different classes,[17] on the basis of 57 variables. Social class (Registrar General's) and age of the population are particularly significant variables in arriving at the classification. In the present survey, the number of observed members (o) was divided by the number of expected members (e) for each town; then for each class of town the arithmetic mean o/e score was obtained. The results were as shown in Table 26.

Individual towns. It is much easier to consider classes of town when the extent of representation of BEA members in any given place is to be considered. An individual activist may succeed in persuading many people in his own small area to join the BEA and, where the population of the area concerned is small, the o/e score can thereby appear very high. Where classes of town are considered, however, the influence of such local initiatives can be reduced. It is, nonetheless, useful to consider more closely those individual towns which deviate considerably from the expectation of one BEA member per unit of 50,000 population. It was found that 24 Moser/Scott towns had no BEA members at all. The largest of these was Coventry, where 5.2 members would be expected. Other notable deviants were Salford (e = 3.6) and West Ham (e = 3.4). All of these were in classes of town in which the BEA was underrepresented in any case. There were, however, some towns with no BEA members in certain classes of town where the BEA was normally overrepresented. These were Peterborough, Lancaster, and York (class 3); Sutton and Cheam (class 9); and Gosport (class 12).

Table 26. *Mean o/e score for Moser and Scott's classes of town*

	o/e
Overrepresented in the following classes of town:	
1. (Mainly seaside resorts)	3.9
6. (Mainly textile centres, Yorkshire and Lancashire)	2.4
12. (Light industry suburbs, national defence centres, towns in sphere of influence of large conurbations)	2.4
2. (Mainly spas, professional and administrative centres)	2.3
3. (Mainly commercial centres with some industry)	1.8
9. (Mainly exclusive residential suburbs)	1.7
11. (Mainly newer mixed residential suburbs)	1.6
Corresponds to national pattern in following classes:	
4. (Including most of the traditional railway centres)	1.3
London Administrative County*	1.3
Underrepresented in the following classes of town:	
5. (Including many of the large ports, plus two Black Country towns)	1.0
7. (Industrial towns of NE seaboard, and mining towns of Wales)	1.0
Huyton with Roby*	0.9
10. (Mainly older mixed residential suburbs)	0.8
13. (Mainly older working-class and industrial suburbs)	0.8
14. (Mainly older industrial suburbs)	0.8
8. (Including the more recent metal manufacturing towns)	0.5

* Listed separately by Moser and Scott, since did not fit into any classes.
Note: Since Moser and Scott's analysis was to be employed, 1951 boundaries and population figures had to be used for arriving at these figures. For each class, the mean o/e was arrived at by summing the o/e figures for the various towns in each class and dividing by the total number of towns in that class. No correction was made for the size of the population of the various towns.

An analysis was also made of those towns where BEA membership was overrepresented. To reduce the possibility that the results might arise from pure chance, examples based on less than five BEA members reported were omitted. Table 27 is a list of the 20 towns where the BEA is at least twice as strong as would be the case if membership were evenly distributed throughout the country.

In this table, the number preceding the town is the class allocated to it by Moser and Scott, the number following it the o/e score.

Table 27. *Overrepresentation of BEA membership in Moser/Scott towns*

6 times* overrepresented:	12	Watford	8.0		
5 times* overrepresented:	1	Bournemouth	7.6	6 Keighley	7.3
	1	Hastings	6.9	1 Southport	6.5
4 times* overrepresented:	3	Ipswich	5.7		
3 times* overrepresented:	3	Norwich	5.0	5 Blackburn	5.0
	2	Exeter	4.0	12 Romford	3.9
2 times* overrepresented:	6	Huddersfield	3.8	9 Coulsdon and	
				Purley	3.8
	3	Southampton	3.6	6 Burnley	3.5
	6	Leicester	3.2	2 Bath	3.1
	3	Bristol	3.0	6 Halifax	3.0
	6	Bradford	2.9	11 Hornchurch	2.9

* I.e. 6, etc., times *or over*.

Individual towns: Scotland and Northern Ireland. Scottish towns are considered by Moser and Scott but do not fit into the English classification. Northern Irish towns are not considered by them at all. The small number of Scottish and Northern Irish towns which exceed 50,000 population is therefore separated into individual components. Table 28 indicates the strength of the BEA in the towns concerned.[18]

The general pattern for English towns is that those towns where the BEA is strong belong to the *classes* of town which have higher-than-average BEA membership: especially Moser and Scott's classes 1, 2, and 3. Such towns tend to have a high proportion of their population in social classes I and II, and a high proportion of old people. In particular Moser and Scott's class 1 towns, mainly sea-side resorts, are clearly the most fruitful source of recruitment to the BEA. These towns tend to be high in social class composition and to have a relatively large number of residents who are elderly and retired, often living in one-person households. The converse also applies. Towns which are low in social class composition and young in age of the population invariably have fewer BEA members than would be the case if they were evenly distributed. This applies to classes 8 and 14, Huyton with Roby, and marginally to class 13. The Scottish towns, which are not classified, are less tractable. No Scottish town is both high in social class composition and aging in population. Motherwell and Wishaw, where the BEA is most over-represented, is a curious exception to the general pattern since it is both low in social class composition and young in population. The Northern Irish towns reflect the underrepresentation of the BEA in Northern Ireland generally.

Table 28. *BEA membership in Scottish and Northern Irish towns*

Town	e	o	o/e
Edinburgh	9.3	18	1.9
Glasgow	21.8	9	0.4
Aberdeen	3.6	3	0.8
Dundee	3.5	4	1.1
Motherwell and Wishaw	1.4	5	3.6
Greenock	1.6	0	0.0
Paisley	1.9	3	1.6
Belfast	8.1	3	0.4
Londonderry	1.1	0	0.0

A general review of the strength of the BEA in Britain demon-strates relatively strong support in Tyneside, seaside towns, the smaller textile centres of Lancashire and Yorkshire, Leicestershire, East Anglia, Berkshire, and the south coast. BEA membership is particularly low in the Midlands; the total absence of BEA mem-bers in Coventry has already been noted. Outside England, the BEA is much weaker. Cardiff has a certain amount of support for the BEA and there is a sprinkling of members along the sea coast of north Wales. In Scotland, the east coast of Fifeshire and Edinburgh are principal sources of recruits. In Northern Ireland, most of the few BEA members reside in County Down.

It appears, therefore, that BEA members are typically to be found in seaside towns, and those inland towns which are spas, watering places, or at least nonindustrial centres of population —

or are centres of light rather than heavy industry. The BEA is remarkably strong in smaller and medium-sized towns of Lancashire
and Yorkshire, and East Anglia generally. The Black Country,
areas based on heavy extractive industry of any kind, and metal-
manufacturing towns, do not in general provide much support for
the BEA.

The findings on geographical distribution largely confirm the
data on social class and age composition of the BEA as derived
from the questionnaire. They do, however, point to the fact that
in these two respects BEA members reflect the milieu in which
they live. Esperanto is thus not a club for old people in a young
neighbourhood, or a club for middle-class people in a working-class
neighbourhood.

EDUCATION

Education is difficult to handle as a face-sheet variable, owing to
its constantly changing structure.[19] This factor is of importance
for the BEA membership since, while it contains both very young
and very old members, the older members predominate. The BEA
membership is also preponderantly male, a matter of some significance when considering the restricted educational opportunities
for females when many BEA members went to school. Thus data
on education must be considered along with data for age and sex.

Members were asked to indicate the age at which they completed
full-time education. The results are presented in Table 29.

Respondents were also asked to indicate the type of school
attended. The results are presented in Table 30.

Tables 29 and 30 show that BEA members are more highly
educated than the population at large. Members are underrepresented among those who completed education under 16 and
overrepresented among those who completed education at 16 or
over. There are some exceptions to this trend, who typically
compensated for their lack of schooling by adult education – and
this has included Esperanto. The overwhelming majority of the
junior members are still undergoing full-time education, reflecting
the better educational opportunities now available. Among the
membership at large, grammar school education predominates. The

Table 29.   *Age on completion of full-time education*

Leaving age	O N	O %	J N	J %	C N	C %	All N	All %
Under 14	15	6	0	0	7	11	16¾	6
14	49	21	0	0	7	11	50¾	19
15	23	10	1	1	6	9	24¾	10
16	46	20	1	2	7	11	48	18
17	29	12	3	7	12	19	32¾	13
18	15	6	1	2	2	3	15¾	6
Over 18	52	22	1	2	21	33	57½	22
Still	1	0	37	84	0	0	10¼	4
No answer	5	2	0	0	2	3	5½	2
Total	235		44		64		262	

Table 30.   *Type of school attended*

Type of school	O N	O %	J N	J %	C N	C %	All N	All %
Elementary or secondary modern	82	35	4	9	18	28	87½	33
Technical or art	10	4	0	0	1	2	10¼	4
Boarding school (any)	19	8	7	16	3	5	21½	8
Grammar, etc.*	97	41	29	66	36	56	113¼	43
Comprehensive	1	0	3	7	1	2	2	1
Educated abroad	7	3	1	2	3	5	8	3
Other	8	3	0	0	0	0	8¼	3
Never at school	1	0	0	0	0	0	1	0
No answer	10	4	0	0	2	3	10½	4
Total	235		44		64		262	

*Grammar, high, independent day, or public day.

figure of 43% for all members contrasts with the 18.3% of the general population who attended grammar school before the introduction of the comprehensive system.[20] These figures assume particular importance when the extension of educational opportunity in the twentieth century is borne in mind; BEA members are particularly well educated considering their age.

Further confirmation of the degree of education of members is given by information on further and higher education and professional qualifications. Table 31 shows the highest qualifications obtained by members. 'Advanced' professional qualifications are taken to be those roughly equivalent to at least a Pass degree, as far as this could be estimated. Teacher training is separately enumerated, but those possessing both a degree and a certificate in education are shown as having a degree only. Those at present studying for a degree or qualification are assumed to possess it already.

Table 31.   *Further and higher education and qualifications*

	O		J		C		All	
	N	%	N	%	N	%	N	%
Degree	30	13	15	34	17	27	38	15
Teacher training	28	12	3	7	4	6	29¾	11
Advanced p.q.	30	13	4	9	9	14	33¼	13
Elementary p.q.	41	17	2	5	15	23	45¼	17
No answer	1	0	0	0	1	2	1¼	0
No qualification	105	45	20	46	18	28	114½	43
Total	235		44		64		262	

Thus a remarkably large proportion of BEA members have undergone further or higher education. The large proportion who have undergone teacher training suggests that many teacher members will be nongraduates.

BEA members are also active in adult education, which is of course one of the ways of learning Esperanto. Apart from Esperanto, members had attended an average of 1.55 adult education classes each, 2.35 if one excludes the 89 members (34%) who attended no evening classes at all. Table 32 shows the subjects attended by at least 10 members.

BEA members can thus be seen to be active in adult education, with academic subjects more popular than 'craft' subjects. Languages are especially popular.

Table 32. *Adult education classes attended by BEA members*

Subject	N	%	Subject	N	%
French	49½	19	Dressmaking/millinery/embroidery	14¾	6
German	40¼	15			
Music	26	10	Italian	14¼	5
Visual Arts	25¼	10	Russian	13¼	5
Psychology	18¼	7	Economics	12	5
Current affairs	18¼	7	Spanish	11½	4
Handicrafts	18	7	Medical subjects	11½	4
English literature	17	6	Biology	10¼	4
History	16½	6	Folk dance	10¼	4
English language	15½	6			

A specific question was asked on knowledge of languages, members being asked to give some indication of fluency. It was discovered that 20% (N = 53) of the entire membership had no knowledge, not even the most rudimentary, of any language other than English and Esperanto. For such persons Esperanto will have opened up important opportunities for overseas contact. However, most members had some acquaintance with foreign languages: indeed, for some members Esperanto was merely the rounding off of a wide range of linguistic achievement. Although 'fluency' is an ambiguous concept, an attempt is made in Table 33 to classify members' pro-

Table 33. *Linguistic proficiency of BEA members*

	Advanced		Intermediate		Elementary		All proficiencies	
	N	%	N	%	N	%	N	%
French	23¾	9	29½	11	125¾	48	179	68
German	11½	4	16¾	6	80¼	31	108½	42
Italian	4¼	2	10¼	4	26¼	10	40¾	16
Spanish	6	2	7¼	3	24¼	9	37½	14
Latin	6	2	7¼	3	16	6	29¼	11
Russian	1¼	1	3¼	1	17½	7	22	8
Dutch	3¼	1	3	1	9½	4	15¾	6

ficiency into 'advanced', 'intermediate', and 'elementary'. 'Elementary' refers to any knowledge from the most rudimentary to a standard approximating to 'O' level; 'intermediate' refers to a standard higher than 'O' level but not higher than 'A' level. 'Advanced' refers to a standard higher than 'A' level, including, for instance, any language taken as a substantial part of a university course, or the respondent's mother tongue if not English.[21] Figures relate to all members.

Percentages are given out of the total number of members in the survey (262). Languages spoken by less than 10 members are not shown. The figures suggest high linguistic ability in languages other than Esperanto. Those languages popular among BEA members are probably those also popular in the wider society.

POLITICS

Members were asked for their voting intentions if a general election were to be held, but were further asked to assume that a candidate for their preferred party was standing. This was the only question that a significant number of members objected to answering. Some argued that this question was 'personal' or that 'Esperanto should not be associated with politics'. Perhaps because of the taboo often felt about politics in the Esperanto movement, the answers to this question were particularly interesting. Members were asked to tick preferences from a list of choices. A few members ticked more than one (mostly 'Lab-Libs'). Choices of this kind were counted as half a vote for each. Table 34 shows members' political preferences.

The most recent general election at the time of the survey was 1966.[22] In that year, 75.8% of the electorate voted. Only the three major parties obtained a national share of the poll which was greater than 1% though the Scottish National Party also did so on the basis of the Scottish vote alone. The national figures in 1966 were as shown in Table 35 (actual *votes*, not voting intentions).

The figures suggest that the BEA contains more supporters of minority parties than are found in the population at large. This should be viewed with caution, however, as the wording of the question about voting on the BEA questionnaire was likely to encourage minority party supporters to indicate such an allegiance.

Table 34. *Voting intentions of BEA members*

	O		J		C		All	
	N	%	N	%	N	%	N	%
Conservative	55	23	12	27	10	15	60.5	23
Labour	82½	35	11½	26	25½	40	91.8	35
Liberal	38½	16	7	16	13	20	43.5	17
Communist	7½	3	1½	3	2	3	8.4	3
Scottish N.P.	5½	2	2	5	0	0	6.0	2
Plaid Cymru	1	0	1	2	0	0	1.3	1
ILP	3	1	0	0	0	0	3.0	1
SPGB	5	2	0	0	1½	2	5.4	2
Monarchist	0	0	1	2	0	0	0.3	0
World Government	0	0	0	0	1	2	0.3	0
Socialist Labour	0	0	0	0	1	2	0.3	0
Anti-Common Market	1	0	0	0	0	0	1.0	0
Independent	1	0	0	0	0	0	1.0	0
Don't know	10	4	3	7	3	5	11.5	4
Wouldn't vote	10	4	5	11	3	5	12.0	5
No answer	15	6	0	0	4	6	16.0	6
Total	235		44		64		262.3	

ILP: Independent Labour Party; SPGB: Socialist Party of Great Britain.

As there were 23½ Scottish members in the survey, the voters for the Scottish National Party would constitute 26% of this total.

Table 35. *National voting figures, 1966 election*

	% of electorate	% of poll
Conservative	31.7	41.9
Labour	36.4	47.9
Liberal	5.6	8.5
Scottish National (Scotland only)	3.8	5.2

The ILP, not mentioned on the questionnaire, is of some significance, as it is the only party which has until recently lent its support to Esperanto.[23] Its weekly newspaper, *The Socialist Leader*, still had a column in Esperanto at the time of the survey. Some who indicated the SPGB may have been confusing it with the Labour Party. The Communist Party appears to be somewhat stronger in the BEA than in the population at large. It appears that the Labour Party is stronger in the BEA than in the population at large and the Conservative Party weaker. The percentage of members who expressed the intention of voting Labour was not substantially different from the proportion of the electorate who voted Labour in 1966 (slightly less, in fact). But account must be taken of the virtual absence of social classes IV and V, and of the large proportion of clerical and professional workers in the BEA; the Labour Party can undoubtedly be seen to be overrepresented. Councillors, who are more middle-class than the membership at large, are also more likely to be left of centre than ordinary members. The commitment may well prove to be anti-Conservative rather than pro-Labour for many members; the Liberal Party is also strong, though it is difficult to estimate whether it is stronger in the BEA than in the general population. Some members will undoubtedly associate Esperanto with left-wing politics, and 9% of the total BEA membership are members either of SAT or *SAT en Britio* (the British workers' Esperanto movement) or both; in other respects the bias against Conservative voting may be a characteristic of social movements generally. A movement aiming to change some aspect of the existing order of things is less likely to be attractive to supporters of a party whose aims, on the whole, are defence of the *status quo*. This matter will be considered further in Chapter 12.

RELIGION

Members were much less reticent on this subject than on politics. Here again the wording of the question has to be taken into account: it is widely known that wording has a considerable effect on questionnaire answers about religion. As with the politics question, members were asked to tick preferences from a list of choices. Many members ticked more than one allegiance (some ticked nearly all of them!). Yet on the whole it was possible to detect a dominant allegiance for most of the members, and this has been used as the basis for Table 36. A comparison is made with the results of a National Opinion Polls survey of religion made in 1965.[24] The results of the NOP survey are answers to the question, 'What is your religion?'

Table 36. *Religious affiliation of BEA members*

Religion or denomination	G.B. %	O N	O %	J N	J %	C N	C %	All N	All %
Church of England	63.4	55	25	13	30	12	20	61¼	25
Nonconformist	10.5	55	25	7	16	13	22	60	24
Roman Catholic	10.1	7	3	5	12	0	0	8¼	3
Presbyterian*	8.9	17	8	2	5	2	3	18	7
Jewish	1.3	1	0	1	2	1	2	1½	1
Atheist/agnostic	1.1	63	29	14	33	26	44	73	30
Other religion	3.0	19	9	1	2	5	8	20½	8
No religion	1.8	3	1	0	0	0	0	3	1
Total classifiable answers		220		43		59		245½	
No classifiable answer		15		1		5		16½	
Total		235		44		64		262	

* Includes Church of Scotland.
Methodists, Congregationalists, Baptists, Quakers, and Unitarians were included under 'Nonconformist'; all other Christian bodies were counted with 'other religion'. Humanists were included with atheists and agnostics.

The proportion of members rating themselves as Church of England is far smaller than in the population at large. For many English people this is a residual category representing religious inactivity. It is likely that members of a movement such as Esperanto will commit themselves for or against religion at the expense of a residual category of allegiance. Nonconformists are overrepresented: in the population at large they tend to be older and more middle-class than members of other major religious groups. This alone may account for the number of Nonconformists in the BEA, though for some members a further factor will be that Nonconformity has been indicative of a reformist outlook favouring allegiance to social movements such as the BEA. Roman Catholics are under-represented. It should be remembered that Roman Catholics tend to be younger and more working-class than the rest of the population, while BEA members are older and more middle-class.[25] This alone could account for the difference. The most striking difference between the BEA and the general population is the large proportion of atheists and agnostics. The different wording of the question in the NOP and the BEA survey will undoubtedly have had some effect on the result, but not to the extent that a large difference would no longer be evident. The figure is even higher for Councillors, 44% of whom are atheists and agnostics. This rejection of dominant values on the matter of religion can be considered alongside a similar rejection on the matter of politics. As Parkin suggests

There exist certain key institutional orders which occupy a key place in the social structure, and the values surrounding which exercise a dominant influence throughout society. Even within a highly diverse and complex normative system, it still makes sense to conceive of, on the one hand, a set of dominant values or core values, which are in a way central to the society, which give the society its defining characteristics; and, on the other hand, a variety of sub-systems which are either opposed to, or in some way "deviant" from the dominant system.[26]

Conservative voting and religious belief are both cited by Parkin as examples of values which accord with the British dominant value system. Another factor is the degree of education of members, which may have had a certain radicalising or liberalising effect. Deviation also extends to support for other religions. This is a very mixed category, including the smaller Christian sects, cults based on mystical experience, and various Eastern religions. Spiritualism was mentioned by 7¼ members (3%). Baha'i, which officially supports the idea of an international language, was mentioned by 2¼ members (1%); while Hillelism, Zamenhof's own proposed religion, was mentioned only by two junior members.

Using 'Christian' in its widest sense, Table 37 indicates religious activity and Table 38 the denominational allegiance of Christian members.

Table 37. *Religious activity of Christian BEA members*

	O		J		C		All	
	N	%	N	%	N	%	N	%
Christian*	4	2	0	0	1	2	4¼	2
Active Roman Catholic	6	3	5	11	0	0	7¼	4
Inactive Roman Catholic	1	0	0	0	0	0	1	0
Inactive Orthodox**	3	1	0	0	0	0	3	1
Active Protestant	82	35	13	30	23	36	91	35
Inactive Protestant	61	23	11	25	11	17	66½	25
Total	157		29		35		173	

* No further indication.
** So returned on the questionnaire, though it is suspected that the respondent was referring to doctrinal orthodoxy, rather than the Eastern Orthodox Church, as was here intended.

A member was considered active if he claimed to attend church at least 'quite regularly' and/or indicated membership of a church or other religious organisation. Those who indicated that they would attend were it not for age or illness were also returned as active.

There is clear evidence for greater religious activity among BEA members than in the population generally. Church attendance is also greater among the Councillors than among rank-and-file members. Yet nominal religiosity is by no means absent. Twenty members, or 8% of the total, were inactive members of the Church of England. This figure is nonetheless considerably smaller than that for the population at large, a majority of which would come into such a category. Nonconformist denominations are more strongly represented among BEA members than in the population at large. The Quakers are particularly well represented, especially considering that this is a small religious organisation. There does in fact appear to be particular compatibility between Quaker beliefs and those associated with the value-oriented interpretation of

Esperanto. Both belief systems emphasise individualism, quietism, and the promotion of peace, and believers perceive of themselves as an enlightened elect.[27]

The general religious composition of the BEA indicates that members are more likely to be irreligious than the population as a whole, less likely to be Anglicans, and, if religious, are more likely to be active in church membership and attendance than is the general population. Such characteristics are those which tend to be found generally in groups which are more highly educated than average.

Table 38.   *Denominational allegiance of BEA members*

	O		J		C		All	
	N	%	N	%	N	%	N	%
Christian (no further indication	4	2	0	0	1	2	4¼	2
Roman Catholic	7	3	5	11	0	0	8¼	3
Orthodox	3	1	0	0	0	0	3	1
Church of England	53	23	13	30	12	19	59¼	22
Methodist	21	9	5	11	4	6	23¼	9
Congregationalist	9	4	2	5	4	6	10½	4
Baptist	8	3	0	0	4	6	9	4
Presbyterian	16	7	2	5	2	3	17	6
Quaker	11	5	0	0	1	2	11¼	4
Unitarian	6	3	0	0	0	0	6	2
Christian Science	2	1	0	0	1	2	2¼	1
Christian Spiritualist	2	1	0	0	0	0	2	1
Christian Community	1	0	0	0	0	0	1	0
Swedenborgian	1	0	0	0	0	0	1	0
Christadelphian	1	0	0	0	0	0	1	0
No denomination	5	2	1	2	2	3	5¾	2
Protestant (no further indication)	7	3	1	2	4	6	8¼	3
Total	157		29		35		173	

MEMBERSHIP OF OTHER ORGANISATIONS

A wide range of other organisations was reported, standing in various positions in relation to societal values: they ranged from the Automobile Association to the Anti-Vaccination League. Many organisations, such as those for teachers, merely reflect the occupational composition of the BEA. Others relate to uncontroversial leisure-time activities, such as gardening and the theatre. Others reflect the religious and political composition of the BEA, which has already been reported on. Attention will be concentrated on those organisational memberships which bring new information about members. These will be considered in turn.

(a) United Nations Association (including United Nations Students' Association). This is supported by a total of 18¼ members (7%) – 14 ordinary members (6%), 3 juniors (7%), and 16 Councillors (25%). There is thus strong individual support for the United Nations. This may be due partly to compatibility of goals, and partly to UEA's explicit lead in this matter. Councillors in particular are strongly committed to both movements.

(b) The National Trust (including Scottish National Trust). A total of 16½ members, or 6% are members of this organisation also.

(c) Pacifist and peace organisations. These include the Campaign for Nuclear Disarmament, the Fellowship of Reconciliation, the Peace Pledge Union, and the War Resisters International. There were 10½ mentions of these organisations, suggesting that the inner idea of Esperanto is supported in other organisations in which certain members are active.

(d) Outdoor organisations. These would include the Scouts, the Youth Hostels Association, the Cyclists' Touring Club, the Ramblers' Association, and the Holiday Fellowship. There are altogether 20 mentions of these organisations.

(e) Vegetarianism. It is frequently observed that vegetarians are particularly well represented among Esperantists. Meetings at which food is provided normally offer facilities for vegetarians. Accordingly an explicit question, 'Are you a vegetarian?' was asked in the survey. Those who said they were not strict were still included, but former or aspirant vegetarians were excluded. The result obtained is shown in Table 39.

Table 39. *Proportion of vegetarians*

	O		J		C		All	
	N	%	N	%	N	%	N	%
Vegetarians	20	9	1	2	9	14	22½	9

The figure of 9% vegetarians can safely be assumed to be far in excess of the proportion to be found in the general population, especially bearing in mind that the survey was done in 1968; the growth in popularity of vegetarianism among certain sections of the population is more recent. Not all were members of vegetarian organisations; the figure for *members* of vegetarian bodies was 6¼, or 3%. A cross-tabulation with voting figures was also made: this revealed that very few vegetarian Esperantists vote Conservative (only two, in fact); the most popular party among them was the Labour Party, supported by 11 members. Investigation also revealed that 2% of members are both vegetarians and members of a pacifist organisation.

It is not easy to interpret data of this kind; indeed, it must be stressed that the overwhelming majority of Esperantists in Britain do not seem particularly deviant in their orientations. The extent of deviation displayed appears to be not much greater than that likely to be found in any reasonably well-educated group of people. Yet not all BEA members are particularly highly educated, and many may have acquired education through evening classes rather than more orthodox means. Members also tend to be rather elderly, and some orientations (e.g. agnosticism) which are not now considered as particularly deviant may be more so for the generation concerned. It remains, however, to explain the presence of a small proportion of highly deviant members – the 'cranks' against whom Lapenna waged a concerted campaign. They are not numerically strong but are often noticeable. The following text from first-hand observation of a BEA Congress (Glasgow – Strathclyde University, 1967) should illustrate this:

Congress lunch, May 28 1967: sat with group from. . . . W, X, Y, and Z are vegetarians, Z only for health reasons (on the advice of a herbalist). They were joined by A and B, two vegetarian ladies from other towns, and the conversation turned to vegetarian problems. B was worried about her pea soup in case it was made with chicken stock. They discussed the problem of vegetarianism and their children. They accepted that it was difficult for them to be vegetarian when younger, but hoped that they would become vegetarians eventually. Also at the table was a member (male) of the Baha'i church. From the next table, leaflets in Esperanto were passed about the duodecimal calculation system.

A questionnaire respondent permits me to quote the following comment:

I have the impression that the movement now has a growing number of members with scientific and technical qualifications or interests, which seems very encouraging if we are to get a more broadly-based movement. The Quaker-pacifist-theosophist-vegetarian-coop elements (not that I personally object to any of these *per se*!) have tended perhaps to be self-perpetuating.

That this is not confined to Britain is evident from Lapenna's reaction to the members of the 1947 Berne World Congress. It remains therefore to explain the presence of these deviants in the Esperanto movement. The deviants do not form a homogeneous group, but some have a number of characteristics in common. There is a consistent strain which rejects in some way the manifestations of urban industrial society. There is a certain tendency to express solidarity with 'nature' and what is 'natural'. This is confirmed by the fact that in the past Esperantists have participated to some degree in certain utopian communitarian experiments such as Whiteway Colony.[28] There are certain suggestions that wars and national boundaries are unnatural, but that a universal language would restore the unity of people across national boundaries.

There is a greater-than-average representation in the BEA of vegetarians and pacifists, even vegetarian pacifists. These two commitments are themselves related. Barkas[29] points to the long-standing association of vegetarian and pacifist commitments, and also claims that meat eating has the effect of increasing aggressive behaviour. In the wider society, willingness to eat meat is assumed, and pacifists have usually been treated with considerable contempt. They are, however, fully accepted in the Esperanto movement. Of a member imprisoned in 1941 for conscientious objection, *The British Esperantist* remarked, 'Whether they agree or disagree with his action, readers will wish him well and appreciate his fidelity to strong religious conviction.'[30]

Many causes of all kinds have been appealed to in the name of promoting world peace, and this opens up the possibility of linking their aims to Esperanto. There are a number of specialist organisations which associate Esperanto with other causes and activities. Esperantists displaying conspicuously deviant orientations are often very active in the movement. Lapenna's criticism of 'cranks' has already been mentioned. The argument is that 'cranks', however small in number, give a 'bad impression' of the movement. George Orwell also voiced such a concern in relation to the socialist movement:

.... There is the horrible – the really disquieting – prevalence of cranks wherever Socialists are gathered together. One sometimes gets the impression that the mere words "Socialism" and "Communism" draw towards them with magnetic force every fruit-juice drinker, nudist, sandal-wearer, sex-maniac, Quaker, "Nature Cure" quack, pacifist and feminist in England. . . to an ordinary man, a crank meant a socialist and a socialist meant a crank.[31]

The statistical results of the questionnaire clearly show that so-called cranks form merely a small but significant minority. They are, however, more easily recognised than 'ordinary' members. Otherwise the membership consists of elderly middle-class people. They tend to be fairly well educated, especially considering their age. Many have been active in adult education. They have sufficient education to pursue their own studies, and at the same time do not have the degree of orthodox formal education that might lead them unquestioningly to support official hostile or indifferent attitudes to Esperanto and other causes that might be regarded as 'cranky'. Esperanto, it must be recalled, is often dismissed out of hand by educationists. For many members Esperanto is itself part of an educational process; in turn it provides satisfactions for members through their participation in the unique activities of the movement. The concept of 'crankiness' will be considered again in the Conclusion.

NOTES

1. For this notion see C.A. Moser, *Survey Methods in Social Investigation*, 1958, pp.76–77.
2. BE, December 1968, p.486.
3. The response might well have been greater: some members wrote regretting inability to fill in the form owing to illness, age, or blindness. Certain enclosures were sometimes sent with the returned questionnaire. Some were elaborations on the answers to the questions; others consisted of items such as religious tracts and leaflets about other social movements to which the member belonged. Hostility and/or total refusal to complete the questionnaire, while not absent, was very rare, though a few objected to certain questions, particularly the one on politics.
4. See G. Sergeant, *A Statistical Source-Book for Sociologists*, 1972, p.12.
5. U.K. population figures drawn from General Register Office, *Census 1966, United Kingdom General and Parliamentary Constituency Tables*, 1969, Table 2, p.3.
6. British figures drawn from General Register Office, *Sample Census 1966, Great Britain Summary Tables*, 1967, p.8.
7. M. Stacey, *Tradition and Change: A Study of Banbury*, 1960, p.78.
8. General Register Office, *Sample Census 1966, Great Britain Economic Activity Tables*, 1969, Part III, Table 30, p.415.
9. T. Bottomore, 'Social stratification in voluntary associations', in *Social Mobility in Britain*, ed. by D. Glass, p.349–382 (p.381).
10. Stacey, *op. cit.*, p.81.
11. *Sample Census 1966, Great Britain Summary Tables, op. cit.*, p.22.
12. General Register Office, *Sample Census 1966, Great Britain Economic Activity Tables*, 1968, Part I, pp.46–50.
13. F. Parkin, *Middle Class Radicalism*, 1968, pp.180–181.
14. C. Campbell, 'Membership composition of the British Humanist Association', *Sociological Review*, 1965, pp.327–337.
15. C.A. Moser and W. Scott, *British Towns*, 1961.
16. Based on 1961 census figures.
17. For details of the towns included in each class, see Moser and Scott, *op. cit.*, pp.17–18.
18. The 'e' column is based on 1961 census figures.
19. See A. Weinberg, 'Education', in *Comparability in Social Research*, ed. by M. Stacey, 1969, pp.1–31 (p.1).
20. G. Sergeant, *op. cit.*, p.51.
21. Members were asked to indicate if they had passed any public examinations in languages.
22. For details see D.E. Butler and A. King, *The British General Election of 1966*, 1966.
23. See G. Thayer, *The British Political Fringe*, 1965, pp.146–148.
24. Reported in R. Goldman, 'Do we want our children taught about God?', *New Society*, 27 May 1965, pp.8–10.
25. *Ibid.*, p.9.
26. Parkin, *op. cit.*, p.21; also in 'Working-class conservatives', *British Journal of Sociology*, 1967, pp.278–290 (p.280).
27. See B.R. Wilson's *introversionist* or *pietist* type of sect, 'An analysis of sect development', in *Patterns of Sectarianism*, ed. by B.R. Wilson, 1967, pp.22–48 (pp.28–

29); also E. Isichei, 'From sect to denomination among English Quakers', *ibid.*,
pp.161–181.
28.   See N. Shaw, *Whiteway, a Colony in the Cotswolds*, 1935.
29.   J. Barkas, *The Vegetable Passion*, 1975.
30.   BE, November/December 1941, p.88.
31.   *The Road to Wigan Pier*, 1937, p.206.

12

Members' Orientations Towards Esperanto and the Esperanto Movement

The social composition of the British Esperanto Association has already been examined. This has involved consideration of, first, 'natural' characteristics of members, such as age and sex; second, their social characteristics, such as occupation, education, and marital status; and third, their ideological orientations, notably politics and religion. The questionnaire used also contained items which dealt with the way in which members related to the Esperanto movement. This involved consideration of factors such as length of time in the movement and motives for learning Esperanto. It also involved consideration of members' attitudes towards Esperanto. The following questions were employed to ascertain the extent to which members perceived Esperanto as a norm- or value-oriented movement:

Some people think that the most important thing about Esperanto is the ideal of peace and world brotherhood through a universal language. Other people tend to emphasise more the practical advantages of an international language in commerce, conferences, and foreign travel.

The next three questions are about how you feel on this question. You may answer "both equally" if you wish, but please try if possible to choose one of the alternatives. You may make whatever comments and qualifications you wish.

30. Which do you think is more important *to you personally* about Esperanto?

(a) The ideal of peace and world brotherhood through a universal language.

(b) The practical advantages of an international language in conferences, commerce, and foreign travel.

(a) . . .　　　(b) . . .　　　Both equally . . .

Comments

31. Which of these two aspects do you think the Esperanto movement should pay more attention to in its activities?
(a) . . .   (b) . . .   Both equally . . .
Comments

32. Which of these two aspects should be stressed more in publicity and advertising of Esperanto?
(a) . . .   (b) . . .   Both equally . . .
Comments

33. Are there any other things about Esperanto that are important to you?

In all tables in this chapter, the letters A, B and C will be used to distinguish the three possible answers to these questions, C being used to represent 'Both equally'. Particular attention will be paid in cross-tabulations to the members' own personal interpretation of Esperanto (question 30); yet it is interesting to note the differences in attitude that members displayed in their answers to all three questions. Whereas question 30 can be seen to relate to expressions of private ·belief, question 31 can be considered as relating to the internal affairs of the movement and question 32 as bearing on the way in which Esperanto and the movement should be presented to the general public. It can be seen that members are likely to prefer private to public expression of idealism. Table 40 makes this clear.

Table 40 suggests that members prefer to see the value-oriented attitude towards Esperanto as something to be confined to private belief, or at least to the social relations of the movement; few wish

Table 40.   *Private and public expression of idealism (all members)*

	A		B		C		Total
	N	%	N	%	N	%	N
30 (personal)	98½	38	109	42	54	21	261½*
31 (movement)	24½	9	135	52	102	39	261½*
32 (publicity)	15¼	6	143¼	54	103	39	261½*

* In all cross-tabulations with idealism, the maximum number of replies will be 261½, not 262, since two Councillors failed to answer the idealism question.

to stress this aspect when presenting Esperanto to the general public. This finding is in line with Zamenhof's distinction between the language Esperanto, compulsory for all, and the idealistic side of Esperanto, 'not compulsory but much more important',[1] which was to be associated particularly with world congresses. A few members suggested that advertising should depend on the audience, but on the whole members' comments on question 32 frequently referred to the general public as 'ignorant' and 'materialistic', suggesting their own self-conception as that of an enlightened elite. Activity in the movement internationally was high. 133¼ members (51%) had attended at least one overseas Esperanto congress or other overseas gathering relating to Esperanto. The really active congress-goers tended to be more idealistic than the rest, though the result was significant only at the 10% level. In Table 41, percentages are given out of the total number of members displaying a given orientation towards Esperanto. In this and all subsequent tables, only the answers to question 30 (personal idealism) will be taken into consideration.

Table 41.   *Attendance at overseas Esperanto meetings and idealism*

Overseas meetings attended	A		B		C		Total	
	N	%	N	%	N	%	N	%
0-5	75	76	96¼	88	44	81	215¼	82
6 or more	23½	24	12¾	12	10	18	46¼	18
Total	98½		109		54		261½	

For 2 degrees of freedom, chi-square = 5.3629.

Another method of investigating the locus of norm- or value-oriented attitudes to Esperanto is to examine the stated motives for learning. These were asked for using the open-ended question, 'Why did you decide to learn Esperanto?' The limitations of such questions are widely known; nonetheless, the answers to such a question are of some interest if they can be shown to bear a meaningful relationship to other variables considered. A coding frame was devised for the answers to this question, using the following categories:

Class N: No choice
> N1 Learned Esperanto from birth.
> N2 Esperanto was part of the school syllabus.
> N   Total with no choice.

Class P: Personal satisfaction
> PA Because of experience of difficulties with other languages.
> PB To help in learning another language.
> PC Because of a general desire to learn another language, without any indication of a hobby or interest in *learning languages*.
> PD As a hobby; curiosity; something to do (with no indication of a hobby or interest in *learning languages*).
> PE As a hobby or interest, with particular mention of an interest in learning languages.
> PF To enable me to understand/communicate with people abroad.
> PG Because of a pre-existing personal relationship (e.g. because husband/wife was an Esperantist).
> PH To take part in the movement's activities.
> PI Because Esperanto might be useful in my job.
> PJ Because of possible use in foreign travel.
> PK To enable me to understand Esperanto radio broadcasts.
> PL To enable me to understand Esperanto literature, periodicals, etc.
> P   Total who learnt Esperanto because of personal satisfaction to be obtained.

Class S: Support for aims
> SX General support for the goals of the movement; 'thought it a good idea'; converted by propaganda literature; converted by an enthusiastic propagandist.
> SI Support for the goals of the movement, but with particular emphasis on idealistic goals: world peace, world friendship, international socialism, etc.
> SP Support for the goals of the movement, but with particular emphasis on *practical* advantages to be brought about by adoption of Esperanto.
> S   Total indicating support for aims of Esperanto.

Many members gave more than one reason, or their answers could only be meaningfully expressed by coding them in more than one way. Thus the total list of motives given will be seen to be greater than the total number of members. The spread of answers is as in Table 42. Percentages are out of the total number of members.

Table 42. *Members' stated motives for learning Esperanto*

N1	From birth	1	(0%)
N2	At school	1¼	(0%)
N	Total no choice	2¼	(1%)
PA	Difficulty in learning other languages	12¼	(5%)
PB	Help in learning another language	3	(1%)
PC	Desire to learn another language	21½	(8%)
PD	Hobby/curiosity/something to do	44¾	(17%)
PE	Hobby or interest in learning languages	41½	(16%)
PF	To understand/communicate with foreigners	23¾	(9%)
PG	Through personal relationship	20¼	(8%)
PH	For movement's activities	7½	(3%)
PI	Use in job	5½	(2%)
PJ	Use in foreign travel	22¾	(9%)
PK	To understand radio broadcasts	1¼	(0%)
PL	To understand literature	2¾	(1%)
P	Total personal satisfaction	206¾	(79%)
SX	General support for goals	75¾	(29%)
SI	Support for idealistic goals	41¾	(16%)
SP	Support for practical goals	7	(3%)
S	Total support for goals	117½	(45%)

Thus the commonest motive mentioned was SX (general support for goals); though PD (as a hobby, nonlinguistic), SI (idealism), and PE (interest in languages) were also mentioned by over 10% of the members. There were certain differences between categories of members in their motives for learning. Councillors were more likely to give PH (to take part in the movement's activities) as a motive (9% as opposed to 3% of the general membership).

It accords with their present position as Councillors that they were originally interested in the *movement* as such. Junior members were more likely to join through interest in Esperanto as a language: PE (interest in languages) was mentioned by 30% of juniors, as opposed to 16% of the membership generally. PC (desire to learn another language) was also popular among junior members (mentioned by 20% of juniors as opposed to 6% of the general membership).

A broad distinction has been drawn between the class of motives beginning with P, which were expressed in terms of personal satisfaction, and those beginning with S, expressed in terms of support for the aims of Esperanto. Class N, those who had no effective choice as to whether or not to learn, is too small for analysis and will not be considered further. Particular attention will also be paid to category SI, consisting of those who learned Esperanto for idealistic motives. This will provide further information about the relationship between norm- and value-oriented interpretations of Esperanto.

It appears that, during the history of the movement, the proportion of those who have joined because of support for the aims of the movement has declined relative to those who have joined for some personal satisfaction. Table 43 indicates the proportions who joined for the two main classes of motive.

Table 43. *Members' motives for learning Esperanto, divided according to the two main classes of motive*

Years since began learning Esperanto	Actual period	P		S		Total reasons
		N	%	N	%	
0–10	1958–1968	88	73	32¼	27	120¼
11–20	1948–1957	27	68	13	33	40
21–30	1938–1947	30¼	57	22¾	43	53
31–40	1928–1937	34¼	61	21½	39	55¾
41–50	1918–1927	15¼	44	19¼	56	34½
51 up	before 1918	12	58	8¾	42	20¾
Total		206¾		117½		324¼

The relationship is striking: there is a consistent tendency for those who learnt Esperanto earlier to be more likely to have done so in support of the aims of the language and movement; more recent recruits are more likely to have learnt for personal satisfaction. There are, however, various possible interpretations of this data. It might merely be the case that those who learnt Esperanto a long time ago were more likely to recollect motives in terms of general support for the aims of Esperanto. However, if the difference is not due to merely technical factors, it may be the case that the more recent recruits to the BEA tend to see Esperanto more as a hobby or specialised interest than as an effective pressure group or utopian social movement. Evidence from the history of the BEA would lend support to such an interpretation. There is, however, another equally likely possibility. It is possible that those who learn Esperanto for personal satisfaction are more likely to lapse in their membership than are those who learn Esperanto in support of its aims. Both tendencies could apply: a growth could have occurred in members' perception of Esperanto as a hobby, together with a tendency for those who perceive Esperanto in this light to drop out more easily.

The proportion who learnt Esperanto specifically for idealistic motives is also worthy of consideration. Table 44 shows these, divided into two classes according to whether they learnt Esperanto before or after 1938.

Table 44.   *Idealistic motives for learning Esperanto*

| Year began | SI | | Total |
learning Esperanto	N	%	N
1938–1968	16½	10	163¾
Before 1938	25¼	26	97¾
Total	41¾		261½

For 1 degree of freedom, chi-square = 10.4765. Significant at 0.5%.

There is thus a highly significant tendency for those who began learning Esperanto before 1938 to be more likely to learn for idealistic motives than those who learnt after that year.[2] It is of course always likely that those recruited for idealistic motives will display a more sustained commitment to the movement.

Figures in Table 44, for idealistic motives, can be corroborated by relating answers to question 30 to the year of learning Esperanto (i.e. before or after 1938). The results are presented in Table 45.

Table 45.   *Idealism and year of learning*

| Year began | A | | B | | C | | Total | |
learning Esperanto	N	%	N	%	N	%	N	%
1938	53½	33	80½	49	29¾	18	163¾	100
Before 1938	45	46	28½	29	24¼	25	97¾	100
Total	98½	38	109	42	54	21	261½	101

For 2 degrees of freedom, chi-square = 9.7191. Significant at 1%.

It can be seen from this table that those of longer standing in the movement tend still to emphasise a value-oriented attitude to Esperanto; while 46% of those who learnt before 1938 are idealists, this is true only of 33% who learnt *since* 1938. Once again there is also the possibility that the idealists tend to be retained in the movement more than the practical-minded.

A related matter is the relationship between age and idealism. Table 46 shows that, provided that data are grouped sufficiently, a highly significant relationship obtains between these variables.

It thus appears that, on the whole, the older a member is the more likely he is to support a value-oriented interpretation of Esperanto. Far from 'youthful idealism' being evident, the opposite seems to prevail. A likely intervening variable is, of course, the length of time in the movement, as has already been shown in Tables 44 and 45.

Table 46.   *Age and idealism*

| | A | | B | | C | | Total | |
Age group	N	%	N	%	N	%	N	%
14–39	11½	22	30	57	11½	22	53	101
40–69	53¾	27	62	42	30¾	21	146½	100
70–94	32	55	15¼	26	10¾	19	58	100
Total	97¼	38	107¼	42	53	21	257½	101

For 4 degrees of freedom, chi-square = 14.3837. Significant at 1%.

A certain relationship prevails between the three categories of members — ordinary, junior, and Councillors — and orientations towards Esperanto. This relationship is shown in Table 47.

Table 47.   *Categories of membership and idealism*

Type of member	A		B		C		Total	
	N	%	N	%	N	%	N	%
Ordinary	90	38	97	41	48	20	235	99
Junior	16	36	24	55	4	9	44	100
Councillors	18	29	24	39	20	32	62	100

The main feature of note is that the Councillors tend to be less idealistic in attitude than either the junior or the ordinary members. Concerned with 'running the system', they appear to have a more mellowed enthusiasm, reflected in the large proportion who put 'both equally'. Service on the BEA Council might attract a greater proportion of 'bureaucrats' rather than 'enthusiasts'.[3]

Additional data, not related to idealism, were tabulated in relation to marriage and the family. A specific question was asked about whether the member had met his or her spouse in connection with any Esperanto activity. The results are of considerable interest, and are presented in Table 48.

Percentages are given out of the total number of members ever married for the category of members in question. Doubtful cases, or cases where the member had married twice, only one spouse having been met in the movement, have been counted as one-half. The figures show that fully 15% of members met their spouses in the movement; for married women members, the figure is as high

Table 48.   *Those who met their spouse in Esperanto circles*

Males						Females						Total	
O		C		All		O		C		All		All	
N	%	N	%	N	%	N	%	N	%	N	%	N	%
12½	11	8½	22	14⅝	12	10	26	2	50	10½	26	25⅛	15

as 26% and the tendency is still more marked for Councillors, of either sex. It has already been noted that married women are underrepresented in the BEA, and it is of additional significance that a substantial proportion of those women who are married met their husbands within the movement. Many marriages between Esperantists are publicised by the movement's literature; this especially applies when such marriages are international, with Esperanto the couple's language in common and future home language. The Esperanto pun *Esperanto-edzperanto* [Esperanto − husband−agent] is usually quoted in connection with such events.

Some Esperantists have advocated the production of native speakers of Esperanto by bringing up children of Esperantists as bilinguals. It appears from the survey that there are very few Esperantists from birth in the BEA; yet there is evidence of wide-spread systematic attempts by members to pass on Esperanto to their children. An open-ended question was asked on this topic. Replies were difficult to analyse: some children of a member's family might speak Esperanto but not others; the children might be too young to learn, or might not have learnt Esperanto until leaving their family of orientation. In a few cases, too, the child(ren) had awakened an interest in Esperanto in the parents. Table 49 shows the proportion of members ever married with children who have systematically passed on Esperanto to the next generation.

Table 49.   *Passing on of Esperanto to the next generation*

O		C		All	
N	%	N	%	N	%
45	42	22	65	50½	44

These results suggest that if one or both parents speak Esperanto this fact is likely to have a certain impact on the children's lives. No doubt the more active the parent is in the movement, the greater the impact, as is suggested by the large proportion of Councillors' children who have learnt some Esperanto. Most of the members of the BEA are middle-class, and therefore their children are likely to attend grammar schools, where a foreign language is taught. A shared interest in the language with which the parent is familiar, but which is not taught in school, is therefore quite likely. This should not be confused with membership of the movement. When the children are old enough to join the movement, i.e. around 14 or older, there is more likely to be a rebellion against parental interests; this is likely to be intensified by the preponderance of late middle-aged and old people in the movement, if the child did show sufficient interest to attend any meetings. Thus learning of the language might be a shared family interest when activity in the movement is not.

The peculiar interest attached to the political composition of the BEA, in a movement which tends to taboo discussion of politics, has already been noted. It was also found to be the case that a strong relationship obtained between politics and idealism. Religion, surprisingly, showed no marked relationship with idealism; the connections proved to be so tenuous and inconclusive that they are not presented here. In the case of politics, only the three main parties had enough representation in the BEA for statistically significant results to be obtained, but the results are of considerable importance. They are presented in Table 50.

Table 50. *Politics and idealism*

	A		B		C		Total	
	N	%	N	%	N	%	N	%
Conservative	13½	22	35¾	59	11¼	19	60½	100
Labour	47⅛	52	28¼	31	16⅛	18	91½	101
Liberal	8¾	20	21½	49	13¼	30	43½	99
Total	69⅜		85½		40⅝		195½	

For 4 degrees of freedom, chi-square = 21.7324. Significant at 0.1%.

If, broadly speaking, the Conservative Party is regarded as right-wing, the Liberal Party as middle-of-the-road, and the Labour Party as left-wing, it can be seen that there is a relationship between right-wing voting and a practical attitude to Esperanto, and between left-wing voting and an idealistic attitude to Esperanto. The Liberals come between the two, though they are closer in their attitudes to the Conservatives than to the Labour supporters. Those who take the middle position in politics are also likely to do so in their attitude to Esperanto: Liberal voters are the most likely to be unwilling to choose definitely between an idealistic and a practical attitude to Esperanto. The differences are substantial but are by no means absolute. There are significant minorities for each political preference which do not correspond to the general pattern. Thus the difference in orientation to Esperanto has never been directly aligned with a party conflict in the history of the British movement.

These results can be corroborated with figures for those who indicated that their motives for learning Esperanto were idealistic. These can be shown to bear a relationship to voting patterns. Table 51 indicates the relationship; there were only sufficient members in the cells for Conservative and Labour voters for the chi-square test to be performed.

Table 51.   *Politics and idealistic motives for learning*

Party.	SI		Total voters
	N	%	N
Conservative	7¼	12	60½
Labour	25	27	91¾

For 1 degree of freedom, chi-square = 5.3697. Significant at 2.5%.

It has already been suggested that a movement aiming to change some aspect of the existing order of things is unlikely to prove attractive to supporters of a party which aims to defend the status quo. Thus non-Conservative voters predominate in the BEA. Yet Conservatives are in no way totally absent; rather it appears that the Conservatives in the BEA do not see Esperanto as a particularly subversive commitment. To most Conservatives, Esperanto is a norm-oriented movement, advocating a practical, scientific innovation.

Even here the distinction is by no means absolute. Some Conservative idealists may be attracted to a certain individualistic strain in the movement and its tendency to suspect the state. Correspondingly, although some Labour supporters are left-wingers (sometimes voting Labour only for want of better), others will be more inclined to stress moderation and the effectiveness of Labour policies in the practical business of living. Thus the norm-oriented attitude is by no means absent among Labour supporters. Liberal supporters tend also to be middle-of-the-road in their attitude to Esperanto. Liberal supporters are nearer to the Conservative than to the Labour supporters in their interpretation of Esperanto. Liberal voting has sometimes been seen as a respectable way of non-Conservative voting for middle-class people (and the bulk of BEA membership is middle-class); thus Liberal supporters might not be inclined to adopt a particularly radical interpretation of Esperanto.

A further factor in the relationship between Labour voting and a value-oriented interpretation of Esperanto is the degree of commitment to the social relations of the movement. There is evidence that, in middle-class neighbourhoods, Labour voters incur a certain amount of social disapproval.[4] Yet they may not necessarily have a high dependence on community ties, and may seek social relations in milieus such as social movements, where their commitment is acceptable. The greater commitment to the social relations of the movement thereby involved is conducive to a value-oriented interpretation of the goals of the movement.

Finally, it may be recalled that there is a notably high proportion of vegetarians in the BEA; these are also likely to vote left. It was found that a close relationship obtained between vegetarianism and idealism. Of the 22½ vegetarian members, 11¼ (50%) expressed the view that idealism was more important (in reply to question 30); 2½ or 11% emphasised the practical side, and 8¾ (39%) emphasised both equally. It has been seen that the vegetarian group, frequently also pacifist, emphasises a certain solidarity with nature and what is 'natural'. This group not only stands for certain distinctive ideals but also displays a strong commitment to the social relations of the Esperanto movement. This corresponds to a value-oriented interpretation of Esperanto.

In conclusion, it can be observed that a number of variables showed no or only minimal relationship to idealism. Among these are occupation and social class; education; family size; meeting of spouse; and knowledge of Esperanto by members' children. To a large extent, too, this was true of religion.[5] Politics emerged as a far more important determinant of attitudes to Esperanto than religion.

Esperanto is a diffuse commitment and is linked with many different activities. It means many different things to different people. It is learnt for a variety of motives. For some members it is just a hobby or spare-time interest. For others it is intimately linked with private domestic relationships of family and marriage. For others it represents a strong ideological commitment, and can be linked with ideologies such as absolute pacifism; or a political commitment to the unity of the workers of the world. There are numerous variations in commitments among BEA members, just as has been the case in the history of the world movement. Thus while as such Esperanto is not a radical, subversive, or even particularly deviant commitment, it is linked by some Esperantists with various radical, subversive, or deviant causes and is felt to be highly compatible with them.

NOTES

1. OV, p.371.
2. Rigorous statistical tests cannot be performed, but an investigation of the strength of idealistic motives was made for each year in the period before 1938. It was found that idealistic motives for learning were particularly strong in the period 1923–1926 (10 out of the 15 motives reported during this period were idealistic). This period coincided with hopeful signs of progress with the League of Nations, with which disillusionment had not yet set in. During this period Esperanto seemed to have a chance of being taken seriously in internationally recognised institutions: certain long-standing members appear to have been recruited at a time when the message of Esperanto as a value-oriented movement was having some fruitful results.
3. The small proportion of junior members who chose 'both equally' can probably be attributed to the relations of the research situation. The rubric to the question on idealism discouraged such a choice, and, appearing on a questionnaire from a university teacher to a population consisting largely of university, college, and school students, might here have proved particularly authoritative.
     For the concepts of 'bureacrat' and 'enthusiast' see Roche and Sachs, *op. cit.*
4. See Stacey, *Tradition and Change, op. cit.*, pp.53–54; F. Parkin, *Middle Class Radicalism, op. cit.*, pp.48–49.
5. A very slight relationship prevailed between membership of smaller denominations, or acceptance of the label 'Humanist', and a greater-than-average support for idealism, but the results were only barely statistically significant.

Conclusion

In this study the Esperanto movement has been examined in a historical and sociological perspective. Part I has been concerned with the dynamics of the organised movement within the broad context of European international relations. Part II has dealt more specifically with Esperanto in the context of British society. Throughout the study particular attention has been focused upon the relationship between norm- and value-oriented interpretations of the aims of the movement. Esperanto has generally been seen by its supporters as 'more than a language' (though with some dissentients), but the kinds of value commitment associated with it have varied over time. Frequently, too, such value commitments have not been clearly articulated and have tended to be rather nebulous.

The distinction between norm- and value-oriented emphases in the Esperanto movement reflects many other dichotomous classifications employed by sociologists. Thus, it could equally well be said that, for the practically minded, the movement is more of a *Gesellschaft* and less of a *Gemeinschaft* than it is for the idealists.[1] The idealists usually appeal to the movement as exemplifying the practical realisation of their ideals and thus attach especial importance to relationships developed in the movement. Likewise, the practitioners have an *instrumental* and the idealists an *expressive* orientation to the aims of the movement. Applied to the study of social movement, such a distinction is suggested by Parkin:

Instrumental activity may be thought of as that which is directly geared to the attainment of concrete and specific goals, generally of a material kind. Emphasis is placed on the ends to be achieved rather than on the means employed in attaining them. Expressive activity is that which is less concerned with specific achievements than with the benefits and satisfactions which the activity itself affords. The rewards are as much in the action itself as in the ends it is directed to.[2]

Parkin goes on to suggest that even left-wing *political* movements will be inclined to discount the power element in politics, preferring to be 'a happy few battling against intolerable odds'.[3] The same standpoint characterises many idealistic Esperantists.

The significance of the Esperanto speech community, which serves to realise the expressive elements of the aims of the movement, will be considered shortly. Initial consideration will be given to the language as such and possible societal reactions to it. It appears, for instance, that certain social controls are exercised in opposition to Esperanto. A number of factors can here be considered. In the first place, the very idea of an artificial language meets with opposition in certain quarters. As Flügel suggests,

It is a strange and indisputable fact that to a large number of cultured people the idea of an artificial language, especially when first encountered, is apt to appear distinctly repellent or *disgusting*.[4]

No systematic data are available on this question, so discussion of the matter must remain rather speculative. Yet impressionistically it does appear that such a reaction is far from unusual, often by those who know nothing about the subject. For instance, Flügel quotes the suggestion, made by an English objector, that to use Esperanto when one could use English would be 'to forsake one's birthright for a mess of pottage'.[5] Flügel seeks an explanation for such reactions in psychoanalytical terms. He suggests the following unconscious motives for opposition to Esperanto:

If the creation of language is, as we have seen, unconsciously regarded as equivalent to the production of faeces or flatus, and if the manipulation of existing natural languages (such as is inevitably involved in the construction of an *a posteriori* artificial language) is similarly regarded as equivalent to playing with faeces, the arousal of disgust is no longer incomprehensible. It becomes still more intelligible when we add to the powerful repressions here involved the influence of the cooperative factors on the allo-erotic level. People who feel disgust at the idea of an artificial language will often discourse at length upon the "beauty" and "sanctity" of "natural" languages, and regard with horror the idea of tampering with this sanctity in order to create an easy artificial language. This process of tampering — in addition to its coprophilic significance — is, we may surmise, for many such persons the equivalent of an attack on the mother, an attack all the more revolting because it is associated with the forbidden coprophilic tendencies and therefore probably conceived in terms of infantile sexual theories of the anal level, thus constituting what might be quite appropriately called a "pollution" of the mother.[6]

Flügel also stresses the importance of the idea of the mother tongue:

The major natural languages, with their imposing literatures and traditions extending over many years, are eminently calculated to attract displacement of the tenderness, admiration, and respect originally attaching to the mother.[7]

It is difficult for the sociologist to assess strictly psychoanalytical explanations of the disgust which can be associated with Esperanto. It can, nonetheless, be observed that the Esperantists have frequently had to combat the suggestion that an artificial language is 'unnatural'. Tönnies makes suggestive observations on the associations of the idea of the mother tongue. He suggests that the fact that language is not invented is one of its key characteristics:

The real organ of understanding, through which it develops and improves, is language. Language given by means of gestures and sounds enables expressions of pain and pleasure, fear and desire, and all other feelings and emotions to be imparted and understood. Language has — as we all know — not been invented and, as it were, agreed upon as a means and tool by which one makes oneself understood. It is itself the living understanding both in its content and in its form. Similar to all other conscious activities of expression, the manifestation of language is the involuntary outcome of deep feelings and prevailing thoughts. It is not merely an artificial means of overcoming a natural lack of understanding, nor does it serve merely the purpose of enabling one to make oneself understood. . . language. . . did not spring from. . . hostility, . . . but from intimacy, fondness, and affection. Especially from the deep understanding between mother and child, mother tongue should develop more easily and vigorously.[8]

The mother tongue is thus a 'natural' phenomenon, one of *Wesenwille* rather than *Kürwille*.[9] This is a frequent objection levelled at Esperanto, which is condemned as 'artificial' or 'unnatural'.[10] Perhaps the significance of this criticism should not be exaggerated; many proposals for innovation and change are often opposed, especially initially, because they are contrary to 'human nature'. Such an objection has frequently been levelled against socialism, women's liberation, and expectations of stable peace. Yet such a criticism of Esperanto seems especially common. Various positions can be taken by opponents of Esperanto, and there are various possible reactions by the Esperantists. If objection is raised to the feasibility of Esperanto on *a priori* grounds, the Esperantists will reply in *a posteriori* terms, appealing to the practical experience of using the language. Frequently, however, the objections to Esperanto may be expressed in a more modified form. It might be argued that Esperanto is acceptable for purely practical purposes but is quite unsuitable for creative and artistic expression, especially for poetry. The Esperantists have found it necessary to reply to this also, and the position taken has been fairly consistent. For a start, Esperanto can be described as a 'constructed' or 'created' language, avoiding pejorative overtones of the word 'artificial'. Esperanto itself can be seen as an artistic creation, and appeal can be made to a broad definition of the word 'art'. Likewise, Esperantists have developed and articulated an affective relationship to the existing structure of the language, as seen especially in the expression 'dear language' (*kara lingvo*). Above all, Esperanto has been widely used by its speakers for literary purposes, original as well as translated works being produced, especially poetry. Thus again the objection has been replied to in *a posteriori* terms. It is significant that not all schemes for constructed international languages have been associated to such an extent with the development of original literature. The strong affective tie of speakers to the structure of the language is also peculiar to Esperanto.

Such persistent argumentation in *a posteriori* terms of practice and tradition is a distinctive feature of the Esperanto movement. It remains to assess sociologically the significance which is attached to the Esperanto speech community. The notion has arisen in the history of Esperanto of an 'Esperantist people' in its own right. It was proposed by Zamenhof, particularly in relation to world congresses. It was continued by UEA's policy of recruitment on a supernational basis. SAT developed the idea of an 'Esperantist people' in a more radical form, particularly in Lanti's ideology of *sennaciismo*. Lanti's own repudiation of his national language and identity is the most extreme development of this pattern. More commonly, emphasis has been placed on the supernational loyalties developed by members through world congresses and other contacts made in the movement. Closely related to the idea of the 'Esperantist people' is the notion of 'neutrality': even SAT considers itself to be neutral in a certain sense. 'Neutrality' can refer merely to a tactful agreement to avoid discussion of contentious issues, but it has also been presented as an ideology in its own right. Conflicts between these two perspectives have taken place. Zamenhof wished also for a universal religion which would link together the Esperantist people. This was, however, unsuccessful since many members were hostile to any kind of religion.

The idea of an Esperantist people has sometimes been articulated in the self-conception of a super-state, as is seen in the term *Esperantujo* [Esperanto-land]. This has involved developments such as the establishment of an Esperanto cheque bank and monetary unit. Some children have been brought up to speak Esperanto as their mother tongue, and there have been developments such as Esperanto-speaking colonies.[11] Such have tended to be fringe activities which have not received general acceptance. Yet there have been widespread appeals to the *analogy* with a state. Radical changes in the composition of the committee of UEA, such as in Stockholm in 1934 and Hamburg in 1974, have been referred to as 'palace revolutions'. Executive Committee members have occasionally been referred to as 'ministers' and subscriptions as 'taxes'. Emphasis has also been placed on Esperanto as the living language of a living people. Those Esperantists who have advocated reforms in the structure of the language have frequently been referred to as 'traitors'. In most cases the analogy with the state has been nothing more than an analogy, albeit a highly influential one. Even the more norm-oriented members will attach importance to the social relations of the movement, given that official adoption of Esperanto scarcely seems an imminent prospect. For a few members, however, the idea of Esperanto-land has been more than a mere analogy: the non-nationalists seriously suggested that their movement aimed at total subversion of existing loyalty to the state.

Also widespread among Esperantists is attachment to shared symbols, apart from the language. Particularly significant has been the original literature, as already noted. From the beginnings of the movement there has been an emphasis on development of such original literature in Esperanto, and such a policy has been pursued by the movement unwaveringly. *La Espero, La Vojo*, and other well-known poems and songs; the green star and green symbolism generally are symbols of cohesion of the Esperanto speech community the world over. The solidarity of the speech community is affirmed at the annual world congresses.

Since the Esperantists claim that their speech community gives rise to an Esperantist 'people' in its own right, it is rather difficult to examine the Esperanto movement within the confines of a single society. Thus attention has been paid to the dynamics of development of the international movement. Yet it is possible to see Esperanto as pre-eminently the product of *European* culture and history. The Esperanto movement can be examined in the context of the international relations of Europe. Its supporters are not confined to Europe, but with few exceptions European countries far outstrip the rest of the world in the strength of membership of Esperanto organisations. It has been shown how Esperanto was produced in relation to a specific situation of strain in Russian Poland. Its source has also been traced to ideas of the Enlightenment and to Positivism, the latter being a continuation of the former into the nineteenth century. A response to the complexity of industrial society was to emphasise the widening of application of science. In such a context, the idea of a 'scientific' solution of the world language problem would seem appropriate. Esperanto was developed in a society where Positivistic ideas were beginning to extend their influence, yet they were only one element in the process. Also important was the Jewish Enlightenment, *Haskalah*, and the 'Jewish dimension' of the ideas of the founder, Zamenhof, has been noted. Zamenhof displayed concern for the situation of the Jewish people, but broadened his interests to a general concern with inter-ethnic relations. Esperanto spread slowly after publication in 1887, chiefly in Russia. Overtly its followers concerned themselves with promotion of a language, but less openly a more value-oriented interpretation developed. When, in 1905, world congresses were initiated, Zamenhof used the opportunity to expound his idealism, initially religious, within the general framework of the movement.

With the turn of the century, the *de facto* international centre of Esperanto shifted, after a brief Swedish interlude, to France and especially Paris. With the move to France occurred a progressive secularisation of the value system with which Esperanto was associated. By 1906 Zamenhof found it necessary to delete any religious overtones to his speech at the world congress; he also found it necessary to stress that norm- and value-oriented interpretations were to be distinguished from one another. The French Esperanto association also affirmed categorically that Esperanto was only a language. The context of Western European thought permitted a wide range of possible interpretations of Esperanto. Positivistic, rationalistic, and scientific currents of opinion began to wane in France by the turn of the century, though Esperanto had a sufficient spiritual dimension to adapt to this greater subjectivism. With the shift to Western Europe, too, came a different kind of value-oriented interpretation of the language. Idealists thought in terms of 'world peace' rather than 'inter-ethnic relations'. By 1908 the most fundamental challenge to the ideology of the movement occurred, namely to the structure of the language itself. Changes had previously been considered in 1894, by the existing supporters of Esperanto, and were rejected. Changes were now proposed by the Delegation, an outside body, which tried to bring Esperanto under the control of rationalistic and Positivistic ideas. Changes proposed were rejected, and the ultimate outcome was schism.

If proposals to change the structure of the language led to schism, proposals for specific values to be associated with the language led rather to specialisation. Thus UEA, founded in 1908, was concerned with 'practical idealism', the organisation of international services for members in the spirit of the values associated with Esperanto. Later, in 1921, SAT associated Esperanto with ideals of world socialism. SAT was organised as a separate association, outside the framework of the neutral or 'bourgeois' movement; but only for a short time was it not possible to be a member of both. Within the neutral movement, a key point of dispute was the problem of establishment of an international organisation to promote Esperanto. One solution was to propose the establishment of a federation of national associations, but UEA exemplified a supernational or cosmopolitan framework. The Contract of Helsinki (1922) provided a compromise between these two conflicting principles, but it proved short-lived. Particularly in the 1930s, powerful nationalistic forces in the wider society brought about polarisation of attitudes to Esperanto, and the schism between UEA and IEL took place in 1936. Finally, Stalinist and Fascist pressures led eventually to eclipse of the movement altogether in certain countries which had previously been important strongholds.

Characteristic of the period since the Second World War has been a unifying and centralising tendency. UEA and IEL were united on a firmer basis than before. Both organisational and ideological unification have been asserted. The value-oriented position has been reaffirmed, but has been related closely to internationalist educational ideals such as UNESCO. Such developments have been largely successful. There has been no major threat to the organisational unity of the movement. Certain East-West tensions have occasionally posed threats to ideological unity, but these have not proved insurmountable.

Thus the background of European history and culture is crucial to the understanding of the Esperanto movement. Even the very structure of the Esperanto language reflects its European base: international roots have been effectively those of European languages. Esperanto (and most other rival projects) drew particularly on vocabulary from the two previously accepted international languages, Latin and French. If the European basis of the language is objected to, Esperantists could reply that Esperanto as a language has an Indo-European rather than a European basis. The Indo-European languages are spoken widely outside Europe: in the Americas, in Australasia. Even in Africa, fears of tribalism have made for the continued use of colonial languages as national. The major exceptions to the Indo-European group are found in the Arab world and in most of Asia. The argument for the use of Esperanto in such countries too tends to be that Esperanto may be European, but it is far easier to learn than English.

Yet not only the language Esperanto, but also the value system traditionally associated with it, has emerged in a European context. The significance of events in European history for the development of the movement has already been noted. The 'world' wars, nationalism, and the development of international peace-keeping bodies have all made their impact. It is particularly noteworthy that internal disputes within the Esperanto movement have tended to increase at times when integrationist tendencies within Europe have been on the decline. This was particularly true of conflict between norm- and value-oriented tendencies within the neutral movement in the interwar period. Internal disputation continued between UEA and IEL on the eve of the Second World War. Conversely, the international Esperanto movement has displayed considerable unity when integrationist tendencies in Europe have been strong. The unity of the movement was apparent when, after the First World War, the League of Nations appeared to be taking seriously the values associated with Esperanto and possibly the language as well. UEA was able to emphasise the unity of concern of all members by its stress on 'practical idealism'. It is true that the League of Nations was not strictly a European institution. Yet it existed at a time when a 'European' war could still be described unselfconsciously as a 'world' war.

An additional characteristic of European societies which has tended to favour Esperanto has been its linguistic diversity. Europe consists of a relatively large number of states, relatively small in geographical area, most of which speak a different language from one another. In many cases these states are densely populated and are relatively wealthy. The key factor in twentieth-century European relations has evidently been the conflict between France and Germany. In such a situation, particularly in the First World War, the values associated with Esperanto could be seen to be relevant. The commitment of the Esperantists was not on the whole sufficiently subversive to make for abstention from the war effort. Rather they concentrated on support for postwar reconstruction and saw a role for Esperanto in moral reform through internationalist education.

In view of the close link between the Esperanto movement and its European context, it is necessary to consider changes in the position of Europe in relation to the rest of the world and the possible implications of these for Esperanto. Joll suggests that

The meeting of the American and Russian armies on the river Elbe in April 1945 symbolised the extent to which the future of Europe was now dependent on the policies of these two powers and on the relations between them.

There is a sense in which the end of the Second World War marked what has been called "The End of European History".[12]

Thus within Europe, the policies of Eastern European nations have on the whole been linked to those of the Soviet Union, those of Western Europe to the policies of the United States. This has gone together with the end of the assumption of a natural European sense of superiority and right to rule.[13] A particularly important force in the world since the Second World War has been American neo-imperialism. It is useful to consider the implications of these changes in the international situation for the development of Esperanto. In the first place, it can be seen that the Esperanto movement has not become a global force and has not succeeded in widening its horizons to recruit large numbers of new members from outside Europe. At the same time American English has become more widespread as a result of American influence in the Third World. English is also particularly widespread outside Europe as a result of earlier British imperialism. Thus the question arises as to whether Esperanto is now destined to remain a vestigial phenomenon, with English having a better chance of official recognition as the world language.

Yet English suffers from the difficulty of being associated with particular nation-states, especially the United States. Diplomatic considerations prevent official recognition of English as the sole language used in United Nations organisations, and preference is given to spending considerable sums of money on translation. The number of official languages of United Nations bodies has further continued to increase. Outside Europe, too, numerous other languages are firmly entrenched: Spanish, French, Arabic, Chinese, and Portuguese, at least, are important international as well as national languages. There seems no immediate likelihood of change in this pattern.[14]

The Esperantists have responded to this situation by concentrating considerable effort on persuading UNESCO to accept Esperanto. It has been seen that such a strategy met with some measure of success, resulting in establishment of consultative relations. Yet this must not be confused with official adoption of Esperanto. Rather it is recognition of the contribution that UEA makes to fulfilling the aims of UNESCO: the movement, rather than the language, has been acknowledged as a significant factor in international life. UEA has continued to pay attention to the United Nations and UNESCO and has drawn attention to the language difficulties in such organisations. So far such activities have been ignored by the bodies concerned. Even the Esperanto *movement* has failed to establish itself as a significant force for international relations *outside Europe* – simply because of a lack of recruitment, at least to international Esperanto associations, in other continents.[15]

The prospects for Esperanto seem somewhat better in the continued linguistic confusion of Europe, especially since the establishment of institutions for European integration. In practice, despite official UEA policy, the largely European-based membership seems even in the 1950s and 1960s to have been especially interested in European problems. Lapenna found it necessary in 1958 to remind members of the Mainz World Congress that, while the campaign for widening the use of Esperanto in Europe was of great value,[16] Esperanto should still be seen as a world and not just a European language. In the very recent past attention has been paid particularly to language problems of the Common Market. The Common Market campaign has been intensified since the admission of the United Kingdom, Denmark, and the Irish Republic, and Pompidou's suggestion that French should remain the Community's principal working language. One basis for his argument was that Europe would in this way be distinguished linguistically from the United States. French has continued to predominate in the Common Market's official proceedings. Yet those who advocate English as a world language are by no means prepared to confine its use to outside Europe. The influence of American capital, and with it the English language, is considerable in Western Europe. In the Common Market, all languages of member states are treated as official. Language problems occur in day-to-day business as well as in formal debates. New states have now been admitted, thus adding to the number of official languages. Thus a review of the linguistic policy of the Community is likely, and the advocates of Esperanto hope to obtain some success.[17]

What has been said about Europe so far applies only to the West. The position is somewhat different in Eastern Europe, where the Soviet Union and the Russian language are dominant. Yet Russian is little known outside Eastern Europe except by those with particular commercial, cultural, or scientific relations with the Soviet Union. Esperanto, too, is not firmly established as a significant force in the Soviet Union itself. The situation is rather different in the smaller Communist countries in Europe, as already noted. In particular, Esperanto enables Western and Eastern Europeans to enjoy face-to-face contact with one another. Thus relations between East and West Europe have become a significant factor in the social relations of the Esperanto movement. This remains at an interpersonal level, internal to the Esperanto movement. Détente and other related exercises have not become sufficiently firmly established to enable the Esperanto movement collectively to incorporate activities related to them as part of its official policy. The potential threat to political neutrality associated with East–West relations in Europe has already been commented upon.

Finally, it should be mentioned that a significant non-European country in the Esperanto world is Japan. The Japanese contingent at world congresses is usually substantial. English is firmly entrenched as a foreign language in Japan, yet it remains difficult for a Japanese to learn and there have been many failures. Esperanto is Western-based, but much easier for a Japanese to learn than English. It is the policy of the Japanese socialist party to introduce compulsory teaching of Esperanto in all Japanese schools.

This brief survey of the world linguistic scene and the prospects for Esperanto in it has been made in order to assess whether or not Esperanto is a 'socially relevant' cause. It is here suggested that, in the world context, language difficulties certainly do occur, and that Esperanto would provide a perfectly feasible solution to them. On the other hand, other more pragmatic, makeshift solutions have been developed to cope with linguistic diversity. Esperanto might be a more satisfactory solution, but existing procedures are not totally unworkable. Thus although language problems do occur, they are not so significant and insurmountable as to encourage strong official international support for a radical solution such as Esperanto. Rather the Esperantists' aims are seen as not an urgent priority. If it is in fact the case that certain subconscious factors exist which make for opposition to the idea of artificial language, these make for further difficulties.

It remains to consider the type of movement represented by

Esperanto. It has been argued that it is difficult to demonstrate that Esperanto has lost or has never had 'social relevance'. Also, as indicated in the Introduction, Esperanto fits uneasily into classic sociological typologies. At the same time it has been noted that the folk-concept of 'crank' has frequently been used to describe Esperanto supporters. It remains to consider the significance of such a societal reaction to Esperanto. In speaking of 'societal re-action' the difficulty arises in an international movement as to which society is being referred to. Thus some of the remaining dis-cussion will use as its basis mostly the British material. The idea of Esperanto as a 'cranky' movement is probably not confined to Britain; yet there is no reason to suppose that Esperanto is thought of as cranky in all societies. But the campaign *within the movement* against cranks has been waged in an international context.

Recapitulating the discussion in Part II on Esperanto in Britain, it has been noted that certain characteristics of the British move-ment depend on the specific situation of Britain. In the first place, Britain speaks the major international language, English. Second, Britain has, although belligerent in two world wars, enjoyed a certain degree of isolation from the most destructive consequences of international conflicts by virtue of being an island. Britain has had a stable political tradition, and in particular has never had a Fascist government. In this context, it has been shown how British Esperantists have supported the legally established political struc-ture; indeed, they have wished to impress it favourably in the hope of securing acceptance of Esperanto. The BEA was formally constituted at an early stage, and has continued to be organi-sationally, if not numerically, strong. There appears always to have been a hard core of members, supplemented by many others whose support has often been short-lived. BEA members have participated fully in the world movement and have supported the development of an international organisation. During the Second World War, the headquarters of IEL was in Britain. The only conflict with the world movement has been in recent times, as a result of suggestions that UEA's policies are mandatory for member states.

The social composition of the BEA has been seen to be elderly middle-class, employed in professional and clerical occupations and especially teaching. Members are relatively highly educated, but not socialised into conventional wisdom to the extent that they would dismiss Esperanto as a 'cranky' movement. They are also employed in occupations outside the field of private industrial enterprise and tend not to live in centres of heavy industry. They tend to be politically left of centre and, to a greater extent than the population at large, are either agnostic in religion or active churchgoers. A significant minority of members support other deviant causes, and this group tends to be labelled as 'cranks'. Older and long-standing members are more idealistic about Esperanto than recent and younger members. Those politically left of centre and vegetarian are more idealistic than conservatives and meat-eaters. Esperanto emerges as a broadly based commitment meaning different things to different people. For some it is just a hobby; for others it is linked with family and marriage; while some members link Esperanto to various radical, subversive, and deviant causes. 'Crankiness', therefore, tends to be a minority phenomenon within the movement.

Discussion of the folk-concept of crankiness must in the present state of knowledge be fairly speculative, but a number of facets can be discerned. It appears, first, that the term tends to be used pejoratively, and by those who would not consider the term to be applicable to themselves. At the same time, those described by such a term will often reply that all progressive ideas were originally considered cranky. The self-description as 'cranks' by the vegetarian group in London has already been noted.[18] Second, it appears that crankiness is something noticeable, something conspicuous. What Wilson says of the sectarian could apply *mutatis mutandis* to the 'crank':

. . .the sectarian is almost always conspicuous by virtue of his religious commitment. Whatever activity he is engaged in, the fact that a man is one of Jehovah's Witnesses, or a Christadelphian, or even a Quaker, tends to become evident sooner rather than later.[19]

There are, however, important differences between the sectarian and the crank. The sect and cranky causes are different kinds of allegiance. The sect will rigidly discipline its members; in some sects the ultimate penalty for apostasy may well be the fires of hell. Sects such as Quakerism do overlap with 'cranky' causes, but there is not much overlap in the case of doctrinally rigid sectarian organisations.[20] The 'crank' is associated typically not so much with sectarian religion as with secular forms of deviant commitment, or if religious with the cult rather than with the sect. The 'crank' may well devote much of his time to various causes; but this level of activity is not normally demanded by the movements themselves, and such movements may consist of many other noncranky members. The question therefore arises as to whether 'crankiness' refers to a distinctive form of commitment or merely to a distinctive behaviour pattern. It is here suggested that any deviant behaviour engaged in by the crank must relate in some way to certain deviant forms of commitment. Deviant behaviour such as personal 'eccentricity' can easily be associated with ideological conservatism. It remains to consider whether crankiness can relate to any kind of commitment, or whether to only certain kinds.

It appears that only certain kinds of movement are particularly liable to be labelled by the outsider as cranky. To label a movement as cranky is to belittle it, to suggest that it is a lost cause rather than a threat to the established order. Cranks are seen as ridiculous; 'nutcases', perhaps (cf. the etymologically related German *krank*), even a nuisance, but not as dangerous. Causes promoted by the crank are simply irrelevant. Cranky causes are minority causes: if they gained significantly in strength, they would cease to be described by such a label. They would then either be seen as a danger to established interests or be absorbed by them.[21]

Typically the crank is associated with nonpolitical forms of deviance. He may not necessarily reject politics and may even be politically active, but the causes he is really interested in contain an important expressive component. Thus the label tends not to be applied to organised radical political movements, however strong the commitment of their members. Such movements, unlike crankiness, are seen as more likely to achieve power and therefore more likely to be a threat to established interests. It can be suggested that Esperanto fits nearest into the 'anarcho-pacifist' tradition outlined by Rigby. The link between anarchism and pacifism can be seen to be close: its converse is well expressed in Clausewitz's dictum that war is a continuation of politics by other means.[22] Anarchism and pacifism as such are perhaps simply extreme developments of a much broader spectrum of nonpolitical deviance. For instance, Rigby suggests that such a current of opinion is typical of the present-day 'alternative society'. He quotes a typical attitude of a communard: 'By living a different way of life, we can make some people sit up and think "maybe there is another way of life, maybe we ought to change our way of life". . .'[23]

Such communitarian movements have roots in philosophical positions expressed notably by Tolstoy: it is interesting that the Tolstoyan commitment has overlapped with Esperanto in a number of places. The emphasis is typically on converting individuals rather than seeking political power. Both Tolstoy and Zamenhof developed their ideas in the context of the repressive Tsarist Russian empire, in which any kind of innovatory idea was suspect. This tradition of thought has continued to be important in the peace movement, which by its very nature displays certain tensions in relation to established political processes. The theologian Reinhold Niebuhr provides a critique of this position. He criticises

. . .the moralists, both religious and secular, who imagine that the egotism of individuals is being progressively checked by the development of rationality or the growth of a religiously inspired goodwill and that nothing but the continuance of this process is necessary to establish social harmony between all the human societies and collectivities.[24]

In his critique, Niebuhr argues that national groupings are too large for religious/ethical/rational principles to be applicable to international relations. He argues that

The relations between groups must therefore always be predominantly political rather than ethical, that is, they will be determined by the proportion of power which a group possesses at least as much as by any rational and moral appraisal of the comparative needs and claims of each group.[25]

He attributes this fact to the 'inevitable limitations of human nature, and the limits of human imagination and intelligence'.[26] He does not, however, reject the value of the insights which this tradition provides:

The realistic wisdom of the statesman is reduced to foolishness if it is not under the influence of the foolishness of the moral seer. The latter's idealism results in political futility and sometimes in moral confusion, if it is not brought into commerce and communication with the realities of man's collective life.[27]

Thus there is a possibility that the *contribution* of this tradition of thinking may be accepted by the established value system as an educational device. Absolute pacifism will not be accepted by any government, yet there can be widespread acceptance of the educational value of 'international understanding'. A tradition of thought thus exists that argues that education can produce harmonious international relations. Waltz[28] suggests that the kinds of explanation of the major causes of war can be grouped under three main headings. The causes of war can be seen as being (a) within man, (b) within the structure of the separate states, and (c) within the state system, i.e. the system of international relations. Correspondingly, prescriptions for peace may concentrate on (a) converting individuals, (b) changing the structure of the various individual states, or (c) changing the organisation of international relations.

Insofar as Esperanto is appealed to as a way of promoting world peace, it is seen mainly in terms of the first image. It is argued that wars take place because 'people do not understand one another'. Language is seen as the chief cause of such lack of understanding, and Esperanto is proposed as the answer. All three images of causes of war overlap, yet far less interest has been taken by the Esperantists in the other two potential causes of war. Esperantists have been particularly unconcerned with the second image, the idea that the internal structure of states needs to be changed in order to secure sustained peace. It has already been observed that the tradition of the movement has been to suspect the state, rather than to suggest the implementation of any radical changes in its structure. The commonest projection of the second image has been the suggestion that the chief cause of war is capitalism.[29] International socialism has been seen as the key to the permanent abolition of war. The tradition of 'political neutrality' of the Esperanto movement has prevented any suggestion of this kind from being adopted as collective policy. Only in SAT did such ideas gain currency; even there, the ideology in its pure form saw the particular role of Esperanto as educational rather than political: the justification for an Esperantist socialist movement was to *educate* the workers *for* world socialism. Members were expected to pursue their other socialist ideas elsewhere, in their own political parties.

The third image has gained greater popularity among Esperantists. Esperanto has not necessarily been seen as logically leading to intergovernmental bodies for world peace: but when these have been proposed by the major world powers, the Esperantists have tended to give them wholehearted support. This was true of the League of Nations and particularly the United Nations, support for which has been incorporated into the official ideology of UEA since the Second World War. Individual Esperantists have often advocated more ambitious schemes for world government; and the *idea* of world government has been regarded as uncontroversial by UEA. The Universal League, an Esperantist organisation advocating world government though not committed to one particular scheme, was listed in UEA returns as a 'neutral' organisation. Yet even in the 1950s and 1960s, particular emphasis has continued to be placed on the first image, the idea that the international situation can be changed for the better, even if only gradually, by educating people for international understanding. Official ideology has particularly concerned itself with the unity of interest of UEA and UNESCO in recent years. More generally, members widely hold to the view that the face-to-face contacts of 'ordinary people' across national and linguistic frontiers, facilitated by the movement, contributes to the ideal of education for international understanding.

Exaggerated claims may well be made by Esperantists and outsiders as to the efficacy of such education. Yet it must be remembered that there is a well-established tradition of advocacy of education as a contribution to world peace in the behavioural sciences.[30] UNESCO, too, stands for recognition of the contribution of education, science, and culture to the maintenance of stable peace. If this is perceived to be a naive view, such naivety is not confined to the Esperantists. UNESCO sees war as beginning 'in the minds of men' and reflects the view of a number of behavioural scientists. Waltz assesses this tradition and points to a number of remedies which have been proposed. These include educational systems that oppose national self-righteousness; increased knowledge of other cultures, which (so it is argued) will lead to increased tolerance; international research in the social sciences; and the application of the findings of behavioural science by those responsible for international policy. Waltz is critical of sweeping claims sometimes made for this kind of approach, but does not reject it as a contribution to a solution of the problem: 'The more fully behavioural scientists take account of politics, the more sensible and the more modest their efforts to contribute to peace become.[31]

A similar position might be held in relation to the value-oriented interpretation of Esperanto: though some Esperantists would see this not as a concession to 'reality' but as a sellout, neglecting the true potential of Esperanto. Lazersfeld and Knupfer, however, suggest that

The social and psychological forces impelling rivalry between nations are too strong to be controlled by a vague allegiance to "all men everywhere", or the ideal of "international cooperation". It seems that a concrete international authority is needed around which people can build up new identifications and supranational loyalties.[32]

Some Esperantists would claim that ultimately this focus of attention is actualised by Esperanto. Some members see 'Esperanto-land' as a microcosm of a future world society. The frequent analogy between the movement and a state has already been commented upon. It should be added that by no means all or even most of those Esperantists who think of their efforts in terms of world peace are in any way articulate about the implications of their commitment in the way that might have been implied here. Esperanto is a sufficiently nebulous commitment to incorporate a wide range of interpretations of its aims, particularly in view of the movement's professed political and religious neutrality.

Particular attention has been paid here so far to the relation of Esperanto to the promotion of peace; and this is indeed the typical value commitment associated with Esperanto. Yet it can be observed that Esperantists are frequently also active in other causes which do not all seem to bear any immediate relation to the contribution that an artificial language might make. Perhaps the commonest is the link between Esperanto and vegetarianism. Here the connection might be indirect, since there exists, as already noted, a close link between vegetarianism and the peace movement. Yet a small but significant number of Esperantists are active in promoting other minority opinions. Such an association between Esperanto and various (some would say various other) 'cranky' causes is worthy of explanation. This has been noted elsewhere. Parkin tenatively suggests that

CND supporters' overall position in relation to central societal values points to what might be called a "deviance syndrome" — that is, the propensity to endorse minority or deviant standpoints on a broad range of public issues. Such an attribute would obviously be an important factor in helping to account for involvement in CND. If the reasonable assumption is made that the supporters subscribed to this particular constellation of deviant values before the emergence of the unilateralist movement, then it makes sense to claim that they were, so to speak, "prepared" for it before the question of nuclear weapons became a major political issue. In other words, an individual's commitment to CND could to a large extent be said to be determined by his existing predisposition to deviance of the kind outlined.[33]

Also that

It would appear that alienation from societal values is not always compartmentalized, but may affect commitment to popularly accepted standards of an apparently neutral type; to take a trivial example, the wearing of beards did appear to be more common among CND supporters than among men in general; also many respondents indicated they were vegetarians. . . . This does suggest that estrangement from certain values may be conducive to deviance in a wide range of social behaviour.[34]

Within the context of religious and analogous collectivities, Campbell points to the existence of the 'cultic milieu':

Such a milieu is defined as the sum of unorthodox and deviant belief-systems together with their practices, institutions and personnel and constitutes a unity by virtue of a common consciousness of deviant status, a receptive and syncretistic orientation and an interpretative communication structure. In addition, the cultic milieu is united and identified by the existence of an ideology of seekership and by seekership institutions. Both the culture and the organizational structure of the milieu represent deviant forms of the prevailing religious and scientific orthodoxies in combination with both instrumental and expressive orientations.[35]

The idea of 'religious *and scientific*' orthodoxies is of some importance in this connection. Campbell suggests that in the twentieth century there has been a decline in the prestige of religion coupled with a growth in the prestige of science. However, scientists cannot effectively control the beliefs of nonscientists, and certain organisations have developed whose aim it is to promulgate scientific 'heresies':

Orthodox science is now at least as important as orthodox religion in defining what is truth and what is error in contemporary culture, if not more so. Scientific "heresies" abound in the cultic fringe... the true heresies are not so much religious beliefs... but beliefs held to be "purely" scientific which are repudiated by the spokesmen of scientific orthodoxy: the flat-earthers, or the flying saucerians who hold that extraterrestrial vehicles actually exist. Fully-fledged scientific theories also abound, notably concerning "ethers", "emanations", "fifth senses", and astral planes together with the many and varied interpretations of the nature of time and space.[36]

Various movements exist to promote heresies in *applied* science. Supporters of such causes do not merely subscribe to and wish to promote knowledge of a certain set of beliefs about the world: they also hold that certain innovations can be applied to the world, thus improving the welfare of mankind. Typical examples of such applied scientific heresies are unorthodox forms of medical treatment. In earlier stages of the development of industrial society, the 'crank' patentee and inventor had a role; but owing to the degree of sophistication of twentieth century technology, the scope for such individual initiative has been much reduced. However, things are known with much less certainty in the social than in the natural world; and, as Banks points out,

... men have invented social techniques and exploited them, much in the same fashion as they have with material techniques. Indeed, only when it is admitted that such social technologies are possible can social movements be regarded as creators rather than as creatures of social change.[37]

'Crank' medicine perhaps stands midway between natural and social technology. The theoretical justification for medicine is found in natural science, yet cause/effect relationships cannot be established with the same degree of certainty as in 'pure' natural science. The case of linguistics is somewhat different and less certain. By no means all linguists have been hostile to the idea of an artificial international language; indeed, some, notably Otto Jespersen, have continuously advocated such a proposal and consciously participated in the development of a suitable instrument.[38] Yet little has been done towards developing an applied interlinguistics at an academic level: this is perhaps largely due to the controversial nature, both politically and linguistically, of an innovation of this kind. Thus the development of an *a posteriori* artificial language for international use has largely been left to amateurs. Esperanto itself was initiated by a doctor of medicine, not by a professional linguist, and is cherished by many 'amateur linguists'. It can thus be seen to be a kind of heresy in applied science. As such it finds its place among those who are inclined to support scientific heresies generally, and these do tend to be of an applied kind — health food, duodecimal calculations, and antivaccination have all been represented among the other commitments of individual Esperantists.

To some degree, innovatory commitments of certain Esperantists take the form of rejection of certain manifestations of industrial society. A sketch of this kind of commitment is seen in Edward Carpenter's *Civilisation: Its Cause and Cure*.[39] Influenced by evolutionary theories of Morgan and Engels, Carpenter expresses concern about the state of 'health', physical and otherwise, of 'civilised' society. He particularly suspects modern medicine, clothing, sex taboos, the state, private property, and indoor life. He advocates a return to nature, and suggests a number of remedies for this condition. These include simple housing and clothing — even nudism; vegetarianism, especially fruit-eating; and Communism. Thus the question arises as to why such a link exists between Esperanto and such forms of deviant commitment.

The characteristics of the Esperantists, as already indicated, might here be of some relevance. It has been noted that, for Britain at any rate, the occupational and geographical location of Esperantists tends to be away from heavy industry. This has also been noted for the CND. Parkin found that

Middle class male CND supporters are to be found predominantly in the employment of state and local authorities, independent bodies such as churches and universities, various non-profit-making organizations including trade unions and Co-operative societies, or in freelance professions. Only about a quarter were employed in private industry and commercial organizations.[40]

Parkin suggests that this is due to the radicalising experience of higher education which has been obtained by the educated middle class. He also suggests that CND members tend to have chosen these occupations since they experience no incompatability in them between their radical commitments and their occupations. The applicability of such an analysis to Esperanto depends on the extent to which *other* commitments of the Esperantists are radical in any way. Esperanto *as such* is far less politically controversial than nuclear disarmament. As already noted, 'cranks' tend to be seen as 'nutcases' rather than as dangerous. Provided that the committment was not too fanatical, it is unlikely that advocacy of Esperanto would prove a barrier in most occupations. It might be added that, while education can have the radicalising effect indicated by Parkin, it is also conducive to socialisation into particular kinds of thought, even particular kinds of radical thought, and may well discourage the espousing of 'cranky' causes. Esperanto is particularly likely to be taken up by those who have shown a certain amount of individual initiative in their education, such as by participation in adult education. Furthermore, Esperantists tend to be typical of an older generation than the CND supporters.

Yet the location of the Esperantists in a situation which lies outside the conflict of capital and labour may be significant, and this characteristic is shared with the CND. Abrams and McCulloch observe that the particular vogue for the CND in the 1960s was short-lived, and that the central political problem has reasserted itself in the 1970s:

After a few years of apparent freedom, politics have as it were been recaptured by capital and labour, now locked again in a series of relations from which the petty-bourgeoisie are excluded.[41]

Following Poulantzas,[42] they suggest that the Marxist concept of the petty bourgeoisie identifies two distinctive economic groups which constitute an ideological and political unity. These are (a) traditional groups engaged in small production, and (b) the 'ideological apparatuses' — found particularly in communication industries, the educational system, and cultural institutions.[43] As examples of the protest movements of this group Abrams and McCulloch indicate the CND, the commune movement, and women's liberation. They also argue:

In a repertoire of petty-bourgeois protest —·anarchism, free-thinking, nudism, civil liberties and the whole gamut of "spiritual-healing" projects — communes are the specific response to an ambivalent discontent with the specific experience of the petty-bourgeois family.[44]

There is some justification for locating Esperanto in this milieu. Particularly, it enables its supporters to open their world to a much wider range of social experience than might otherwise have been available to them. Merchant's biography of the pioneer of Esperanto in England, Joseph Rhodes, makes this point:

Joseph Rhodes was born on the 9th of July, 1856, in a small house in Aireworth Street, Keighley, and he died in that same small Yorkshire town sixty-three years afterwards, on the 28th of February 1920. From those two facts, one can immediately note what a tremendous factor in his life Esperanto undoubtedly became, opening to him the doors of the Wide World across the sea, and introducing him to the exchange of thought and sympathy with the peoples of other nations in all continents. Some other man, born and living in those same circumstances for many years, would be set in narrow-minded opinions, would see life generally from a parochial viewpoint, and would remain one of the most unintelligent and uninteresting individuals. But what a contrast is evident in our old friend! Examining more carefully his opinions and viewpoints, we find that, like Bacon, he "made the whole world his province", or that, like Pistol in *Merry Wives of Windsor*, he could say, "Why, then, the world's mine oyster, which I with sword will open". But in Rhodes's case, he wisely used the pen instead of the sword.[45]

Abrams and McCulloch see such movements as expressions of petty-bourgeois individualism, as an escape from capitalism rather than a confrontation with it. Although they argue that the term 'petty bourgeois' should not be seen as intended derogatively, in fact the tone of their account of communes is highly critical. At this point particularly the question of value judgements inevitably arises. Rigby, whose view of communes tends to be favourable, suggests that 'one's assessment of the revolutionary potential of any dissident group will depend on one's basic value-position'.[46] This factor should be borne in mind in the present discussion.

In the first place, some Marxists might reject the suggestion that Esperanto is doomed as such to be a form of petty-bourgeois protest. Indeed, Lapenna, while still a Marxist, argued that Esperanto could be and should be rescued from the grip of the petty bourgeoisie. He made such criticisms of manifestations of 'crankiness' at the 1947 Berne World Esperanto Congress.[47] He was critical of this kind of expression within the movement as such, and wished to enhance its respectability by discouraging 'crankiness'.

Yet the question arises as to whether discussion of social movements can only be appropriately carried on in Marxist terms. Also, if 'cranky' movements do not have as their focus of attention the conflict between capital and labour, it does not follow *a priori* that such movements do anything to bolster capitalism. Indeed, as Orwell was painfully aware, there was no shortage of 'cranks' in the socialist movement of his period. If cranks are to be criticised for failing to concentrate their efforts on a critique of capitalism, does this imply that no social change should be sought unless capitalism is abolished, or that, if socialism were established, all promotional groups would cease to be necessary? There seems no reason to assess a movement like Esperanto invariably in terms of what contribution it might make to the establishment of socialism, especially since there are so many competing definitions of 'true socialism'.

However, the discussion of communes and other movements in the anarcho-pacifist tradition which Abrams and McCulloch provide gives a clue to the definition of crankiness. Cranks, they would argue, are out of touch with 'reality'. It needs to be considered how far there is justification for such a degree of certainty about the social world. Rather it might appear that, by the side of dominant values there exist certain deviant values, whose supporters wish to change some key area of the dominant value system. Cranks, typically, concentrate their efforts on issues which are not central to either the dominant or the accepted deviant value system. Typically, cranks are fervent supporters of their cause. Often support for a cranky cause may demand a certain degree of effort on the part of the adherent. The crank may be expected to discipline himself to eat certain kinds of food; to go to the trouble of learning a

language; to live in an unconventional domestic unit; or to overcome inhibitions about parading naked in mixed company on
certain occasions.

Thus it has been suggested that 'crankiness' implies (a) a certain
kind of commitment, and (b) conspicuous fervent support for this
commitment. Frequently, conspicuous 'cranks' form only a minority of members of a movement, and this is the case with Esperanto. Yet for outsiders, support for a cause of this kind is seen as
ipso facto cranky, and therefore unacceptable. The behaviour of
the 'cranks' in a movement is conspicuous: the cranks are also the
mainstay of the membership and will renew their subscriptions
whether their cause is popular or not. Such is not so true of many
other members, who may join if the cause shows signs of being
taken seriously but will lapse if less attention is paid to it. In the
recent history of the movement, the policy has been to draw public attention to the contribution that Esperanto can make, and
manifestations of 'crankiness' have been discouraged. Yet Esperanto
has not been adopted officially by any major organisation, state,
or group of states. Thus to some degree certain members are liable
to continue to display characteristics of the 'deviance syndrome'.

NOTES

1.   F. Tönnies, *Community and Association (Gemeinschaft und Gesellschaft)*, 1955.
2.   Parkin, *Middle Class Radicalism, op. cit.*, p.34.
3.   *Ibid.*, p.35 (quoting an observation by Roy Jenkins).
4.   J.C. Flügel, 'Some unconscious factors in the international language movement
      with especial reference to Esperanto', *International Journal of Psychoanalysis* 6,
      1925, pp.171–208. The notion of 'disgust' has also been commented upon in legal
      circles, notably by Lord Devlin (P. Devlin, *The Enforcement of Morals*, 1965,
      pp.viii–ix). It appears that there are certain kinds of change to which societies are
      peculiarly resistant.
5.   Flügel, *op. cit.*, p.201n.
6.   *Ibid.*, pp.199–200.
7.   *Ibid.*, p.201.
8.   F. Tönnies, *op. cit.*, pp.54–55.
9.   For definition of the concepts *Wesenwille* ['natural' or 'essential' will] and *Kürwille*
      ['rational' or 'elective' will] see F. Tönnies, *op. cit.*, p.119.
10.   M.D. Biddis, *op. cit.*, p.42, observes that at the Universal Races Congress of 1911,
      Tönnies spoke against Esperanto but was prepared to accept a modified version of
      Latin as a world language.
11.   A colony of this kind (*Bona Espero* in Brazil) has now begun to function.

12. Joll, *op. cit.*, p.468.
13. For discussion of these trends see *ibid.*, Ch.16, *passim*.
14. For discussion of the 'internationality' of various languages see P. Burney, *Les Langues internationales, op. cit.*; R. Breton, *Géographie des langues*, 1976; M. Pei, *One Language for the World*, 1958; H.N. Shenton, *op. cit.*
15. See Ch. 1 for geographical spread of the Esperanto movement.
16. Lapenna, *Elektitaj paroladoj kaj prelegoj, op. cit.*, pp.48–54.
17. See W. Bormann, *Bona ŝanco*, 1970, for assessment of such possibilities.
18. See p.273.
19. B.R. Wilson, *Religion in Secular Society*, 1966, p.182.
20. The term 'sect' is, of course, a broad category, as Wilson himself recognises. See B.R. Wilson, 'An analysis of sect development', *Patterns of Sectarianism, op. cit.*, pp.22–48.
21. The use of the term 'crank' has also been reported from colonial Central Africa (P. Gibbs, *Avalanche in Central Africa*, 1961, p.71). It has characteristically been used to refer to white people who are prepared to be friendly to black Africans and invite them to their homes. This usage reflects the unusually high degree of social control exerted in situations of this kind, and the unusually high degree of ostracism for deviants. But by referring to the deviants as 'cranks' the supporters of dominant values in the white community in such circumstances are able to belittle them, and can do so successfully provided that the deviation is not widely indulged in (as indeed it was not). The deviants are able in their turn to seek social relations among the black population, thus compensating for their rejection by the white community.
22. C. von Clausewitz, *On War*, 1968, p.119.
23. A. Rigby, *Alternative Realities, op. cit.*, p.37.
24. R. Niebuhr, *Moral Man and Immoral Society*, 1934, p.xii.
25. *Ibid.*, p.xxii.
26. *Ibid.*, p.xxiii.
27. *Ibid.*, p.288.
28. K.N. Waltz, *Man, the State and War*, 1954, Ch. I.
29. *Ibid.*, Ch. V.
30. *Ibid.*, Ch. III.
31. *Ibid.*, p.79.
32. P.F. Lazersfeld and G. Knupfer, 'Communications research and international cooperation', in *The Science of Man in the World Crisis*, ed. by R. Linton, p.466 (quoted in Waltz, *op. cit.*, pp.69–70).
33. Parkin, *Middle Class Radicalism, op. cit.*, pp.29–30.
34. *Ibid.*, p.29n.
35. C. Campbell, 'The cult, the cultic milieu and secularization', in *A Sociological Yearbook of Religion in Britain* 5, ed. by M. Hill, 1972, pp.119–136 (pp.134–135).
36. *Ibid.*, p.126.
37. Banks, *op. cit.*, p.15.
38. See F. Bodmer, *op. cit.*, pp.470–471; H. Jacob, *Otto Jespersen: His Work for an International Language, op. cit.*
39. E. Carpenter, *Civilisation: Its Cause and Cure*, 1889.
40. Parkin, *Middle Class Radicalism, op. cit.*, p.142.
41. P. Abrams and A. McCulloch, *Communes, Sociology and Society*, 1976.
42. N. Poulantzas, 'On social classes', *New Left Review* 78, 1973, pp.27–54.
43. Abrams and McCulloch, *op. cit.*, pp.195–196.

44.   *Ibid.*, p.127.
45.   J. Merchant, *op. cit.*, pp.9–10.
46.   Rigby, *op. cit.*, p.308.
47.   See pp.233–234.

Appendix I

The Sixteen Rules of Esperanto Grammar (from *Fundamento de Esperanto*, pp.57-61)

(A) THE ALPHABET

Aa, a as in 'last'
Bb, b as in 'be'
Cc, ts as in 'wits'
Ĉĉ, ch as in 'church'
Dd, d as in 'do'
Ee, a as in 'make'
Ff, f as in 'fly'
Gg, g as in 'gun'
Ĝĝ, j as in 'join'
Hh, h as in 'half'
Ĥĥ, strongly aspirated h, 'ch' in 'loch' (Scotch)
Ii, i as in 'marine'
Jj, y as in 'yoke'
Ĵĵ, z as in 'azure'

Kk, k as in 'key'
Ll, l as in 'line'
Mm, m as in 'make'
Nn, n as in 'now'
Oo, o as in 'not'
Pp, p as in 'pair'
Rr, r as in 'rare'
Ss, s as in 'see'
Ŝŝ, sh as in 'show'
Tt, t as in 'tea'
Uu, u as in 'bull'
Ŭŭ, u as in 'mount' (used in diphthongs)
Vv, v as in 'very'
Zz, z as in 'zeal'

Remark: If it be found impracticable to print works with the diacritical signs (ˆ, ˇ), the letter *h* may be substituted for the sign (ˆ), and the sign (ˇ), may be altogether omitted.

(B) PARTS OF SPEECH

1. There is no indefinite, and only one definite, article, *la* for all genders, numbers, and cases.

2. Substantives are formed by adding *o* to the root. For the plural, the letter *j* must be added to the singular. There are two cases: the nominative and the objective (accusative). The root with the added *o* is the nominative, the objective adds an *n* after the *o*. Other cases are formed by prepositions;

thus, the possessive (genitive) by *de*, 'of'; the dative by *al*, 'to'; the instrumental (ablative) by *kun*, 'with'; or other prepositions as the sense demands. E.g. root *patr*, 'father'; *la patr'o*, 'the father'; *la patr'o'n*, 'the father' (objective); *de la patr'o*, 'of the father'; *al la patr'o*, 'to the father'; *kun la patr'o*, 'with the father'; *la patr'o'j*, 'the fathers'; *la patr'o'j'n*, 'the fathers' (obj); *por la patr'o'j*, 'for the fathers'.

3. Adjectives are formed by adding *a* to the root. The numbers and cases are the same as in substantives. The comparative degree is formed by prefixing *pli* (more); the superlative by *plej* (most). The word 'than' is rendered by *ol*, e.g. *pli blank'a ol neĝ'o*, 'whiter than snow'.

4. The cardinal numerals do not change their forms for the different cases. They are:

unu (1), *du* (2), *tri* (3), *kvar* (4), *kvin* (5), *ses* (6), *sep* (7), *ok* (8), *naŭ* (9) *dek* (10), *cent* (100), *mil* (1,000).

The tens and hundreds are formed by simple junction of the numerals, e.g. 583 = *kvin'cent ok'dek tri*.

Ordinals are formed by adding the adjectival *a* to the cardinals, e.g. *unu'a*, 'first'; *du'a*, 'second', etc.

Multiplicatives (as 'threefold', 'fourfold', etc.) add *obl*, e.g. *tri'obl'a*, 'threefold'.

Fractionals add *on*, as *du'on'o*, 'a half'; *kvar'on'o*, 'a quarter'. Collective numerals add *op*, as *kvar'op'e*, 'four together'.

Distributive prefix *po*, e.g., *po kvin*, 'five apiece'.

Adverbials take *e*, e.g., *unu'e*, 'firstly', etc.

5. The personal pronouns are: *mi*, 'I'; *vi*, 'thou', 'you'; *li*, 'he'; *ŝi*, 'she'; *ĝi*, 'it'; *si*, 'self'; *ni*, 'we'; *ili*, 'they'; *oni*, 'one', 'people', (French *'on'*).

Possessive pronouns are formed by suffixing to the required personal, the adjectival termination. The declension of the pronouns is identical with that of substantives. E.g. *mi*, 'I'; *mi'n*, 'me' (obj.); *mi'a*, 'my', 'mine'.

6. The verb does not change its form for numbers or persons, e.g. *mi far'as*, 'I do'; *la patr'o far'as*, 'the father does'; *ili far'as*, 'they do'.

Forms of the Verb:

(a) The present tense ends in *as*, e.g. *mi far'as*, 'I do'.
(b) The past tense ends in *is*, e.g. *li far'is*, 'he did'.
(c) The future tense ends in *os*, e.g. *ili far'os*; 'they will do'.
(c) The subjunctive mood ends in *us*, e.g. *ŝi far'us*, 'she may do'.
(d) The imperative mood ends in *u*, e.g. *ni far'u* 'let us do'.
(e) The infinitive mood ends in *i*, e.g. *fari*, 'to do'.

There are two forms of the participle in the international language, the changeable or adjectival, and the unchangeable or adverbial.

(f) The present participle active ends in *ant*, e.g. *far'ant'a*, 'he who is doing'; *far'ant'e*, 'doing'.

(g) The past participle active ends in *int*, e.g. *far'int'a*, 'he who has done'; *far'int'e*, 'having done'.

(g) The future participle active ends in *ont*, e.g. *far'ont'a*, 'he who will do'; *far'ont'e*, 'about to do'.

(h) The present participle passive ends in *at*, e.g. *far'at'e*, 'being done'.

(h) The past participle passive ends in *it*, e.g. *far'it'a*, 'that which has been done'; *far'it'e*, 'having been done'.

(i) The future participle passive ends in *ot*, e.g. *far'ot'a*, 'that which will be done'; *far'ot'e*, 'about to be done'.

All forms of the passive are rendered by the respective forms of the verb *est* (to be) and the participle passive of the required verb; the preposition used is *de*, 'by'. E.g. *ŝi est'as am'at'a de ĉiu'j*, 'she is loved by every one'.

7. Adverbs are formed by adding *e* to the root. The degrees of comparison are the same as in adjectives, e.g., *mi'a frat'o kant'as pli bon'e ol mi*, 'my brother sings better than I'.

8. All prepositions govern the nominative case.

(C) GENERAL RULES

9. Every word is to be read exactly as written, there are no silent letters.

10. The accent falls on the last syllable but one (penultimate).

11. Compound words are formed by the simple junction of roots (the principal word standing last), which are written as a single word, but, in elementary works, separated by a small line ('). Grammatical terminations are considered as independent words. E.g. *vapor'ŝip'o*, 'steamboat' is composed of the roots *vapor*, 'steam', and *ŝip*, 'a boat', with the substantival termination *o*.

12. If there is one negative in a clause, a second is not admissible.

13. In phrases answering the question 'where?' (meaning direction), the words take the termination of the objective case; e.g. *kie'n vi ir'as*? 'where are you going?'; *dom'o'n*, 'home'; *London'o'n*, 'to London', etc.

14. Every preposition in the international language has a definite fixed meaning. If it be necessary to employ some preposition, and it is not quite evident from the sense which it should be, the word *je* is used, which has no definite meaning; for example, *ĝoj'i je tio*, 'to rejoice over it'; *rid'i je tio*, 'to laugh at it'; *enu'o je la patr'uj'o*, 'a longing for one's fatherland'. In every language different prepositions, sanctioned by usage, are employed in these

dubious cases, in the international language, one word, *je* suffices for all. Instead of *je*, the objective without a preposition may be used, when no confusion is to be feared.

15. The so-called 'foreign' words, i.e. words which the greater number of languages have derived from the same source, undergo no change in the international language, beyond conforming to its system of orthography. — Such is the rule with regard to primary words, derivatives are better formed (from the primary word) according to the rules of the international grammar, e.g. *teatr'o*, 'theatre', but *teatr'a*, 'theatrical' (not *teatrical'a*), etc.

16. The *a* of the article, and final *o* of substantives, may be sometimes dropped euphoniae gratia, e.g. *de l'mond'o* for *de la mond'o; Ŝiller'* for *Ŝiller'o*; in such cases an apostrophe should substituted for the discarded vowel.

Appendix II

Correlatives

	Indefinite some (any)	Interrogative or Relative which, what	Demonstrative that	Universal each, every, all	Negative no
Quality kind, sort	*ia* of some kind, some kind of	*kia* of what kind, what kind of, what a . . . !	*tia* of that kind, that kind of, such a . . .	*ĉia* of every kind, every kind of	*nenia* of no kind
Motive reason	*ial* for some reason	*kial* for what reason, why, wherefore	*tial* for that reason, therefore, so	*ĉial* for every reason	*nenial* for no reason
Time	*iam* at some time, ever	*kiam* at what time, when	*tiam* at that time, at all	*ĉiam* at every time, at all times, always	*neniam* at no time, never
Place	*ie* in some place, somewhere	*kie* in what place, where	*tie* in that place, there, yonder	*ĉie* in every place, in all places, everywhere	*nenie* •in no place, nowhere
Manner way	*iel* in some way, somehow	*kiel* in what way, how, as	*tiel* in that way, thus, so as, like that	*ĉiel* in every way	*neniel* in no way, nohow
Possession one's	*ies* someone's somebody's	*kies* which one's whose	*ties* that one's	*ĉies* everyone's each one's everybody's	*nenies* no one's nobody's

(continued)

	Indefinite some (any)	Interrogative or Relative which, what	Demonstrative that	Universal each, every, all	Negative no
Thing	*io* some quantity, somewhat	*kio* what quantity, how much, how many	*tio* that quantity so (much), as (many)	*ĉio* the whole quantity, all of it	*nenio* no quantity, not a bit, none
Individuality one	*iu* someone, some (person or thing)	*kiu* which (one), who,	*tiu* that (one)	*ĉiu* every (one), each (one), everybody	*neniu* no (one), nobody

Appendix III

La Vojo [The Way]

Tra densa mallumo briletas la celo,
Al kiu kuraĝe ni iras
Simile al stelo en nokta ĉielo,
Al ni la direkton ĝi diras.
Kaj nin ne timigas la noktaj fantomoj
Nek batoj de l'sorto, nek mokoj de l'homoj
Ĉar klara kaj rekta kaj tre difinita
Ĝi estas, la voj' elektita.

Nur rekte, kuraĝe kaj ne flankiĝante
Ni iru la vojon celitan!
Eĉ guto malgranda, konstante frapante;
Traboras la monton granitan.
L'espero, l'obstino kaj la *pacienco* —
Jen estas la signoj, per kies potenco
Ni paŝo post paŝo, post longa laboro,
Atingos la celon en gloro.

Ni semas kaj semas, neniam laciĝas,
Pri l'tempoj estontaj pensante.
Cent semoj perdiĝas, mil semoj perdiĝas, —
Ni semas kaj semas konstante.
"Ho ĉesu! mokante la homoj admonas, —
Ne ĉesu, ne ĉesu!" en kor' al ni sonas:
"Obstine antaŭen! La nepoj vin benos,
Se vi pacience eltenos".

(continued overleaf)

Se longa sekeco au ventoj subitaj[1]
Velkantajn foliojn deŝiras,
Ni dankas la venton, kaj, repurigitaj,
Ni forton pli freŝan akiras.
Ne mortos jam nia bravega anaro,
Ĝin jam ne timigos la vento, nek staro,
Obstine ĝi paŝas, provita, hardita,
Al cel' unu fojon signita!

(repeat the second verse).

Translation:

Through dense darkness twinkles the goal,
To which we courageously make our way
Like a star in the night sky,
It tells us the direction.
And the ghosts of the night do not frighten us
Nor the blows of fate, nor the mockery of men
As clear and direct and very defined
Is the chosen way.

Only directly, courageously, not turning aside
Let us go on our intended way!
Even a little drop, hitting constantly,
Bores through the granite mountain.
Hope, steadfastness and *patience*
Here are the signs by whose power
We, step by step, after long work,
Will reach our goal in glory.

We sow and sow, and never tire,
Thinking of future times.
A hundred seeds are lost, a thousand seeds are lost
We sow and sow constantly.
"Give up" men exhort us, mockingly, —
"Don't give up", don't give up" sounds in our hearts
"Steadfastly forward! Your grandchildren will bless you
If you hold out patiently".

1.   The first four lines of this verse are often quoted as a comment on schismatic
     tendencies.

If long drought or sudden winds[1]
Tear away wilting leaves,
We thank the wind, and, cleansed,
We acquire renewed strength.
Our intrepid membership will not die just yet,
It will not be frightened by the wind, or standing still
Steadfastly it sets forth, tried, hardened
To the goal once marked!

1.   The first four lines of this verse are often quoted as a comment on schismatic
     tendencies.

Appendix IV

World Esperanto Congresses (Neutral Movement)

	Year	Place	No. of members
1.	1905	Boulogne, France	688
2.	1906	Geneva, Switzerland	1,200
3.	1907	Cambridge, Britain	1,317
4.	1908	Dresden, Germany	1,500
5.	1909	Barcelona, Spain	1,500
6.	1910	Washington, U.S.A.	357
7.	1911	Antwerp, Belgium	1,800
8.	1912	Cracow, Poland	1,000
9.	1913	Berne, Switzerland	1,203
10.	1914	Paris, France. Cancelled owing to the war: 3739 had enrolled	
11.	1915	San Francisco, U.S.A.	163
12.	1920	The Hague, Netherlands	408
13.	1921	Prague, Czechoslovakia	2,561
14.	1922	Helsinki, Finland	850
15.	1923	Nuremberg, Germany	4,963
16.	1924	Vienna, Austria	3,400
17.	1925	Geneva, Switzerland	953
18.	1926	Edinburgh, Britain	960
19.	1927	Danzig	905
20.	1928	Antwerp, Belgium	1,494
21.	1929	Budapest, Hungary	1,200
22.	1930	Oxford, Britain	1,211
23.	1931	Cracow, Poland	900
24.	1932	Paris, France	1,650
25.	1933	Cologne, Germany	950
26.	1934	Stockholm, Sweden	2,042
27.	1935	Rome, Italy	1,442

	Year	Place	No. of members
28.	1936	Vienna, Austria	854
29.	1937	Warsaw, Poland	1,120
30.	1938	London, Britain	1,602
31.	1939	Berne, Switzerland	765
32.	1947	Berne, Switzerland	1,370
33.	1948	Malmö, Sweden	1,761
34.	1949	Bournemouth, Britain	1,534
35.	1950	Paris, France	2,325
36.	1951	Munich, Germany (F.R.)	2,040
37.	1952	Oslo, Norway	1,614
38.	1953	Zagreb, Yugoslavia	1,760
39.	1954	Haarlem, Netherlands	2,353
40.	1955	Bologna, Italy	1,687
41.	1956	Copenhagen, Denmark	2,200
42.	1957	Marseilles, France	1,468
43.	1958	Mainz, Germany (F.R.)	2,021
44.	1959	Warsaw, Poland	3,256
45.	1960	Brussels, Belgium	1,930
46.	1961	Harrogate, Britain	1,646
47.	1962	Copenhagen, Denmark	1,550
48.	1963	Sofia, Bulgaria	3,472
49.	1964	The Hague, Netherlands	2,512
50.	1965	Tokio, Japan	1,710
51.	1966	Budapest, Hungary	3,975
52.	1967	Tel-Aviv, Israel (transferred to Rotterdam owing to the war)	1,265
53.	1968	Madrid, Spain	1,769
54.	1969	Helsinki, Finland	1,857
55.	1970	Vienna, Austria	1,987
56.	1971	London, Britain	2,071
57.	1972	Portland, Oregon, U.S.A.	923
58.	1973	Belgrade, Yugoslavia	1,638
59.	1974	Hamburg, Germany (F.R.)	1,651
60.	1975	Copenhagen, Denmark	1,227
61.	1976	Athens, Greece	1,266
62.	1977	Reykjavik, Iceland	1,199
63.	1978	Varna, Bulgaria	4,414
64.	1979	Lucerne, Switzerland	1,630
65.	1980	Stockholm, Sweden	1,807
66.	1981	Brasilia, Brazil	1,749

Appendix V

Local Esperanto Groups in Britain: 1964 Survey

The following figures are derived from the publication *Listo de lokaj Esperanto-societoj*, published by the Research and Documentation Centre of UEA.

Town	No. of members	Town	No. of members
Barking	11	Glasgow (railwaymen's)	16
Birmingham	20	Halifax	12
Blackburn	20	Hamilton	12
Blackpool	12	Havering	18
Bournemouth	32	Hexham	19
Bournemouth (Diservo)*	30	Hull (co-operative)	12
Bradford	45	Ilford	14
Bridlington	21	Ilford (youth)	10
Brighton	20	Ilford (Redbridge)	?
Bristol	47	Ipswich	20
Burnley	24	Keighley	30
Cambridge (University)	10	Kircaldy	13
Chester	21	Leeds	45
Crawley	12	Leicester	35
Croydon	30	Letchworth	18
Denton (school)	11	Liverpool	22
Edinburgh	73	London	210
Enfield	20	London (Diservo)*	25
Exmouth (Glenorhia)	6	Manchester	60
Folkestone	10	Nelson	10
Glasgow	30	Newcastle	30

* A group for the purpose of arranging religious services in Esperanto, organised separately so as to conform to the principle of religious neutrality.

Town	No. of members	Town	No. of members
Norwich	15	Stoke-on-Trent	20
Nottingham	32	Sunderland	20
Plymouth	12	Sutton	8
Reading	14	Walthamstow	12
Rochdale	12	Watford	24
Sheffield	14	West Hartlepool	14
Southampton	19	Worthing	10
Southend	15		
Stockport (International Language Group)	23		

Appendix VI

Questionnaire and Accompanying Letter
THE UNIVERSITY OF HULL

SOCIOLOGICAL SURVEY OF THE BRITISH ESPERANTO
ASSOCIATION

Dear Member,

I am carrying out a study of the Esperanto movement in Britain, and would be most grateful for your help. Your name has been selected as part of a sample of members of the B.E.A. living in the United Kingdom, and I would be very grateful if you could complete the enclosed questionnaire.

Although it may seem long, the questionnaire will take only a few minutes to complete, as many of the questions can be answered simply by putting a tick against the appropriate word. A stamped addressed envelope is enclosed for your reply. All information will be treated as *strictly* confidential, and will certainly not be revealed to any other member: nor will any officer of the B.E.A. be responsible for sorting out the replies. The information will be used for statistical tables from which it will not be possible to identify any individual. As well as contributing to sociological research, it is hoped that the statistics will be of use to the B.E.A. in planning its future policy. You will find a code number in the top right-hand corner of the questionnaire: this is simply to enable me to check up on any questionnaire which might have gone astray.

The survey is being carried out independently of the B.E.A., but I am acting in friendly collaboration with the Executive Committee, who have been kind enough to allow me to draw a sample of members in this way. Answering the questions will commit you to nothing, and no further correspondence will be entered into on the basis of your replies. Some statistical tables on the basis of the survey will be published in due course in the *British Esperantist*.

Many thanks in advance for your co-operation.

Yours sincerely,

(signed)
Peter G. Forster, M.A. (Econ.),
Assistant Lecturer in Sociology
University of Hull.

BRITISH ESPERANTO ASSOCIATION SURVEY:
QUESTIONNAIRE   No. ——

Where alternative answers are given, please tick the appropriate answer. If you
wish to modify or amplify your answers in any way, please do so on plain
paper or on the back of the questionnaire. Where dates are asked for, please
give the nearest year. Approximate dates and figures will suffice if you cannot
remember them exactly.

    1. How did you first learn about the Esperanto movement? (the organised
Movement, not just the name of the language).

    2. When did you first start to learn Esperanto? (year) . . . . . .

    3. Why did you decide to learn Esperanto?

    4. Are you a member of the Universala Esperanto-Asocio? Yes . . . .
No. . . . . (i.e. *individual* member, J–MJ, or above)
(if yes) In what year did you first join? . . . . . .
(if you *first* joined the Internacia Esperanto-Ligo, please give the date when
you joined I.E.L.)

    5. Are you a member of any of the following organisations? If so, please
tick and give the year in which you first joined the organisation.

(a) Universala Ligo . . . .   First joined . . . .
(b) Society of British Christian
     Esperantists . . . .   First joined . . . .
(c) Internacia Katolika Unuigo
     Esperantista . . . .   First joined . . . .
(d) Sennacieca Asocio Tutmonda . . . .   First joined . . . .
(e) Esperanto Teachers' Association
     (or S.B.E.T.) . . . .   First joined . . . .
(f) Junularo Esperantista Brita . . . .   First joined . . . .
(g) Skolta Esperantista Ligo . . . .   First joined . . . .
(h) Kvakera Esperantista Societo . . . .   First joined . . . .
(i) Esperantista Spiritista
     Societa . . . .   First joined . . . .
(j) Any other specialist Esperanto organisations:
     Name of Organisation   *Date first joined*

(k) A local Esperanto group or regional Esperanto federation:
     Name of group or federation   *Date first joined*

    6. Are you, or have you been, an official or committee member of any of
the organisations mentioned in your replies to question 5, or of UEA or IEL?

(at any level: local, regional, national, international). If yes, please give details below:

    7. In what year did you first join the BEA? ......

    8. (*Present* councillors only):

(a) In what year did you first join the BEA council? ......

(b) Apart from BEA council membership, do you hold or have you held an official position at any level in the BEA? If yes, please give details:

    9. (*all* other members, including former councillors). Do you hold or have you held an official position at any level in the BEA? If yes, please give details.

(all members resume replying here)

    10. Have you ever attended a British Esperanto congress?

Yes .... No .... (if yes) how many have you attended? ......

    11. Have you ever attended a UEA or IEL congress? Yes .... No ....

(if yes) how many have you attended (a) in Britain ......

                           (b) overseas ......?

    12. Have you ever attended a universal SAT congress?

(if yes) how many have you attended (a) in Britain ......

                           (b) overseas ......?

    13. Have you ever attended any other *international* congress, conference, seminar, holiday, school, or other gathering of Esperantists? If yes, please give details below:

    14. Of what organisations other than Esperanto are you a member? (Please include everything here: Local, regional, national, international; political, peace, religious, professional, trade union, social, recreational, charitable, etc.) Please give the names of these organisations below:

    15. Are you or have you been an official or committee member of any of the organisations you mention in question 14? If yes, please give details.

    16. In which part of the country were you born? If in Britain or Ireland please give town or village, and country; if born abroad, give name of country only.

    17. Are you married ......   widowed ......

                  single ......   divorced ......

                             separated ......?

IF YOU ARE SINGLE, GO ON TO QUESTION 21; OTHERWISE ANSWER Q. 18, 19, 20.

    18. Did you meet your husband/wife in connection with any Esperanto activity?

Yes ...... No ......

    19. Have you any children? Yes .... No ....; if yes, how many? ....

20. (if you have children) Do your children know any Esperanto? How much?

21. In what year were you born?

22. What is your occupation? Please be as specific as possible: e.g. if civil servant, what grade? If teacher, what type of school? etc. (If you are retired, please record former occupation.)

23. (married women only) What is your husband's occupation (or what was your husband's last occupation). Please be specific, as above.

24. What is or was your father's occupation? (Please be specific, as above.)

25. Have you a degree or any professional qualifications? Yes . . . . No . . . .
If you have or are studying for a degree or professional qualifications, please give
(a) subject(s)
(b) *where* you studied or are studying for them, and whether this is/was *part* or *full* time
(c) (if degree) title of degree (i.e. B.A., Ph.D., B.D. etc.)

26. Have you ever attended an evening class or adult education class, other than Esperanto?
Yes . . . . . . No . . . . . .
If yes, please give the subjects of these classes below:

27. Do you hold any diplomas or certificates in Esperanto? Yes . . . .
No . . . . If yes, please give grade (where applicable) and name of awarding body:

28. How old were you on completing full-time education?
   Under 14 . . . . . .   17 . . . . . .
          14 . . . . . .   18 . . . . . .
          15 . . . . . .   over 18 . . . . . .
          16 . . . . . . still receiving full time education . . . . .

29. What type of secondary school did you attend?
Elementary or secondary modern   . . . . . .
Technical or Art   . . . . . .
Public or other boarding school   . . . . . .
Grammar, High, independent day, or public day   . . . . . .
Comprehensive   . . . . . .
Educated abroad   . . . . . .
Other (please state)
(if you are still at school, give the school you at present attend)

Some people think that the most important thing about Esperanto is the ideal of peace and world brotherhood through a universal language: other people tend to emphasise more the practical advantages of an international language in commerce, conferences, and foreign travel.

The next three questions are about how you feel on this question. You may answer "both equally" if you wish, but please try if possible to choose one of the alternatives. You may make whatever comments and qualifications you wish.

30. Which do you think is more important *to you personally* about Esperanto?

(a) The ideal of peace and world brotherhood through a universal language.

(b) The practical advantages of an international language in conferences, commerce, and foreign travel.

(a) . . . . . .   (b) . . . . . .   Both equally . . . . . .

Comments

31. Which of these two aspects do you think the Esperanto movement should pay more attention to in its activities?

(a) . . . . . .   (b) . . . . . .   Both equally . . . . . .

Comments

32. Which of these two aspects should be stressed more in publicity and advertising of Esperanto?

(a) . . . . . .   (b) . . . . . .   Both equally . . . . . .

Comments

33. Are there any other things about Esperanto that are important to you?

34. Have you ever read a book on the life of Zamenhof or on the history of the Esperanto movement (i.e. a full-length book, not an article in a magazine, newspaper or encyclopedia)?

Yes . . . .   No . . . .

35. Some people think that too many new root-words are being introduced into Esperanto; but other people say that Esperanto needs more root-words. Which of these statements most nearly expresses your views on the subject:

There are definitely too many new root-words being introduced . . . .

I think there may be too many new root-words . . . .

I don't know what to think . . . .

I think Esperanto may need more root-words . . . .

Esperanto definitely needs more root-words . . . .

36. If a general election were held tomorrow, for which party would you vote? (If you are not eligible to vote, which party would you vote for if you could? Assume that a candidate for your party is standing in your area.)

Conservative . . . .   Communist   . . . . Unionist   . . . .
Labour   . . . . Plaid Cymru   . . . . Mebyon Kernow   . . . .
Liberal   . . . . Scottish nationalist . . . . Socialist Party of G.B.   . . . .
Don't know . . . .   Wouldn't vote   . . . . Other (please state)   . . . .

37. Are you:

Christian . . . .   Jewish   . . . .   Theosophist   . . . .   Agnostic   . . . .
Buddhist . . . .   Hindu   . . . .   Anthroposophist . . . .   Humanist   . . . .
Muslim   . . . . Baha'i   . . . .   Atheist   . . . .   Spiritualist . . . .

Any other religious or philosophical allegiance (please state) . . . . . .

If you are a Christian, please answer the following questions:

(a) Are you Protestant . . . . . .
     Roman Catholic   . . . . . .
     Orthodox Church   . . . . . .

(b) Do you attend religious services
     Regularly   . . . . . .
     Quite regularly . . . . . .
     Occasionally   . . . . . .
     Hardly at all   . . . . . .
     Never   . . . . . .

(c) Protestant Christians: what denomination do you belong to?

   38. Are you a vegetarian? Yes . . . .   No . . . .

   39. What languages other than Esperanto and English do you know?
(Please give some idea of fluency. If you have passed any public examinations
in these languages, you should mention this.)

   40. Any other comments

Thank you very much for your co-operation in filling in the questionnaire.
Please return it as soon as possible in the enclosed stamped addressed envelope.

Glossary

The following expressions occur at various points in the text. For the convenience of the reader not otherwise familiar with the Esperanto movement, they are collated here. Unless the Esperanto term is the one generally used in the text, the English expression is given first. This is followed by the Esperanto term, where appropriate, and the Esperanto abbreviation (if any).

For a list of World Esperanto Congresses see Appendix IV.

ACADEMY (*Akademio*)
The supreme linguistic authority of the Esperanto movement. Originally established in 1908 as a superior body elected by the Language Committee, but absorbed the latter in 1948.

AGREEMENT OF COLOGNE: see Cologne.

BOULOGNE, DECLARATION OF (*Deklaracio de Boulogne*)
A document accepted by the first World Esperanto Congress in 1905, officially defining the aims of the Esperanto movement. It stressed, among other things, the neutrality of the Esperanto movement, and acceptance of the *Fundamento* as binding.

BRITISH ESPERANTO ASSOCIATION (*Brita Esperantista Asocio*, BEA)
An association, founded in 1904, concerned with all aspects of the promotion of Esperanto in Britain.

CENTRAL OFFICE (*Centra Oficejo*, CO)
Originally the secretariat, founded by the private initiative of General Sébert in 1906, of the institutions set up in 1905 by the Boulogne World Esperanto Congress. The name was subsequently used to refer to the headquarters of the Universal Esperanto Association.

COLOGNE, AGREEMENT OF (*Interkonsento de Kolonjo*)
An agreement made in 1933, replacing the Contract of Helsinki and strengthening the influence of the national Esperanto associations in the Universal Esperanto Association.

CONTRACT OF HELSINKI: see Helsinki.

DECLARATION OF BOULOGNE: see Boulogne.

DECLARATION OF TYRESÖ: see Tyresö.

DELEGATE (*Delegito*, D.)

An unpaid representative of UEA in various towns throughout the world, whose duty it is to answer inquiries from members and assist travellers who are members of UEA.

DELEGATION POUR L'ADOPTION D'UNE LANGUE AUXILIAIRE INTERNATIONALE

An organisation formed in 1901 aiming to request the International Association of Academies to choose a constructed auxiliary language. If this association was unwilling to make the choice, the Delegation itself would elect a committee for this purpose. This turned out to be necessary. The committee elected met in 1908, and adopted Esperanto in principle provided that certain modifications were made on the lines of Ido. The Esperantists rejected proposals for change, and Ido was adopted.

DUA LIBRO [Second Book]

The second book in Esperanto, published by Zamenhof in 1888, containing exercises in the language and some translated material.

EKZERCARO [Exercises]

A set of elementary exercises in the language, published in 1894 and reissued as part of the *Fundamento*.

ESPERANTO ASSOCIATION OF NORTH AMERICA (*Esperanto-Asocio de Norda Ameriko*, EANA)

The original American promotional association for Esperanto, established in 1908. In 1957 this body was forced to withdraw from the Universal Esperanto Association for displaying McCarthyite tendencies, and was replaced by the Esperanto League for North America.

ESPERANTO LEAGUE FOR NORTH AMERICA (*Esperanto-Ligo por Norda Ameriko*, ELNA)

An organisation for promotion of Esperanto in America. This was set up as a result of McCarthyite tendencies in the original Esperanto Association of North America. When the former was forced to withdraw from the Universal Esperanto Association, the new organisation was officially recognised.

ESPERO, LA [Hope]

The official Esperanto anthem.

FROSTAVALLEN, PRINCIPLES OF (*Principaro de Frostavallen*)

A set of principles officially developed by the Universal Esperanto Association in 1956, dealing with the appropriate manner of presenting Esperanto to the general public.

FUNDAMENTA KRESTOMATO [Fundamental Chrestomathy]

A book of short stories, articles and poems in Esperanto, published in 1903 with contributions by various authors, including Zamenhof. It was recommended by Zamenhof as an example of good Esperanto style.

FUNDAMENTO DE ESPERANTO [Basis of Esperanto]

A book published in 1905, containing the *Ekzercaro*, the *Universala Vortaro* and the sixteen rules of Esperanto grammar. Change in those aspects of the language which appear in the *Fundamento* is not permitted, though additions to the material contained therein are acceptable.

GREEN STANDARD (*Verda standardo*)

The Esperanto flag, on which a green star appears. Also applied to the nebulous value system associated with Esperanto, especially world congresses.

GREEN STAR (*Verda stelo*)

The symbol of Esperanto, widely used as a sticker and a badge.

HELSINKI, CONTRACT OF (*Kontrakto de Helsinki*)

A contract signed at the 1922 World Esperanto Congress in Helsinki, establishing a unified neutral Esperanto association by the setting up of a committee to link existing organisations together. This committee (the International Central Committee) was elected partly by representatives of the national Esperanto associations, partly by the Universal Esperanto Association.

HILLELISM (*Hilelismo*)

A project initially published by Zamenhof in 1901, designed to apply the thoughts of Hillel the Elder to the solution of the 'Jewish problem'.

HOMARANISMO

(No exact equivalent: roughly 'the philosophy of membership of Humanity') A project for a universal religion, developed by Zamenhof from Hillelism and published by him, initially anonymously, in 1906.

IDO

A schismatic project for a world language, based on Esperanto, but incorporating certain changes, notably in the alphabet and the system of derivation. This project was adopted by the Permanent Committee of the *Délégation pour l'Adoption d'une Langue Auxiliaire Internationale*, in 1908, after attempts to persuade the Esperantists to accept the changes had proved unsuccessful.

INNER IDEA (*Interna ideo*)

The nebulous value orientation, involving peace, solidarity, friendship, and justice, which is traditionally associated with Esperanto.

INTERNATIONAL CENTRAL COMMITTEE (*Internacia Centra Komitato*, ICK)

A committee set up in 1922 in accordance with the Contract of Helsinki, linking together elected representatives of the national Esperanto Association.

For a brief period after its establishment it was known as the Central Esperanto Committee (*Centra Esperanto-Komitato*).

INTERNATIONAL ESPERANTO LEAGUE (*Internacia Esperanto-Ligo*, IEL)
A new organisation for promoting and using Esperanto at an international level. This was set up by the Executive of the Universal Esperanto Association in 1936, when it was found to be constitutionally impossible for the head-quarters of this body to be moved from Switzerland. In 1947 this organisation rejoined the Universal Esperanto Association.

INTERNATIONAL OF PROLETARIAN ESPERANTISTS (*Internacio de Proletaj Esperantistoj*, IPE)
An international Communist Esperanto movement, controlled by Moscow, having split off from the World Association of Non-Nationalists in 1932.

LANGUAGE COMMITTEE (*Lingva Komitato*, LK)
The original supreme linguistic authority for Esperanto, initiated at the 1905 Boulogne World Congress. After 1908 it elected the Academy and was absorbed by the latter in 1948.

LINGVAJ RESPONDOJ [Language Replies]
A collection of replies given by Zamenhof to various points of Esperanto grammar, and published in certain Esperanto periodicals. They extended over three periods: 1889–1895; 1906–1908; and 1911–1912.

PERMANENT CONGRESS COMMITTEE (*Konstanta Kongresa Komitato*, KKK)
An international committee set up in 1906, concerned with the organisation of World Esperanto Congresses. In 1924 this work was taken over directly by the International Central Committee.

PERMANENT REPRESENTATIVES (OF THE NATIONAL SOCIETIES) (*Konstanta Representantaro*, KR)
A committee set up in accordance with the Contract of Helsinki in 1922, for cooperation and exchange of information between the national Esperanto organisations.

PRINCIPLES OF FROSTAVALLEN: see Frostavallen.

RESEARCH AND DOCUMENTATION CENTRE (*Centro de Esplorado kaj Dokumentado*, CED)
A section of the Universal Esperanto Association, founded in 1952, concerned with systematic information about Esperanto and research on matters relating to it.

SOCIETE FRANÇAISE POUR LA PROPAGATION D'ESPERANTO
The French promotional association for Esperanto, founded in 1904 on the basis of an earlier association founded in 1898.

SOVIET ESPERANTO UNION (*Sovetlanda Esperantista Unuiĝo*, SEU)

The promotional association for Esperanto in the Soviet Union, founded in 1921, made illegal in 1937.

TYRESÖ, DECLARATION OF (*Deklaracio de Tyresö*)
A document produced in 1969 by the World Esperantist Youth Organisation. It urged a radical stance on linguistic and all other forms of discrimination.

UNIVERSALA VORTARO [Universal Dictionary]
An Esperanto dictionary in five languages, published in 1893 and incorporated into the *Fundamento*.

UNIVERSAL ESPERANTO ASSOCIATION (*Universala Esperanto-Asocio*, UEA)
Originally founded in 1908, this organisation aimed to create a link of solidarity between its members the world over, and to provide a range of services through local representatives in different towns. Membership was initially of the world movement directly, without the mediation of national associations. After 1933, and the conclusion of the Agreement of Cologne, the influence of national Esperanto associations was strengthened in UEA. Between 1936 and 1947 UEA became independent again. In 1947 on the basis of a new agreement, UEA was reconstituted and incorporated the International Esperanto League. Membership is now partly through national associations and partly through direct subscription to UEA.

UNUA LIBRO [First Book]
The first book about Esperanto, published by Zamenhof in 1887, in Warsaw, in Russian, French, German, and Polish. It contained the grammar of Esperanto and a basic vocabulary, together with some translated and original work in Esperanto.

WORLD ASSOCIATION OF NON-NATIONALISTS (*Sennacieca Asocio Tutmonda*, SAT)
A broadly based workers' Esperanto association, founded in 1921, designed to educate the workers for world socialism.

WORLD ESPERANTIST YOUTH ORGANISATION (*Tutmonda Esperantista Junulara Organizo*, TEJO)
An organisation of Young Esperantists originating in 1938, the word 'Esperantist' (*Esperantista*) being added to its name in 1952. Originally an independent body, in 1956 it became the youth section of the Universal Esperanto Association.

WORLD PEACE ESPERANTO MOVEMENT (*Mondpaca Esperantista Movado*, MEM)
An organisation aiming to use Esperanto in the cause of world peace. It tends to support the Soviet standpoint.

Bibliography

1. WORKS OF REFERENCE

The Academic Who's Who (1973-1974), London, Black.

Baltea, J., M. Barroux, and M. Prévost (1933), *Dictionnaire de biographie française*. Paris, Letonzey et Ane.

Bibliothèque Nationale (Paris) (1897), *Catalogue général des livres imprimés*. Paris, Ministère de l'Instruction Publique et des Beaux-Arts.

Encyclopaedia Judaica (1971), Jerusalem, Keter.

General Register Office (1967), *Sample Census 1966, Great Britain Summary Tables*. London, HMSO.

— (1968), *Sample Census 1966, Great Britain Economic Activity Tables*, Part I. London, HMSO.

— (1969a), *Census 1966, United Kingdom General and Parliamentary Constituency Tables*. London, HMSO.

— (1969b), *Sample Census 1966, Great Britain Economic Activity Tables*, Part III. London, HMSO.

2. SOCIOLOGICAL AND RELATED WORKS

Abrams, P., and A. McCulloch (1976), *Communes, Sociology and Society*. Cambridge, Cambridge University Press.

Aron, R. (1964), *German Sociology*. Glencoe, N.Y.: Free Press.

Asad, T., editor (1973), *Anthropology and the Colonial Encounter*. London, Ithaca.

Ashworth, A.E. (1968), 'The sociology of trench warfare 1914-1918', *British Journal of Sociology*: 407-423.

Banks, J.A. (1972), *The Sociology of Social Movements*. London, Macmillan.

Beattie, J. (1964), *Other Cultures*. London, Cohen and West.

Becker, H.S. (1963), *Outsiders: Studies in the Sociology of Deviance*. New York, Free Press.

Berger, P. (1957), 'Motif messianique et processus social dans le Bahai'sme', *Archives de Sociologie des Religions* 2(4) (July-December): 93-107.

Berry, D.R. (1970), *The Sociology of Grass Roots Politics*. London, Macmillan.

Billington, R.H.C. (1976), 'The women's education and suffrage movement, 1850-1914: innovation and institutionalisation'. Unpublished Ph.D. thesis, Hull.

Bottomore, T. (1954), 'Social stratification in voluntary associations', in *Social Mobility in Britain*, ed. by D. Glass, 349-382. London, Routledge and Kegan Paul.

Butler, D.E., and A. King (1966), *The British General Election of 1966*. London, Macmillan.

Campbell, C. (1965), 'Membership composition of the British Humanist Association', *Sociological Review*: 327-337.

– (1969), 'Humanism in Britain: the formation of a secular value-oriented social movement', in *A Sociological Yearbook of Religion in Britain* 2, ed. by D. Martin, 157-172.

– (1971), *Toward a Sociology of Irreligion*. London, Macmillan.

– (1972), 'The cult, the cultic milieu, and secularization', in *A Sociological Yearbook of Religion in Britain* 5, ed. by M. Hill, 119-136.

Carr, E.H. (1961), *What is History*? London, Macmillan.

Comte, A. (1851-1854), *Système de politique positive*. Paris, Mathias.

Coser, L. (1971), *Masters of Sociological Thought*. New York, Harcourt Brace.

Durkheim, E. (1912[1915]), *The Elementary Forms of the Religious Life*. London, Allen and Unwin. (First French edition 1912.)

– (1895[1964]), *The Rules of Sociological Method*. New York, Free Press. (First French edition 1895.)

Engels, F. (1969), 'Letter to J. Bloch', in *Basic Writings in Politics and Philosophy* by K. Marx and F. Engels, ed. by L.S. Feuer, 436-439. London, Collins.

Faris, R.E.L., editor (1964), *Handbook of Modern Sociology*. Chicago, Rand McNally.

Forster, P.G. (1973), 'Empiricism and imperialism: a review of the New Left critique of social anthropology', in *Anthropology and the Colonial Encounter*, ed. by T. Asad. London, Ithaca.

Friedland, W.H. (1964), 'For a sociological concept of charisma', *Social Forces* (October) 43(1).

Glass, D., editor (1954), *Social Mobility in Britain*. London, Routledge and Kegan Paul.

Gluckman, M. (1964), *Closed Systems and Open Minds; The Limits of Naivety in Social Anthropology*. Edinburgh and London, Oliver and Boyd.

Goldman, R. (1965), 'Do we want our children taught about God?', *New Society*, 27 May: 8-10.

Gusfield J.R. (1963), *Symbolic Crusade: Status Politics and the American Temperance Movement*. Urbana, University of Illinois Press.

Heberle, R. (1951), *Social Movements: An Introduction to Political Sociology*. New York, Appleton-Century-Crofts.

Highet, J. (1950), *The Churches in Scotland Today*. Glasgow, Jackson.

Horton, R. (1964), 'Ritual man in Africa', *Africa* 35: 85–104.

Isichei, I. (1961), 'From sect to denomination in English Quakerism', in *Patterns of Sectarianism*, ed. by B.R. Wilson. London, Heinemann.

Jones, R.K. (1975), 'Some sectarian characteristics of therapeutic groups with special reference to Recovery, Inc. and Neurotics Nomine', in *Sectarianism*, ed. by R. Wallis, 190–210. London, Owen.

Killian, L.M. (1964), 'Social movements', in *Handbook of Modern Sociology*, ed. by R.E.L. Faris. Chicago, Rand McNally.

King, C. Wendell (1956), *Social Movements in the United States*. New York, Random House.

Kornhauser, W. (1960), *The Politics of Mass Society*. London, Routledge and Kegan Paul.

Kruijt, J.P. (1959), 'The influence of denominationalism on social life and organisation patterns', *Archives de Sociologie des Religions* 4(8) (July–December): 105–111.

Lofland, J. (1966), *Doomsday Cult*. Englewood Cliffs, N.J.: Prentice-Hall.

Lukes, S. (1974), *Power: A Radical View*. London and Basingstoke, Macmillan.

Marx, K., and F. Engels (1969), *Basic Writings on Politics and Philosophy*, ed. by L.S. Feuer. London, Collins.

Merton, R.K. (1968), *Social Theory and Social Structure*. New York, Free Press.

Messinger, S. (1955), 'Organisational transformation: a case study of a declining social movement', *American Sociological Review*: 3–10.

Moser, C.A. (1958), *Survey Methods in Social Investigation*. London, Heinemann.

Moser, D.A., and W. Scott (1961), *British Towns*. Edinburgh and London, Oliver and Boyd.

Newton, K. (1969), *The Sociology of British Communism*. London, Allen Lane.

Parkin, F. (1967), 'Working-class conservatives', *British Journal of Sociology*: 278–290.

— (1968), *Middle Class Radicalism*. Manchester, University Press.

— (1971), *Class Inequality and Political Order*. London, MacGibbon and Kee.

Poulantzas, N. (1973), 'On social classes', *New Left Review* 78: 27–54.

Redfield, R. (1956), *Peasant Society and Culture*. Chicago, University of Chicago Press.

Rigby, A. (1974), *Alternative Realities*. London, Routledge.

Roche, J.P., and S. Sachs (1955), 'The bureaucrat and the enthusiast: an explanation of the leadership of social movements', *Western Political Quarterly*: 248-261.

Sergeant, G. (1972), *A Statistical Source-Book for Sociologists*. London, Macmillan.

Shenton, H.N. (1933), *Cosmopolitan Conversation*. New York, Columbia University Press.

Smelser, N.J. (1959), *Social Change in the Industrial Revolution*. London, Routledge and Kegan Paul.

– (1962), *Theory of Collective Behaviour*. London, Routledge.

Spiri, M.E. (1956), *Kibbutz: Venture in Utopia*. Cambridge, Harvard University Press.

Stacey, M. (1960), *Tradition and Change: A Study of Banbury*. London, Oxford University Press.

–, editor (1969), *Comparability in Social Research*. London, Heinemann.

Thayer, G. (1965), *The British Political Fringe*. London, Blond.

Tomasson, R.F. (1970), *Sweden: Prototype of Modern Society*. New York, Random House.

Tönnies, F. (1955), *Community and Association (Gemeinschaft und Gesellschaft)*, translated and supplemented by Charles P. Loomis. London, Routledge and Kegan Paul.

Wallis, R., editor (1975), *Sectarianism*. London, Peter Owen.

Waltz, K.N. (1954), *Man, the State and War. A Theoretical Analysis*. New York, Columbia University Press.

Weber, M. (1964), *The Theory of Social and Economic Organisation*, translated by A.M. Henderson and T. Parsons. London, Collier-Macmillan.

Weinberg, A. (1969), 'Education', in *Comparability in Social Research*, ed. by M. Stacey, 1-31. London, Heinemann.

Wilson, B.R. (1961), *Sects and Society*. London, Heinemann.

– (1966), *Religion in Secular Society*. London, Watts.

–, editor (1967), *Patterns of Sectarianism*. London, Heinemann.

Worsley, P. (1968), *The Trumpet Shall Sound* (second edition). London, MacGibbon and Kee.

Yinger, J.M. (1957), *Religion, Society and the Individual*. New York, Macmillan.

Zald, M.N., and R. Ash (1966), 'Social movement organizations: growth, decay and change', *Social Forces*: 327-341.

3. WORKS ON LANGUAGE

Bodmer, F. (1944), *The Loom of Language*. London, Allen and Unwin.

Breton, R.J.-L. (1976), *Géographie des langues*. Paris, Presses Universitaires de France.

Burney, P. (1962), *Les Langues internationales*. Paris, Presses Universitaires de France.

Ghosh, S.K., editor (1972), *Man, Language and Society*. The Hague and Paris, Mouton.

Pei, M. (1958), *One Language for the World*. New York, Devin-Adair.

Sadler, V., and U. Lins (1972), 'Regardless of frontiers: a case study in linguistic persecution', in *Man, Language and Society*, ed. by S.K. Ghosh, 206–215 The Hague and Paris, Mouton.

Sapir, E. (1949), *Selected Writings of Edward Sapir: Language, Culture and Personality*, ed. by D.G. Mandelbaum. Berkeley and Los Angeles, University of California Press.

Thomas, L.L. (1957), 'Some notes on the Marr school', *American Slavic and East European Review* 16(3) (October): 338–364.

4. WORKS ON HISTORY

Biddiss, M.D. (1971), 'The Universal Races Congress of 1911', *Race* 13(1) (July): 37–46.

Carr, E.H. (1961), *International Relations Between the Two World Wars (1919–1939)*. London, Macmillan.

Dyboski, R. (1933), *Poland*. London, Benn.

Fischer, G. (1958), *Russian Liberalism from Gentry to Intelligentsia*. Cambridge, Harvard University Press.

Goodrich, L.M. (1960), *The United Nations*. London, Stevens.

Guitton, J. (1968), *Regards sur la pensée française, 1870–1940*. Paris, Beauchesne.

Hudson, G.F. (1968), *Fifty Years of Communism: Theory and Practice 1917–1967*. London, Watts.

International Anti-Communist Entente (1939), *The Red Network: The Communist International at Work*. London, Duckworth.

Joll, J. (1973), *Europe Since 1870*. London, Weidenfeld and Nicholson.

League of Nations (1930), *Ten Years of World Cooperation*. Geneva, League of Nations Secretariat.

Lefranc, G. (1953), *Le Syndicalisme en France*. Paris, Presses Universitaires de France.

Montreuil, J. (1946), *Histoire du mouvement ouvrier en France des origines à nos jours*. Paris, Aubier.

Rappart, W.E. (1931), *The Geneva Experiment*. Oxford, Oxford University Press.

Reddaway, W.F., J.H. Penson, O. Halecki, and R. Dyboski, editors (1951), *The Cambridge History of Poland from Augustus II to Pilsudski, 1697–1935*. Cambridge, Cambridge University Press.

Smith, W.S. (1967), *The London Heretics*. London, Constable.

Spiller, G., editor (1911), *Papers on Inter-Racial Problems, Communicated to the First Universal Races Congress, London 1911*. London, King.

Treadgold, D.W. (1959), *Twentieth Century Russia*. Chicago, Rand McNally.

5. INTERNATIONAL LANGUAGE MOVEMENT: PERIODICALS

The dates quoted indicate the run of the periodical concerned which has served as a source of data for the present study. They should not necessarily be taken to indicate the total life-span of the periodical concerned.

American Esperanto Magazine (or *Amerika Esperantisto*), 1950–1963.

La Belga Sonorilo, 1902–1908.

La Brita Esperantisto, 1974–date.

The British Esperantist, 1905–1973.

Esperantista Laboristo, 1920–1921.

L'Espérantiste, 1898–1913.

La Esperantisto, 1889–1895.

Esperanto, 1905–1936. Continued as *Esperanto Internacia*.

Esperanto, 1951–date.

Esperanto (Geneva), 1936–1942 and 1946. Absorbed in *Esperanto Internacia*.

Esperanto Internacia, 1937–1950. Continued as *Esperanto*.

Heroldo de Esperanto, 1920–date.

Internacia Esperanto-Ligo, Jarlibro, 1936–1947.

Internacia Kulturo, 1930–1933, 1939.

Konkordo, 1927.

Kontakto, 1963–date.

Lingvo Internacia, 1895–1920.

La Monda Lingvo-Problemo, 1969–date.

Nica Literatura Revuo, 1955–1962.

Progreso, 1908–1914.

La Revuo, 1906–1914.

Ruslanda Esperantisto, 1906.

Sennacieca Asocio Tutmonda, Jarlibro, 1922–date.

Sur Posteno, 1934–1938.

Universala Esperanto-Asocio, Jarlibro, 1908–date.

Volapükagased, Vol. 24 (1959).

6. INTERNATIONAL LANGUAGE MOVEMENT: BOOKS, PAMPHLETS AND REPORTS (GENERAL DOCUMENTATION)

General note: Needless to say, these works vary widely in quality and accuracy. A number, however, are of value as more than mere source material and can provide a good basis for further study. Among these can be mentioned Privat (1923, 1927), a useful concise history which unfortunately goes no further than 1927. This is best read in conjunction with Privat, 1963, since in the earlier work the author modestly excludes his own contribution. Durrant (1943) continues the history up to the Second World War. Other particularly useful sources are Lapenna (1954) and Lapenna et al. (1974). The latter work incorporates Lins (1973), a particularly useful analytical history of persecution of Esperanto and Esperantists.

It is fortunate for the researcher that Zamenhof's original works have been collated and edited in two important collections, i.e. Zamenhof (1929, ed. by Dietterle) and Zamenhof (1948, ed. by Waringhien). The latter work contains much astute editorial comment.

On the general question of the international language movement, particularly useful are Couturat and Leau's two works (1903 and 1907). Further material is contained in Drezen (1928, Esperanto translation 1967). Guérard (1922) provides a useful synthesis and suggests some new hypotheses.

In tracing documentary sources Stojan (1929) is particularly useful. A more recent work is Tonkin (1977) which, while short, is of value to the researcher who does not himself read Esperanto, since most of the works listed are in English.

Auld, W., editor (1963), *Esperanta antologio*. La Laguna, Regulo.

Aymonier, C. (1914), *Histoire d'une délégation pour l'adoption d'une langue auxiliaire internationale*. Paris, Société des Amis de l'Espéranto.

Bandet, A. (1923), *La Conférence internationale de Venise pour l'adoption d'une langue commerciale commune. Rapport, dont les conclusions ont été adoptées par la Chambre de Commerce de Paris*. Paris, Chambre de Commerce.

De Beaufront, L. (n.d.), *L'Espéranto: seule vraie solution de la langue internationale*.

Benaerts, L. (n.d.), *Louis Couturat*. Coulommiers.

Berger, R. (1937), 'Li ver historie del lingue internationale', *Cosmoglotta* (August): 65–80 (special number on history of international language).

Blanke D., editor (n.d.), *Sociopolitikaj aspektoj de la Esperanto-movado*.

Boningue, A.M. (A. Michaux) (1909), *Metode de international lingue*. Boulogne.

Bormann, W. (1970), *Bona sanco*. La Laguna, Regulo.

Borsboom, E. (1976), *Vivo de Lanti*. Paris, SAT.

Boulet, P. (1905), *Unua universala kongreso de Esperanto en Boulogne-sur-Mer: Kongresa libro*. Boulogne, Hamain.

– ('Kongresinto') (1965), *Boulogne 1905: Testo kaj triumfo*. Marmande, Esperantaj Francaj Eldonoj.

Boulton, M. (1960), *Zamenhof, Creator of Esperanto*. London, Routledge and Kegan Paul.

– (1962), *Zamenhof, aŭtoro de Esperanto*. La Laguna, Regulo.

Braga, I.G. (1940), *Monumento de Carlo Bourlet*. Rio de Janeiro, Livraria da Federaçao E. Brasileira.

Brinton, D.G., M. Phillips, and M.B. Snyder (1888), 'The scientific value of Volapük', *Nature* 38 (August): 351–355.

British Association for the Advancement of Science (1922), *Report of the Eighty-ninth Meeting, Edinburgh, September 7-14, 1921*. London, Murray.

British Esperanto Association (n.d.), *Handbook and Booklist*.

De Bruin, G.P. (1936), *Laborista esperanta movado antaŭ la mondmilito*. Paris, SAT.

Bureau International de l'Union Télégraphique (1925), *Documents de la Conférence Télégraphique Internationale de Paris* (2 volumes). Paris.

Cart, T. (1922), *Korektoj de la eraraj tradukoj en 'Universa la Vortaro'* (English edition: also issued for other languages in which the *Universala vortaro* appeared; all are reprinted in Zamenhof, *Fundamento de Esperanto*, 1963 edition). British Esperanto Association.

– (1927), *Vortoj de Profesoro Th. Cart*, ed. by S. Grenkamp and R. de Lajarte. Jaslo, Esperantista Voco.

Caubel, A. (1959), 'Nekonato: la Zamenhofa Homaranismo', *Sennacieca Revuo*: 3–16.

Cavanagh, B. (n.d.), *A First Foreign Language for All Mankind*. London, British Esperanto Association.

Ĉefeĉ, E. (H.V. Hoveler) (1911), *La Elementoj kaj la vortfarado, gramatiko kaj sintakso en Esperanto*. Paris, Warnier.

– (1912), *Pluaj argumentoj por pruvi, ke la teorio, 'La radikoj en Esperanto havas gramatikan karakteron' kontraŭstaras la intencojn de la Fundamento*.

Centro de Esplorado kaj Dokumentado (1964), *Listo de lokaj Esperanto-societoj*.

Courtinat, L. (1964), *Historio de Esperanto* (*movado kaj literaturo*) (3 volumes). Agen.

Couturat, L. (1907), *Etude sur la dérivation en Espéranto*. Coulommiers, Brodard.

– (1909), *Le Choix d'une langue internationale*. Paris, Revue du Mois.

– (1912), *L'Echec de l'Espéranto devant la délégation*. Paris, Chaix.

–, and Leau, L. (1903), *Histoire de la langue universelle*. Paris, Hachette.

—, and – (1907), *Les Nouvelles langues internationales*. Coulommiers, Brodard.

—, and – (1910a), *Compte rendu des travaux du Comité*. Coulommiers, Brodard.

—, and – (1910b), *Conclusions du rapport sur l'état présent de la question de la langue internationale*. Coulommiers, Brodard (privately circulated in 1907).

Cresswell, J., and J. Hartley (1957), *Teach Yourself Esperanto*. London, English Universities Press.

Drezen, E. (1928[1967]), *Za vseobshchim yazykom*. Moscow and Leningrad, Gosudarstvennoe Izdatel'stvo. (Esperanto translation, *Historio de la mondolingvo*, by N. Hohlov and N. Nekrasov. Third edition, Oosaka, Pirato, 1967.)

– (1929), *Zamenhof*. Moscow, Mospoligraf. (Reprinted in *Socipolitikaj aspektoj de la Esperanto-movado*, ed. by D. Blanke, 125-165.)

– (1931), *Analiza historio de la Esperanto-movado*. Leipzig, Ekrelo.

Durrant, E.D. (1943), *The Language Problem: Its History and Solution*. Rickmansworth, Esperanto Publishing Company.

Dyer, L.H. (1923), *The Problem of an International Auxiliary Language and its Solution in Ido*. London, Pitman.

Ellis, A.J. (1888), 'On the conditions of a universal language', *Transactions of the Philological Society*: 59-98.

Dr. Esperanto (L.L. Zamenhof) (1887), *Mezhdunarodnyi yazyk: Predislovie i polnyi uchebnik*. Warsaw, Kelter.

Flusser, W. (1927), *Die internationale Konferenz 'Durch die Schule zum Frieden', Prag, 16-20 April 1927*. Prague, Verlag des vorbereitenden Ausschusses der Konferenz.

Forster, P.G. (1975), 'La ideologio de Esperanto kaj la koncepto de superŝtato', *Eŭropa Esperanto-Revuo* 1(7): 2-3.

Fruictier, P. (1914), *La esperanta vortfarado laŭ la Fundamento*. Paris, Le Monde Espérantiste.

Gale, W.A. (1910), *Konkordanco de la 'Sentencoj de Salomono'*. London, Stead.

– (n.d.), 'Konkordanca vortaro de "Marta"'. Unpublished manuscript in BEA Library.

'Gomo Sum' (1901), *Gillelizm: proyekt resheniva yevreiskago voprosa*. St. Petersburg, Sklad.

Grosjean-Maupin, E. (1910), *Kompleta vortaro Esperanto-franca*. Paris, Hachette.

—, A. Esselin, S. Grenkamp-Kornfeld, and G. Waringhien (1930), *Plena vortaro de Esperanto*. Paris, SAT.

Guérard, A.L. (1922), *A Short History of the International Language Movement*. London, Fisher Unwin.

Hagler, M. (1971), 'The Esperanto Language as a Literary Medium'. Unpublished Ph.D. thesis, Indiana University, Bloomington.

Hodler, H. (n.d.), *Esperantism*. Geneva, UEA.

Holzhaus, A. (1969), *Doktoro kaj lingvo Esperanto*. Helsinki, Fondumo Esperanto.

– (1973), *Wilhelm Heinrich Trompeter*. Essen, Schroter.

De Hoog, H.R. (1964), *Nia historio*. Kristana Esperantista Ligo Internacia.

Hureau, E. (1920), *Le Problème de la langue internationale*. Paris, Emancipanta Stelo.

Internacia Konferenco pri la Instruo de Esperanto en Lernejoj (1922), *Resuma raporto*. Geneva, Lernejo por Edukaj Sciencoj J.J. Rousseau.

Jacob, H. (1934), *Internacia lernolibro por Esperantistoj*. Stockholm, Sueda Ido-Centro.

– (1943), *Otto Jespersen: His Work for an International Auxiliary Language*. Loughton, International Language (Ido) Society of Great Britain.

– (1946), *On the Choice of a Common Language*. London, Pitman.

Janton, P. (1973), *L'Espéranto*. Paris, Presses Universitaires de France.

Jespersen, O. (1928), *An International Language*. London, Allen and Unwin.

– (1930). *Novial lexike*. London, Allen and Unwin.

Kalocsay, K., and G. Waringhien (1932), *Parnasa gvidlibro*. Budapest, Literatura Mondo.

Van Kleef, C. (1965), *La Homaranismo de D-ro L.L. Zamenhof*, translated from the Dutch by C. Ribot. Agen, Editions Françaises d'Espéranto.

Lanti, E. (1922), *For la neŭtralismon*. Paris, SAT.

– (1928), *La laborista Esperantismo*. Paris and Leipzig, SAT.

– (1930), *Naciismo: Studo pri deveno, evoluado, kaj sekvoj*. Leipzig, SAT.

– (1931 [1970]), *Manifesto de la sennaciistoj, kaj dokumentoj pri sennaciismo*. Paris, SAT.

– (1931), *Vortoj de kamarado Lanti*. Leipzig, SAT.

– (1934), *Absolutismo*. Paris and Amsterdam, SAT and FLE.

– (1940), *Leteroj de E. Lanti*, ed. by G. Waringhien. Paris, SAT.

–, and Ivon, M. (1935), *Ĉu socialismo konstruiĝas en Sovetio?* Paris, Esperanto.

Lapenna, I. (1950), *Retoriko*. Paris.

– (1954a), *Conceptions soviétiques de droit international public*. Paris, Pedone.

– (1954b), *La Internacia Lingvo: Faktoj pri Esperanto*. London, UEA (CED).

– (1960), *Memorlibro eldonita okaze de la centjara datreveno de la naskiĝo de D-ro L.L. Zamenhof*. London, Centro de Esplorado kaj Dokumentado.

– (1963), *State and Law: Soviet and Yugoslav Theory*. London, Athlone.

– (1966), *Elektitaj paroladoj kaj prelegoj*. Rotterdam.

– (1968), *Soviet Penal Policy*. London, Bodley Head.

– (1975), *Hamburgo en retrospektivo*. Sarbrucken, Sarlanda Esperanto-Ligo.

–, U. Lins, and T. Carlevaro (1974), *Esperanto en perspektivo*. London and

Rotterdam, Centro de Esplorado kaj Dokumentado pri la Monda Lingvo-Problemo.

Laurat, L. (1951), _Staline, la linguistique et l'impérialisme russe_. Paris, Les Iles d'Or.

League of Nations (1922), _Esperanto as an International Auxiliary Language_. Geneva, League of Nations.

— (1923), _Committee on Intellectual Cooperation: Minutes of the Second Session_. Geneva, League of Nations.

Lins, U. (1966–1967), 'Esperanto dum la Tria Regno', _Germana Esperanto-Revuo_ (July–August 1966): 76–78; (October 1966): 99–101; (January 1967): 5–8. (Reprinted in _Socipolitikaj aspektoj de la Esperanto-movado_, ed. by D. Blanke.)

— (1973), _La danĝera lingvo: Esperanto en la uragano de persekutoj_. Kyoto, L'Omnibuso.

London Chamber of Commerce (1923), _Commercial Conference at Venice, 2 to 5 April, 1923; Report of the Delegate_. London, Chamber of Commerce.

Maimon, N.Z. (1978), _La kaŝita vivo de Zamenhof: Originalaj studoj_. Tokyo, Japana Esperanto-Instituto.

Merchant, J. (n.d.), _Joseph Rhodes kaj la fruaj tagoj de Esperanto on Anglujo_, translated by L. Briggs. Bradford, Federacio Esperantista de Yorkshire.

Nitobe, I. (1922), 'The language question and the League of Nations', _League of Nations Official Journal_ (January–March): 295–298.

The Office (1888), December 8.

Oficiala Raporto di la Unesma Internaciona Kongreso por la Linguo Internaciona Ido (1921), Stockholm, Sueda Ido-Editerio.

Oficiala Raporto dil Duesma Internaciona Kongreso por la Linguo Internaciona Ido (1922), Frankfurt-am-Main, Werner and Winter.

Oficiala Raporto dil Triesma Internaciona Kongreso por la Linguo Internaciona Ido (1923), Frankfurt-am-Main, Englert and Schosser.

Oficiala Raporto dil Quaresma Internaciona Kongreso por la Linguo Internaciona Ido (1925), Luxemburg, Solimpa.

Paris: Grupo Esperantista (1914), _Carlo Bourlet_. Paris, Grupo Esperantista.

Preliminary Conference for an International Agreement on Wireless Telephony (1924), _Report of the Proceedings_. Geneva.

Premier Congrès International des Radio-Amateurs, Paris, 14–18 April, 1925 (1926), _Report of the Proceedings_. Paris, Chron.

Privat, E. (1920), _Vivo de Zamenhof_. Rickmansworth, Esperanto Publishing Co.

— (1923, 1927), _Historio de la lingvo Esperanto_ (2 volumes). Leipzig, Hirt. (Vol. 1: 1923; vol. 2: 1927.)

— (1963), _Aventuroj de pioniro_. La Laguna, Regulo.

Ratkai, A. (n.d.), 'La internacilingva movado kiel kreinto de la Internacia

Lingvo' in *Socipolitikaj aspektoj de la Esperanto-movado*, ed. by D. Blanke, 166-181.

Regulo-Perez, J. (1961), *La zamenhofa Esperanto: Simpozio pri* ATA/ITA La Laguna, Regulo.

Rosenberger, W. (1902), *Wörterbuch der Neutralsprache (Idiom-Neutral)*. Leipzig, Haberland.

De Saussure, R. (1907), *Elementale gramatiko de la lingwo internaciona kun exercaro di Antido*. Geneva, Kundig.

– (1910), *Teoria ekzameno de la lingvo Esperanto kun fonetika internacia alfabeto, sistemo Antido N-o 2*. Geneva, Kundig.

– (1911), *Principes logiques de la formation des mots*. Geneva, Kundig.

– (1919), *Fundamento de la Internacia Lingvo Esperantida*. Berne.

Schleyer, J.M. (1880), *Volapük, die Weltsprache. Entwurf einer Universalsprache aller Gebildeten der ganzen Erde*. Sigmaringen.

Sennacieca Asocio Tutmonda (1925), *Petro: kursa lernlibro por laboristoj*. Leipzig, Eldona Fako Kooperativa.

– (1935), *Historio pri la skismo en la laborista Esperanto-movado*. Paris, SAT.

– (1953), *Historio de S.A.T.*, Paris, SAT.

Ŝirjaev, I., L. Kokeny, V. Bleier, and K. Kalocsay (1933-1934), *Enciklopedio de Esperanto* (2 volumes). Budapest, Literatura Mondo.

Springer, G.P. (1956), *Early Soviet Theories in Communication*. Cambridge, Mass., M.I.T. Center for International Studies.

Stettler, E. (1928), *Hector Hodler: Lia vivo kaj lia verko*. Geneva, UEA.

Stojan, P.E. (1929), *Bibliografio de internacia lingvo*. Geneva, UEA.

Sudre, J. (1866), *Langue musicale universelle, par le moyen de laquelle tous les différents peuples de la terre, les aveugles, les sourds et les muets peuvent se comprendre réciproquement*. Paris.

Tonkin, H. (1977), *Esperanto and International Language Problems: A Research Bibliography*. Washington, Esperantic Studies Foundation.

UNESCO (n.d.), Documents: 7C/PRG/11 and 8C/PRG/3.

Universala Esperanto-Asocio (1968), *Statuto kaj regu* laroj *de Universala Esperanto-Asocio*. Rotterdam, UEA.

Verdiro (pseudonym: J.W. Leslie) (1962), *Elingita glavo*. La Laguna, Regulo.

Wackrill, A.E. (1907), *Konkordanco de 'Ekzercaro' de D-ro L.L. Zamenhof*. Paris, Hachette.

De Wahl, E. (1922), *Occidental, unic natural vermen neutral e max facil e comprensibil lingue por international relationes*. Reval.

Waringhien, G. (1953), 'La ideologia dramo de L.L. Zamenhof', *Sennacieca Revuo*: 2-9.

– (1959), *Lingvo kaj vivo*. La Laguna, Regulo.

– (1967), *Aktoj de la Akademio*, Rotterdam and Paris, UEA and SAT.

–, editor (1970), *Plena ilustrita vortaro*. Paris, SAT.

Wells, J. (1969), *The E.U.P. Concise Esperanto and English Dictionary*. London, English Universities Press.

Williams, N. (1963), *Application to the Secondary School Examination Council: Esperanto 'O' Level Subject for G.C.E.*. Denton, Egerton Park County Secondary School.

–, editor (1968), *British Esperanto Congress 1968*. Manchester.

Wüster, E. (1923), *La oficiala radikaro kun enkonduko kaj notoj*. Berlin, Ellersiek and Borel.

– (1927), *Zamenhof-Radikaro*. Leipzig, Hirt.

Zamenhof, L.L. (1888), *Dua Libro de l'lingvo internacia*. Warsaw, Kelter.

– (1889a), *Adresaro de la personoj, kiuj ellernis la lingvon Esperanto (1-1000)*. Warsaw.

– (1889b), *Aldono al la Dua Libro de l'lingvo internacia*. Warsaw, Kelter.

– (1894a), *Ekzercaro de la lingvo internacia Esperanto*. Warsaw, Gins.

– (1894b), *Universala Vortaro*. Warsaw, Gins.

– (1896), *Adresaro de la Esperantistoj. Serio XVI (3001-3602), 1.10.93-1.10.95*. Warsaw, Gins.

– (1900), *Adresaro de la Esperantistoj. Serio XX (4661-5025), January 1899-January 1900*. Nuremberg, Tummell.

– (1903[1954]), *Fundamenta krestomatio de la lingvo Esperanto* (seventeenth edition). Rickmansworth, Esperanto Publishing Co..

– (1905), *Adresaro de la Esperantistoj. Serio XXV, 1.1.04-1.1.05 (9261-11199)*. Coulommiers, Brodard.

– (1905[1963]), *Fundamento de Esperanto*. Marmande, Esperantaj Francaj Eldonoj.

– (anonymous) (1906), *Homaranismo*. St. Petersburg.

– (1910), *Lingvaj Respondoj aperintaj en La Revuo*. Paris, Hachette.

– (1913a), *Homaranismo*. Madrid, Rosenorn.

– (1913b), *Lingvaj Respondoj: nova serio*. Paris, Central Office.

– (1925), *Lingvaj Respondoj: plena kolekto*, Paris, Brodard.

– (1929), *Originala verkaro*, ed. by J. Dietterle. Leipzig, Hirt.

– (1948), *Leteroj de L.L. Zamenhof* (2 volumes), ed. by G. Waringhien. Paris, SAT.

– (1973). *Unuaj libroj por Esperantistoj. Iam kompletigota plena verkaro de L.L. Zamenhof, kajero 1*, ed. by Tacuo Hugimoto. Kyoto, Ludovikito.

– (1975), *Zamenhof Leteroj*, ed. by A. Holzhaus. Helsinki, Fondumo Esperanto.

– (1976), *Hebreo el la geto: de Cionismo al Hilelismo. Iam kompletigota plena verkaro de L.L. Zamenhof, kajero 5*, ed. by Tacuo Hugimoto. Kyoto, Ludovikito.

Ziolkowska, M. (1959), *Doktoro Esperanto/Doktor Esperanto* (parallel text Esperanto/Polish). Warsaw, Wiedza Powszechna.

7. MISCELLANEOUS

Barkas, J. (1975), *The Vegetable Passion*. London, Routledge and Kegan Paul.

Carpenter, E. (1889), *Civilisation: Its Cause and Cure*. London, Allen and Unwin.

Von Clausewitz, C. (1968), *On War*, translated by J.J. Graham. Harmondsworth, Pelican.

Couturat, L. (1901 [1961]), *La Logique de Leibniz d'après des documents inédits*. Hildesheim, Olms.

– (1903), *Opuscules et fragments inédits de Leibniz*. Paris, Alcan.

Dalgarno, G. (1661), *Ars signorum, vulgo character universalis et lingua philosophica*. London, Hayes.

Descartes, R. (1897), 'Letter to Mersenne, 20 November 1629', in *Oeuvres complètes*, vol. 1: 76–82. Paris, Cerf.

Devlin, P. (1965), *The Enforcement of Morals*. London, O.U.P.

Flügel, J.C. (1925), 'Some unconscious factors in the international language movement with especial reference to Esperanto', *International Journal of Psychoanalysis* 7: 171–208.

Funke, O. (1929), *Zum Weltsprachenproblem in England im 17. Jahrhundert*. Heidelberg, Winter.

Gibbs, P. (1961), *Avalanche in Central Africa*. London, Arthur Barker.

Goldin, J. (1946), 'Hillel the Elder', *Journal of Religion*: 263–277.

Hitler, A. (1943), *Mein Kampf* (English translation by R. Manheim). Cambridge, Mass., Riverside.

Leibniz, G.W. (1840), *God. Guil. Leibnitii opera philosophica*, ed. by J.E. Erdmann. Berlin, Eichler.

Maude, A. (1910[1930]), *The Life of Tolstoy*. London, Oxford University Press.

Niebuhr, R. (1934), *Moral Man and Immoral Society*. New York, Scribner.

The Open Road (1923).

Orwell, G. (1937), *The Road to Wigan Pier*. London, Gollancz.

Review of Reviews (1902-1903).

Roth, L. (1960), *Judaism – a Portrait*. London, Faber.

Russell, B. (1967), *The Autobiography of Bertrand Russell, 1872-1914*. London, Allen and Unwin.

Saw, R.L. (1954), *Leibniz*. Harmondsworth, Penguin.

Shaw, N. (1935), *Whiteway, a Colony in the Cotswolds*. London, Daniel.

Simmons, E.J. (1960), *Leo Tolstoy* (2 volumes). New York, Vintage.

The Times (1905), 8 August.

UNESCO Courier (1957-1964).

Wilkins, J. (1668), *Essay towards a Real Character and a Philosophical Language*. London, Gellibrand.